# AMERICAN FURNITURE

*Also by Helen Comstock*
100 Most Beautiful Rooms in America

# AMERICAN FURNITURE

Seventeenth, Eighteenth, and Nineteenth
Century Styles

## by HELEN COMSTOCK

BONANZA BOOKS • NEW YORK

517106183

Copyright © MCMLXII by The Viking Press, Inc.

Library of Congress Catalog Card Number: 62-18074

This edition is published by Bonanza Books, a division of Crown Publishers, Inc. by arrangement with The Viking Press, Inc.

abcdefgh

Manufactured in the United States of America.

# Contents

Preface 7

1. Jacobean — William and Mary: 1640–1720 10

2. Queen Anne: 1720–1755 71

3. Chippendale: 1755–1790 115

4. Classical Period: 1790–1830 191

5. Early Victorian: 1830–1870 275

Notes 312

Selected Bibliography 319

Acknowledgments 325

Index 327

# Preface

The need for a book on American furniture which coordinates widely scattered material has been evident for some time. Reprints of Nutting, Lockwood, Miller, and Kettell, all useful, do not answer the present purpose. Charles Nagel's *American Furniture,* and Meyric R. Rogers' *American Interior Design* are out of print. Recent specialized studies, loan-exhibition catalogues, and, particularly, many articles in *Antiques* Magazine presenting fresh material over the years have added to our store of information.

I have attempted to write an introduction to the subject of American furniture coordinating some of this material, and in doing so have based the treatment on design characteristics of styles from Jacobean to Early Victorian. I have presented American furniture styles in relation to the European background and have indicated fundamental points of difference which show American individuality. Since architecture was so often the source of furniture ornament I have mentioned contemporary developments in architecture. Furniture forms distinctive of the various periods are traced in their origin and development, and technical terms are explained chiefly through illustrated examples. Passing references to contemporary writings which throw light on domestic life are introduced as a suggestion for further reading.

My subject is primarily a history of style. Construction, a subject which should be covered in detail if it is to have any value, is only incidently mentioned, while problems of restoration and fakes are outside the province of this book. Suggestions for decoration with antiques, not specifically given, may be found in the illustrations of interiors which are introduced at frequent intervals, sometimes in color. These show the forms under discussion in appropriate settings.

The plan of the book is the result of my own search for answers to questions relating to identification of furniture styles. The method is pictorial. The first section combines Jacobean with William and Mary because of their close relationship. This is followed by chapters on Queen Anne, Chippendale, the classical period (in which Hepplewhite, Sheraton, and Empire furniture is considered) and, finally, Early Victorian. After 1870 the mechanization of industry, which had begun in the second quarter of the nineteenth century, deprived the craftsman of his individual, creative role and opened a new epoch which I feel is of more interest when treated as a separate study in relation to developments in the twentieth century.

The introduction of each period is followed by a chart which sums up distinctive and new forms, characteristics of design, and techniques of decoration. Also indicated are contemporary changes in England and, in the case of the later periods, in France.

Illustrations are arranged alphabetically according to form, and the descriptions are written in predominantly technical terms in order to illustrate them by example. This unavoidably leads to repetition. I have tried to give each subject, and each period, as much completeness as possible, so that the book may be consulted at random or in the sections of greatest personal interest to the reader. The use of reference notes, which means turning repeatedly to the back of the book, or looking at the bottom of a page, I have held to a minimum. Wherever it has seemed possible to insert an acknowledgment or explanation directly in the text, I have done so.

A selected bibliography at the end of the book contains the titles of books and articles which I have found helpful in a number of years of study of American furniture. There are without doubt other works which should be mentioned, but a list of over two hundred already exceeds the requirements of an introductory work. (The bibliography is limited to modern studies; influential publications of the seventeenth, eighteenth, and early nineteenth centuries are given in notes and outlines.) I have referred to most of the works in the bibliography while preparing to write this book, and my feeling of obligation, in making use of work done by others, is great.

Throughout I have constantly referred to *Dictionary of English Furniture* by Macquoid and Edwards and the files of the magazine *Antiques,* 1922-1962. Nutting, Lockwood, and the handbook of the American Wing by Halsey and Cornelius as revised by Downs have accompanied me from the Jacobean through the classical period. I have turned again and again to the writings of Joseph Downs, not only to his *American Furniture* for the Queen Anne and Chippendale periods, but to his many contributions in the *Bulletin* of the Metropolitan Museum and his articles in *Antiques,* always with admiration for both the style and content of his writings. For the Chippendale period I have frequently consulted, in addition to Downs, the works of Hipkiss, Carpenter, and Hornor. E. Milby Burton on Charleston and V. Isabelle Miller on New York makers have proved helpful. For a concise review of the Chippendale style in England I have depended to a large extent on Peter Ward-Jackson.

A foundation for the study of American furniture of the nineteenth century has been offered in a series of articles in *Antiques,* 1958-1959, by Robert C. Smith, which is so illuminating that I have made it the point of departure in the treatment of the Empire, Late Empire, and Early Victorian styles. For the Victorian period I have also relied on the writings of Marvin D. Schwartz for American and Peter Floud for English developments. Giedion's *Mechanization Takes Command* has thrown light on such specifically Victorian types as upholstered furniture and patent furniture.

For all periods of English furniture I have found much information in the *Connoisseur Period Guides — Tudor, Stuart, Early Georgian, Late Georgian, Regency,* and *Early Victorian,* especially in contributions by Ralph Fastnedge, E. T. Joy, John Fleming, and Clifford Musgrave; also in articles in *The Connoisseur* by R. W. Symonds, Ralph Edwards, and F. J. B.

Watson. Books by these distinguished writers on English furniture, given in the bibliography, have been found essential.

My brief notes on makers in each section have gained through my having Ethel Hall Bjerkoe's *Cabinetmakers of America* for further reference. The compilations from early newspapers by George F. Dow, Arthur Coxe Prime, and Rita Gottesman Susswein have proved as invaluable to me as to every historian of the decorative arts.

Illustrations have been chosen chiefly from public collections, since these are accessible to the reader, but many examples from private collections are also included. While an effort has been made to secure a great many less familiar examples, the selection has been determined by the extent to which a subject fills a place in a dictionary-style presentation of American furniture design.

Regional traits are stressed here, but the book is not devoted solely to this subject, which is one that could well be made the basis of an entire book. An early instance of the coordination of observations on regional styles may be found in the catalogue of the Girl Scouts Loan Exhibition by Louis Guerineau Myers (1929). In retrospect, the origin of regional studies may be seen more clearly than elsewhere in *Antiques,* which, since its founding in 1922, has shown consistent interest in research regarding the work of different areas. Homer Eaton Keyes, editor from its founding until his death in 1938, may have been first to recognize the existence of regional traits. Certainly he did more than anyone to further the study of local characteristics of New England, Pennsylvania, New York, and the South, while his editorial notes are so perceptive that it inspires the wish that he had given more extended form to his own findings. He encouraged Esther Stevens Fraser in her study of Pennsylvania-German and Massachusetts painted furniture; Dr. Samuel Woodhouse in research on Philadelphia makers; Dr. Irving P. Lyon in his extensive review of the oak furniture of seventeenth-century Ipswich; Fiske Kimball and Mabel M. Swan in lengthy studies of Salem. Luther described the Hadley chest in *Antiques* in 1925, a decade before the publication of his book. A study of Charleston cabinetmakers was offered by Jennie Haskell Rose in 1933. Mary Ralls Dockstader was investigating other Southern furniture, particularly from Georgia, 1931-1934.

Extended observations on regional traits in Downs' *American Furniture* have been of great value to me in making comparisons of illustrations of the work of Boston, Newport, New York, Philadelphia, Connecticut, Baltimore, and Charleston. Admittedly indications of origin in a definite area are not always present, and there are many exceptions and contradictions, but the vitality of American work is most evident in the special shaping according to the manner of a certain region. The life of a locality is imprinted on the arts of its people, and the study of the work of the American craftsman in regional variations offers one way to bring the past to life with a deeper appreciation of our cultural heritage.

— HELEN COMSTOCK

February 1962
South Peacham, Vermont

# 1. Jacobean – William and Mary

## 1640 - 1720

When colonies were founded at Jamestown and Plymouth in 1607 and 1620, James I was King of England. English furniture of the first half of the seventeenth century is called Jacobean (from *Jacobus,* the Latin word for James).

In America the Jacobean style persisted throughout the seventeenth century, but during the last quarter new fashions began to appear. These reflected the Continental influence introduced into England with the restoration of the monarchy in 1660. Late seventeenth-century American furniture is classified as in the William and Mary style, although it also shows the influence of Restoration fashions which antedated that style.

While Colonial Jacobean and William and Mary styles have many differences, they have many more characteristics in common; and it has become usual to treat both periods as a unified phase in the development of American furniture. Little but the rudest sort of furniture could have been made in the Colonies during the hardships of settlement, and most of the earliest American pieces in museum collections today are dated about mid-century. Among these are the court cupboard (No. 74) probably made in Virginia, and the Parmenter cupboard (No. 75), originating in the Ipswich-Salem-Boston area of Massachusetts. Both pieces are remarkably like contemporary English work. They have the same general design, the same bulbous supports, carved, foliated scrolls, fluting, palmate panels, and strapwork which the Jacobean joiner, turner, and carver inherited from their Elizabethan predecessors. It is clear, however, that American Jacobean is not English. The carving in American work is flatter and less finished, the selection of ornament is more restricted, and the whole feeling bold, vigorous, and primitive by comparison. The conditions of pioneer living worked a form of discipline which resulted in a style that to our eyes today is extremely appealing in its simplicity.

10

I. The hall, or keeping room, in Hempsted House, the oldest structure in New London, built in 1678. *(The Antiquarian and Landmarks Society of Connecticut.)*

*The First Born.* By Samuel Dirkes von Hoogstraten (1627-1678); Dutch School. *(Springfield Museum of Fine Arts.)*

Wicker cradles of this type were known to the Pilgrims. The similar cradle of Peregrine White, who was born on the *Mayflower,* is at Pilgrim Hall, Plymouth. It was probably made in Holland.

*Above:* Top of Prince-Howes family press cupboard, Plymouth, Massachusetts; seventeenth century. *(Nutting Collection, Wadsworth Atheneum.)*

*Far left:* Spanish foot on William and Mary stool, No. 109. *(New Hampshire Historical Society.)*

*Left:* Cup turning on William and Mary lowboy, No. 120. *(Nutting Collection, Wadsworth Atheneum.)*

For two centuries English influence dominated American furniture design, although there were always variations and modifications in style which give it a distinctive character. The moderate differences, which can be seen in the two court cupboards, were magnified before the century was over and culminated in the eighteenth century, when the typically American forms of Philadelphia Chippendale and Newport blockfront were produced. However, the basic relation is there, and any study of American furniture must begin with the English prototypes.

SOURCES OF ENGLISH DESIGN. It may seem strange to find Italian Renaissance versions of the acanthus and guilloche on the first American furniture made by craftsmen whose first concern was survival. But these forms bear witness to the fact that, a full century before, England had responded to the fascination of Italian Renaissance ornament. By the time the great migration brought thousands of settlers to the Massachusetts Bay colony in the 1630s, simplified versions of Renaissance motifs were the stock patterns of provincial craftsmen. Transplanted to American soil, they continued in existence after they were outmoded in Europe.

In sixteenth-century England, when classic arcaded panels supplanted the linen-fold pattern on paneling, a new element in furniture design appeared. This is recognizable in the exaggerated dimensions of the bulbous supports on tables and cupboards. The style was of Flemish or possibly German origin and was introduced by Flemish-Huguenot craftsmen working in England. It was also known from Flemish pattern books. The more progressive forms of Continental furniture design were thus communicated to a somewhat backward England whose brilliant Tudor age was yet to come. From Flemish sources came the interpretation of the age-old motif of interlacing bands, partly geometric and partly scrolled, called strapwork. Strapwork was used in many crafts, including those of the goldsmith and plasterer as well as the carver. Ornament became exuberant and vigorous, and, although this was a debased classicism that dominated English sixteenth-century ornament on Elizabethan flagons, on the plasterwork ceilings of Jacobean houses, and on the richly carved cupboards displaying silver plate in the nobleman's hall, there was nothing weak or uncertain about its application. The same may be said of the carved chests and cupboards of Essex County, Massachusetts, where the late Elizabethan style is seen in brilliant afterglow.

THE PILGRIM PERIOD. For the Jacobean phase of American furniture design the term Pilgrim has come into use. While there is some justification for this, the term is not used as a classification in this book, where broader ones are sought. Strictly speaking, "Pilgrim" should be reserved for the Plymouth colony and not be applied to the Puritan communities of the Massachusetts Bay colony such as Boston, Ipswich, and the North Shore in general. It would have dismayed those Separatists, whom we call Pilgrims, and the Puritans to know that future generations would have so little regard for the differences between them. However, it seems probable now that the term Pilgrim will remain in use as a general classification for New England work in the Jacobean style.

Undoubtedly furniture was being made at an early date in Virginia and the Carolinas, but most early Southern work has disappeared. Pennsylvania and the other middle colonies are represented by little that can be dated before the late 1600s. Pilgrim furniture, so closely associated with the founding of our country, alone offers a tangible impression of the first American homes.

AMERICAN JACOBEAN FORMS. The most important pieces of furniture in the Jacobean style were the court and press cupboards. These were owned by the wealthier families. The court cupboard had a shelf above (or below) for the display of silver, delftware, and other treasured possessions, and also included a closed section for the storage of utensils in everyday use. An excellent example is seen in the seventeenth-century Hart Room at the Winterthur Museum (No. 106). Present-day usage in England associates term "court cupboard" with a form with open shelves only, but apparently this type was not made in America. Yet there are many inventory listings of court cupboards, and it seems obvious that these referred to the kind of cupboard seen in Nos. 74-76.

While the court cupboard was intended chiefly for ornaments and utensils, the chief purpose of the press cupboard, with its capacious drawers and cupboard sections, was for clothing (No. 77). The upper part was used for display.

The chest was essential in every home, and served as a place of storage and as a table or bench. Clothing, linens, blankets, and household equipment were originally kept in it, but after the development of the chest of drawers it became more specifically a linen and blanket chest. These chests were usually of framed-panel construction, and were the work of a joiner.[1] The arcaded chest (No. 47) was one of the more elaborate types, and this was carved with a wide range of Tudor and Jacobean ornament. Slightly later examples show geometric paneling (No. 51). Of entirely different construction was the simpler "borded chest" formed of planks nailed or pegged together by the carpenter or semi-skilled joiner (No. 49).

The chest of drawers (No. 59) gradually developed from the chest which had one drawer below. The number of drawers was gradually increased until eventually the chest section was abandoned altogether. The chest of drawers was not an American innovation, nor even an English one, but came from the Continent. It was used in the 1640s in England, where it supplanted the chest and press cupboards for clothing. The earliest examples have drawers on side runners, the drawer being grooved to fit a runner attached to the carcass. American inventories mention chests of drawers in the 1640s, but a Massachusetts example dated *1678,* which belonged to the Staniford family of Ipswich (and is now in the Winterthur Museum), may be the earliest recorded American example in existence.

Large rectangular tables with turned baluster legs joined by rectangular stretchers are called stretcher tables (No. 114). In old records this type is generally named a "long joined table." It served many uses as a center and dining table, and was among the better furnishings of the early home. In everyday use for dining was the trestle table, which was constructed of a removable board resting on a trestle (No. 112). Both stretcher tables and trestle tables, when used for dining, were accompanied by joint stools and benches or forms.

In the seventeenth-century house, where chairs were few, the joint (joined) stool was the basic piece of seat furniture. That more of these stools do not exist today is the result of hard usage. In Elizabethan England joint stools were the first individual seats at the dining table, except for the chairs that were reserved for the master and mistress. Before that, people sat side by side on benches which had no backs. After use, the joint stools were placed under the table or were laid across the stretchers. Joint stools were made throughout the seventeenth century in America, but the early, heavy baluster turnings seen on the stool in the Hart Room (No. 106) gave place to vase-turnings (No. 107). These stools look like small tables, with a height of about twenty to twenty-two inches. Their legs are raked for stability.

Large armchairs, known as "great chairs," were restricted in number and were not known in every home. They were generally used with a cushion, and their seats were dished to receive it. "Great chairs" included the wainscot chair, made by the joiner, and the Brewster, Carver and slat-back chairs which were made by the turner.[1] The wainscot chair (No. 24) was made of oak, and was frequently richly carved. The name comes from the Dutch *wagonschot,* a fine grade of oak plank which was exported from the Continent. A wainscot chair with partly plain and partly paneled back is shown in No. 23. The joiner may have applied to the turner for the shaping of the massive posts, or, as was likely in the Colonies, he may have been a turner himself.

Brewster and Carver chairs are named after chairs now in Pilgrim Hall, Plymouth, which are believed to have been owned by Elder William Brewster (1567-1644) and Governor John Carver (died 1621). The Brewster chair, No. 16, resembles the original, with spindles in the back and below the arms and seat rail. Those below the seat and in the back are arranged in tiers, by which the Brewster is distinguished from the Carver chair. It is customary, however, to use the name Brewster for chairs that have spindles below the seat, even if none are present below the arms. Carver chairs (No. 18) have spindles in the back only. There are also intermediate types. The earliest examples have massive posts (possibly exceeding two and a half inches in diameter) and large, turned finials on the back posts. The large balls, originally on the front posts, are apt to be much worn or missing.

Slat-back chairs (Nos. 30-35) are of turned construction except for the slats. The earliest slat-backs were contemporary with Carver and Brewster chairs but the form survived longer because, with slats curved outward, they were more comfortable. They were made in the eighteenth century with modifications (country versions were very simple), and were given a handsome transformation in the Chippendale ladder-back chair. In the nineteenth century the Shaker slat-back chair gave the design new vitality and in less distinguished forms it has survived to the present.

Small upholstered chairs (No. 27) with seats covered in leather or needlework (such as appear in Dutch genre paintings of the seventeenth century) were immensely popular in England in Oliver Cromwell's time, which explains their popular modern name, "Cromwellian chair." They were made in America and used in the homes of the well-to-do in the late 1600s.

Seat furniture also included the bench and settle. In old records, these terms were used interchangeably, but modern usage generally reserves "settle" for the long seat with arms and back. The bench without a back was called a "forme," as mentioned in many inventory records. However, an American joined form of the seventeenth century, as seen in the Seventeenth-Century Room at the Winterthur Museum (No. 7), is extremely rare today.

The earliest American beds in existence are of the low-post variety with simply turned posts and plain, low headboards (No. 1). Sometimes they are mentioned in early inventories as stump bedsteads or low bedsteads. Most of those extant, and there are only a few, are of the late seventeenth century, but they probably perpetuate an earlier type.

High-post beds were undoubtedly known, even if none of seventeenth-century date exist today, for there is frequent mention of curtains and valances accompanying the bedstead (the word bed being reserved for the featherbed or its equivalent). The impression gained from the inventories is of the draped bed as the dominant article of furniture in almost every room.[2]

Boxes with hinged, slanting lids were variously used for books, as desks, and for the safe-keeping of valuables when equipped with a lock. The popular name for the type is "Bible box." William Clark of Salem, who died in 1647, kept silver and "wampon" in his "desk."[3] The desk of the greater part of the seventeenth century was a desk box, and only at the end of the century were larger forms of writing furniture introduced. The slanting lid of the desk or book box made it suitable for both writing and reading. Its form was basically that of the medieval scholar's book box which in turn was inspired by the ecclesiastical lectern. The early boxes (Nos. 12-15) are of especial interest because they are often finely carved with many of the same designs found on the chests of the period.

Small cabinets, or cupboards, small enough to stand on a table (No. 73) were sometimes used as "dressing boxes." One of these is mentioned in an inventory taken in 1691 of the estate of John Bowles of Roxbury, Massachusetts. Some of these small cabinets were divided into compartments for the storage of spices (as still indicated by the aroma), and are popularly referred to as "spice cabinets."

JACOBEAN DESIGN. The distinctive feature of Jacobean furniture is the use of turned members. Generally these are of bulbous outline, although occasionally in the earliest work the straight columnar outline is found. The source of both the columns and curving, vase-shape forms is to be traced to Italian Renaissance architecture. For the curving forms, the terms baluster, vase, and spindle are used almost interchangeably, but there are distinctions.[4] The baluster serves as a support (No. 110), and when split lengthwise and applied it becomes surface ornament (No. 81). Some of the turnings are formed as balls or knobs, as on the stretchers of chairs (No. 27) and on tables. The ball, too, may be cut in half and applied, becoming the boss that produces a jeweled effect when grouped on drawer fronts (No. 54).

Carving was applied lavishly to Jacobean furniture. It must have been so time-consuming that possibly something more than fashion recommended the use of the geometric paneling, which was often combined with it. Diamond and other shapes were formed of strips of molding which were applied to larger panels, breaking the area into geometric forms (No. 48). A frequent procedure was to outline drawer fronts with beveled moldings (No. 77). Applied spindles were almost invariably present (No. 76). Painted ornamentation was also used on Jacobean pieces, appearing first as ebonizing of bosses but finally in designs used for their own sake. Painted floral and heraldic designs (No. 67) were especially popular in the early 1700s.

ENGLAND: AFTER 1660. The later seventeenth century brought new influences from France, Holland, and Portugal as trade and politics resulted in closer relations between England and the Continent. The heavy oak furniture popular in the time of James I and Charles I was supplanted by light, plain-surfaced walnut furniture. This type, belonging to the period of Charles II, shows a logical development of practical and pleasing forms, disciplined in ornament, and befitting the new intellectual age of Dryden and Locke. The seventeenth century was also an epoch of political and religious strife. In spite of two civil wars and the austerity of the Commonwealth, the rise of the English landed gentry provided so much work for craftsmen that the making of fine furniture appears to have continued unhindered.

New techniques such as caning and veneering were introduced from the Continent into England shortly after 1660. New furniture forms, such as the high chest, fall-front desk, daybed and tall-back chair, appeared between 1660 and 1680. The gateleg table, known in small size in the early 1600s, became the large oval dining table.

16

The new techniques had appeared as a result of England's friendly relations with Holland in the time of Cromwell, and they increased noticeably in the reign of Charles II. After the Great Fire which wiped out most of London in 1666, houses were built in a new style. New furniture of a lighter type than Jacobean oak was required. For this walnut was used, which was not only lighter but had fine pattern suitable for veneering, an art which Flemish craftsmen working in London taught their English counterparts. They also taught them the art of marquetry, which was inlay in elaborate designs formed of various-toned woods. A third skill was the art of making drawers of all sizes, which fitted to perfection. A craftsman who was master of these skills was a cabinetmaker. The word came into use in the 1680s, and thereafter the cabinet-maker supplanted the joiner and turner in importance.

An unusual number of new forms were introduced about the last decade of the seventeenth century. The desk-on-frame, slope-front desk, and a combination of desk and bookcase (secretary) indicate that writing and reading played an increasingly important role in daily life. The dressing table or lowboy and the tea table were innovations, and the high chest became an important form.

William and Mary furniture displays fine surface pattern in burl and crotch veneers outlined with herringbone inlay. New design elements included the Flemish scroll (a baroque S-scroll), trumpet turnings, and the arched and shaped skirt on case pieces, the lines of which were repeated in the flat, shaped stretcher which united the legs. The scrolled knuckle of the armrest on chairs became the ram's horn, and the turned leg often ended in an S-scroll. As a result of improved techniques developed by the cabinetmaker, drawer sides were no longer so heavy.

WILLIAM AND MARY STYLE IN AMERICA. Fashions introduced in England after Charles II returned to the throne in 1660 began to be apparent in American furniture some fifteen years later, and these merged with the fresh wave of Continental influence in the reign of William and Mary. In regard to American furniture, these new fashions of the second half of the seventeenth century are said to be in the William and Mary style, although the origin of the tall-back chair (No. 36), the high chest on a frame with twist-turned legs (No. 69), the fall-front desk (No. 96), and the daybed (No. 88) antedated 1690.

The high chest, popularly called the highboy in America, replaced the press and court cupboards as the most important piece in the interior (Nos. 69-72). Handsomely patterned veneers of walnut and ash burl and the finer interior construction of these chests indicate that the cabinetmaker, rather than the joiner and turner, had become the most important figure in furniture making. The high chest, which appeared in the time of Charles II, was inspired by the Oriental lacquer cabinet on a decorative stand. On the more utilitarian high chest, a chest of drawers became the upper portion, and the support was a stand with a single drawer. More drawers increased the depth of the stand, and an arched skirt was added. Until about 1720 the American highboy closely followed English styles. The origin of the word highboy is not known, but it is no older than the nineteenth century.

The lowboy (No. 120) was the support for the high chest, but it was also made as a separate piece serving as a dressing table to accompany the high chest in the bedroom. The addition of side drawers to the single-drawer stand created the graceful lowboy. On both sides of an arched opening, convenient for the sitter, were tiers of drawers for the cosmetics, pomades, lip salve, powder, rouge, brushes, and combs required for the toilet. An easel mirror stood on top accompanied by jewel boxes, salvers, and candlesticks.

The word lowboy was in use in the eighteenth century, although infrequently. It has fallen into disuse in England but is still retained in America.

Developments in new forms of the desk resulted from the increase of letter writing in the late 1600s. National postal service was established in England, and there was a deputy postmaster general for North America in 1692. There had been a few experiments in writing tables in the reign of Charles II, but these did not reach America. However, the fall-front desk, already mentioned, was occasionally made. In the William and Mary period three new types appeared: the desk-on-frame, slope-front desk, and desk and bookcase, or secretary. The desk-on-frame (No. 90) was the former desk box on a stand. In place of the slanting lid, a new writing surface was made possible by small slides on which the open lid could rest. The lid was hinged, so that it opened outward instead of lifting up.

The slope-front desk (No. 94) originated when the desk box was placed on a chest of drawers, and as this provided valuable extra drawer space it eventually outmoded the desk-on-frame.

The desk and bookcase, or secretary (No. 98), was merely the slope-front desk with a cupboard section added. William and Mary secretaries are rare in America, and the form does not appear frequently until the Queen Anne period.

The easy chair, or wing chair, was an important addition to the late seventeenth-century room (No. 43). To the all-over upholstered chair, which had been known for a century in England, wings were added in the Restoration period. The form was the result of experiments of the upholsterer with a "sleeping chayer," which had a back that could be let down with a ratchet, and wings that protected the occupant from drafts. The general usefulness of this type of chair was soon realized, and it began to be made without the ratchet device. The name easy chair was given to it in the seventeenth century.

Caned furniture appeared in America in the late 1600s, after its introduction into England from Portugal and Holland around 1660 or later. The trade of the East India Companies had made Oriental caning familiar. By the 1680s, cane-chair making was a specialized industry in England. Apprentices learned to split imported Indian canes, and skilled frame-makers and carvers completed the product. England's export of cane chairs was prodigious; many reached the Colonies, where patterns were soon copied by local chairmakers. As a rule English chairs were made of beech, a wood occasionally used in American examples, although most often in combination with maple or ash. These chairs, fashionable in England in the 1680s, were of the tall-back type with cane panel, carved crests, and Flemish scroll stretchers.

The banister-back chair seen in Nos. 38-42 was of simpler form and was frequently made in America. Its design, with a back composed entirely of a series of banisters, is unlike the English equivalent with its few banisters combined with cane. The row of banisters forming the back of the American chair seems to have represented a practical simplification. Generally the banisters are flat, but sometimes they are true split balusters, and have a rounded surface on one side. When these are turned to the back, the chair seems out of balance; when they are turned toward the sitter the chair is uncomfortable.

There is a scarcity of existing examples of William and Mary beds. Illustrated in Nos. 3 and 4 are folding trestle beds which have abbreviated testers suggesting the English William and Mary half-tester type. Daybeds were useful extra beds in the small seventeenth-century house, and possibly more examples survive from the William and Mary period than from any other. Daybeds were so-called in Tudor days, although the boxlike form of these early examples was unlike the Charles II style on which Nos. 88 and 89 are based. The construction is like an extended chair with eight legs (usually) and either a canted or adjustable back. Caning is usual, but a laced-sacking bottom is frequently found on early eighteenth-century pieces. A squab or long cushion covered with embroidery, velvet, damask, wool, or other fabric contributed to comfort. Daybeds were generally called couches by our ancestors, and many books today classify them as such, but as there are so many kinds of couches the earlier name remains a clearer identification.

Tables of the late 1600s have lighter turnings than those of the Pilgrim period and are more varied in form. The gateleg table, introduced about 1675, was made in various sizes (Nos. 122-127). A small gateleg table had been in use in England from about 1600, but during the reign of Charles II a larger, oval-top gateleg table was made for dining. This type was frequently made in America. However, instead of the twist-turning used in England most American gatelegs have vase-turnings or, on rare occasions, a ball-and-ring turning.

The most popular American table of the period was the butterfly table (Nos. 117 and 118). This is sometimes considered to be of American origin, but tables with a hinged leaf were also known in Europe, and the precise connection is not clear. Whatever the source of the design, the New England craftsman gave a personal stamp to his butterfly table, with its raked legs and gracefully designed wings. If not entirely of American origin, it became a distinctively American form.

A more comfortable standard of living in the William and Mary period is suggested by the number of medium-sized tables for such purposes as reading, writing, for breakfast, cards, or tea. Most of these tables have modern names, such as porringer table (No. 131), tavern table (No. 135), splay-leg table (No. 132), and Spanish-foot table (No. 127). There were also a side table now called a mixing table (No. 130), with a slate or marble top impervious to hot or strong liquids, and a hutch table, which was a country-type descendant of the Pilgrim chair table (No. 128).

The tea table (No. 137) made a rare appearance in America in the William and Mary style. As a special form it was made in England about 1680. Tea had been introduced around 1650 but was so costly at first that it was used chiefly as a medicinal drink. Increased importation into England by the East India Company gradually reduced the price, and tea drinking by Catherine of Braganza, the Portuguese princess who became the wife of Charles II, made it fashionable. In the 1670s silversmiths began making tall cylindrical teapots, and not long afterward cabinetmakers made small tables for serving it. The first record of a purchase is in 1690 when, according to the *Dictionary of English Furniture,* Lord Bristol paid ten pounds for a "tea-table and two pairs of china cupps." The development of the tea table, however, belongs to the Queen Anne period.

The looking glass became a decorative feature of the late seventeenth-century interior, but surviving American examples are rare (Nos. 99 and 100). There was a distinction in terminology between the "looking glass," which hung on the wall, and the "mirror," which was a hand glass. The long slender pier glass came into existence to fill the empty space on the pier between the windows in the new type of house Sir Christopher Wren was designing in the late seventeenth century. It hung over the pier table. As the manufacture of mirror glass was perfected, plates of larger size became available and joining of more than one plate resulted in English pier glasses of imposing size. As looking glasses were exported in quantity to the Colonies, the identification today of American-made examples is often difficult; this continues to hold true throughout the Queen Anne and Chippendale periods. The rare early examples which have claim to American origin are of the simplest type.

BLENDING OF STYLES. The William and Mary style did not supplant the Jacobean entirely, but modified it. Throughout the entire seventeenth century, furniture was characterized by rectangular forms and turned members. Regardless of changes in techniques and the introduction of new furniture forms, basic harmony is apparent. In America new types, such as the Connecticut and Hadley chests, fundamentally Jacobean, were originated at the time when William and Mary high chests and slope-front desks were being introduced. At that point the two styles ran concurrently. There was also an influence from the William and Mary style which modified the Jacobean, bringing about the use of slender vase turnings rather than heavy baluster supports of earlier type. Time has destroyed many of the earliest examples of Jacobean furniture made in America, and it is frequently necessary to study the style in later versions. For these reasons it has become customary to consider the two first styles together.

THE QUESTION OF DATES. Assigning dates to early furniture is always difficult, especially in regard to Jacobean and William and Mary pieces. Documentary evidence is rare; inscribed dates are few, and some may be commemorative and therefore misleading. To suggest a decade or twenty-year span is by many students considered unjustified; a half-century would come nearer to fact. Dates are given guardedly with each illustration, but dates must be given, and in decades where possible, so that the sequence of changes in design is indicated.

# Makers

Comparatively few seventeenth- and early eighteenth-century makers are known by documented works. The most important was *Thomas Dennis,* who was born in England about 1638 and trained there as joiner and carver. He was in Portsmouth, New Hampshire, in 1663 and by 1688 was working in Ipswich, Massachusetts. Dennis was a maker of wainscot chairs and richly carved chests with late Tudor and Jacobean ornament, including strapwork, guilloche, foliated S-scrolls, arcading, and palmate panels. Recent studies have shown that it is no longer tenable to assign to him the many examples credited him in the past (see No. 24) but his reputation as a craftsman is secure through works which have come down in his family. For works which have been attributed to Dennis see Nos. 47, 78, 79, 80.

*Nicholas Disbrowe* (1612/13-1683), Hartford, Connecticut, is another maker to whom attributions have been given too liberally. Like Dennis, he was born and probably trained in England. He was one of the first settlers of Hartford. The inventory of his estate shows that he owned many tools of a joiner. Governor John Winthrop's wainscot chair, which now belongs to Wesleyan University at Middletown, Connecticut, is well established as his work, but Mary Allyn's chest has a signature no longer credited to him by most students (see No. 55). The typical Connecticut or Hartford chest with tulip and sunflower carving, which was once tentatively associated with him, has been shown by Houghton Bulkeley to be propably the work of *Peter Blin* of Wethersfield (see No. 53).

Makers of the Hadley chest (No. 56) form a distinct group because of the marked individuality of the type, but they were scattered along the Connecticut River from Hartford to the Vermont border. The chief makers lived in Hadley, Massachusetts, or in that part of it which became Hatfield. They included *John Allis* (1645-1691) and *Samuel Belding* (1633-1713), followed by their sons, *Ichabod Allis* (1675-1747) and *Samuel Belding, Jr.* (1637-1737). *Samuel Allis,* brother of John, worked for the firm of Belding and Allis. *John Hawkes,* born in Hatfield in 1643, moved to Deerfield, where his work is still to be seen in Memorial Hall. Several other makers are recognized in the group, which perfected an original form of hope chest with tulip and leaf carvings in flat relief against a matted ground which covered the entire face of the chest. The best account of the type is still to be found in the Reverend Clair Franklin Luther's *The Hadley Chest,* published in 1935.

The names of makers of documented furniture in the William and Mary style are unfortunately lacking. *John Gaines* (1704-1743) of Portsmouth, New Hampshire, is known for chairs which descended in his family. These chairs show Queen Anne influence but have many points of the William and Mary style. Gaines was born in Ipswich, Massachusetts, the son of the turner John Gaines (1677-c.1750). The latter's account book, now in the library of the Winterthur Museum, contains so many references to different types of chairs that it is considered possible to discover his hand in work (see No. 37) which is closely related in style to that of the son. The subject has greatly interested students, and further findings may identify pieces by the elder John Gaines and another son, Thomas, who continued to work in Ipswich after the younger John Gaines moved to Portsmouth.

Gaines, senior, was primarily a maker of turned chairs, but he also turned furniture parts for others and did architectural work for houses and churches. Beyond that, his activities as farmer and storekeeper, blacksmith and butcher, were manifold. He was business agent in a small way. He and his sons thatched roofs, plowed fields, and went on errands to Salem or Boston for more affluent townsmen. The number and variety of household and farm tools they made was endless, from button molds, rolling pins, and hoe handles to spindles and whorls for the spinner. Seldom does a ledger present such a vivid impression of the life, the skills, and the ingenuity of an early New England craftsman.

# *Chart:* Jacobean — William and Mary, 1640–1720

*Jacobean*
   Arcaded chest; book box (bible box, desk box); Brewster chair, Carver chair; court cupboard, press cupboard; slat-back chair; stretcher table; upholstered (Cromwellian) chair; wainscot chair.
*William and Mary*
   Banister-back chair; butterfly table; cane chair; daybed; desk-on-frame; dressing table (lowboy); easy chair; fall-front desk; gateleg table; high chest (highboy); mixing table, splay-leg table; tavern table; tall-back chair.

PRINCIPAL WOODS

*Jacobean*
   Oak, pine.
*William and Mary*
   Walnut, maple.

DECORATIVE TECHNIQUES

*Jacobean*
   Carving, ebonizing, inlay (rare), painting, turning.
*William and Mary*
   Inlay, japanning (advertised in Boston, 1712), painting, turning, veneering.

DESIGN

*Jacobean*
   Applied bosses and spindles (No. 54).
   Arcaded panels (No. 47).
   Ball turnings (No. 27).
   Bulbous supports of baluster form (Nos. 74-81).
   Geometric panels (No. 77).
*William and Mary*
   Arched skirt (apron) formed of cyma (ogee) scrolls (No. 71).
   Fielded panels (No. 96).

Flemish scroll (No. 88).
Trumpet turning and variations (Nos. 70, 71, 121).
Vase-turning (No. 126).

# English Background

*Early 1600s*
   Small gateleg table; the so-called Cromwellian chair, a small chair upholstered in leather or Turkey work. As it was not common until midcentury it has acquired the modern name.

*Mid-1600s*
   Chest of drawers, 1640s.
   Restoration of Charles II, 1660.
   Caning, veneering and japanning introduced from the Continent. Technique of fine cabinetmaking in inlay, lighter drawer construction, introduced through Dutch and Flemish workmen.
   Walnut becomes the most important wood, supplanting oak in fashionable work.
   New forms: daybed; high chest; fall-front desk. The gateleg table was made larger, seating eight or ten persons, and became the usual dining table in the "dining parlor" of the new type of house built by Sir Christopher Wren in London after the Great Fire of 1666.
   The tall-back chair was introduced into England about 1685 and was popular until 1710.
   Stalker and Parker's *Treatise of Japanning,* Oxford, 1688, gave practical instructions for imitating with varnish and paint the true Oriental lacquer, which was done with the sap of the tree, *Rhus vernicifera;* also supplied designs of Oriental character showing Dutch influence.

*Late 1600s*
   *William and Mary, 1688.*
   New forms: desk and bookcase (secretary); dressing table (lowboy); high chest reaches perfected form; slope-front desk and desk-on-frame; tea table; pier glass.

1

1. A New England Jacobean low-post bed of oak. It has turned posts, molded rails, and low headboard. The paneled cradle, also of oak, has a hood of open construction and turned rocking posts. From the Thomas Hart house parlor, Ipswich, Massachusetts, about 1640. (*Metropolitan Museum of Art.*)

2. Jacobean oak cradle, with pine panels and top made in the mid-1600s. It is of framed-panel construction; the galleried hood is complete with a cap, notched after the manner of early desk boxes. Spindles forming the gallery are elaborately turned, and there are rocking posts. This cradle descended in the family of Samuel Fuller of Plymouth, a *Mayflower* arrival. (*Nutting Collection, Wadsworth Atheneum.*)

2

**3.** New England folding trestle bed of pine with six legs, made in the early 1700s. It is constructed so that it can easily be folded against the wall and concealed behind a curtain. The simple framework was not intended to be seen, the foot being hidden by a coverlet. The square headposts are visible, and a small tester supports a valance and hangings which, like the coverlet, are of crewelwork (wool embroidery). At the foot of the bed is a late seventeenth-century joint stool. (*Room from Hampton, New Hampshire, Metropolitan Museum of Art.*)

**4.** This folding trestle bed of walnut, made in the early 1700s, is a finer example of the type shown in No. 3. Its turned footposts and headposts (of late Jacobean form) support bed hangings in the style of the William and Mary half-tester bed. The valance, hangings, and coverlet of eighteenth-century crewelwork have a widely spaced floral motif, characteristic of American work. The room is furnished with other pieces of the William and Mary period. (*The Walnut Room, H. F. du Pont Winterthur Museum.*)

3

4

**5.** Walnut cradle with paneled, flaring sides, open hood, and rocking posts. The cradle, of type seen in Dutch genre paintings, is considered to have been made in the Hudson River Valley, about 1700. Here it accompanies a rare seventeenth-century *kas* or wardrobe (see Nos. 82-84). (*Philipsburg Manor, Upper Mills, Sleepy Hollow Restorations.*)

**6.** Trundle beds, mentioned in the earliest records of American homes, were used for children. This example, when closed, appears to be no more than a fielded panel in the footboard. The red painted bed with simply turned headposts and low headboard is probably later than 1720 but represents the kind used with furniture of the early 1700s as seen here. The bed has rust-red bed curtains of homespun linen and antique yellow-green linsey-woolsey coverlet. The room is in Hempsted House, New London, built in 1678. (*The Antiquarian and Landmarks Society of Connecticut.*)

**7.** Jacobean form of the late 1600s, made of oak and maple with a pine top. As early inventories so often list together the table, form, and joint stool (Nos. 106-108), a permanent arrangement in proximity with each other is suggested, as in this hall or "keeping room," which was kitchen, dining room, and bedroom. This interior is from an Essex, Massachusetts, house built in 1684. These forms were in general use in the days when chairs were few. Here the form accompanies a stretcher table and other turn-of-the-century pieces. (*Seventeenth-Century Room, H. F. du Pont Winterthur Museum.*)

7

8

9

10

**8.** New England pine settle of about 1710 with maple ball- and baluster-turnings and sloping arms as seen on wainscot chairs. The back has raised and fielded panels which indicate the William and Mary period. Beveled edges of the center are recessed so that the faces of the panels project forward slightly. This style of paneling distinguished the houses of Sir Christopher Wren in England in the last quarter of the seventeenth century and reached America about 1700. In his *Furniture Treasury*, Nutting states that this settle was made in Connecticut. (*Nutting Collection, Wadsworth Atheneum.*)

**9.** Early eighteenth-century hooded settle of pine. The lobed armrests suggest New Jersey or Pennsylvania origin. In New England armrests generally taper to a blunt point. The back of this one has five fielded panels and continues to the floor, as a protection from drafts. Trestle feet are scrolled in cyma (ogee) curves. Hooded settles were made in New England and the middle colonies for so long a period that examples are difficult to date. (*Metropolitan Museum of Art.*)

**10.** William and Mary settle of walnut and leather made about 1700. The leather upholstery, although unpadded, shows that comfort was a consideration, and this piece undoubtedly belonged to a home of more than usual luxury. The back, as usual, extends almost to the floor. The arms show a new modification in design; instead of being of the early drooping type they are horizontally scrolled. (*Metropolitan Museum of Art.*)

11. The William and Mary leather-upholstered bench in this Hall from Morattico, Richmond County, Virginia, was made about 1700. The undulation in the swelling and diminishing lines of the slender vase-turned stretchers were obtained by skillful manipulation of the cutting instrument while the wood revolved in the lathe. The turner's art is also well represented by other pieces in this interior, which includes a late seventeenth-century joint stool and, representing styles of the early 1700s, a Spanish-foot easy chair, a William and Mary desk-on-frame, and a chest of drawers on ball feet with exceptionally well-painted floral scrolls in imitation of marquetry. The cane armchair (which resembles the Charles II chair of England more closely than is usual in American work) and the cane side chair with Flemish-scroll foot are of the late 1600s. (*H. F. du Pont Winterthur Museum.*)

12

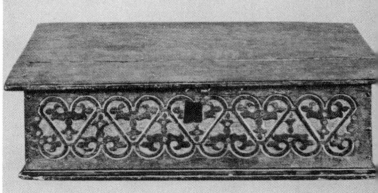

14

15

**12.** A Jacobean book or desk box of about 1680 from New England. It is painted green. The carved design in flat relief against an incised ground is formed of favorite devices of the seventeenth-century carver, the S-scroll and reversed S-scroll. Used in pairs, these scrolls produced a heart-shaped design. The scrolls here are vertical, but they were frequently horizontal. (*Brooklyn Museum.*)

**13.** New England Jacobean book or desk box, probably made in Massachusetts about 1650-1680. The bottom is white oak and the cleat hinges, red oak. Carved initials *P P*, framed in carved strapwork, appear on the lid of the box. The band of rosettes across the front is executed in gouge, or chip, carving, a crude form of intaglio. Traces of red and black paint remain. (*H. F. du Pont Winterthur Museum.*)

**14.** New England book, or desk, box in pine, painted bluish-green (Jacobean, 1680-1700). This somewhat crudely carved design is handsome in scale, a simply rendered tulip and leaf pattern silhouetted on a punched ground. The tulip, while rendered differently, suggests comparison with the Connecticut Sunflower chests and the Hadley chests (Nos. 53, 56). (*Detroit Institute of Arts.*)

**15.** Box with Friesland carving, made in the late 1600s. While similar to No. 13, the intaglio design of rosettes, diaper work, and geometric motifs is more closely integrated in Friesland ("Friesian") carving, which seems to have been done all along the Atlantic coast. The style was doubtless copied from European work, but whether from Dutch originals is not certain. (*Brooklyn Museum.*)

13

11

16

16. New England Brewster chair made of ash around 1640. This Jacobean chair descended in the family of William Bradford (1589/90-1657) and probably belonged to him. Bradford, governor of the Plymouth colony for thirty years, may well have written some of his history of the Plymouth colony while sitting in this chair, although it was not his only "great" chair, his estate listing no fewer than six, an unusually large number for the time. Originally the front posts, which are of the heavy, early type, would have been surmounted by balls. These posts have been worn down at the base as far as the stretcher. The seat is dished for a cushion. (*Pilgrim Society, Pilgrim Hall, Plymouth, Massachusetts.*)

17. Brewster-type child's armchair, made of maple and elm, in the late 1600s. The simpler turnings indicate a later date than the chair in No. 16. Also, maple began to appear in later examples. (*Art Institute of Chicago.*)

18. New England Carver chair made of ash around 1650-1660. The massive, well-turned spindles in the back of this chair make it superior to the one which gave the name to the type. The posts, however, are not quite so heavy as those on John Carver's chair. (*Nutting Collection, Wadsworth Atheneum.*)

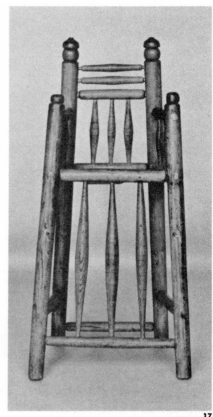

17

18

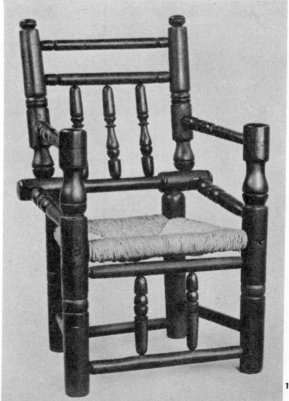

19

**19.** Turned great chair of ash in Jacobean style, about 1675, with dished seat and plain stretchers. The chair, owned by the Stryker family of New York, has a Carver-type back and spindles below the seat, which relate it to a Brewster chair. An almost identical chair has belonged to the Connecticut Historical Society for over a hundred years. The distinguishing feature is the canted back, which rests on a turned rail supported above the seat frame by the back posts. By this means the back is given a slant to provide greater comfort. (*Metropolitan Museum of Art.*)

**20.** Southern Carver chair of maple and hickory, made in the early 1700s. Carvers are occasionally found in the southern states and have the local characteristic of an arm projecting over the front post. The spindles here are lightly turned and the posts have good vase turnings. The seat of split white oak is new. (*Collection of Frank L. Horton.*)

**21.** Jacobean turned chairs at Hempsted House, New London, Connecticut, are seen in the hall or "keeping room." A small chair of Brewster type, at left, has elaborate turnings. The Carver chair at end of table has light spindles, moderately heavy posts and finials, suggesting a date in the last quarter of the seventeenth century. At right, an early slat-back armchair with the usual three slats; finials resemble those on early Carver and Brewster chairs. (*The Antiquarian and Landmarks Society of Connecticut.*)

20

21

22

23

22. Jacobean chair-table of oak, probably made in Connecticut about 1650-1675. Chair-tables are mentioned as early as the 1630s. The dual function, served by raising and lowering the back, made it popular in houses with limited space. Here is a rare example of columnar turnings of legs and arm supports instead of vase-shapes. This is primarily the work of a joiner and has pegged mortice and tenon joints. Originally there was a drawer in the frame under the seat. The sides are carved with crude imbrication. (*Greenwood gift, Smithsonian Institution.*)

23. Jacobean oak wainscot chair from Essex County, Massachusetts; made in the late 1600s; the carved back panel shows a guilloche motif enclosing rosettes under a flat cresting rail carved with segments of arches. This once belonged to the early collector, Charles F. Waters of Salem. It is one of a scant half-dozen or so examples known having the squared baluster in the posts and the same general treatment of the back. The quality of carving here is superior, but the tapering feet are questioned (the chair had undergone incorrect restoration while in the Waters collection); probably the original form was square. The squared foot is seen on what is probably the prototype of the group, now at Pilgrim Hall, Plymouth, Massachusetts, and in an example at Winterthur (No. 106). (*Museum of Fine Arts, Boston.*)

24. Wainscot chair in oak from Essex County, Massachusetts, made in the late 1600s, and formerly attributed to the Ipswich joiner and carver Thomas Dennis.[5] The back is richly carved with floral forms rising from a cartouche in the central panel, strapwork, S-scrolls and reverse S-scrolls. Flanking the design are carved terminal figures, frequent in Jacobean work in England, not in America. The carving is similar to that on a closely related chair belonging to the President of Bowdoin College, Brunswick, Maine. Both chairs descended in the Dennis family, but while the latter is a justifiable attribution to the Ipswich maker, this chair may have been the work of an apprentice. (*Essex Institute, Salem.*)

24

**25.** Jacobean wainscot chair of oak from New Jersey. It is painted black and carved with the date *1695* and initials *R / R I* for Robert and Janet Rhea of Freehold. (J becomes I in the Latin form.) That Robert Rhea was a Scottish carpenter and joiner doubtless explains the prominence given to the thistle in the carved design on the back panel, with the conventionalized tulip and rose. A very wide crest, such as this, is sometimes seen on sixteenth-century English wainscot chairs. Stretchers are knob-turned and the front posts are unbroken at the seat rail in the early manner. (*Monmouth County Historical Association.*)

**26.** Jacobean upholstered armchair of the late 1600s, made of beech and covered in leather. The spiral turning, seen here in the front stretcher and in the arm and back supports, appears rarely in America, although it has been noted in New York and in the South. This chair, once in the Bolles collection, resembles (in its turnings) the walnut side chairs in the Philadelphia Museum of Art and Winterthur Museum which are traced to New Jersey. (*Metropolitan Museum of Art.*)

**27.** Jacobean upholstered chair, the so-called Cromwellian chair; with uprights and ball-turned front stretcher made of maple and the remaining parts of oak. The date is about 1690. This type, covered in leather or Turkey work, long antedated the period of Cromwell in England but became widely popular in the mid-1600s, when it supplanted the joint stool at the dining table.[6] They were probably made in America during the last quarter of the seventeenth century, but were never common. In the right foreground of No. 29 there is a glimpse of such a chair which has its original Turkey-work upholstery, a form of needlework which imitated the Turkey carpet. (*Metropolitan Museum of Art.*)

**28.** Leather-upholstered maple chair from New England, with bulbous front stretcher and block-and-vase-turned legs. Although in general character this is a William and Mary chair (about 1720) there are indications of the approach of the Queen Anne style. The uprights are molded instead of turned, the cresting is in a continuous line with the uprights, and the "bended back" has an undulating curve adapted to the form of the occupant. (*George Dudley Seymour Collection, Connecticut Historical Society, Hartford.*)

25

26

27    28

**29.** Seventeenth-century Jacobean chairs. At left, a leather-upholstered ("Cromwellian") chair with ball-turnings; at the table, a Carver chair with the earliest type of finial on the back posts. The back is canted slightly, for comfort. This type of construction is even more pronounced in the early slat-back armchair at the wall. Its mushroom arms are of the large size found on early slat-backs. Three slats are also typical of the early period. Both this and the Carver chair have the early, plain stretchers. Slightly later sausage-turning is found on the handsomely proportioned slat-back armchair with winged slats by the fireplace. (*Oyster Bay Room, H.F. du Pont Winterthur Museum.*)

**30.** Jacobean slat-back armchair of oak from New England. The heavy posts and three broad slats represent the early type. The date *1691* is scratched on the back of the upper slat, with initials *J P* for John Picard of Rowley, Massachusetts, in whose family the chair has descended to the present. (*Greenwood gift, Smithsonian Institution.*)

**31.** Late Jacobean slat-back armchair from New York or Connecticut, made of maple and ash with a rush seat (1660-1690). Under black paint are traces of an earlier coat of red. Here are fine, heavy, ring-turned posts with mushroom finials on the front posts, ball finials on the back ones, and turned lateral spindles below the arms. (*No. 8, "Furniture by New York Cabinetmakers, 1956-1957," Museum of the City of New York; catalogue by V. Isabelle Miller. Ex Coll. Behrend. Art Institute of Chicago.*)

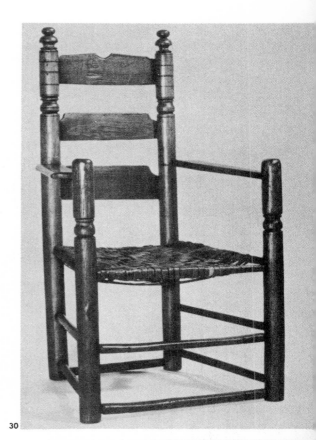

**32.** Slat-back armchair of oak and ash, made in New England about 1700. This late-Jacobean example is the concluding form of the "great" slat-back of the seventeenth century, with posts two to three inches thick. The unevenly graduated slats were obviously designed with comfort in mind. The inverted bulbous finials succeeded the type at left in No. 33. (*Henry Ford Museum.*)

**33.** Slat-back armchairs with rush seats, made in New England in late 1600s. The chair at left has the same style of finial seen on early Brewster and Carver chairs and may have been made about 1680. It retains traces of old red paint. Chair at right, made about 1690, has mushroom arms. The mushroom is a large flattened disk that caps the front post and is turned in one piece with it. Two of the more usual forms of slats are represented here. Slats may be curved, scooped, indented, pointed, scrolled, or winged. The woods most often used were oak and ash, and sometimes maple. (*Shelburne Museum.*)

32

**34.** Slat-back armchair, with rush seat, made in Connecticut between 1710-1730. Oak and an unidentified wood were used in its construction. The chair has five slats, sausage-and-ball-turned stretchers, and a delicately turned medial crosspiece under the arms. It came from the Captain Charles Churchill house, Newington, Connecticut. This form, made after 1700, shows the influence of the English tall-back chair of 1680-1710. (*George Dudley Seymour Collection, Connecticut Historical Society.*)

**35.** Slat-back maple armchair of the Pennsylvania–New Jersey type, made about 1725. The arched slat is characteristic of the Delaware River Valley. For a time after 1700 the development here as elsewhere was toward greater height and a greater number of slats. Then, as the design became the concern of the country chairmaker, the height and number of slats were both decreased. The ringed bulbous front stretcher is finely turned. (*Henry Ford Museum.*)

33

34

35

37

38

39

36

40

**36.** William and Mary tall-back cane chair, made in New York about 1690.[7] The wood is maple and beech. This is an American version of the English chair used with the new tables for the serving of tea. The New York chair makes full use of the Flemish scroll, a florid "S," which appeared in English work about 1675. The crest is contained between the uprights, in the manner of Charles II chairs. The next development was to place the crest on top of the uprights. (*Bequest of Herbert Lee Pratt, 1945, Metropolitan Museum of Art.*)

**37.** A maple Spanish-foot cane chair made in New England between 1710-1720. The chair has certain points in common with chairs attributed to John Gaines of Portsmouth (No. 46), but it is of an earlier date. The similarity of the pierced crest, the Spanish foot, and the bulbous front stretcher have given rise to the suggestion that this chair may be the work of the father, John Gaines (1677-c.1750) of Ipswich, Massachusetts, a turner and chairmaker whose account book,[8] now at the Winterthur Museum, shows he was an active craftsman. In the days when the son learned his trade from his father, such stylish affiliations can be inferred. (*Ex Coll. Louis E. Brooks. Henry Ford Museum.*)

**38.** William and Mary banister-back armchair, with crown crest and ram's-horn arms, made in New York about 1700.[9] The wood, maple and hickory, is painted black. Noteworthy are the richly turned stretchers, the bulbous form across the front, the medial stretcher, the balusters at the sides and the simple vase-shaped stretcher at the back. This chair has been in the two most important exhibitions of New York furniture, at the Metropolitan Museum in 1934 and the Museum of the City of New York, 1956-1957. (*Ex Coll. Mrs. J. Insley Blair. Museum of the City of New York.*)

**39.** William and Mary banister-back side chair of the early 1700s. Although constructed of beech, the design, typical of New England, frees the chair of possible English origin. It has a crown crest, banister-back, bulbous front stretcher, block-and-vase-turned legs. (*Connecticut Historical Society.*)

**40.** William and Mary banister-back armchair made in New England about 1690-1720. It has pine uprights and legs, maple cresting and cross-rail above the seat, and oak stretchers and banisters, all painted black. The high, pierced crest has a triple tier of spirals in the center and cornucopia-shaped openings at the sides. The contoured arms end in ram's-horn hand rests. Block-and-ring-turned front legs have Spanish feet, and there are reel-shaped turnings in the center of the front stretcher. (*Henry Ford Museum.*)

**41.** This William and Mary banister-back armchair with heart-and-crown crest was made in New England about 1700-1730. While not strictly a banister-back, this chair, with its straight, vertical slats, is classed with them. Shadow molding of the slats relieves the severity of straight lines. There are turned cross supports under the arms. The cresting has become a silhouette of the crown, and is pierced with a heart-shaped opening in a design used often enough to make this a recognized type. The wood is maple. (*Gift of Katharine Prentis Murphy, New-York Historical Society.*)

**42.** Here banister-back chairs of later form are drawn up at a hutch table. Turnings have become more rudimentary; the back of one has a crest showing a simple curve, the other has a low, unpierced silhouette of a crown. In the background is an exceptionally fine Brewster-type oak armchair with its three horizontal spindles in the back surmounted by a central finial. The New England slat-back armchair at the fireplace is also seen in No. 32. (*Plympton House, Henry Ford Museum.*)

**43.** William and Mary easy chair of about 1700. The arched crest and narrow lines are typical of the earliest period. The frame shows the block-and-vase-turned leg, medial stretcher, and Spanish foot. The upholstery, not original but of the same

41

42

43                                                          44

date as the chair, is of blue and white printed linen. The origin of this "blue resist" fabric with large floral patterns and ogival bands has proved puzzling, but it is known to have been in frequent use in eighteenth-century America. (*Gift of Mrs. J. Insley Blair, Metropolitan Museum of Art.*)

**44.** This New England William and Mary easy chair was possibly made in Ipswich about 1710-1730. It is of maple and painted black. The chair shows a well-executed Spanish foot, carved with a slight scroll at the side, and a bulbous medial stretcher with block-and-spindle side stretchers. Both this example and No. 43 have the horizontally rolled arm, like the first English easy chairs. This type was retained as a rule only on Philadelphia chairs, while Massachusetts and New York adopted the vertically rolled arm. This chair descended in the family of Theophilus Parsons (1750-1813), First Chief Justice of Massachusetts Supreme Court. (*Bayou Bend Collection, Houston.*)

45

46

**45.** William and Mary corner chair of the early 1700s, found in New Hampshire. The wood is undetermined. The central leg ends in a Spanish foot. The earliest corner chairs, such as this, had no splats. The type, used for writing and at the card table, was designed to accommodate the voluminous costume of the time. The term corner chair was used in the eighteenth century. (*Prentis Collection, New Hampshire Historical Society.*)

**46.** Spanish-foot side chair of maple, made about 1725 and attributed to John Gaines (1704-1743) of Portsmouth, New Hampshire.[10] The chair is a transition type between the Queen Anne style (note shape of the splat) and the William and Mary style, of which the bulbous front stretcher, block-and-vase-turned leg, and Spanish foot are familiar details. Like many examples of American furniture combining elements of two periods, this piece has the vitality of both. (*Prentis Collection, New Hampshire Historical Society.*)

47

**47.** Arcaded chest from New England made about 1675. It is of oak throughout and has a three-board lid, sides with two panels, and channeled rails and stiles. The carving, done in a more graduated relief than is usual in American work, combines late Tudor and Jacobean motifs, including arcaded panels enclosing the acanthus and foliation, a guilloche on the top rail, palmate panels on the stiles, and faceted ornaments alternating with whorls on the bottom rail. The center panel with acanthus rising from a cartouche is closely related to the design on the wainscot chair shown in No. 24, but is more skillfully carved. Both pieces have long been attributed to Thomas Dennis (c. 1638-1706) of Ipswich, but it is now believed that few of the nearly sixty former attributions to him can be sustained.[5] This chest from the Bolles collection has no recorded history, but if superiority is accepted as proof of the work of Dennis it should continue to bear his name. (*Metropolitan Museum of Art.*)

**48.** New England Jacobean chest of oak with a pine top, made about 1680. The "shuttle" lunette, formed of opposing lunettes, on the top rail, was a favorite design in America. Diamond panels, also frequently used both in America and in seventeenth-century England, here show imbrication on the borders of the diamonds and on the muntins between the panels. (*George Dudley Seymour Collection, Connecticut Historical Society.*)

49

**50**

**49.** Six-board chest made in New England in 1673. The "borded chest" of solid planks pegged (and in later years, nailed) was known in medieval Europe. Stamped designs are characteristic, but decoration occasionally was carved. These chests were often made of plain boards or wall sheathing. The ends form the "feet," and were cut to a V-shape, rounded to an arch, or were scrolled as here. Many examples are of flush construction at front and back, the ends cut to receive the front and back planks. When this was not done, as in the case here, a bracket was sometimes added to the awkward projection. The design consists of hearts, diamonds, dotted lines, the initials *I W*, and the date *1673*. (*Old Sturbridge Village.*)

**50.** Fourteen-panel Jacobean chest of oak, used in New Hampshire but probably made in Massachusetts about 1680. This chest is unusual for its all-around paneling which suggests that the piece was intended to stand free from the wall and to be seen from all sides. This is plain paneling of an early type, the molding being worked directly on the framework of the panels and not applied. At the tops of the panels the molded surface stops before it reaches the corners. (*Greenwood Gift, Smithsonian Institution.*)

**51.** Small Jacobean chest of oak with oak till, cleat hinge, and geometric paneling, made in New England about 1680-1690. Applied turnings in the form of split spindles, painted black to simulate ebony, were a feature of American work after 1675. This chest displays typical Jacobean paneling with geometric designs composed of mitred moldings. An heirloom of the Revere-Little family, it was in the sale of the collection of Miss Laura Revere Little, September 1947. (*Old Deerfield.*)

**52**

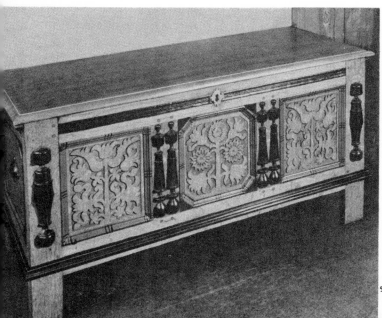

**52.** One-drawer walnut chest, made in the early 1700s. It has fielded panels (see No. 8); and a shaped skirt below the drawer. The secondary wood is southern hard yellow pine,[11] and this, with its discovery in the South, is probably indicative of its origin. (*No. 65, Exhibition of Southern Furniture, Virginia Museum, January 1952. Collection of Frank L. Horton.*)

**53.** Connecticut Sunflower chest, of oak with a pine top made probably about 1680-1700. The spindles and channeling are painted black. The tulip-and-sunflower design, peculiar to Connecticut, has recently been attributed to Peter Blin (working about 1675-1725) of Wethersfield.[12] The tulip motif, a popular decoration in Restoration England (to which it came from Holland), was also much used along the Connecticut River. The "sunflower," possibly a development of the Tudor rose, sometimes has rounded petals, sometimes pointed ones. Both are seen in the central panel here. Most Sunflower chests have two drawers below; this has none. (*Old Sturbridge Village.*)

53

54

55

**54.** Sunflower two-drawer oak chest made in Connecticut, about 1680-1700. Like No. 53, this chest of the late Jacobean period belongs to a group now associated with Peter Blin. The Sunflower chest can be called a characteristically American type, since the design elements, although English, are used in a manner peculiar to Connecticut. The carving is not as intricate as Essex County work (see No. 47), and compared to English pieces the geometric detail is simpler and the applied split spindles and bosses more prominent. (*Ex Coll. Luke Vincent Lockwood. Bayou Bend Collection, Houston.*)

**55.** Two-drawer oak chest of the late Jacobean period made about 1680. This famous chest, with its inscription, *Mary Allyns Chistt — Cutte and Joyned by Nich: Disbrowe*, is frequently published as the earliest signed piece of American furniture. While the validity of the inscription is no longer accepted by students, this does not lessen the intrinsic value of the chest as a fine example of Connecticut work. The design in flat relief raised against an incised, flat ground consists of tulips, leaves, scrolls, and a vine trail entirely covering the panels, drawer fronts, stiles, and rails. The piece is similar to the Hatfield type of Hadley chest attributed to John Allis, although it is finer than the example carved *A A* in the Cleveland Museum and the *H A* chest at the Wadsworth Atheneum. It has much in common with the handsomer *E A* and *L A* chests, Nos. 4 and 6 in the Reverend Clair Franklin Luther's definitive study, *The Hadley Chest*, but whether as prototype, relative, or member of this group, which John Allis made for his daughters, is a subject for further study. It is worth noting that the initials carved in the panels are *M A*. (*Bayou Bend Collection, Houston.*)

**56.** Hadley chest, marked *I P* for Joanna Porter (1687-1714), who in 1704 was married to John Marsh, representative to the General Court. Hadley chests, first noted in the vicinity of Hadley, Massachusetts, were made about 1675 to 1740 in the valley of the Connecticut River. Over one hundred and twenty have been recorded. They are chiefly one- or two-drawer oak chests with tulip and leaf carving in flat relief against a flat, matted ground. The chests, characteristically, are painted red, black, shades of brown, and sometimes green. Incised lines ending in scrolls define the design. The chief makers were Samuel Belding, senior and junior, John Allis and his son Ichabod, all of Hatfield.[13] Others were John Taylor of Hadley and Hatfield, John Hawkes of Deerfield, and John Pease of Enfield. This particular chest resembles work attributed to Belding and Allis. (*C. Sanford Bull Collection, Yale University Art Gallery.*)

56

**57**

**58**

**59**

**60**

**57.** Late Jacobean chest-on-frame, made in the 1690s and found at Ipswich, Massachusetts. The woods used are oak, pine, and maple. The turnings, bosses, and small panels are stained black. In later periods the chest-on-frame consisted of two separate pieces, but this seventeenth-century type was a single unit. The spool-turnings seen here did not appear in American work until the late 1600s. The chest section is characterized by the use of very narrow panels intercepted by cross pieces with bosses. These panels are formed by grooves cut in the solid wood and outlined with a narrow cyma molding. Other Essex County pieces show similar decoration. None of the five pieces known to have been made by Thomas Dennis of Ipswich (to whom it has been attributed) displays this "small panel" style,[5] and this piece is probably to be traced to some other maker in Essex County. (*Art Institute of Chicago.*)

**58.** Chest-on-frame of oak, pine, and maple, made in Massachusetts about 1700. It has vase-and-ring-turned stretchers, lift-up top, and cleat hinge. The chest, which descended in the Hancock family, represents the popularity of painted ornament as distinct from solid color, which began to be evident in American furniture around 1680.[14] The panels are red, the trees black and white, and the body of the chest is stained to imitate graining. (*Brooklyn Museum.*)

**59.** Chest of drawers of oak with a yellow pine top and back made about 1675-1700 in New England. This two-drawer chest, with front carved with leaf and palmette in lunettes, and a vine design around the stiles and rails, has been attributed to Nicholas Disbrowe. It has been difficult to isolate the work of Disbrowe, who was evidently responsible for mucn furniture made in Hartford, of which he was one of the founders in 1636. He is generally credited with the President's chair at Wesleyan University. However, as the inscription on the chest illustrated in No. 55 has been doubted, the attribution of the piece illustrated here is weakened; but a Connecticut origin seems likely. (*Metropolitan Museum of Art.*)

**60.** Chest of drawers, probably made in New England about 1675-1700. The effect of the elaborate inlay or marquetry, characteristic of English work in the late seventeenth century, was sometimes imitated in America in the form of painted, or painted and carved design, as here. This late Jacobean three-drawer chest of oak is one of the earliest American pieces of its kind. It has a boldly carved palmette and heart design joined by straight lines and semicircles on a black background. The stiles have a leaf panel terminating in a highly conventionalized fleur-de-lis. (*Metropolitan Museum of Art.*)

**61.** A chest of drawers of oak and pine, made about 1690, and once in the Fairbanks house at Dedham, Massachusetts, the oldest framed house in America. The chest appears to have eight drawers, but in reality it has only four. The others are suggested by panels with beveled moldings. The paneling on the stiles is intercepted by knob turnings of early type, and there are two panels on the ends as found on early press cupboards. The chest has flattened ball feet in front and stiles that continue as feet to the floor at the back. Cast brass drop handles supplanted wrought-iron handles in the late 1600s. (*Shelburne Museum.*)

61

**62.** This double chest of drawers, made in Massachusetts about 1690, is the forerunner of the chest-on-chest of greater height. Its flush construction makes it appear to be a single chest of four drawers; in others of this rare type molding marks the division. The drawer fronts have geometric paneling simulating eight drawers. The drop handles are partly original. Like No. 61, this oak chest came from Dedham, Massachusetts. (*George Dudley Seymour Collection, Connecticut Historical Society.*)

**63.** William and Mary chest of drawers with walnut burl veneer and herringbone banding. This piece was owned by the Reverend Thomas Prince (1687-1758) of Boston, associate pastor of the Old South Church and owner of the land on which Princeton, Massachusetts, was settled. The date *1687* painted on the bottom was added at a later date, apparently to commemorate the year of his birth. The chest may have been made in 1719, the time of his return from an extended visit to Europe and England and the year of his marriage. The veneering and inlay represent the work of a highly trained cabinetmaker. Knowledge of these skills came to England from Flanders and Holland in the reign of Charles II and to America around 1700. (*Greenwood Gift, Smithsonian Institution.*)

62

63

**64.** This oak chest of drawers, made in the late seventeenth century, has drawer fronts paneled with beveled moldings. Between the drawers are single-arch moldings, a method of construction familiar in England in the period of Charles II and copied in America around 1690 and later (see Nos. 94 and 95). The painted floral design, an elaborate one, is still subsidiary to the geometric style but anticipates the popularity of painted designs on New England furniture in the early 1700s. (*Gift of Mrs. J. Insley Blair. Metropolitan Museum of Art.*)

**65.** One-drawer oak chest made in New England, possibly Massachusetts, about 1690. Combination of geometric elements in the paneling and applied split spindles with a floral design indicates the early period of painted ornament. Painted design on American furniture of the late 1600s takes the place of marquetry on English furniture. Japanning was used on more costly American pieces. The bold design of conventionalized roses surviving on the panels and top rail of this chest gives some idea of the brilliant effect it must have had in the seventeenth-century room. (*Bayou Bend Collection, Houston.*)

**66.** One-drawer chest made in the early 1700s. Oak forms the main part, with pine for the panels and the top. The painted tree and bird design suggests the inspiration of a needlework pattern. Colors are red, green, and black on the natural tone of the wood. The flattened ball feet are attached to extended stiles, and the top has the usual thumbprint-molded edge seen in early work. The fielded panels at the ends are seen here in an early example of their use on American furniture and indicate the William and Mary period. (*Old Deerfield.*)

**67.** Guilford chest with one drawer made in the early 1700s.[15] It is of oak painted green with a superimposed white and polychrome design. Oak chests with this design have been found chiefly in the region of Guilford, Connecticut. They have armorial decoration, combining the crown, fleur-de-lis, Tudor rose, and thistle of Scotland, traced to seventeenth-century book ornament. No exact prototype in English furniture has yet been discovered. Other decorations may include an urn and floral design. The ends (as here) generally display a pheasant or bird of indeterminate species. The design also occurs on a chest-on-frame in the Metropolitan Museum and on a chest of drawers in the Wadsworth Atheneum. (*Henry Ford Museum.*)

64

65

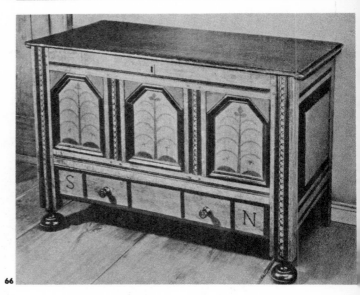

66

67

**68**

**68.** Painted chest of drawers with ball feet made in New England about 1690. It is of maple, with pine used as the secondary wood. The red and white design on a black ground was probably added in the early 1700s, in the vicinity of Boston. The decorator or artist must have drawn on various sources, such as japanned decoration and needlework motifs, for this elaborate ornamentation. (*Shelburne Museum.*)

**69**

**69.** William and Mary high chest (highboy) made in New York about 1690.[16] The use of gumwood (bilsted) and the spiral-twist leg are found on some half-dozen pieces with a New York history. This chest was made for the Mitchell family of Port Washington, Long Island. It is interesting that these rare pieces from the New York area show the single-twist turning of Dutch-Flemish type rather than the double or "barley sugar" twist of so much English work. The highboy was destined for a longer life in America than in England, where it disappeared after the Queen Anne period. This example has the shaped, flat stretcher of William and Mary pieces but otherwise belongs to the Carolean period. (*Metropolitan Museum of Art.*)

**70**

**70.** William and Mary high chest (highboy), with six legs, arched skirt, and shaped stretcher, made about 1690-1720. This is a finely veneered piece with matched panels of crotch walnut and bands of diagonal inlay around the drawers, which have the single-arch molding between them. The turned legs represent the tapering lines of the William and Mary period. This is called trumpet-turning, but the variations are described as cup-turning, bowl-turning, and trumpet, and there are intermediate forms. This example is cup-turned; No. 71 is trumpet-turned, No. 121 bowl-turned. William and Mary highboys usually have six legs, sometimes five, and at the end of the period four indicate the approach of the Queen Anne style. (*New-York Historical Society.*)

71

72

**71.** William and Mary high chest (highboy) with trumpet-turned legs made about 1720. Walnut crotch veneer with birch and maple. The William and Mary period brought curved lines into fashion, seen here in the cyma or ogee curves in the skirt, which are repeated in the front and side stretchers. The brasses are the first to show the loop handle with engraved backplate. A new refinement is seen in the cockbead (a narrow, half-round molding) on the drawer frame, a style used in England about 1720 to 1750, and longer in America. The lower section, with deep side drawers, represents a growing characteristic form. (*Metropolitan Museum of Art.*)

**72.** William and Mary high chest (highboy) made about 1710-1725. It is of birch with walnut-burl veneer. Four legs and a cross-stretcher are rare on highboys of the period, but were often seen on the lowboy, or dressing table. The six-legged type with shaped stretchers (as in Nos. 70 and 71) was usual. The slender legs here are cup-turned, and the double-arch molding around the drawers is a method of construction adopted from English precedent around 1700. (*Metropolitan Museum of Art.*)

73

74

**73.** Small cupboard or cabinet of oak and pine made in Massachusetts about 1660-1690. The serrated molding (see also No. 77) is associated with Plymouth. The type, often called a spice cabinet, is seen again in No. 106. (*Art Institute of Chicago.*)

**74.** Jacobean court cupboard (c. 1640) found near the Maryland-Virginia border. It is made of oak, with southern yellow pine[11] as the secondary wood. The bulbous supports (balusters) are unusually heavy. The panels are carved in low relief with tulip and rosette motifs; foliated S-scrolls appear at top and on the drawer below, and a serrated leaf design decorates the stiles. The old suggestion that the term "court" may have come from the French word *court*, meaning short, is sustained in the *Dictionary of English Furniture*. Present usage in England reserves the term "court cupboard" for the kind with three open shelves. As this type was apparently unknown in America, the many inventory records of court cupboards must have referred to examples like this and Nos. 75 and 76. (*Nutting Collection, Wadsworth Atheneum.*)

**75.** Jacobean court cupboard of oak with pine shelves made in Massachusetts about 1640-1660. All the turnings are stained black. Inlay, frequently seen in English work, makes a rare appearance here in Pilgrim furniture. Tudor and Jacobean motifs are represented by the faceted ornaments, fluted arches, horizontal S-scrolls in flat carving, palmate panel in center, and leaf panels on doors in low relief carving. The last have geometric framework. In his *Furniture Treasury*, Nutting says this piece from the Parmenter family was in Sudbury in 1683, but its style suggests an earlier date. (*Nutting Collection, Wadsworth Atheneum.*)

**76.** This court cupboard of oak with southern yellow pine[11] in the interior was made about 1660-1680. It is mentioned in the will of Thomas Vines of Yorktown, Virginia, who died about 1700, as an "old court cupboard." The ringed baluster supports are unusually elaborate and approximate English Jacobean turnings. The applied split spindles are also elaborately turned. As opposed to New England court cupboards, this Southern example has the enclosed cupboard section below. (*No. 91, Exhibition of Southern Furniture, Virginia Museum, 1952. Collection of Frank L. Horton.*)

**77.** Jacobean press cupboard of oak with pine top and maple turnings, from Plymouth County, Massachusetts (1660-1680). This cupboard, with its heavy balusters, serrated moldings, geometric paneling, and applied beveled moldings on the lower drawers, is closely related to the Prince-Howes press cupboard (Nutting, *Furniture Treasury*, No. 455), which has a long history connected with Plymouth. (*Gift of Mrs. J. Insley Blair, Metropolitan Museum of Art.*)

**77**

**75**

**76**

**78**

**79**

**78.** Jacobean press cupboard of oak and pine made about 1680-1700 in Massachusetts, probably Essex County. It has been attributed to Thomas Dennis[5] of Ipswich, but was more probably the work of one of his contemporaries. Unusual is the recessed cupboard below. The upper part has the splayed front seen on some court cupboards. Carved foliated scrolls enclose the fleur-de-lis motif. Similar turnings, with pronounced curves, are seen on many pieces with an Ipswich history. (*Museum of Fine Arts, Boston.*)

**79.** Jacobean press cupboard of oak and pine made about 1680-1720 in Massachusetts, probably Essex County. A similar cupboard in the Metropolitan Museum (dated 1699) was once attributed to Thomas Dennis,[5] and so this piece was also assigned to him. Both examples have geometric paneling on the drawers, splay-front upper sections supported by balusters, and side doors divided in double arches. It is now realized that much of the work formerly credited to Dennis was made by equally skilled craftsmen whose names are now emerging from the records of Essex County. The regional style is marked by the use of intricately turned split spindles, and bulbous supports with tapering outlines. (*William Rockhill Nelson Gallery of Art and Atkins Museum.*)

**80.** Jacobean press cupboard of oak with pine top, ebonized maple balusters, and applied turnings and bosses. It was probably made in Essex County, Massachusetts, about 1680-1700. This type, with projecting upper section, belongs to a small group of which one is dated 1680.[17] The design, and the use of turned, pendent drops, is reminiscent of the treatment of the overhang of the seventeenth-century house, with monumental oak pendants or, as they were called, "pendills." This piece, once attributed to Thomas Dennis,[5] was found in Salem, where it was acquired by the early collector, Henry F. Waters. Later it was owned by Dwight M. Prouty of Boston and by Joseph Downs, curator of the Winterthur Museum. (*Henry Ford Museum.*)

**80**

81

82

83

84

**81.** This Jacobean press cupboard of oak with ebonized turnings, made about 1680-1700, is from Connecticut and resembles the Sunflower chest. Almost identical pieces are illustrated in Nutting's *Furniture Treasury,* one of which is traced to an original owner in Wethersfield and may have been made by Peter Blin.[12] The distinctive form of the ringed baluster supports, the fretwork hearts above the heavy spindles, and the diagonal dentil of the cornice are characteristic of these Connecticut press cupboards. (*Museum of Fine Arts, Boston.*)

**82.** An oak kas (the word is derived from the Dutch *kast*) made in the early 1700s in the Hudson Valley. The kas was also made in New Jersey and parts of Pennsylvania. A few examples (such as the one seen in No. 5) are of seventeenth-century date, and they continued to be made in much the same style through most of the eighteenth century. The form is Dutch-Flemish, with heavy cornice and large ball feet. The seventeenth-century kas usually has paneled doors and stiles without the heavy-faceted applied ornament seen on the typical eighteenth-century form. (*Art Institute of Chicago.*)

**83.** Hudson Valley kas of hard yellow pine found at Saugerties near Kingston. This example, made c. 1690, is of a simpler form than No. 82. It is without cornice or ball feet, but the painted design of pendent fruit, birds, and flowers (based on baroque carved ornament) is characteristic of one type of kas. The ground is gray, the design in blue-grays, brown, orange, and white. (*Ferry House, Van Cortlandt Manor, Croton; lent to Sleepy Hollow Restorations by Mitchel Taradash.*)

**84.** A painted kas occupies a natural and prominent position in this bedroom from the Hardenbergh house in Ulster County, New York. The house, built in 1762, is in an early Dutch style, untouched by English influence. The design in grisaille on the kas shows pendent fruit painted in the manner of a *trompe l'œil.* Other pieces in the low-ceiled room with broad beams are a seventeenth-century stretcher table with sausage turnings and vase-and-ring-turned legs; a canopied bed; and a Queen Anne rush-bottomed chair, painted red and black, with the turned, straight leg typical of the Hudson Valley. (*Hardenbergh Bedroom, H. F. du Pont Winterthur Museum.*)

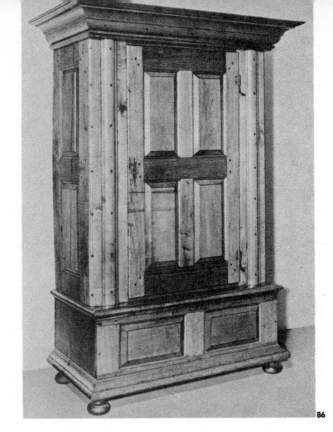

**85.** Unusual kitchen cupboard of chestnut with coved sides in an elongated C-scroll. The shape in profile suggests a type of New England settle. Its date is about 1700. (*Old Sturbridge Village.*)

**86.** William and Mary clothes press or wardrobe made in eastern Pennsylvania in the early 1700s. The back is of oak, and inside the wardrobe is a shelf of the same wood. There is a chest section in the lower part. The door has fielded panels, repeated on the sides and across the bottom. The wide, molded cornice is reminiscent of the kas, although in eastern Pennsylvania English influence predominated. (*Chester County Historical Society.*)

**87.** Wall cupboard or cabinet of oak with arched-panel door and flattened ball feet in the William and Mary style. It was made to stand on a table or hang on the wall from a wrought-iron strap. The glazed door and sides were designed for the display of china. The arched form indicates probable origin after 1700. (*Old Sturbridge Village.*)

88

**88.** William and Mary day bed or couch, probably made in New England about 1690-1700. The frame of birch or maple encloses a cane seat and back. It has eight block-and-vase-turned legs, a canted back, Flemish scroll stretchers enclosing a leaf design, and cushions of eighteenth-century flamestitch embroidery. The crest on the back is in the style of William and Mary chairs. (*Prentis Collection, New Hampshire Historical Society.*)

**89.** William and Mary maple day bed or couch, made in Pennsylvania about 1710-1740. The scrolled and crested back is let down with a ratchet and chain, which is usual in Pennsylvania work. There is a laced-sacking bottom under the velvet cushion. (*Bayou Bend Collection, Houston.*)

89

90

92

91

**90.** William and Mary desk-on-frame made of pine and maple (1690-1720). The finest examples of the desk-on-frame are of the William and Mary period. After Queen Anne the form was outmoded by the more practical slope-front desk. The first step in changing the former desk box into the desk as we know it today was taken by making it larger and constructing the lid so that it opened outward and rested on slides. This was placed on a supporting frame. (*Art Institute of Chicago.*)

**91.** William and Mary desk-on-frame made of gumwood (bilsted). The front is paneled to suggest a drawer. The lid was the actual writing surface and the user must have stood. It is hinged to lift upward, giving access to writing materials. The desk was made in New York about 1700. (*Metropolitan Museum of Art.*)

**92.** William and Mary desk-on-frame made about 1710-1730 in Pennsylvania. It is of walnut and tulip poplar (tulipwood). The shape of the vase turning of the leg — long and slender above a swelling curve — is noted in eastern Pennsylvania. The lid opens forward and rests on slides. This desk has a long history of ownership in Chester County. (*Chester County Historical Society.*)

**93.** William and Mary desk-on-frame made of pine and maple in Sudbury, Massachusetts, about 1720. It still has the original red paint on the exterior and blue on the interior. The construction of the drawer with an ovolo-molded (or lip-molded) edge, was introduced in England in the Queen Anne period and appears in American work around 1720. (*Greenwood gift, Smithsonian Institution.*)

**94.** William and Mary slope-front desk of walnut-burl veneer and maple. It was made in New York about 1690-1710. The interior has ten pigeonholes and five small drawers. (*Van Cortlandt Manor, Croton: Sleepy Hollow Restorations.*)

**95.** This William and Mary slope-front desk of walnut-burl veneer and maple is from Massachusetts. The drawers are banded with walnut in herringbone pattern. A movable lid in the writing section gives access to a well or "secret" drawer with eight small drawers made of pine. It was made about 1700. (*Henry Ford Museum.*)

These two desks, so similar in general appearance, are shown together to illustrate what is meant by single-arch molding around the drawers (No. 94) and double-arch (No. 95), composed of two half-round moldings. These forms were adopted from England about 1690 and 1700 respectively.

94

95

**96**

**97A**

**96.** William and Mary fall-front desk made in Philadelphia by Edward Evans.[18] Walnut is used with red pine and white cedar. The desk is constructed in two sections. A brand on the base of one of the small drawers in the upper section displays the mark *Edward Evans 1707*, which establishes this as the earliest signed and dated piece of Philadelphia furniture. The front, with a mitred panel enclosing a large fielded panel, is an early example of this architectural treatment and is of special importance because the piece is dated. (*Raleigh Tavern, Colonial Williamsburg.*)

**97B**

**97.** Interior of the fall-front desk shown in No. 96, and the mark displayed in detail on the drawer. This kind of desk, long made in England, was rare in America.

**98.** William and Mary desk and book-case of walnut with an interior in hard southern yellow pine and oak. The ball feet are of hard pine. The piece was probably made about 1720 and was found near Edenton, North Carolina, where it would seem a considerable amount of fine furniture was produced. The ogee or cyma curve, seen here in the arched panels, appears on the skirts of William and Mary highboys and lowboys. Its use on paneled doors became characteristic of the Queen Anne period. (*No. 114, Exhibition of Southern Furniture, Virginia Museum, January, 1952. Frank L. Horton Collection.*)

**98**

99

100

**99.** William and Mary looking glass, with convex-molded frame, of walnut veneer on pine. It was made about 1690-1700, and has the original glass. These glasses of rectangular shape were the earliest to be used on the wall. Sometimes they had a crest. Contemporary prints show such mirrors above a table with tall candlestands on either side. In England matching sets were made after the French and Dutch-Flemish fashion, but these were probably not known in America. (*Nutting Collection, Wadsworth Atheneum.*)

**100.** William and Mary looking glass made about 1700 and originally owned by the Pepperrell family of Kittery, Maine. The frame is painted in tortoise-shell effect and the matching crest is cut from thin wood. White pine establishes the New England origin of this looking glass, which is one of the earliest surviving American examples to be found in such excellent condition. The proportions indicate that taller plates of glass were now available and that the pier glass was coming into existence. The design of the pierced crest, partly floral, partly geometric in character, is a more ambitious rendering of the type seen on the chair in No. 40. (*H. F. du Pont Winterthur Museum.*)

**101.** A pine-top trestle stand, with maple turnings made in the late 1600s. It has a well-turned vase-shaped stretcher. The top is pegged to the crosspieces. Unusually long supports measure over fifteen inches. Nutting assigns this example to Connecticut. (*Nutting Collection, Wadsworth Atheneum.*)

101

**102.** Candlestand with turned column and cross-base, made about 1690-1710. This typical early form was supplanted to a large extent by the screw candlestand and other adjustable forms. Later, in the eighteenth century, the columnar candlestand emerged in more sophisticated styles designed by Chippendale and Sheraton. (Nos. 353 and 539.) (*Nutting Collection, Wadsworth Atheneum.*)

102

103

104

105

**103.** Triangular stand with drop leaves. In extended position the leaves are held in place by pivoting the top. When the top is swung back, the leaves fall. The slender vase turnings and the use of mahogany suggest an approximate date of 1725. (*Metropolitan Museum of Art.*)

**104.** Maple stand with drawer and vase-and-ring-turned legs and stretchers. The piece is of interest as a descendant of the joint stool of the late 1600s and a forerunner of the sewing table or work table of the late 1700s. (*George Dudley Seymour Collection, Connecticut Historical Society.*)

**105.** Small cross-base stands, such as this one made in the early 1700s, were often used as tea tables. Under the brown paint are a pine top, a maple column, and cross-base of white oak. The vase-ball-and-ring turning is more elaborate than usual. On the stand is an American pewter tea set with English scratch-blue salt-glaze tea cups. A Queen Anne easy chair stands at the fireplace. The paneled room is from a house in Ulster County, New York, built in 1762 but representing the style of the early 1700s. (*Hardenbergh Parlor, H. F. du Pont Winterthur Museum.*)

**106.** A Jacobean joint (joined) stool is seen here in company with other New England pieces and a gateleg table from Pennsylvania. This oak stool, with baluster-turned legs and slightly projecting top, is an exceptionally fine example of the oldest American joint stools extant. Its date of origin is probably in the third quarter of the seventeenth century. The Essex County court cupboard, dated 1684, was originally owned by the Foster family of North Andover, Massachusetts, and may have been made by Joseph Parker, Jr., an Andover joiner who died in 1684. (See *Antiques*, October 1960, the article by Helen Park on Essex County makers.) The splayed front of the cupboard provides extra space for the display of choice household pieces. A rare object is the small cabinet or spice cabinet, with geometric paneling. The piece bears the initials and date *T H 1679* for Thomas Hart, whose father built the house in Ipswich which contained this room. (*Hart Room, H. F. du Pont Winterthur Museum.*)

107

108

109

**107.** Joint stool made about 1690-1700 and found in Maine. The vase-and-ring-turnings which began to supplant the heavy baluster in the late 1600s are executed here with unusual character. The wider top may have been a concession to comfort. (*Nutting Collection, Wadsworth Atheneum.*)

**108.** Joint stool of cherry made about 1700-1725. The baluster-turnings here are much simpler and less vigorous than those of the older stool illustrated in No. 106. The use of cherry suggests an eighteenth-century origin. (*Metropolitan Museum of Art.*)

**109.** William and Mary upholstered stool with Spanish foot, made about 1710-1720 and found in New Hampshire. This maple piece has fine bulbous turnings and a well-formed carved and scrolled foot. The slip seat is covered in flame-stitch embroidery. Upholstered stools were used in England as early as 1600, but really only came into their own after the Restoration. They were never common at any period in America. At first they were articles of luxury and in later periods were outmoded by the more comfortable "back stool" or side chair. (*Prentis Collection, New Hampshire Historical Society.*)

The illustrations of tables show first those with heavy turnings, generally of the Jacobean or Pilgrim style (Nos. 110-116) then those of the late Jacobean and William and Mary style, which have lighter turnings and represent an increasing number of types (Nos. 117-137).

**110.** Jacobean draw-table made in the mid-1600s. This is one of the great early tables and well known as a rare American example of its type. The side leaves are missing but the cross-board can be seen in the photograph. The present length of six feet could have been stretched nearly to eleven by the missing leaves. The ringed-baluster turnings, which are of the heavy, early type, are of oak, like the frame, although turnings were frequently made of maple. References to these "drawing tables," as the inventories called them, were few in the Colonies. (*Connecticut Historical Society.*)

110

**111.** Jacobean folding-top table of oak and maple, made in Essex County, Massachusetts, about 1675-1700. The top, when open, is supported by a single gate which rests on the lower shelf. The type existed in the mid-1600s in England, where such a table may have been used for cards. Its comparatively small size fitted it for occasional use. This table is crudely painted to represent marbelizing.[19] (*Gift of Mrs. J. Insley Blair. Metropolitan Museum of Art.*)

112

113

**112.** This Jacobean trestle table of oak with a pine top was made in the mid-1600s and is over twelve feet long. The trestle table is one of the earliest table forms. Surviving examples in England date back to the 1400s, possibly earlier. The separate top was supported on a frame so the table could easily be moved to the side of the room after use and the top placed against the wall. The supports are joined by a truss or brace held in position by pegs. Trestle tables are found listed in early inventories as a "table bord" accompanied by a "frame" or "tressell." (*Metropolitan Museum of Art.*)

**113.** Jacobean stretcher table of oak made in New England, about 1680. It has bulbous supports, a deeply scrolled and bracketed skirt with pendants, a channeled frieze, and a removable top with battens at the ends. (*Nutting Collection, Wadsworth Atheneum.*)

114

**114.** Late Jacobean oak stretcher table with pine top made in Massachusetts about 1700. While this piece indicates that the period of massive vase-turning has passed, the generally heavy and simple members of the table keep it in the Pilgrim category. (*Greenwood gift, Smithsonian Institution.*)

**115.** Jacobean stretcher table of oak with a pine top made in Plymouth, Massachusetts, about 1660-1680. The frieze is carved with intersecting (shuttle) lunettes above the imbrication. The baluster-turned legs are joined by rectangular stretchers, molded on top. These large tables with drawers may be considered a form of center table, the forerunner of library and parlor tables. (*Greenwood gift, Smithsonian Institution.*)

115

**116.** This early William and Mary stretcher table, of walnut with inlay of ash and rosewood and a tulipwood drawer, was made in the late 1600s. The top has indented corners. The tapering baluster form of the turned legs and flat stretcher suggest Dutch influence. This table belonged to the family of Aert Middagh (1707-1777) and is a rare example of an early New York table. Exhibited No. 7, Furniture by New York Cabinetmakers, Museum of the City of New York, 1956-1957. (*Lea S. Luquer Collection.*)

116

117

117. Connecticut butterfly table of maple, made about 1690-1700. The full turning of the legs and stretcher and decided rake of the legs are strong points. Most butterfly tables are oval when open, but a few have rectangular tops. Tables on which brackets support a leaf are known in Europe, but the American form is so distinctive that it owes little to a foreign source. (*Collection of Mr. and Mrs. Frederick K. Barbour.*)

118. Butterfly table of maple, made in New England about 1700-1710. The brackets, or wings, by which the butterfly table is chiefly judged, should be of good design, as here; many are either too elaborate or too plain. It is also desirable that both stretchers and legs be turned. (*Collection of Mrs. Giles Whiting.*)

118

119. William and Mary dressing table (lowboy); made in New England c. 1700. The wood, maple, is painted red. Frequent use of this color is to be noted in New England painted furniture. The earliest lowboys were shallow and had a single drawer. The full turnings combine vase, ball, and ring. Diagonal, shaped stretchers represent the William and Mary style. (*Shelburne Museum.*)

119

**120**

**121**

**120.** William and Mary dressing table (lowboy) of walnut, made in New England about 1700-1720. Typical of the developed form of lowboy are the deep drawers on either side of a central drawer, and shaped skirt, with pendants which have their complement in the turned finial on the cross-stretcher. (*Nutting Collection, Wadsworth Atheneum.*)

**121.** William and Mary dressing table (lowboy) made in the early 1700s in New England. It has a plain, arched skirt and double-arch molding around the drawers instead of the single-arch seen in the preceding example. The legs have bowl-turnings in contrast to the former's cup-turnings. Both styles are in the general class of trumpet-turnings (see No. 71). (*No. 580, J. K. Byard Sale, Parke-Bernet Galleries, March 1960.*)

**122.** Late Jacobean table with trestle gate, made in New York about 1680-1700. The trestle table with a swinging gate was one of the earliest forms of dropleaf table in England, but the gates were generally turned and not severely plain as here. In America they were frequently plain, although members of the gate are sometimes molded. This piece was used as a field table during the Revolution by General Philip Schuyler of Albany, whose daughter Elizabeth married Alexander Hamilton. (*Collection of Mr. and Mrs. Mitchel Taradash.*)

**122**

**123.** Late Jacobean oak and pine table with double gates and ball-and-ring-turning. It was made in Massachusetts in the late 1600s. Ball-and-ring-turning was a refinement over the plain ball (No. 27) and shows an attempt to follow the more elaborate turnings of English furniture. The usual construction of the large gateleg table, with double gates on each side, and twelve legs, is seen here. This type supplanted the long stretcher table (No. 7) for use as a dining table. (*Art Institute of Chicago.*)

**123**

124

124. William and Mary gateleg table of walnut, made in New England about 1690-1725. Here is another example of the typical large gateleg, but it shows the more usual vase-and-ring-turning. This table and No. 123 represent the fully developed style. A famous example of the earlier, more primitive form is the table supposedly used by Governor Edward Winslow (died 1655) of Plymouth in his council chamber and now at Pilgrim Hall, Plymouth. It has massive turnings and is broad in the central section, having only one gate on each side. The double gates of the present table were better fitted to support a heavy top. (*Metropolitan Museum of Art.*)

125. William and Mary gateleg table of Santo Domingan mahogany, made in New York, c. 1700. The construction is unusual, with gates pivoting outward from the center, and inner-legs that do not extend to the floor. This makes it an eight-leg table in spite of its great size (it extends to 71 inches). The table once belonged to Sir William Johnson (1715-1774), Superintendent of Indian Affairs for George III, whose home, Johnson Hall at Johnstown, New York, is now maintained as a historic site. His property was confiscated during the Revolution and at the sale of furnishings from the house it was purchased by John Taylor of Albany, in whose family it descended. (*Albany Institute of History and Art.*)

126. Gateleg table of walnut in William and Mary style, made in New England probably in the early 1700s. It has single gates on each side and eight legs. This small table with oval top, opening to 24½ inches, may be considered an occasional table with many uses — as a breakfast table, tea table, or work table. The vase-turnings have both vigor and delicacy. (*Nutting Collection, Wadsworth Atheneum.*)

125

127. William and Mary Spanish-foot gateleg table of walnut, made between 1710 and 1720. There are only a few Spanish-foot gateleg tables known, one being in the Winterthur Museum, another in the Wadsworth Atheneum. The so-called Spanish foot appears frequently in American work, often in primitive form and rarely in the well-carved type with small scroll at the side seen here. (See also Nos. 44, 46, 109, 132, 133.) The foot was made separately, and attached to the turned leg by means of a dowel. (*Allen House, Old Deerfield.*)

126

127

128

**128.** Hutch-table made in the Hudson River Valley in the early 1700s. The hutch-table was a humble relative of the chair-table (No. 22). The top, supported on trestle ends, pivoted to a vertical or horizontal position to serve as a chair or table. This one also includes a small chest of drawers. Hutch-tables continued to be made for a long period, and the dating of an example is difficult. (*Ferry House Bar, Van Cortlandt Manor, Sleepy Hollow Restorations.*)

**129.** Eighteenth-century hutch-table of pine and maple, made in New England. The seat slides out to give access to the storage section. The top turns on large pins which secure the cross-braces to the arms. (*George Dudley Seymour Collection, Connecticut Historical Society.*)

**130(A).** William and Mary walnut mixing table made in New England about 1690-1710. It has a Swiss export top with a slate center bordered in marquetry. The term "mixing table" is modern and refers to side tables with tops of marble, slate, or tile, impervious to hot or strong liquids. Earlier they would have been called slab tables or, as in this instance, a slate table. A Boston inventory of 1699 mentions, "in the lower room a slate table £1:10:1."[20] The Swiss export tops may have come to America through trade with Holland. Similar examples are seen in Swiss museums. (*Metropolitan Museum of Art.*)

**130(B).** A detail showing the slate center with wide inlaid border containing plain and strapwork panels. The confronting lions in the end panels are characteristic of Swiss export tops.[21] Woods used are generally walnut and fruitwoods.

129

130 A

130 B

**131**

**132**

**133**

**131.** Porringer table of maple and cherry, made in New England about 1710-1720. The table has vase-turned legs of lighter form than earlier ones, a characteristic prevailing at the end of the William and Mary period. The stretcher is the forerunner of the block-and-spindle seen on Queen Anne chairs. The skirt is scrolled in deep cyma curves and the projecting corners of the top (useful for candlesticks) are as round as porringers and suggested the modern name. It may have been used for reading, for writing, or as a tea table. (*George Dudley Seymour Collection, Connecticut Historical Society.*)

**132.** William and Mary splay-leg table with Spanish foot, made in New England about 1700. The legs are maple, the top pine. It descended in the Appleton family of Ipswich, Massachusetts. The legs on the splay-leg table rake in four directions. The form is graceful and the table light, using less wood than those of rectangular construction. This is not a recognized English type, and its appearance in America was comparatively brief. It was outmoded by the butterfly table, which is also of the splay-leg type, and has the advantageous dropleaf. The design of the shaped frieze suggests the arched skirt of a William and Mary lowboy. (*Bayou Bend Collection, Houston.*)

**133.** William and Mary splay-leg, Spanish-foot table of maple with pine top, made in Massachusetts, c. 1700. It has original red paint on the base and traces of it on top. This is another version of the rare splay-leg table with Spanish foot. It differs from the preceding example in the use of a turned instead of a plain stretcher. Although the splay-leg table had a brief existence in northern sections, it continued in fashion much longer in the South, frequently appearing in the Queen Anne period and occasionally with the claw-and-ball foot of American Chippendale. (*Shelburne Museum.*)

**134.** William and Mary five-stretcher or high-stretcher table, made about 1720 in the South. The wood is walnut with hard yellow southern pine used in the drawer. The table has slender block-and-spindle-turned legs and stretchers. The cockbead carried from the bracketed skirt across the top of the legs is a finely worked out detail. The table top has a thumbprint-molded edge, which is a seventeenth-century treatment, and a drawer with lip-molding. The latter detail was used in English drawer construction shortly after 1700 and reached America as the William and Mary period closed. (*Governor's Palace, Colonial Williamsburg.*)

**134**

**135.** William and Mary tavern table of maple with a pine top, made in New England about 1720. The drawer has a lip-molded edge. The term "tavern table" is a modern one used for a light, easily moved table set before a visitor at an inn or tavern. Many such tables were in domestic use as well. This example is commendable for superior turnings combining vase, ball, and ring. (*Nutting Collection, Wadsworth Atheneum.*)

**136.** William and Mary tavern table, made in Connecticut about 1720-1730. It is of maple with a whitewood top, painted a Venetian red. This table has a spindle-turned stretcher joining similarly turned legs, which are slightly raked. The skirt is bracketed. Compared with No. 135 the turnings tend to become less clearly defined. The table was found in Guilford, Connecticut. (*George Dudley Seymour Collection, Connecticut Historical Society.*)

137

135

136

**137.** Walnut tea table with dished top, cyma-scrolled skirt, and columnar legs. It was found in the South and was probably made there in the early 1700s. Tea tables in the William and Mary style are very rare. This one is seen in a room with other William and Mary furnishings at West St. Mary's Manor, which was built in the early 1700s in southern Maryland. (*Colonel and Mrs. Miodrag Blagojevich.*)

138

**138.** Queen Anne four-post beds are so rare that this tall Rhode Island bed (height, 8 feet) with four identical posts is probably unique. Back-posts are usually plain but here they have the same cabriole legs with pad foot seen on the front posts. Maple is unusual in Rhode Island work but Job Townsend is known to have used it and it appears again in the Newport desk at right, which is rare for the shell carving on the knee. The bed was made between 1735 and 1750 and the desk is of about the same period. The crewelwork hangings and trellis-pattern coverlet (inherited by John Hancock from his uncle, Thomas) are in shades of blue, green, rose, and yellow. Other Queen Anne furnishings include a Newport side chair, at left; dressing table and Newport comb-back corner chair of walnut. The room comes from the Pickard house, Cecil County, Maryland, built in the first half of the eighteenth century. (*H. F. du Pont Winterthur Museum.*)

# 2. Queen Anne

## 1720-1755

By the time the Queen Anne style reached the Colonies, a century had passed since the founding of Plymouth. Roads had improved and the cities along the Atlantic coast were more closely connected. A marked difference had been brought about between 1704, when Madam Knight made her difficult journey on horseback by the shore route from Boston to New York,[22] and the year 1744 when Dr. Alexander Hamilton traveled with comparative ease in the same manner from Annapolis to Maine.[23] By 1736 a stage was running between Boston and Newport, and many families owned their own carriages. At the beginning of the second quarter of the century, elegant houses with garden, coach house, and stable were being built. In Newport, Doctor Hamilton was able to visit the large stone mansion and garden of Colonel Godfrey Malbone (the grandfather of the famous miniature painter), who profited from the privateering in which Newport specialized. Inside these luxurious new houses were marble mantelpieces and wainscoted walls with fielded panels above and below a dado. Inventories show an increase in personal possessions and more frequent mention of plate and other luxuries. These were the days when men wore the broad-skirted frockcoat and deep-pocketed waistcoat as seen in portraits by John Smibert and Robert Feke. About 1725, ladies were wearing broad hoopskirts, and in 1740 the "jewels, patches, and gay apparel" worn in Boston were criticized by the clergyman Whitefield.

For some years life had been more comfortable and secure in the cities and older communities. During the first decades of the 1700s it was more secure in America than in Europe, which was suffering under the War of the Spanish Succession. This conflict did not greatly affect America, where it was named Queen Anne's War. However, the severe depredations of the French and Indians in central Massachusetts culminated in the massacre at Deerfield in 1704.

That was also the year when Marlborough's victory at Blenheim broke the power of Louis XIV, though the war did not officially end until 1713, when the Treaty of Utrecht brought peace. England had emerged supreme in Europe and there were consequent advantages to the Colonies. English capital was invested anew in colonial expansion, and the individual merchant continued to gain by it. The natural resources of America reached a wider market in Europe and the West Indies. Her forests provided naval stores, masts for the Royal Navy, and lumber for furniture and building. Fish came from New England, grain from Pennsylvania, tobacco from Virginia, indigo and rice from South Carolina. These were the staples of an expanding trade, carried on in a new and larger type of vessel, the schooner. In an active coastwise trade the Colonies helped each other, and ultimate political unity was fostered.

Trade was important, and those who profited most by it imitated the English gentry in their interest in new homes and fine furnishings. Like the wealthy middle class in England, prosperous American merchants, shipowners, and planters were the patrons of cabinetmakers. This meant that fine furniture could be produced in greater quantity, and there was an advancement of skill in every branch of the cabinetmaker's craft.

THE QUEEN ANNE HOUSE. By 1725 some of the distinguished houses which can be seen today had recently been finished or were about to be built. One of the earliest, now known as the Warner House, was built in Portsmouth, New Hampshire, by a Scottish sea captain, Archibald Macphaedris. It is of the Anglo-Dutch boxlike style developed in the late seventeenth century in England but called Queen Anne because this type of architecture was so prevalent in her reign. In 1719 the Trent House at Trenton, New Jersey, another of this type, was begun by William Trent, a business associate of James Logan's. Logan, who was Penn's secretary, was a great bibliophile and scientist as well as successful merchant, and he built historic Stenton at Germantown in 1728. Thomas Lee began to build Stratford about 1725, and although its H-shaped form is reminiscent of the Tudor period it has a fine Palladian great hall which shows that the builder was abreast of the times. Other Virginia houses — Berkeley, home of the Harrisons; Shirley, owned by the Carters; and Westover, belonging to the Byrd family — were built approximately between 1725 and 1735. In New England, Isaac Royall, a wealthy Antigua merchant, was remodeling a handsome house at Medford in 1732. Drayton Hall was built in 1740 in South Carolina.

In none of these houses today is there a Queen Anne interior so complete in all respects as the parlor from Readbourne (No. 156) which is now installed at the Winterthur Museum. The house was built in Queen Anne's County, Maryland, in 1733. Typical are the fully paneled walls above and below a dado, with fielded panels rising to a heavily molded cornice. The chimneybreast is set across the corner of the room in Anglo-Dutch style. A bolection molding and Dutch tiles surround the fireplace. The parlor is furnished with pieces in the Queen Anne style, early and late, beginning with the easy chair which has a narrow back reminiscent of the William and Mary period, and ending with a New York tea table which, with claw-and-ball feet, indicates the beginning of Chippendale.

DESIGN IN THE QUEEN ANNE PERIOD. It is evident that, compared with William and Mary furniture, the pieces in the Readbourne parlor represent a decided change in furniture design. The side chairs drawn up at the table embody these changes in the vase-shape of the splats and their undulating form (the conformal splat or "bended back"). In the rake of the rear

72

legs there is a difference from the straight lines of earlier chairs. Another change is to be seen in the absence of a crest. The uprights now form a continuous curving line in the hoop-back, or yoke-back. Most revolutionary of all is the shape of the leg — the cabriole, with curving knee. It was developed from a classic shape, revived and modified in Italy and France before it came to England about 1700. The French version was called *pied de biche* (doe's foot), and some of the early examples in England had the hoof termination. In its simplicity and elegance, a balance of curves that produces stability, the cabriole seemed the ultimate solution for a supporting member, and it dominated furniture design in Europe and America through much of the eighteenth century.

The S-shaped scroll, called a cyma or ogee scroll, was a favored line in the Queen Anne period, dominating the broken-scroll pediment on case pieces (No. 183), the frieze of tea tables (No. 230) and the skirt of lowboys (No. 222). The pad foot is the usual terminal on furniture legs. When pointed, it becomes the slipper foot (No. 166). The trifid is an elaboration of the pad (No. 148). An innovation at the end of the Queen Anne period was the claw-and-ball foot (No. 171).

The shell is used everywhere as a carved motif on furniture of this period. Combined with the husk it is the favorite decoration for the knee of the cabriole (No. 143). It is the central ornament on the top of chairbacks (No. 150) and is inset on seat rails. Under rococo influence it takes more fanciful forms (No. 149) and when geometrized, is referred to as a fan or a sunburst (No. 182). The shell is also the characteristic ornament for the drawers of highboys and lowboys.

FURNITURE FORMS OF THE QUEEN ANNE PERIOD. The Queen Anne period did not produce as many new forms as that of William and Mary, but it modified many of the earlier types. The dished-top tea table was given a cabriole leg in the Queen Anne style, and it became an important eighteenth-century form. It was not common before 1740 because the habit of tea drinking became general only in the 1730s. The rectangular form of tea table was particularly popular in New England (No. 230) and also appears in New York (No. 156). The tripod tea table with a bird-cage attachment which made it possible to tilt and turn the top appeared shortly before 1750 (No. 233) and had its great popularity in the Chippendale period.

New in America was the folding-top card table of square form with rounded corners (No. 215). The high chest or highboy, which in the William and Mary style closely followed contemporary English design, received its characteristic American form in the Queen Anne period, with a scrolled pediment and large, carved shells on the upper and lower drawers (No. 184). The design does not duplicate any English form, and remained basically unchanged in America during the Chippendale period.

The desk and bookcase, or secretary, was seldom designed with the flat top that distinguished examples of the William and Mary period, and is generally seen with the broken-scrolled pediment (No. 200). The quick acceptance of the broken scroll may have been the result of the importation of early Georgian style mirrors with architectural pediments which were fashionable in England when the Queen Anne style was taking form in America.

The daybed (Nos. 194 and 195) remained an important furniture form in the Queen Anne period, for houses were not large, and an extra bed in this convertible type was desirable. When larger houses began to be built in mid-eighteenth century, the daybed was less often made, and by that time it also had a rival in the long sofa.

The slope-front desk outlived the desk-on-frame, although there are some very pleasing examples of the latter (No. 196). But the greater usefulness of a desk which has a chest of drawers below was the reason for the long life of this form.

The new dining table was a modification of the gateleg. It was a large table of the dropleaf type with leaves supported on either side by a single cabriole leg attached to a swinging gate (No. 218).

The place of the court cupboard was taken by cupboards either built in the wall, as seen in No. 189, or of a free-standing corner type, represented by No. 191. There were also dressers (No. 193) and the china press (No. 192) of utilitarian character. The cyma-scrolled sides, which entered into the design of many cupboards and dressers (No. 190), may have had a source in interior architecture. Such scrolls are conspicuous on the alcove cupboard built in the paneling of an early eighteenth-century room from Fiskdale, Massachusetts, which is now installed in the Museum of Fine Arts, Boston.

The upholstered settee was slow to appear in America although its close relative, the easy chair, was being made from the late 1600s. The earliest ones, such as No. 206, show the influence of the tall-back chair in the shape of the back. More characteristic of later Queen Anne developments is the lower, straight back seen in No. 207. The chair-back settee, so often seen in English furniture of the William and Mary and Queen Anne periods, does not appear in America but was occasionally made in the Chippendale period (No. 350).

A unique American example of a Queen Anne sofa with undulating back is illustrated in No. 208. This form, the predominant design of the Chippendale period, resembles English sofas of the 1740s. The difference between a sofa and settee is slight and often goes unspecified. The settee is a small sofa, and the latter, to be called a sofa, should be long enough for reclining, according to the *Dictionary of English Furniture*. Sofas are upholstered over the seat frame and have upholstered arms, but this is not necessarily the case with settees.

WOODS AND TECHNIQUES OF DECORATION. Mahogany was imported soon after 1700, but did not become the predominant wood for furniture until the Chippendale period. Black walnut was the most important wood of the first half of the eighteenth century. White walnut (butternut) was also used, particularly in country pieces, and maple and cherry were in frequent use. Maple was particularly favored in New England and Pennsylvania, and cherry in Connecticut and New York. New York continued to favor red gum (bilsted). By 1750 Newport was using the heavy, dark Santo Domingan mahogany which is usual in furniture by the Townsend-Goddard cabinetmakers.

For the ornament of furniture, carving became more important than inlay. Carved finials of urn and corkscrew forms surmounted pediments. Inlay was generally restricted to the variegated star and to the sunburst patterns, and triple bands of stringing were used on drawer fronts (No. 220). Chair splats were frequently veneered to show finely patterned wood. Japanning (No. 184) achieved great popularity in Boston, where a number of decorators are known to have been working from 1712. In New York too, japanning was practiced, and was advertised in 1736 by Gerardus Duyckinck. A japanned high chest at Winterthur, attributed to Connecticut, indicates that this elaborate craft was also practiced there.

REGIONAL CHARACTERISTICS. Regional characteristics began to be pronounced in the Queen Anne period, and it is frequently possible to say whether a piece of furniture was made in New

**II.** A Queen Anne New England tea table, Newport side chairs, and walnut lowboy attributed to Benjamin Frothingham furnish the living room in a Connecticut house built in 1771. *(Home of Mr. and Mrs. William C. Harding.)*

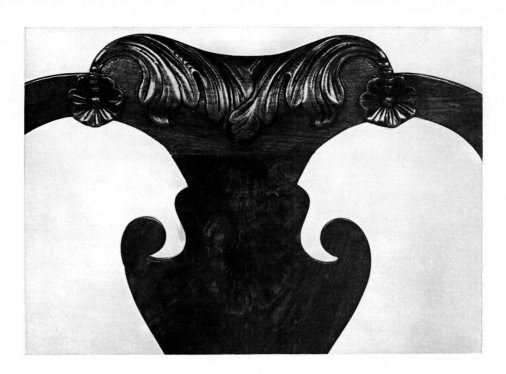

Carving on Queen Anne armchair, No. 148. *(Henry Ford Museum.)*

Queen Anne cockle shell and leaf; paneled trifid
foot; on Philadelphia side chair.
*(Karolik Collection, Museum of Fine Arts, Boston.)*

*Opposite: Portrait of John Cort-
landt.* Artist unknown. *(Brooklyn Museum.)*

This portrait of about 1730 shows the
costume worn when the Queen Anne
style prevailed in American furniture.
It portrays one of the children at Van
Cortlandt Manor (see No. 164). John
was the fourth son of Philip Van
Cortlandt. Children wore the same
dress as their elders, represented here
by the long flaring waistcoat buttoned
at the waist, biblike cravat, turned-
back cuff, and square-toed shoes.

**III.** Queen Anne japanned highboy (No. 184) made in Boston about 1735. *(Metropolitan Museum of Art. Photo courtesy Shell Oil Company.)*

England, New York, or Philadelphia simply from the design and construction. However, identification cannot be made in every case.

Massachusetts furniture is characterized by spare proportions and delicacy of form. Highboys are narrow and slender and have delicately shaped cabriole legs (No. 184). The uprights of narrow-backed chairs are slim and rather straight. The vase-form splat (No. 157) is almost pinched compared to New York's broad type and Philadelphia's scrolled form. The slenderness of Massachusetts chair legs may explain the persistence of the stretcher, which remained on chairs of that region after it was dispensed with elsewhere. The slender lines of Massachusetts furniture may perhaps be best appreciated in the card table, pier table, and tea table, as in these pieces the tall, thin, delicately formed cabriole stands out with emphasis.

Newport developed a style of cabinetmaking which is possibly the most original of any in America, but the full flowering of Newport work came in the following period. In mid-century Newport harbor was filled with merchant ships and privateers, and within sight of the wharves were the homes of the shipowners who prospered through trade with the West Indies or from the cargo captured from Spanish merchantmen. Also within sight of the wharves, notably on Easton's Point (where the Goddards and Townsends established their shops) were the furniture makers who worked for the wealthy townsmen and also made simpler types of furniture for export. Furniture was part of the "venture" cargo which the captain of a Newport vessel used as his stock in trade in southern ports.

Newport characteristics include the use of the heavy, dark Santo Domingan mahogany, mentioned previously, and the early adoption of the claw-and-ball, which soon became oval in form, with slender, outstretched talons. Sometimes the claw-and-ball form is pierced, as in English work, and pieces with this detail are attributed to John Goddard (No. 221). The shell on the cresting rail of a Newport chair is silhouetted, as it is on pieces made in New York, but the splat is narrower and frequently scrolled (Nos. 159 and 160). Also characteristic of Newport is the flat serpentine stretcher on chairs, although this occasionally appears also in Philadelphia work. There are no rules for which exceptions do not exist.

There is little direct influence of Dutch design in New York furniture of the eighteenth century, yet there is something characteristically Dutch about the sturdy, vigorous forms and proportions of typical pieces that were made there. The chair-back is squarer and the cabriole heavier than those on Boston and Philadelphia examples. The New York claw-and-ball foot is somewhat square in outline, and the rear leg is rounded and tapering, ending in a small, squared foot. The latter treatment is also found on English chairs. On No. 159 can be noticed, at the base of the splat, a scroll called the "cupid's bow," which is also of English origin.

Philadelphia produced the finest Queen Anne chairs (No. 151). These are remarkable for their rhythmic grace. Characteristic features are the S-shaped spiral on the hooped cresting, curved scrolls and volutes on the splat, and the concave center of a horseshoe-shaped seat ornamented with a carved shell. The shell on the cresting is held within the framework (No. 167) and is not silhouetted as in Newport and New York work. The trifid foot is almost exclusively Philadelphia's and is frequently paneled (No. 148). Similar paneling is found on the slipper and club foot. This peculiarity, once thought to belong solely to Philadelphia, has been traced to Irish design.[24] The rear leg on Philadelphia chairs is generally the severely plain round form known as the stump leg, and this is occasionally chamfered.

The subject of regional characteristics is of great importance in regard to American furniture, in which local differences play a much greater role than they do in English work. In England there was only one furniture capital — London. In America many cities along the Atlantic Coast were centers of style for the surrounding regions. In each of these furniture centers, English styles were developed in a local idiom which became gradually less distinct as roads, travel, and communications brought cities closer together in the late eighteenth and early nineteenth centuries.

DATE OF THE QUEEN ANNE PERIOD. Although there was evidence of coming change around 1720, the Queen Anne style was not firmly established in American furniture until about 1730. The change came slowly, and there are transitional forms between William and Mary and Queen Anne styles which are singularly harmonious (No. 28). Again, as the Chippendale style reached America, there are many instances, particularly in chair design, which show the use of elements of earlier and later date, such as the pierced splat and claw-and-ball foot used on chairs with Queen Anne hoop-backs (No. 149). The Queen Anne style lingered through most of the century, and is seen in the continuing use of the pad foot and arched-panel door. Simplicity of line, particularly agreeable to most American cabinetmakers, persisted especially in furniture from Connecticut, New Hampshire, and the South. The Queen Anne style did not end in 1755, but the height of its influence passed with the coming of the new forms in the rococo, Gothic, and Chinese manner.

# Makers

*William Savery* (active 1740-1787), Philadelphia. He is the best known American maker who worked in the Queen Anne style. Most of the labeled examples by this excellent craftsman belong to the Chippendale period. It was the discovery of his label in a Chippendale lowboy in the Van Cortlandt mansion in New York that for many years caused most fine Philadelphia work to be attributed to him. A labeled Queen Anne daybed and side chairs are illustrated by Hornor in the *Blue Book of Philadelphia Furniture* (plates 82, 314, 462.) The transition from Queen Anne to Chippendale is represented by a side chair at the Raleigh Tavern, Williamsburg (No. 176), and the same blending of styles is seen in a labeled armchair at the Winterthur Museum.

The *Townsend-Goddard* cabinetmaking family was founded in Newport by Job and Christopher Townsend and John Goddard. They began their activities in the Queen Anne period. Job Townsend's labeled secretary is illustrated in No. 201, and a lowboy attributed to John Goddard is seen in No. 221. However, the majority of the great works of the Townsend-Goddard makers belong to the following period, and an account of them has accordingly been reserved for the Chippendale chapter.

*Thomas Elfe* (active before 1747), Charleston, South Carolina. Elfe came to Charleston presumably from London, was active in the Queen Anne period, but he too is included among the Chippendale cabinetmakers because the pieces attributed to him are in the latter style.

*Thomas Johnston* (or *Johnson*), who was active in Boston between 1732 and 1766, was an engraver as well as a japanner. A trade card engraved for his shop in Ann Street shows cherubs' heads, which also appear as part of the decoration on a few pieces of japanned furniture of great quality. The Metropolitan Museum's matching highboy and lowboy (Nos. 184 and 185) are two examples. The highboy is seen also in color plate III.

*Robert Crosman* (active about 1730-1799), Taunton, Massachusetts, made the so-called Taunton chest represented by No. 180. Crosman's highly individual designs are characterized by vine patterns in which C-scrolls form the leaves. Bird motifs also appear in some instances. The collection at Historical Hall, Taunton, includes a dated blanket chest of 1729 which is also attributed to this maker.

*John Gaines,* (died 1743), Portsmouth, New Hampshire, is mentioned in the account of furniture makers in the preceding period. Gaines continued to work in Portsmouth, until his death, but any furniture he may have made purely in the Queen Anne style has not yet been identified.

# *Chart:* Queen Anne, 1720–1755

NEW FORMS

Card table with folding top; corner cupboard; side chair with vase-shaped splat; tea table with dished-top and cabriole leg.

PRINCIPAL WOODS

Walnut, maple, cherry, mahogany, (c. 1750).

DECORATIVE TECHNIQUES

Carving, inlay, painting, japanning, veneering.

DESIGN

Arched panel on doors (No. 201).
Broken-scroll pediment on case pieces (No. 200).
Cabriole leg (No. 142).
Hoop-back (yoke-back) on chairs (No. 157).
Pad foot (No. 143) and variations, slipper (No. 194), web (No. 208), and trifid (No. 206).
Vase-shaped splat on chairs (No. 146).

CLOCKMAKERS

Bartholomew Barwell (active 1749), New York. (No. 188.)
Gawen Brown (1719-1801), Boston. (No. 187.)
William Claggett (active 1720-1740), Newport, Rhode Island. (No. 186.)
Peter Stretch, arrived from England, 1702; worked in Philadelphia.

## English Background

*1720s*
Chair backs are lower; splats are pierced. Claw-and-ball foot, introduced in early 1700s, becomes usual.
Kneehole desk, or dressing table, a new form.

Repeal of duty on mahogany (1721) opens way for wider use, but walnut remains fashionable to midcentury.
James Gibbs, *A Book of Architecture* (1728).

*1730s*
Bowed cresting replaces hoop-back on chairs.
Architectural style in furniture developed by William Kent (1685-1748); carved lion and satyr masks, Vitruvian scroll, festoons, eagle's-head terminal on arms; lion's-paw foot; bookcase with broken pitch-pediment; console table.

*1740s*
The rococo style, introduced from France, begins to affect furniture design, at first in looking-glass frames and wall lights.
Matthias Lock's *New Drawing Book of Ornaments* (1740), the first successful interpretation of French rococo style in cartouches, shields, etc.; no designs for furniture.
New forms: breakfront bookcase; tripod (piecrust) tea table.
Batty and Thomas Langley, *City and Country Builders and Workman's Treasury of Designs* (1740).
Thomas Chippendale (c. 1718-1779) moves to St. Martin's Lane (1748).

*1750s*
Gothic and Chinese design blend with rococo in the Chippendale style.
Lock and Copland, *New Book of Ornaments* (1752).
William Hogarth, *Analysis of Beauty* (1753).
Thomas Chippendale, *Gentleman and Cabinet-Maker's Director* (1754; 2nd ed., 1755; 3rd ed., 1762).
Edwards and Darly, *New Book of Chinese Designs* (1754).
Horace Walpole restores Strawberry Hill in Gothic style.
French scrolled toe replaces the claw-and-ball foot. Sectional dining table, known earlier, becomes usual. "Ribband back" chair design used (but not invented) by Chippendale.

**139.** Low-post walnut bed, made in Philadelphia about 1750-1760. It has turned club-shape rear legs and cabriole front legs ending in a claw-and-ball foot indicating the approach of the American Chippendale period. The room is from an eighteenth-century house in Coombs Alley, Philadelphia. Local pieces include a maple armchair at the fireplace, resembling labeled examples by William Savery, and a small walnut chest-on-stand, with inlay work typical of Chester County (see Nos. 178, 197). Above it is a pine watch case, painted red, which shows an ingenious manner of giving a watch the importance of a clock. (*H. F. du Pont Winterthur Museum.*)

**140.** Field bed of maple, with Spanish foot, made about 1725-1750, probably in Connecticut. Eighteenth-century advertisements repeatedly mention field beds. The *Dictionary of English Furniture* (revised by Ralph Edwards, 1954) states that they were presumably intended for use in war and traveling. Sheraton remarks that they were used in homes, under low ceilings (*Cabinet Dictionary*, 1803). Arched testers adjusted them to the sloping lines of attic rooms. Sheraton says they have received their name because they are "similar in size and shape to those really used in camps." The difference between the bed for domestic use and the camp bed was that the latter was constructed so that it could readily be taken down and transported. Tent bed is another name for this type. (*Israel Sack, Inc.*)

**141.** Southern cellaret of walnut on a stand with cherry sides, made probably before 1750. The interior is designed for nine bottles. The cellaret, for the storage and safe-keeping of bottled spirits, as distinct from the wine cistern for cooling them, is typically a Southern form although frequently made in England. This Queen Anne example is rare. The broad dovetailing of the sides suggests an early date. Straight tapering legs are common on Southern furniture in the Queen Anne style. (*Collection of E. Ross Millhiser.*)

**142.** The transition from William and Mary to Queen Anne is evident in the use of the Queen Anne cabriole leg with block-and-turned rear legs and stretchers, scrolled arms, and towering cresting rail in the earlier style. The squared cabriole with grooving on the edge is sometimes found in Connecticut work. This walnut and cane armchair was probably made in New England between 1700 and 1725. (*No. 11, Downs, American Furniture. H. F. du Pont Winterthur Museum.*)

**143.** Upholstered walnut armchair, made about 1740-1750 in Newport. Upholstered chairs of the Queen Anne period are rare today but frequently appear in early portraits. The carved shell and husk motif on the knee is often seen on English chairs of the George I period. In Newport the shell was frequently designed with the small scroll at the side as seen here. The chair is covered in eighteenth-century plum-colored moreen, a watered (moiré) fabric. (*No. 15, Downs, American Furniture. H. F. du Pont Winterthur Museum.*)

141

142

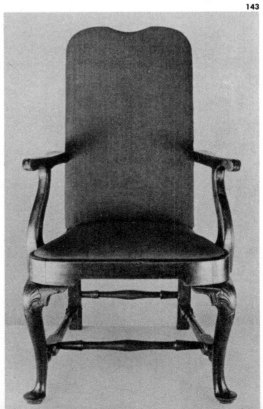

143

**144.** Upholstered walnut armchair, made about 1730-1750 in New York. The James family of Flushing once owned this and a companion chair, while a matching set of six from another New York family is at Winterthur. Although these are called Queen Anne chairs in America, they are derived from a Georgian prototype with a lower back. Their outward-flaring arms were designed to accommodate wide hoopskirts. The looped arm, rare in American work, is more often seen on Philadelphia chairs. (*Metropolitan Museum of Art.*)

**144**

**145**

**145.** The forerunner of the familiar Martha Washington chair of the late eighteenth century (No. 438) is seen in this upholstered walnut open-arm chair, made in New England about 1740-1760. This lady's chair has a seat about fourteen inches from the floor. (*No. 20, Downs, American Furniture. H. F. du Pont Winterthur Museum.*)

**146.** New York armchair made in the Hudson Valley about 1720-1740. It is of maple and cherry grained to imitate walnut. The survival of the turner's chair is evident here, where the curving crest of Queen Anne design is superimposed on turned backposts of an earlier type. Characteristic of the Hudson Valley are the straight, trumpet-turned legs ending in pad feet (see also Nos. 163, 164). Note the tilting of the foot as it rests on the supporting disk. The wide splat is typical of New York. (*No. 24, Downs, American Furniture. H. F. du Pont Winterthur Museum.*)

**146**

**147**

**147.** A masterpiece of New York chairmaking is represented by this walnut armchair, made between 1730 and 1750. It is one of a large set which came from the house built by Stephanus Van Cortlandt, first lord of the manor of Van Cortlandt, who died in 1700. The house, which was on Cortlandt Street, New York, was probably the residence of his son Philip at the time these chairs were made. They are richly carved with a pierced crest silhouetting a shell above undercut leaf scrolls, an eagle's head on the arms, and shell and husk on the knee. The claw-and-ball foot has New York's typical squared outline. The cupid's bow at the base of the splat is often found on New York chairs. (See also No. 161.) (*No. 26, Downs, American Furniture. H. F. du Pont Winterthur Museum.*)

**148**

**148.** The height of the Queen Anne style in Philadelphia is represented by this walnut armchair with its bold and symmetrically balanced curves. It was made about 1740-1760. The use of a crest of acanthus and rosettes instead of volutes and a shell is unusual. The splat is veneered with figured crotchwood. Typically Philadelphian are the concave arm supports, the paneled trifid foot and the scrolled splat. The block-and-spindle stretcher is seen more often on New England chairs. (*Ex Coll. Louis E. Brooks. Henry Ford Museum.*)

**149.** This Philadelphia armchair made of walnut about 1750-1760 represents the ultimate enrichment of the Queen Anne style. The breadth of the outward flaring arms gives a monumental effect to a chair of delicate lines. The design has no English parallel, for here a Georgian pierced splat is contained within the Queen Anne hoop-back with voluted cresting. In place of a realistic cockle shell on the cresting is a transformed palmette-like shell, pierced for added depth and light. A naturalistic flower and acanthus appear on the cabriole. (*Bayou Bend Collection, Houston.*)

**149**

**150**

151

**151.** For a full appreciation of their design, chairs should be seen from the back and side, and this grouping of Queen Anne chairs provides such an opportunity. Characteristic Philadelphia details are the web, pad, and trifid foot, the horseshoe-shaped seat that contracts sharply at the back rail, the scrolled splat, and the concave arm support. The chair in the foreground has a molded rear leg, a deviation from the customary stump leg. (*Vauxhall Room, H. F. du Pont Winterthur Museum.*)

**150.** Philadelphia armchair of walnut, made about 1750. The original owner is thought to have been Samuel Powel (1738-1793), mayor of Philadelphia, who lived in a handsome house at 244 South Third Street, represented today by rooms in the Metropolitan and Philadelphia Museums. Powel, who made the Grand Tour in 1768, had a sophisticated taste and his ballroom was one of the finest rococo interiors in America. This chair represents a Philadelphia type with concave seat rail and inset shell, voluted cresting with shell enclosed, looped arm, and stump rear leg. (*Philadelphia Museum of Art.*)

152

153

**152.** Newport corner chair of mahogany made about 1750-1760. The corner chair which in the earlier period had no splats (No. 45) is improved here by their inclusion. Interlacing scrolls were favored in Rhode Island. The chair has the cushioned pad foot often used in New England. The cyma curves of the seat rail are repeated on the shaped backrail which ends in a scrolled knuckle. (*No. 20, Carpenter,* Arts and Crafts of Newport. *R. W. Maynard Collection.*)

**153.** Philadelphia corner chair of walnut with original cowhide upholstery. Made about 1750 for the Duncan family. The unusual inverted vase-shaped splats introduce breadth at a point which conforms with the swelling line of the arm rests. The cabriole legs, capped with beaded lambrequins, end in pointed web feet. The knuckles terminate in finely carved spirals. (*Bayou Bend Collection, Houston.*)

**154.** Newport corner chair of walnut with comb back, made about 1735-1750. The straighter lines of the William and Mary style are present in this chair which slightly antedates Nos. 152 and 153. The block-and-turned posts and cross-

154

stretcher contrast with the curving lines of the splats, the seat, and the cabriole leg which ends in the Queen Anne pad foot. The shape of the scrolled splat is characteristic of Newport and may be compared with No. 160. (*No. 64, Downs,* American Furniture. *H. F. du Pont Winterthur Museum.*)

**155.** Easy chair of walnut and cherry made in New England about 1725-1750. The basic design of the easy chair, from the time of its origin in the seventeenth century through the eighteenth, changed less than any other form. Characteristic of New England is the turned stretcher used here, and the vertically rolled arms. (*Gift of Mrs. J. Insley Blair, Metropolitan Museum of Art.*)

155

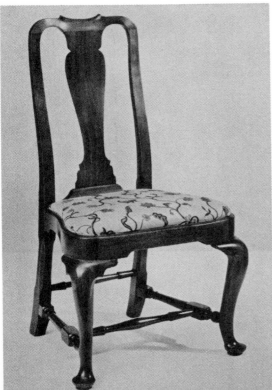

**156.** A Philadelphia Queen Anne easy chair with scrolled arm is seen in this room of the 1730s. The period of the chair (1735-1750) is recognizable in the tall back and narrow proportions. Other pieces here include Philadelphia chairs with shell-carved cresting rails, a New York tea table with claw-and-ball foot, a japanned mirror (originally owned by the Bleecker family), quillwork sconces with silver candle branches (made by Jacob Hurd of Boston) and a portrait by Wollaston over the fireplace. The blue of the Dutch tiles is repeated in the eighteenth-century Italian velvet window draperies. The parlor comes from Readbourne, a house built in Queen Anne's County, Maryland, about 1733. (*H. F. du Pont Winterthur Museum.*)

**157.** Walnut side chair made in Massachusetts about 1740-1750. This is one of a set of six which belonged to Edward Holyoke, president of Harvard College, 1737-1769. All the attributes of the New England Queen Anne side chair are combined in the Holyoke chairs — the tall, slender back, narrow vase-shaped splat, yoke-back with molded top, the cabriole leg ending in a cushioned pad foot, and the block-and-spindle stretcher. (*Garvan Collection, Yale University Art Gallery.*)

New York and Newport chairs, so much alike in some respects, are contrasted in these two examples (Nos. 159 and 160). Both chairs have the shell silhouetted on the cresting and both, unlike Philadelphia and Massachusetts chairs, have broad backs. However, the New York splat is not scrolled at the sides like the Newport example, and the curve of the uprights breaks much higher. There is a cupid's bow on the base of the New York splat and a tapering rear leg ends in a squared foot. The Newport chair has a block-and-spindle stretcher so frequently used in New England.

**158.** New England maple side chairs, seen from various angles, appear compact and restrained, yet graceful. Compared with Philadelphia designs they show moderation in the use of the curved line. This interior is from a mid-eighteenth-century house, once occupied by Joseph Pearson, first Secretary of State of New Hampshire, and now moved in its entirety from Exeter to Dearborn, Michigan. It is furnished with New England pieces suggested by the inventory of Pearson's estate. (*Secretary House, Greenfield Village, Henry Ford Museum.*)

**159.** New York side chair of mahogany made about 1740-1750. (*Norvin Green sale, 1950. Parke-Bernet Galleries.*)

**160.** Newport side chair of walnut made about 1740-1750. (*Rhode Island School of Design.*)

160

161

**161.** One of a set of eight New York walnut chairs which originally belonged to the Apthorp family, owners of two Pre-Revolutionary houses in New York. The chair, made about 1740-1750, has a veneered splat of richly figured grain, a pierced shell crest with elaborately imbricated undercut scrolls, and a carved shell on the knee. The flat, shaped stretcher is generally seen in Newport, occasionally in Philadelphia, but rarely in New York. This chair resembles the Van Cortlandt family chairs (No. 147). (*Ginsburg and Levy.*)

**162.** Newport side chairs in a stair hall, from a house built by John Banister in 1756 near Newport. Like New York chairs, these have square proportions, broad splats, and silhouetted shell. The Newport splat is generally scrolled, the New York one usually (but not always) plain. The Newport shell on the cabriole has the typical spiral — or volute — at the sides, seldom used on New York chairs. The marbleized hall stairway has a massive newel post turned and pierced in a broad spiral — a specialty of New England carvers. (*Banister Stair Hall, H. F. du Pont Winterthur Museum.*)

162

**163.** Hudson Valley side chair of the early 1700s with yoke cresting imposed on turned back posts. It has a vase-shaped splat and straight trumpet legs instead of the usual Queen Anne cabriole. The wood is pine, maple, and hickory, painted black. Surviving from the William and Mary period is the bulbous front stretcher (see also No. 146). The design of the pad foot, as if tilted on a flat disk, is a Hudson Valley trait. (*Van Cortlandt Manor, Sleepy Hollow Restorations.*)

**164.** Hudson Valley chairs (similar to No. 163, but grained to imitate mahogany) surround a Queen Anne oval dropleaf cherry table. The slope-front desk is veneered in walnut burl. The curtains are of eighteenth-century resist-dyed linen. This is Van Cortlandt Manor's old parlor, antedating the additions of 1749 when Pierre Van Cortlandt took up residence there. It represents the days when Stephanus Van Cortlandt and his son Philip used the house as a trading post and has been restored with furnishings of the early 1700s. The only family pieces are the Dutch still-life and the antlers of a deer which family tradition states was a pet of John Van Cortlandt's. (*Van Cortlandt Manor, Sleepy Hollow Restorations.*)

163

164

**165**

**165.** Philadelphia side chair of walnut with veneered splat and seat rail made about 1730-1750. Philadelphia traits are seen in the slipper foot with tongue, the scrolled splat, curving uprights, and chamfered rear leg. The shaped stretcher occurs occasionally on Philadelphia pieces, more often in Newport work. This, the simplest form of the Philadelphia Queen Anne chair, has the same subtle curved lines of more elaborate examples. (*No. 112 Downs, American Furniture. H. F. du Pont Winterthur Museum.*)

**166.** Side chair of walnut made in Connecticut about 1740-1750. Similarities sometimes exist between Connecticut and Philadelphia work. These are more apparent in the Chippendale period, but can also be seen here in the general form of the hoop-back. The Connecticut chair is less sophisticated in design, but also has the slipper foot, and the chamfered rear leg, and it starts the curve in the uprights only a little above the seat frame. The lambrequin on the knee is an unusual detail. (*Brooklyn Museum.*)

**167.** This Philadelphia walnut side chair represents the Queen Anne style at a high point of development. It is without the Georgian influence seen in Nos. 168 and 169. Typical Philadelphia details are the voluted crest enclosing a shell, the scrolled splat, and the channeling on the outer edge of the uprights. The paneled trifid foot, a detail noted in Irish furniture[24] is also indicative of a Philadelphia origin. (*Ex Coll. Louis E. Brooks. Henry Ford Museum.*)

**168.** Philadelphia walnut side chair made about 1745-1755. The elaboration of ornament which distinguished the later phases of the Queen Anne style is seen here in the concave seat rail with carved shell, in the increasing enrichment of the knee of the cabriole with a leaf-carved bracket, and in the carved, textured effect of the acanthus which surrounds a daisy-like motif. (*No. 115, Downs, American Furniture. H. F. du Pont Winterthur Museum.*)

**166**

**167**

**168**

169

**169.** Philadelphia walnut side chair made about 1750-1760 for the Garrett family. The particular form of pierced splat on this chair shows a progression toward the Chippendale style. The sculpturesque claw-and-ball foot is a characteristic of Philadelphia. Spiral volutes on the hoop-back mark the climax in the development of balanced curves. (*Plate 304, Hornor,* Blue Book of Philadelphia Furniture. *Israel Sack, Inc.*)

**170.** Philadelphia walnut side chair with original needlework seat made about 1750-1760. This rare type of chair, with rounded uprights, is from a set made for the Waln family. The pierced splat (a faithful rendering of an English Georgian splat), the cabochon on the knee, and the new version of the acanthus, all are indicative of the approach of the rococo Chippendale style. (*Plate 41, Hornor,* Blue Book of Philadelphia Furniture. *On loan from the Commissioners of Fairmount Park to the Philadelphia Museum of Art.*)

**171.** New York side chair of walnut. The cipher carved in the back, *R M L,* stands for Robert Livingston and Margaret Beekman, who were married in 1742 and were the parents of Fulton's associate in steamboat transportation. The Livingstons may have used this chair at Clermont, on the Hudson River, or in their town house near Bowling Green. New York chairmakers adopted the claw-and-ball foot before 1750. The tapering rear leg and silhouetted shell are familiar characteristics, but in other respects this has unusual grace for a New York chair. (*Bayou Bend Collection, Houston.*)

**172.** An early treatment of the Georgian scrolled and pierced splat is shown in this Newport side chair of walnut made about 1740-1750. The scrolled design was of pre-Chippendale origin although in American furniture pierced splats are usually classed as Chippendale. No designs resembling this are to be found in Chippendale's *Director* but Manwaring brought some of them together in his *Cabinet and Chair-Makers' Real Friend and Companion* (1765). However, this particular chair, originally owned by General James of Providence, antedates it. (*No. 14, Carpenter,* Arts and Crafts of Newport. *Arthur B. Ladd Collection.*)

171

172

**173.** The chairs in this Newport interior show a further development of the design seen in No. 172, as they have claw-and-ball instead of pad feet and the backs are entirely pierced. The room has a fine Newport Chippendale blockfront chest of drawers by the Townsend-Goddard cabinetmakers and a Rhode Island easy chair of maple and walnut made about 1740-1750. The room comes from the same house as the stair hall in No. 162. (*H. F. du Pont Winterthur Museum.*)

**174.** New England walnut chair from a set which descended in the Winthrop-Blanchard family. The Oriental-lacquer decoration of birds, landscape, and flowers in gold, green, and red on a black ground is combined with Western acanthus scrolls and a coat-of-arms. It is thought that these chairs, made in the mid-1700s, were sent to China to be decorated at the end of the century. The chair offers an interesting contrast to the furniture in Western styles made and decorated in China for the Bowditch and Low families, which was shown in the China Trade Exhibition at the Metropolitan Museum of Art in 1941. (*Bayou Bend Collection, Houston.*)

175

**175.** Newport slipper chair of walnut made about 1750. It has a cushioned pad foot, square seat, and block-and-spindle stretcher and belongs to a small group of side chairs with low seats, twelve to fourteen inches from the floor, to which the modern term slipper chair is given. These chairs were also made in Pennsylvania and the South, and were without doubt intended for women. In England they are sometimes called nursery chairs. The earliest Rhode Island examples (1730-1740) have a taller back, later ones the claw-and-ball foot. The chair illustrated has an early foot, but the later, and lower, back. (*Old Deerfield.*)

**176.** Philadelphia side chair of the mid-1700s with the label of William Savery: *All sorts of Chairs and Joiners Work Made and Sold by William Savery. At the Sign of the Chair, a little below the Market, in Second Street, Philadelphia.* It is made of walnut and has the intaglio (inverted) leaf carving on the knee, frequently taken as indicative of Savery's hand. The piece has many of the characteristics of the Queen Anne chair, but with two new elements of design — a rectangular back and bowed cresting — from which the Chippendale period can be seen to have begun. Savery was working in Philadelphia from about 1740 until his death in 1787. (*Colonial Williamsburg.*)

**177.** Newport side chair showing the transition from Queen Anne to Chippendale. Characteristic is the rectangular back and the broad simple cresting, which is really the Queen Anne hoop straightened into an almost horizontal line. This part of the design, rather than the pierced splat, introduces the Chippendale period. (*Collection of Ralph E. Carpenter, Jr.*)

176

177

179

180

**178.** Chest of drawers from Chester County, Pennsylvania, made about 1730. It is made of walnut and has an inlay of light-toned woods in geometric scrolls ending in a conventional trefoil. The inlaid furniture (1720-1760) of Chester County represents an interesting local style of unidentified origin. Something like it is seen in the Shenandoah Valley of Virginia and inland Georgia. Other Chester County examples are shown in Nos. 139 and 197. (*Chester County Historical Society.*)

**179.** Chest-on-frame made in Massachusetts about 1730-1750. It is painted red and has a drawer in the torus molding of the cornice. The frame has an arched center, with cyma scrolls at the sides and on the ends. Country furniture was sometimes homemade but was generally the work of a local craftsman with modest training and limited materials. The honesty of his work, the ingenuous manner in which he combines old and new styles (the deep cyma-scrolled skirt of the William and Mary period with the stubby Queen Anne cabriole and pad foot) gives it character and charm. Extensive collections of country furniture are found at Sturbridge, Massachusetts, and the New York State Historical Association at Cooperstown. (*Old Sturbridge Village.*)

**180.** Small one-drawer pine chest probably made for a child. It measures only 20½ inches in height. The painted decoration is attributed to Robert Crosman[25] of Taunton, Massachusetts, who worked from 1730. The design, with a delicate tree pattern springing from a base of wavy lines, and the leaves delineated like C-scrolls, suggest his work. The form of the one-drawer chest is typical of the seventeenth century. It consists of a chest with lift-up lid and a single long drawer below. (*Art Institute of Chicago.*)

**181.** New England high chest or highboy of mahogany, made about 1720-1740. Matched crotch veneer is inlaid on the drawers. This exceptionally beautiful example of the early Queen Anne highboy has the flat top and herringbone inlay of the William and Mary period but the Queen Anne cabriole leg and pad foot. Mahogany, although infrequently used before 1750, was well known by 1730. In 1708 it was to be found in a Philadelphia cabinetmaker's shop (Hornor, *Blue Book of Philadelphia Furniture*) and is mentioned in a New York inventory of 1733 given by Downs, *American Furniture,* No. 16. (*Essex Institute.*)

**182.** A high chest, or highboy, of cherry with original step-top, probably made in Connecticut about 1740-1760. A fan is carved on the top and bottom drawers, and a sunburst on the step-top. The drawers are lip-molded and the cabriole leg has a scrolled bracket. A few highboys, mainly from Connecticut, have survived with their original step-tops designed for the display of ornaments.[26] "Steps for China ware" are mentioned from 1733 and may have been common, but as only a few were an integral part of the construction the stands have generally been lost. The step-top here is not attached. This method of displaying valued possessions seems to have been typical in America and does not follow any English design. The detail shows the highboy arranged with ornaments of Astbury-Whieldon type. (*Henry Ford Museum.*)

181

182 B

182 A

183

**183.** This high chest, or highboy, of walnut was made for the Woodward family, probably in Boston between 1730 and 1750. This is the fully perfected form of Queen Anne highboy, with broken-scroll pediment, fluted pilasters, and carved shells. Veneering of matched panels of crotch wood is outlined with triple bands of stringing. The sides of both sections are inlaid with a variegated star so that the sum total of the ornament answers to the early terms, "stringed," "feneered" (veneered), and "star and scallup." The matching lowboy is seen in No. 220. (*Ginsburg and Levy.*)

**184-185.** New England japanned highboy and matching lowboy, probably decorated by Thomas Johnston (or Johnson) of Boston, who was working between 1732 and 1767. They were made about 1735 and originally belonged to the Pickman family of Salem. Japanning reached a higher state of development in Boston than elsewhere in America.[27] Paint, varnish, and metal leaf have been employed with whiting and size on a core of maple and pine. On an imitation tortoise-shell ground, produced by streaking vermilion with lamp-black, there is a partly raised design of Chinese figures and architecture combined with Western motifs — winged cherubs and classic columns. (See color plate in introductory text.) (*Metropolitan Museum of Art.*)

184

185

**187.** Clock by Gawen Brown (1719-1801) of Boston, signed and dated *1766.* The pine case has original japanned decoration on a red and black "tortoise-shell" ground. Although this clock was made after 1750 the case is in typical Queen Anne style, with arched dial, and domed top over an arched cornice. (*Henry Ford Museum.*)

**188.** Clock by Bartholomew Barwell, who worked in New York between 1749 and 1760. In 1749 Barwell advertised himself as "lately from the city of Bath." The coved pediment on the hood is typical of early Georgian design. The oak case has a japanned decoration on a "tortoise-shell" ground which may have been the work of Gerardus Duyckinck, Jr., who advertised in New York between 1746 and 1772. (*Brooklyn Museum.*)

Tall clocks made in America earlier than 1750 are extremely rare. Three of the main types of case, representing English William and Mary, Queen Anne, and early Georgian designs, are illustrated together here for the sake of comparison.

**186.** Clock (1720-1740) by William Claggett, who was born in Wales and advertised in Boston in 1715 five years before he settled in Newport. This clock, signed on the dial, is in a walnut and walnut-burl case of William and Mary type, with a domed superstructure, flat on top, and with a straight cornice over an arched dial. (*Henry Ford Museum.*)

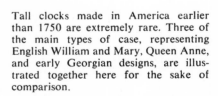

**189.** In the second quarter of the 1700s, cupboards with paneled doors or glazed doors, and also many without doors, were built in corners or set in side walls beside the fireplace. The built-in cupboard soon became popular and was often used instead of a separate piece of furniture. Almost invariably the built-in cupboard had a top carved as a cockle shell and an interior painted dark red, vermilion, or light green. A typical Queen Anne example is seen in this parlor at Marlpit Hall, Middletown, New Jersey. It has a simple keystoned arch, fluted pilasters, fielded panels in the spandrels, and paneled doors enclosing the lower section. The parlor was added when the original house of 1684 was enlarged between 1720 and 1750. (*Monmouth County Historical Association.*)

**190.** This New England pine cupboard with fielded panels and cyma-scrolled framework around the open shelves was made about 1730-1750. The cyma scroll, which entered into the design of cupboards and dressers, may have had its source in interior architecture. Similar scrolls frame an alcove cupboard in an early eighteenth-century room from Fiskdale, Massachusetts, now in the Museum of Fine Arts, Boston. (*Ashley House, Old Deerfield.*)

191

192

193

**191.** Southern corner cupboard in two sections, made of walnut with a hard yellow southern pine interior, arched-panel doors, straight bracket foot, chamfered sides, and a dentil molding on the cornice. Its date is about 1750. The corner cupboard as a separate piece of furniture was not inspired by the built-in cupboard, as is sometimes assumed. Separate corner cupboards were known from the William and Mary period. Lockwood refers to them in inventories of the 1720s.[28] Cupboards with paneled doors were especially popular in the South, while in the middle states and New England glazed doors became more common. (*Collection of Raymond C. Power.*)

**192.** Southern china press with arched-panel doors below and glazed doors above, probably made in Tidewater Virginia, about 1750. Southern yellow pine is used throughout. The repetition of the arched form in the glazed section, the paneled sides, and the dentil course over bead and reel represent a high level of craftsmanship expended on a predominantly utilitarian piece. (*Governor's Palace, Kitchen, Colonial Williamsburg.*)

**193.** This pine dresser, with traces of slate-gray paint, was made in Long Island during the second quarter of the eighteenth century and originally belonged to the Cowenhoven family of Brooklyn. The superstructure of shelves, which is the distinguishing feature of the eighteenth-century dresser, usually has a back instead of being open as here. The cyma-curved sides are in Queen Anne style. Dressers were familiar in eighteenth-century kitchens along the Atlantic coast, and later the form remained popular in country furniture. Dressers are seen in Dutch seventeenth-century genre paintings, but in America their general use is due mainly to English influence. (*Philipsburg Manor, Upper Mills, Sleepy Hollow Restorations.*)

194

195

**196.** Maple desk-on-frame with original brass loop handles, made in New England about 1735-1740. The frame has lip-molded drawers and a handsome concave shell. One of the happiest combinations in furniture design was that of the Queen Anne lowboy with a desk box, but it yielded to the more convenient slope-front desk, with chest of drawers below. This piece was discovered by Dwight Blaney of Boston, who was collecting actively before 1900. (*Formerly in the collection of Margaret Blaney.*)

196

**194.** Philadelphia walnut daybed or couch with six legs, a pair of scrolled splats, molded hoop-shaped cresting rail, and undulating back supports, made about 1730-1740. The rear legs are chamfered; the remaining four are of cabriole shape ending in a slipper foot. A similar example is attributed to William Savery in Hornor's *Blue Book of Philadelphia Furniture.* The present piece was in the Reifsnyder sale of 1929. Daybeds attained their finest form in Philadelphia Queen Anne examples. (*Henry Ford Museum.*)

**195.** Philadelphia eight-leg walnut daybed or couch with scrolled double splat made about 1730-1740. The carved shell in the spiraled cresting complements the shell on the front cabriole leg. During the Queen Anne period the daybed was still a furniture form of first importance, but by the mid-eighteenth century, when larger houses were built, it was less often made. Although the long, rectangular form of the daybed poses a design problem, the Philadelphia maker gave it dignity and grace. (*Bayou Bend Collection, Houston.*)

**197.** Slope-front walnut desk, made in Pennsylvania, probably Chester County, between 1725 and 1740. It has herringbone banding around the drawers, turned, bulbous feet, and a bookrest on the lid. This is an unusually elaborate example of Chester County inlaid furniture. The design is characterized by the geometric quality of its scrolls, which suggest conventionalized vine tendrils ending in trefoils (see also Nos. 139 and 178.) (*Collection of Mrs. Giles Whiting.*)

**198.** This mahogany desk-on-frame made in Connecticut in the mid-1700s represents the next step (after No. 196) in the development of the conventional slope-front desk. Shells are carved in the writing compartment and on the center of the scrolled skirt of the frame. The well-formed short cabriole ends in a cushioned pad foot. It was originally owned by Nathaniel Brown of Hartford and is accompanied by his commission as captain in Connecticut's Sixth Regiment, dated May 25, 1770. (*Teina Baumstone.*)

**199.** Slope-front desk of curly maple with pad foot and double cushion, made in New Hampshire in the mid-1700s. Curly maple was well liked in New England. According to Downs, the curly grain is found in the white or silver maple (*acer saccharinum*) and in the swamp or red maple (*acer rubrum*). "The curly figure is produced by fibers which develop spirally . . . giving a tiger-stripe pattern much prized by collectors." The tiger is well represented here. (*Henry Ford Museum.*)

**200.** New England walnut desk and bookcase (secretary), probably made in Boston about 1730. It is only about two and a half feet wide and is reminiscent of the small English secretary designed to stand against the pier between windows. The broken-scrolled pediment (bonnet top form) is an early example, with small opening and broad molding. The orna-

**200**

**201**

**202**

mentation is exceptionally rich. On the face is a large varie-gated star, one of five, inlaid in rosewood and satinwood. Bands of mahogany, ebony, and satinwood surround the fielded panels of the arched doors. The elaborate inlay is repeated around the crotch-veneered panels on the drawer fronts and on the lid. (*Karolik Collection, Museum of Fine Arts, Boston.*)

**201.** Mahogany desk and bookcase (secretary) with arched paned doors made in Newport by Job Townsend about 1730-1750. This is one of the most important examples of American furniture. It is the only labeled piece by Job Townsend so far discovered, although a signed desk has lately appeared in the market. Job Townsend and his son-in-law, John Goddard, founded the Townsend-Goddard line of Newport cabinetmakers, who specialized in pieces of blockfront-and-shell construction. In the writing section is an early example of the Newport shell, combined with blocking. Its full development can be followed in later work (Nos. 298, 305, 316, 324, 330). The lowboy, No. 221, also shows an intaglio shell with the edge contained in the segment of a circle, as here. In later work (No. 298) the shell has a serrated outline. (*Rhode Island School of Design.*)

**202.** Connecticut cherry desk and bookcase on frame, made about 1740. This is the forerunner of typical Connecticut case pieces associated with the Chapins and Aaron Roberts. The upper section has carved serrated leaf panels framing the doors, reminiscent of seventeenth-century New England motifs but unusual in the Queen Anne period. The vine trail was typical in later Connecticut decoration. (*Henry Ford Museum.*)

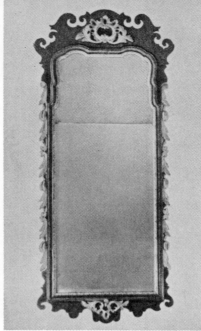

**203.** Looking glass, made about 1735-1745, probably in New York, where it was originally owned by Isaac Van Keuren. It is of pine with japanned decoration showing Chinese designs in gold on a black ground. This may be the work of Gerardus Duyckinck senior, the only japanner advertising in New York at the time. On January 6, 1735, his first announcement appeared in the *New-York Weekly Journal*. In 1746 his son, Gerardus, advertised that he had succeeded to the business. The favored form of the Queen Anne mirror in America is characterized by a scrolled crest and apron. (*Ginsburg and Levy.*)

**204.** Looking glass of walnut veneered on pine with the beveled glass in two sections. It was made in New England in the mid-1700s and is one of a pair. Mirror glass was made in small sizes, and this method of extending the length is seen in Queen Anne mirrors. The pier glass was hung over a side table, as seen in No. 205. The carved, gilt molding next to the glass was an addition made to the frame in the second quarter of the century. This example shows elaborate fretwork, and the applied gilt ornaments in fanciful shell and leaf form are in rococo style. The pendants of carved and gilt leaves, blossoms, and fruit were inspired by the English architectural-looking glass of the George I period. (*Karolik Collection, Museum of Fine Arts, Boston.*)

**205.** The parcel-gilt pier glass in the dining room of Van Cortlandt Manor is probably of New York workmanship. It is of pine, painted black, and was made in the mid-1700s. The pier table under the mirror has a skirt bordered with the rather coarse gadrooning typical of New York. This too is a Van Cortlandt family piece. New York side chairs, from another New York State family, are illustrated in the Chippendale section, No. 273. (*Van Cortlandt Manor, Sleepy Hollow Restorations.*)

**206.** Walnut settee (upholstered in mauve velvet) made about 1735 in Philadelphia for Stenton, the home of James Logan (1674-1751), who was secretary to William Penn. Stenton was built in 1728, and its great library passed in 1751 to the city of Philadelphia. The upholstered settee was slow to appear in America even though its close relative, the easy chair, was being made from the late 1700s. The tall back with scrolled outline is unusual but typical of chair backs of the late 1700s. Particularly handsome are the cabriole legs with scrolls at the knee, beaded bracket, carved shell, and trifid foot. (*Metropolitan Museum of Art.*)

206

**207.** Settee made in New York before 1750. It is of mahogany with cherry underframing, upholstered in early eighteenth-century quilted linen, and comes from the Beekman house on Van Brugh Street. This has New York details in the square claw and ball, and a tapering back leg ending in a square foot. The plain, lower back of straight design became fashionable at the end of the reign of Queen Anne. The first upholsterers' advertisements in New York were published in 1749. Stephen Callow, "from London," and James Huthwaite, "Upholsterer and Chair Stuffer from London," advertised individually but were working in partnership in 1750. Among Callow's accomplishments was the making of "Seattees." (*Metropolitan Museum of Art.*)

**208.** Unique American Queen Anne sofa. It is of walnut (covered in leather) with carved web feet and cabriole legs with knee blocks. The arrow-shaped stretchers are unusual. This, probably the earliest American sofa with undulating back, was made in Philadelphia about 1740-1750. It is shown again, in its setting at Winterthur, in No. 156. (*No. 269, Downs,* American Furniture. *H. F. du Pont Winterthur Museum.*)

207

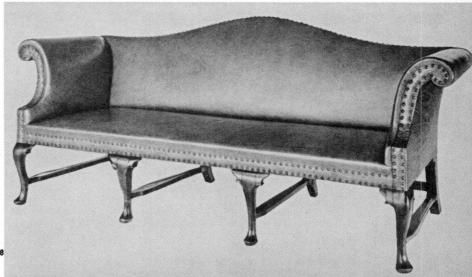

208

209

210

211

**209.** Candlestand and firescreen of cherry made between 1740-1750. In describing this unusual piece Downs was able to mention two Pennsylvania records, one of a "Screen Candlestick" in 1737, and of a "Table & Candle Skreen" in 1744. American examples of the Queen Anne period are rare, but the period is substantiated by the simple baluster of the shaft. The screen is fixed rather than adjustable as was the case in later pieces. (*No. 235 Downs,* American Furniture. *H. F. du Pont Winterthur Museum.*)

**210.** Mahogany candlestand made in Philadelphia about 1745. The size of this very small table (height twenty-nine inches, diameter twenty) would suggest that its purpose was to support a candlestick, yet the dished top indicates its probable use as a tea table as well. The bird-cage attachment made it possible to tip and turn the top. The arched tripod, ending in snake feet, supports a ring-turned, tapering shaft with a slightly flattened ball that represents an early evolutionary stage of Philadelphia's flattened ball on tripod tables (No. 402). (*Henry Ford Museum.*)

**211.** Screw-type candlestand of maple. The table and candle-arm can both be adjusted to the height required. The table has a dished top and the pole ends in a modified acorn finial. These candlestands are difficult to date, as the type was developed about the first quarter of the eighteenth century and continued to be made for a long period. (*Nutting Collection, Wadsworth Atheneum.*)

212

**212.** Newport stool made of walnut, with maple in the slip-seat frame. The covering is flamestitch embroidery. The height (twelve inches) is from three to six inches lower than the average stool and approximately that of the "slipper" chairs of which Newport produced a number of examples (see No. 175). Eighteenth-century American stools are rare but generally of fine quality. This one was made about 1720-1740. Through most of the seventeenth century, chairs were scarce but the joint stool was widely used. As chairs became more common, stools then lost favor in the average household but continued to be used in luxurious homes, sometimes as part of a set with chairs. It is often difficult to establish an American origin, but maple here substantiates it. (*No. 292, Downs,* American Furniture. *H. F. du Pont Winterthur Museum.*)

213. Maple breakfast table[29] with shaped skirt made in Massachusetts about 1725-1740. The pad foot has a hock, a feature of French furniture as far back as the late 1600s and called *pied de biche* (doe's foot). Small gateleg tables had undoubtedly been used in the seventeenth century as breakfast tables. In the eighteenth century the cabriole leg instead of the gateleg marked the principal change in design of the small dropleaf breakfast table which also served for tea, cards, writing, or as a candlestand. New England led in the production of such small tables with oval tops. (*No. 304, Downs*, American Furniture. *H. F. du Pont Winterthur Museum.*)

**213**

**214**

**215**

214. Walnut breakfast table made in New England about 1730. The "straight" cabriole leg ends in a cushioned pad foot. A table designed for a place in a corner when not in use has a triangular frame and three stationary legs and one that pivots. The triangular, folding leaf has suggested the popular name, "handkerchief table." This design was frequently made both in New England and in the South. (*John S. Walton.*)

215. Mahogany card table made in Massachusetts (probably Boston) about 1735. The slender cabriole legs and shallow frame are typical of New England. The table has checkered inlay on the skirt, drawer front, and top. The rounded corners (turret ends) were designed for the circular-based candlesticks of the period. This example, which has the original needlework covering, is one of the rare American card tables extended by concertina (accordion) action.[30] It descended in the family of Peter Faneuil, the wealthy Huguenot merchant who built Faneuil Hall for Boston in 1742. (*Bayou Bend Collection, Houston.*)

**216.** Mahogany card table made about 1740. This unusually early example from Newport follows the usual Queen Anne form. The rounded, or turret, corners are given more than usual prominence by the molding of the frieze which is enriched with a small carved shell. The bracket of the cabriole ends in a long, beaded C-scroll of crisp outline. The slender, almost straight leg displays an early use of the claw-and-ball foot. There is a long drawer characteristic of New England card tables. (*Bayou Bend Collection, Houston.*)

216

**217.** Center table made in Massachusetts about 1720-1740. It is of walnut with an imported red and gray Brescia marble top. The stamp *I Hill* in the soft pine lining may be that of an unrecorded maker. In the eighteenth century this would have been called a slab table[20] or a marble table. It is finished on all sides, which shows that it was intended to stand free of the wall. (*No. 353, Downs, American Furniture. H. F. du Pont Winterthur Museum.*)

**218.** Newport dining table made about 1730-1750. The fine figured grain of the heavy Santo Domingan mahogany is the chief ornament of this plain but well-designed table. The cabriole is square at the knee, and, as frequently noted in Newport work, the substantial thickness in the upper portion of the leg tapers off to a slender ankle. The large, oval dropleaf table that could seat eight persons is rarely found today, although (as successor to the gateleg

217

table of the late 1600s) it was the favored form of dining table of the Queen Anne period. (*Henry Ford Museum.*)

**219.** This New England mahogany dressing table, or lowboy, with cabriole leg and pad foot was made about 1750 and descended in the Stearns family of Salem. The inset shell, or fan, is a distinguishing feature of Queen Anne lowboys and highboys. Two tiers of drawers give this piece a more boxlike form than the William and Mary lowboy (Nos. 119-121), but the shaping of the skirt, although less deeply arched, and the use of turned pendants are reminiscent of the earlier type. The molded edge of the top has incurved corners. Queen Anne lowboys of the mid-eighteenth century frequently have Chippendale brasses. (*John S. Walton.*)

218

**220.** New England walnut dressing table (lowboy) made about 1735 and decorated with a carved, gilt intaglio shell, triple bands of stringing, and variegated inlaid on top and sides. This Queen Anne lowboy matches the highboy, No. 183. Both pieces were owned by the Woodward family of Massachusetts and Connecticut. They were probably made in Boston which, in the year 1744, Dr. Alexander Hamilton found more like a European capital than any other city along the Atlantic coast.[23] Boston produced the richest American Queen Anne furniture in her japanned work and in parcel-gilt pieces such as this. (*Ashley House, Old Deerfield.*)

**221.** Dressing table or lowboy of flame-grain mahogany, with a single tier of drawers and scalloped skirt, made in Newport about 1755, and attributed to John Goddard (1723-1785). The shell, contained in the segment of an arch instead of forming its own serrated outline (No. 298), is of the early type on Townsend-Goddard furniture. The silhouette at the lower edge of the shell joins the flowing lines of the skirt. This is an early example of the Newport claw and ball, the ball oval in form, the claw extended. It is also undercut and pierced and therefore suggests the work of John Goddard, as on the Jabez Bowen tea table at the Winterthur Museum. The rear legs have the claw-and-ball foot instead of the more usual pad foot. (*Bayou Bend Collection, Houston.*)

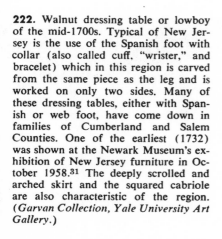

**222.** Walnut dressing table or lowboy of the mid-1700s. Typical of New Jersey is the use of the Spanish foot with collar (also called cuff, "wrister," and bracelet) which in this region is carved from the same piece as the leg and is worked on only two sides. Many of these dressing tables, either with Spanish or web foot, have come down in families of Cumberland and Salem Counties. One of the earliest (1732) was shown at the Newark Museum's exhibition of New Jersey furniture in October 1958.[31] The deeply scrolled and arched skirt and the squared cabriole are also characteristic of the region. (*Garvan Collection, Yale University Art Gallery.*)

**223**

**223.** Dressing table or lowboy, made about 1745-1760, probably in Maryland.[32] Walnut was used with tulipwood and white cedar as secondary woods. The trifid foot represents the Queen Anne style; otherwise the design comes close to the Chippendale lowboy. Its pierced skirt is without parallel. The rectangular, box-like form so unlike the New England lowboys with scrolled and arched skirts, agrees with English precedent. (*No. 324, Downs,* American Furniture. *H. F. du Pont Winterthur Museum.*)

**224.** Charleston dressing table or lowboy of walnut with cypress as secondary wood, made in the mid-1700s. This is the first shell-carved Charleston lowboy to come to light. The knee is carved with an inverted husk motif suggesting a fleur-de-lis, and the inside of the cabriole is C-scrolled. The shaping

**224**

of the central arch and the broad pad foot resemble Charleston work in the Exhibition of Southern Furniture at Richmond, 1952. This lowboy is one of the richest pieces of Charleston furniture of the Queen Anne style so far discovered. (*Collection of Frank L. Horton.*)

**225.** This Southern dressing table or lowboy of walnut with a hard yellow southern pine interior was made in the mid-1700s. It has ogee scrolls on either side of a plain central arch and a cabriole leg with cushioned pad foot. Simplicity of design combined with good craftsmanship is characteristic of Southern furniture. This typical form of Queen Anne lowboy, with a single tier of drawers, continued to be made in the South through the greater part of the century. (*Collection of John C. Goddin.*)

**226.** Mixing table of maple, painted black, made in Massachusetts about 1720-1740. The dished top contains blue and white Dutch tiles illustrating scenes from the Old and New Testaments. The only other known Queen Anne table with tile top is at the Winterthur Museum. A William and Mary example is shown in Lockwood's *Colonial Furniture* (Vol. II). Mixing tables were generally made with marble or slate tops, impervious to strong or hot liquids. (*Henry Ford Museum.*)

**225**

**226**

227

228

229

**227.** Porringer table of curly maple made in Newport about 1735-1750. The top has cyma scrolls and rounded or porringer corners. The term "porringer" is a modern one, suggested by the round corners, given to an occasional table used for writing, cards, tea, or as a breakfast table. (*No. 301, Downs, American Furniture. H. F. du Pont Winterthur Museum.*)

**228.** Mahogany console table with a marble top, made in Newport about 1740-1765. This is literally a console, as the back attaches directly to the wall. This is a very rare American form in any period. The elongated claw-and-ball foot of Newport is recognizable but it is a more robust version than that seen in the later work of the Townsend-Goddard cabinetmakers, to whom this table may be attributed. The shaping of the skirt, the lambrequin on the knee, and the vigorous scroll at the side of the leg are noteworthy. It was presented to the Essex Institute in 1916 by the Salem family in which it had descended. (*Essex Institute.*)

**229.** New York side table of mahogany with marble top, made about 1750. A variegated star is inlaid on the frieze and there is a scrolled bracket on the cabriole leg, which ends in a raised slipper foot. The massive, sturdy lines of New York furniture are seen in this large slab table, as it would have been called at the time it was made.[20] It was originally in the mansion at 3 Wall Street built by Gulian Verplanck, who died in 1751. Verplanck had many dealings with Peter Faneuil of Boston, whose delicate table (No. 215) expresses the sophisticated refinement of Boston while this one suggests the solid worth of Dutch New York. (*Metropolitan Museum of Art.*)

**230.** Tea table of walnut and cherry made about 1730-1740. It has a dished top characteristic of the New England tea table, which is generally rectangular in form. The perfect proportions of this piece, the narrow frieze of curly-grain cherry, shaped convex skirt, and slender cabriole legs, represent the extreme refinement of Massachusetts cabinetmaking. (*No. 365, Downs, American Furniture. H. F. du Pont Winterthur Museum.*)

230

231

232

**231.** Because of the tall slender cabriole, narrow frieze, and narrow convex scrolled apron, this cherry tea table at first glance suggests New England workmanship of the mid-1700s. However, the thick-soled slipper is not characteristic. In describing a table with a similar foot at the Winterthur Museum, Downs wrote, "New York furniture in the Queen Anne style often has a distinctive slipper foot not unlike a modern platform shoe." A Long Island highboy with an almost identical foot was exhibited with New York furniture at the Museum of the City of New York, 1956-1957. It also had the tall, slender cabriole. This table, made in the mid-1700s, has been attributed to Connecticut, but may possibly represent Long Island work. (*Garvan Collection, Yale University Art Gallery.*)

**232.** Cherry and birch tea table, probably made in Connecticut in the mid-1700s. Everything about this little piece represents the characteristic New England tea table — dished top, scrolled frieze, cabriole leg, and pad foot. The angular cabriole and the use of cherry suggest Connecticut but are not conclusive. (*J. K. Byard Sale, Parke-Bernet Galleries, 1960.*)

**233.** Tripod tea table made in Philadelphia in the mid-1700s. The birdcage makes it possible for the top to revolve and to be turned to a vertical position. The piecrust edge is generally associated with the Chippendale period, but details here suggest an earlier date. The shell and husks on the cabriole resemble the ornament on Queen Anne chairs and the baluster (larger above) is a tentative form antedating the flattened ball and shaft used almost exclusively later. The workmanship relates it to a tea table, Plate 74, in Hornor's *Blue Book of Philadelphia Furniture*, which is thought to have come from Charles Norris' house. (*Bayou Bend Collection, Houston.*)

**234.** This tripod tea table of mahogany with a plain molded rim made between 1740-1750 is a simpler version of No. 233. It shows the beginning of the development of Philadelphia's flattened ball on the column, which was to assume still wider proportions in later work. Although the table is sparingly carved, its claw-and-ball foot is rendered in the best Philadelphia style. Like the former example, it might also be considered an early Chippendale table, but early traits are present. (*Los Angeles County Museum.*)

233

234

# 3. Chippendale

## 1755-1790

The Colonies in which the Chippendale style developed were already approaching the time of open conflict with England. Realization of the struggle that was likely to come was noted by the Finnish traveler, Peter Kalm.[33] During his stay in America, between 1748 and 1751, Kalm gained a strong impression that the people to whom he talked expected someday to be independent, and this seemed to be inevitable. There was new feeling of strength and confidence in the Colonies in 1763, when the French and Indian War ended in a victory which they had materially helped to bring about. Shortly following the Treaty of Paris which ended the war, England revised the hated Navigation Acts. Since the mid-seventeenth century these Acts had plagued commerce, and England's new restrictions of 1766 began to bring things to a head. The Stamp Act and its repeal, followed by Townshend's further devices for taxation, then the Boston Tea Party and the Boston Port Bill, occupied the years up to 1774, during which many colonials still believed that a way out would be found without a definite break with England. Philip Vickers Fithian,[34] whose journal provides a description of life in Tidewater Virginia in 1773-1774, observed that in the great plantation households which he visited a toast to the King was customary at dinner, yet there was general approval of the Boston Tea Party, and people were singing "Liberty Songs."

Despite the growing unrest, an extraordinary amount of building went forward after the mid-eighteenth century, and many of the finest historic houses which are open today as museums are of this date. Considering this, and also the fact that so many examples of fine furniture were made during the same period, it is evident that anxiety over the future was not sufficient to affect creative activity.

PALLADIAN ARCHITECTURE IN ENGLAND AND AMERICA. In the years 1755-1775 master builders and house carpenters, whose names are generally unknown, were adapting the Palladian style to American needs. This style was dominant in England from 1715 to 1760, and was based on the work of the Italian Renaissance architect Andrea Palladio (1518-1580). Palladio's manner of using classic design in Italian villas profoundly influenced the two chief English exponents of the style, Lord Burlington (1695-1753) and William Kent (1684-1748). In the early seventeenth century, classical influence had been introduced by Inigo Jones (1573-1652) and had passed through a free and vigorous interpretation, the baroque, by Sir Christopher Wren (1632-1723) and John Vanbrugh (1664-1726) in the late 1600s. Classical design was not new to English builders, but certain details received new emphasis, particularly the Roman temple portico, with a row of columns supporting a triangular pediment. Doors and windows were usually pedimented, and there was frequent use of the Palladian window, an integral grouping of three lights of which the center and tallest was round-topped, the whole enframed in pilasters. Architects' designs published in builders' guides enabled the house carpenter in America to create an American version of the simpler type of Georgian house as lived in by well-to-do merchants and the professional class in England. Among these books are *A Book of Architecture* (1728) by James Gibbs (a follower of Wren); Batty and Thomas Langley's *City and Country Builders and Workman's Treasury of Designs* (1740); Abraham Swan's *Designs in Architecture* (1757); William and John Halfpenny's *The Modern Builder's Assistant* (1757); and Isaac Ware's *Complete Body of Architecture* (1756).

One of the richest Palladian interiors of the period to be seen in America is the drawing room at Gunston Hall, Lorton, Virginia. This house in Fairfax County, now open as a museum, was begun about 1755 by the Virginia statesman George Mason. In that year William Buckland (1734-1774), having completed an apprenticeship in England, came over to work for him under indenture for four years as "carpenter and joiner." The gifted Buckland (to be known later for his houses in Annapolis) displays his skill as a carver in an interior which rivals any of the Philadelphia houses. Fluted pilasters frame doors and windows and enclose the built-in cupboards that flank the fireplace. Richly carved entablatures and modillioned cornice combine lavish details from contemporary builders' manuals. It is known that Buckland possessed a library of seventeen architectural works, the largest owned by any early builder.

Another distinguished house in the Palladian style is Woodford, in Fairmount Park, Philadelphia. When it was remodeled in 1756 for William Coleman it was given a façade with a Palladian window and projecting pedimented central section, a treatment which began to be seen on fine homes of the period. At Mount Vernon, a pediment was added to the west front during the alterations carried out by George Washington about 1774, and a sketch for this exists in his own hand. At Kittery Point, Maine, tall pilasters of the Ionic order on both sides of the pedimented section rise to the full height of the Lady Pepperrell house, which was built in 1760.

Other great houses of the period are Mount Pleasant in Philadelphia, (see color plate IV), Mount Morris in New York, the Jeremiah Lee house in Marblehead, Massachusetts, the Corbit house in Odessa, Delaware, and the Hammond-Harwood house in Annapolis. John Adams called Mount Pleasant the "most elegant seat in Pennsylvania." It was begun in 1761 as a country house on the Schuykill for John Macpherson, a Scottish sea captain who amassed a fortune privateering in West Indian waters. Both the exterior and interior of Mount Pleasant display a full range of Palladian detail. The Great Chamber contains a chimneypiece surmounted by a broken-scrolled pediment with a new element in design, the rococo. This is present in an asymmetrical leaf carving such as is frequently seen on Philadelphia Chippendale highboys of the 1760s and 1770s.

Mount Morris in New York (also known as the Jumel Mansion) was built in 1765 and offers an early example of the two-story portico, which was to become common in the nineteenth century. The Jeremiah Lee house (1768) is famous for its English painted wallpaper showing Roman ruins, based on designs by Pannini and Vernet, of which examples are rare even in England today. The Corbit house (1772) has a carved chimneybreast, probably derived from the works of Abraham Swan, and a Chinese railing crowning the roof which reflects the popularity of Chinese designs in the mid-eighteenth century. The Hammond-Harwood house (1774) represents the last work of William Buckland. The severely plain brick façade has one of the finest doorways of the period. Introduced here, with the traditional Palladian motifs of pitch pediment and Ionic columns, are festoons of roses over the fanlight, indicating use of naturalistic floral forms, which then were seen also on rococo furniture.

All these houses may be taken as representative of the original homes for which furniture in the Chippendale style was made.

ARCHITECTURAL INFLUENCE ON FURNITURE. The Palladian style affected English furniture design in the 1720s and 1730s. This is evident in the work of William Kent, which, although elaborate in the extreme, was well suited to the grandiose settings for which it was intended. The Palladian style also influenced design at a more modest level. Simpler forms of George II furniture show proportions of a classic and often geometric character.

In his *Vitruvius Britannicus* (1715), Colen Campbell expressed a significant view when he said that the "Square and Circle . . . in my weak Opinion are the most perfect Figures." Nowhere is this more noticeable in furniture than in the Georgian chair, with its square design, which contrasts with the taller Queen Anne and William and Mary forms. Also introduced were ornamental details taken from the classic entablature of architrave, frieze, and cornice. The broken pediment (already present in the broken-scrolled form developed in the baroque style) appeared with the straight lines of the triangular (or pitch) pediment. Pilasters on case pieces were suggested by those which flanked the entrance or the chimneybreast. The looking-glass frame drew so completely on these motifs that a type with classical entablature is referred to as the architectural mirror.

ENGLAND — ARRIVAL OF THE ROCOCO. In the 1730s and 1740s, while Palladian elements remained in evidence in furniture design, three new and quite different sources of ornament began to engage attention. These were the rococo style, developed in France; Chinese designs, known from Oriental porcelains, lacquer, and wallpaper; and the Gothic style, which remained part of English tradition. The fusion of these three elements in the design of furniture of classical proportions is known as the Chippendale style.

Earlier Georgian elements remained present in the baroque broken-scrolled pediment on case pieces of this period and in the pierced vase-shaped splat on chairs. The latter had been developed in the 1720s, and, although pierced strapwork designs in vase form disappeared from the more fashionable English chairs after the middle of the eighteenth century, they were too practical and pleasing to be abandoned altogether. Robert Manwaring illustrated many of these designs together with Chinese and rustic forms in his *Cabinet and Chair-Maker's*

*Real Friend and Companion* (1765). The claw-and-ball foot, which originated in the Chinese dragon claw and pearl (one of the Oriental motifs entering English design at the end of the seventeenth century) was retained, although it was no longer at the height of fashion. The acanthus carved on the cabriole leg of tables and chairs, and the eagle's head as a terminal of the armrest on chairs are, when present on Chippendale furniture, evidence of the survival of the fashions of the 1720s and 1730s.

The most important of the new elements in English furniture design was the rococo. The style began to attract English designers in the 1730s and was widely accepted in the 1740s. In a natural reaction to rigid symmetry, English designers had begun to look with interest at the curving lines of the rococo style, already brought to perfection in France.

Before the end of the reign of Louis XIV in 1715, France had begun to develop lighter forms with flowing lines, and by 1720 the continuous curve had entered the basic structure as well as the ornament of furniture. André Charles Boulle, Jean Bérain, Jean le Pautre, and Daniel Marot (the last also worked in England) were the forerunners of the rococo style, created by such designers as Juste-Aurèle Meissonier (c.1693-1750), Gilles-Marie Oppenord (1672-1742), and Jean Pillement (1728-1801).

The term "rococo" was not in use until late in the eighteenth century. Chippendale, on the title page of his *Director,* called it the "modern" style. The meaning of rococo is "rockwork," referring to the rock forms (*rocailles*) which, with shell motifs (*coquilles*), had long been popular in French garden ornament. These shapes, appearing in an endless variety of exaggerated designs in all the decorative arts, are the distinguishing features of the new style. But there were other aspects of rococo. Chinese motifs were adapted from porcelain, lacquer, and painted wallpaper, all of which became increasingly familiar as European trade with the Far East continued to develop. A third element was the naturalistic rendering of plant and animal forms; and a fourth (an almost abstract creation) was the flamboyant framework given to the cartouche, or ornamental tablet. The latter, which took on an almost plastic character, was used in countless variations. In its simplest form it was the cabochon on the knee of the cabriole and in its most resplendent it was the pierced cartouche finial for a pediment.

Chief credit for the popularization of rococo in England must go to Matthias Lock, author of *A New Drawing Book of Ornaments* (1740), which contained designs for carved mirror frames and wall lights. Lock published several similar works before preparing a work with a similar title, *A New Book of Ornaments* (1752) with H. Copland (first name unknown). Copland had published rococo designs of his own in 1746. In these and later English design books, including Chippendale's *Director,* the rococo style is adapted to the ornamentation of existing English furniture forms. The basic lines of French furniture were not adopted in England except for the already accepted cabriole leg, and the English cabriole (as opposed to the French design) never lost its feeling of verticality in the way it joined the seat rail. Bombé and serpentine lines were also used to some extent in case pieces, but without disturbing the rectilinear mass of the design. The first furniture designs published in England which show rococo influence are found in some crude plates in Batty and Thomas Langley's *City and Country Builders and Workman's Treasury of Designs.*

CHINESE INFLUENCE. Chinese influence on the decorative arts of England took two forms — the Westernized version of Chinese motifs, *chinoiserie,* a component part of the French rococo; and second, the adaptation of actual forms in straight-leg furniture, and the use of

Chinese lattice and frets. William Halfpenny's *New Designs for Chinese Temples* (1750) was the first to show Chinese lattice designs — not for furniture but for use on staircases and in garden architecture. More influential were Edwards and Darly's *New Book of Chinese Designs* and Chippendale's *Director*, both published in 1754. The source of all these illustrations was not actual Chinese furniture but delineations of furniture on porcelain and wallpapers. Consequently, their use in furniture design had a pseudo-Chinese character. Quite different were the types offered by Sir William Chambers in his *Designs of Chinese Buildings, Furniture, Dresses, Machines and Utensils,* published in 1757. Chambers had gone to China in the 1740s and made drawings while there. These and other works gave English furniture makers a refreshingly new fund of ideas, not derived, as was usual in England, from France or Holland.

Regarding the first form of Chinese influence, *chinoiserie,* England had its own early source in Stalker and Parker's *Treatise of Japanning* (1688), but it was the growing importation of Far Eastern wares which made Chinese decoration really familiar. The designs on lacquer and porcelain illustrated architecture, figures, dragons, chi-lins, flowers, and emblems, all depicted with complete disregard of the canons of symmetry and perspective, and therefore perfectly in accord with the concepts of the rococo. Chinese motifs took their place illogically yet at the same time logically with the rockwork, C-scrolls, and naturalistic motifs of rococo design.

GOTHIC INFLUENCE. Gothic influence had long since departed from English furniture, but it was still evident in church and public architecture when Kent used it in the late 1720s for a gatehouse on a country estate. In the 1740s Sanderson Miller was building imitation Gothic ruins on gentlemen's estates, and pseudo-Gothic designs for buildings were offered in Batty Langley's *Gothic Architecture Improved* (1742). Horace Walpole purchased Strawberry Hill in 1747 and spent many years remodeling it in the "charming venerable Gothick." He even had furniture constructed which copied details from Gothic monuments. Furniture in Gothic designs was first published in Darly's *New Book of Chinese, Gothic and Modern Chairs* (plates dated 1750 and 1751), but these are of little importance and only indicate that Chippendale was not entirely an innovator when he offered a variety of Gothic designs in 1754. Among the Gothic motifs found on English furniture are lancet and ogee arches, trefoils, and cusps in chair splats; crockets (bunched leaves) on pediments; and foliated designs from tracery forming the astragals (glazing bars) on doors of bookcases and cabinets.

Gothic forms, like the Chinese, were not copied literally on English furniture. They were so harmonized with Chinese and rococo motifs that analysis is often difficult. The real worth of the Chippendale style is in the imagination with which these were transformed and united.

THOMAS CHIPPENDALE, 1718(?)-1779. Following the publication of *The Creators of the Chippendale Style* by Fiske Kimball and Edna Donnell (*Metropolitan Museum Studies.* Vols. I and II, 1929), the personal reputation of Thomas Chippendale suffered by their conclusion that he had made use of other men's designs, particularly those of Matthias Lock and H. Copland. This view has been widely accepted in England and America, but the subject has been reviewed recently by Peter Ward-Jackson of the Victoria and Albert Museum in *English Furniture Designs of the Eighteenth Century* (1958), where evidence is offered in support of Chippendale. The book describes in detail the drawings for the *Director* in the museum. All these drawings are in the same hand, and are quite different from those identified with Lock. Furthermore, each drawing is signed *T. Chippendale Invent. et delin.,* and the authenticity of the signature is not questioned. Mr. Ward-Jackson can find no reason for doubting that these are what they purport to be. He also notes that the argument sometimes advanced that the busy tradesman would have had no time to make his own drawings is disproved by a letter[35] from Chippendale to his patron, Rowland Winn of Nostell Priory, in which he mentions the drawings he had been making for furniture at Harewood House. In addition, Chippendale makes several references to his own work on designs in the preface of the *Director*. All that is definitely known of Copland's designs for furniture is based on six plates he contributed to Manwaring's *Cabinet and Chair-Maker's Real Friend and Companion*, in a style totally unlike anything in the *Director*. H. Copland is an obscure figure, and no original drawings of any kind are known to be his. Consequently the attempt to assign to him the drawings for the *Director* in the Metropolitan Museum on the basis of comparison with his engravings seems to Mr. Ward-Jackson insufficiently based. The question is left open, with the weight of evidence in favor of Chippendale.

Thomas Chippendale was born about 1718 in Otley, Yorkshire, of a family of joiners and carpenters. He was in London by 1748, when he was married, and in 1753 moved to St. Martin's Lane, the most fashionable address for a London cabinetmaker. He worked there until his death in 1779, and was succeeded by his son Thomas and his partner, Thomas Haig. His best-known work was done for Nostell Priory and Harewood House, records of which exist, while his accounts show that he worked for many of the great houses of the time. Among subscribers to the *Director* were twenty members of the nobility, but what was more important in relation to Chippendale's reputation were the craftsmen subscribers who made use of his designs — ninety cabinetmakers, twenty upholsterers, ten carvers, nine joiners, and four carpenters, as well as picture-frame makers and plasterers.

The first edition of *The Gentleman and Cabinet-Maker's Director* by Chippendale appeared in 1754, the second (unchanged) in 1755. In the third edition (1762) a number of plates were omitted and over a hundred new ones added. Previous publications of furniture designs had been scanty in number. Batty Langley had included a few among the architectural plates in his *Treasury of Designs*, and Lock had shown looking-glass frames and girandoles (wall lights), but Chippendale was the first to illustrate furniture of all kinds.

A French edition of Chippendale's *Director* was published in 1762; his influence spread to Germany in the work of the Roentgen family, and his work was sold in Spain, Portugal, and the Low Countries. The use of his name to represent a phase of eighteenth-century furniture design began in the late nineteenth century, probably after the English firm of Wright and Mansfield began to make furniture after designs in the *Director*.

AMERICAN CHIPPENDALE. While English Chippendale furniture displays a great variety of rococo, Chinese, and Gothic designs in combination with Georgian classical forms, American Chippendale is more faithfully Georgian. In American work there is also more evidence of the survival of Queen Anne details — for instance, in the arched-panel doors of case pieces such as No. 336. In rural areas the Queen Anne pad foot was used to the end of the century.

New elements in Chippendale design are seen in the Gothic arch on chair backs (No. 272), in Gothic fret carving (No. 271) and a Chinese fret (No. 334). Occasionally there is a Chinese lattice, as represented by a Philadelphia chair (No. 276) and a Charleston table (No. 371). The straight-leg furniture of the 1770s (No. 370) shows the influence of actual Chinese furniture forms as depicted by Sir William Chambers. And the rococo influence is seen in the pierced cartouche finial which made a handsome terminal for many of the Philadelphia high chests (No. 311).

American Chippendale furniture may be divided into three groups: (1) the distinctively American; (2) new forms; (3) continuing forms.

An example of the first category can be found in both the high chest and dressing table (highboy and lowboy), which were often made as matching pieces. Distinctively American is the combination there of Queen Anne forms with Chippendale at a time when the Queen Anne style went out of fashion in England. The American Chippendale highboy, with its tall, scrolled pediment and shell-carved drawers at top and bottom has no parallel in English furniture. The Philadelphia Chippendale lowboy, with its carved deep skirt, inset quarter columns and shell-carved drawer, is also unmistakably American. Original to America is the combination of blockfront construction and shell carving found in Newport work (No. 330).

New forms include the pembroke table (No. 360), frequently used as a breakfast table. Its shallow leaves and its wide center reverse the proportions of earlier dropleaf tables. The bookcase, consisting of a cabinet above an enclosed section, sometimes with a projecting center which explains the name "breakfront," was new, and also rare, in America (No. 240).

The sofa made a gradual appearance in America, developing from the Queen Anne settee represented by Nos. 206 and 207. The early Chippendale style of the mid-1700s is represented by No. 346, which has a longer seat and lower back than the Queen Anne type. A later stage in the Chippendale style is seen in No. 347, a serpentine-back sofa with horizontally rolled arms. No. 348 is similar but has the Marlborough leg, a broad, straight leg, generally ending in a block, which was developed in Philadelphia about 1770.

The tripod tea table (piecrust table) with a top supported by a device called a birdcage had made a rare appearance in the 1740s, but the final development of the design belongs to the Chippendale period (No. 402). The gallery-top china table, an elaboration of the Queen Anne rectangular tea table with a pierced or raised gallery around the edge (No. 373) was new.

Reflecting the period's increasing luxury in interior furnishings was the appearance of such small new pieces as basin stands, kettle stands, and tall stands for candlesticks. New also was the blockfront chest of drawers (No. 298), made in New England and New York. A variant of this with a kneehole section, sometimes called a kneehole desk, served as a dressing table (No. 381).

Forms which continued in favor during the Chippendale period were the desk and bookcase (secretary) and chest-on-chest. The slope-front desk was made in great numbers. The chest of drawers might have plain, straight lines or be given serpentine (and reverse serpentine) construction. Occasionally it had a top drawer fitted with compartments for cosmetics and other dressing-table articles, which made it a dressing chest (No. 302). The side table, often constructed with a marble top as in the Queen Anne period, remained in style. This piece, antedating the sideboard, was considered essential in most dining rooms. The dining table of the dropleaf type continued to be made, but the pad foot of the Queen Anne period was replaced by claw and ball, and the top was square rather than oval in newer designs.

Looking glasses became larger and more imposing. So many were imported from England that American makers had every opportunity to copy them closely. For this reason it is often difficult to distinguish between the imported examples and those that were made in America. Highly prized by collectors are the mirrors labeled by John Elliott of Philadelphia, but, as his label states that he imported English looking glasses, supporting evidence in construction must be present in order to designate an example as American work. Boston, Philadelphia, and New York were the chief centers of mirror production. Three main types were made: the architectural mirror, with a broken-scrolled pediment and entablature (No. 344); the gilt mirror, with *chinoiserie* and rococo ornament (No. 343); and the old favorite, the fretwork looking glass (No. 340). The design of the latter was an elaboration of the Queen Anne form.

REGIONAL STYLES. In the second quarter of the eighteenth century, Philadelphia became the leading city of the Colonies. Manufactures and the crafts flourished there, and trade with the interior, the West Indies, and Europe offered its citizens opportunities for rapid accumulation of wealth. Samuel Powel I, carpenter, John Bringhurst, cooper, and George Mifflin, shopkeeper, were among the many Philadelphians of humble origin who followed the path to prosperity marked out by James Logan, Penn's secretary, through trade and ship-owning. In the *Map of the Improved Part of the Province of Pennsylvania* which Nicholas Scull, surveyor-general, published in 1759, is a roster of great Philadelphia families who owned the country seats in the vicinity. Here are listed the homes of Norris, Pemberton, Wharton, Mifflin, Waln, and others who indulge in Penn's taste for country living after prospering in town.

The new State House (now Independence Hall), one of the earliest Palladian buildings in America, was completed in 1744. It looked down on a city which, in 1748, impressed Peter Kalm as possessing "grandeur and perfection . . . by no means inferior to . . . the most ancient towns of Europe." The city which George Heap drew from the Jersey shore about five years later (seen in the Scull-Heap *View,* engraved in London in 1754) is imposing with its long waterfront. Among the landmarks are the spire of Christ Church, the towers of the State House and Court House, the simple block of the Quaker Meeting House, and the slender spire of the Academy.

The greatest number of craftsmen from Europe were attracted to Philadelphia between the mid-eighteenth century and the Revolution. In 1788 more than one hundred cabinet and chair-makers and their journeymen marched in the procession celebrating the ratification of the Constitution. No other center can match a list which includes Thomas Affleck, Benjamin Randolph, James Gillingham, Benjamin Gostelowe, Thomas Tufft, John Folwell, William Savery, and Jonathan Shoemaker.

In Boston, only John Cogswell's fine bombé case pieces and Benjamin Frothingham's distinctively blocked furniture have been identified. New York work is represented by documented chairs by Gilbert Ash and case pieces by Thomas Burling and Samuel Prince. Newport is represented by Job, Edmund and John Townsend, John Goddard, and other members of the Townsend-Goddard family. Charleston had a distinguished maker in Thomas Elfe. Connecticut Chippendale developed somewhat late in the period but had skillful craftsmen, including Eliphalet and Aaron Chapin.

American furniture is of simpler design than the English; it is less square in proportion and emphasizes the vertical line. Chairs are narrower, carving is not so elaborate, and the rake of the rear leg of chairs is less pronounced. This may be said as a generalization, but there are local traits as well.

Massachusetts retained as a regional characteristic the slender forms of the Queen Anne period. The cabriole leg is of great refinement, and its delicacy is probably the reason for the retention of the block-and-spindle stretcher. The claw-and-ball foot is carved with precision, and the side talon turns back sharply, forming a triangle with the center claw when the foot is

**IV.** The Great Chamber at Mount Pleasant in Fairmount Park, Philadelphia, which was built in 1761, has a magnificently carved chimney piece and alcove cupboards. Furniture includes fine examples of Philadelphia Chippendale. *(Philadelphia Museum of Art.)*

*Portrait of a Man.* By John Mare (active 1760-1774). *(Metropolitan Museum of Art.)*

It is tempting to believe that this may be a portrait of a New York chairmaker, perhaps Gilbert Ash (1717-1785). The painting is signed and dated, *1767*. Gilbert Ash, "in Wall-Street, near the City-Hall," was advertising "ready made Chairs, Mahogany and Black Walnut" in 1763. The design of the chair suggests that it might have been inspired by Chippendale's *Director,* 1762, Plate IX, but is, of course, much more elaborate than any known New York chair.

*Below: The Congress Voting Independence.* Engraving by Edward Savage after a painting by Robert Edge Pine. *(The Old Print Shop—Harry Shaw Newman.)*

Benjamin Franklin and Charles Carroll of Carrollton are seen in windsor chairs similar to No. 290, which is known to have been made for the State House (Independence Hall). Pine had his studio in this room in 1784, so his painting has documentary value even though painted after the event. It seems reasonable to assume that windsors were used at the Signing.

*Above:* Philadelphia rococo-carved pediment on mahogany highboy, 1760-1770. *(Karolik Collection, Museum of Fine Arts, Boston.)*

*Right:* Philadelphia claw-and-ball foot; mahogany highboy, 1760-1770. *(Karolik Collection, Museum of Fine Arts, Boston.)*

*Right:* Newport pierced claw foot; attributed to John Goddard, 1760-1765; tea table in collection of R. H. I. Goddard. *(No. 77, Carpenter, Arts and Crafts of Newport.)*

*Far right:* New York claw-and-ball foot on mahogany card table, 1760-1770. *(Collection of Mrs. Giles Whiting.)*

Newport blockfront-and-shell desk and bookcase by the Townsend-Goddard cabinetmakers, 1760-1775. *(Karolik Collection, Museum of Fine Arts, Boston.)*

**V.** A Pennsylvania German dresser and corner cupboard filled with Gaudy Dutch and spatterware lend color to an informal setting with country furniture in this breakfast room. *(Home of Mr. and Mrs. Mitchel Taradash.)*

viewed from the side (No. 272). Massachusetts card tables, side tables, and tea tables (the last generally of rectangular form) have tall, slender cabriole legs. Table frames are frequently severely plain and do not show the gadrooning seen in New York and Philadelphia work. A rare type of tea table in Massachusetts is the turreted or buttress type (No. 393), on which semicircular projections provide an individual place for teacups and saucers. Massachusetts secretaries and chests-on-chests are likely to have engaged pilasters framing the upper section (No. 329). Corkscrew finials are usual, and the more costly pieces may have carved figures, as on the desk and bookcase in the Metropolitan Museum which has figures by the Skillins of Boston. The use of the bombé form (kettle-base) for chests and other case pieces is typical. Blockfront furniture was popular, and blocking is generally somewhat flat (No. 380).

Newport's Townsend and Goddard families were responsible for the fine examples of blockfront-and-shell furniture of the 1760s and 1770s. The maritime importance of Newport never revived after the Revolution, and the patronage which produced fine furniture was lacking. But in the decades preceding the conflict Newport developed the most original style in America (Nos. 305, 324, 330, 381). Blocking seldom occurs in English furniture but is characteristic of Dutch work, and its adoption in America has not been satisfactorily explained. The undulating surface is formed of projecting sections alternating with concave ones, generally cut from the solid wood but sometimes with the relief sections applied. The carved shell, a favorite of the baroque period retained by William Kent, was given great emphasis in Newport. It was carved in relief and incised; shells in high relief were generally applied. The pliant lobes curve outward from a palmette or petal-like center which varies in design. A distinctive Newport characteristic is the small spiral scroll which may be observed on the ogee-bracket foot (No. 305). Newport secretaries and double chests generally have a bonnet-top closed at the back, and paneling which is carried up into the pediment (Nos. 305 and 330). The claw-and-ball foot is oval in form and the talons slender and outstretched. Sometimes the talons are undercut, as on English furniture. This detail has been found on work by John Goddard, and is frequently associated with him (No. 392). Another Newport characteristic is the combination of intaglio carving and relief in the delineation of the palmette which often adorns the knee of the cabriole leg (No. 394).

Connecticut furniture frequently shows the stylistic influence of Philadelphia and Rhode Island. Benjamin Burnham and Eliphalet Chapin worked in Philadelphia, which would explain lattice pediments (No. 314) and the scalloping on skirts of case pieces. The origin of Connecticut's blockfront-and-shell, which shows Rhode Island influence, has not yet been traced, but it is no longer attributed to the fact that John Townsend of Newport worked in Middletown, Connecticut, for this has recently been disproved by Houghton Bulkeley. The Connecticut blockfront has flatter blocking than is seen in Newport work, and the shell is more simply carved (No. 299). Connecticut makers liked carved sunbursts, sometimes of spiral or "pinwheel" type (No. 306). Fluted, chamfered corners are characteristic. The Queen Anne pad foot was long retained in this region, and the claw and ball was rather crudely carved.

New York had little use for rococo but occcasionally employed Gothic motifs (No. 273). George II forms, long-lived in America, were particularly favored in New York, as in the use of the tassel and ruffle on the splats of chairs (No. 247), and in the strapwork enclosing a diamond (No. 260). The serpentine form in New York card tables represents a rare expression of rococo influence (No. 367). Stiff gadrooning is often seen on the skirts of chairs. New York chairs were squarer and somewhat heavier than those elsewhere in America. The manner of cutting the claw and ball is also characteristic. The claws grasp the ball with box-like angularity (No. 368). The rear leg of chairs follows an English type, tapering rather sharply toward a squared foot (No. 259). This is sometimes found in Boston work, but generally indicates a New York origin. No New York scroll-top highboys have yet been discovered, but there are pitch-pedimented secretaries, as seen in No. 334.

Philadelphia made use of rococo, Gothic, and Chinese design in Chippendale style with more facility and imagination than elsewhere in America. The Gothic arch and trefoil appear on chair backs (No. 270), Gothic frets are carved on case pieces (No. 308), and rococo pierced shells and pierced cartouches are elaborate (No. 336). The tripod table with piecrust edge (No. 402) reached its finest American form in Philadelphia, and a flattened ball at the base of the baluster is typical. The claw-and-ball foot is finely sculptured in Philadelphia, and the hollows above the claws are finely articulated (No. 389). The French scrolled toe, rarely used in America, is found in the work of Randolph (No. 275). For reasons unknown, Philadelphia's straight-legged furniture was called the "Marlborough" style. Generally the leg ends in a block or plinth (No. 253), although it may be plain. Serpentine-back sofas were favored, and inset quarter columns are generally seen on case pieces. The hairy paw foot, occasionally used in Massachusetts, was used in Philadelphia and distinguishes a choice group of furniture represented by No. 274. The knee of the cabriole is sometimes carved with a cabochon (Nos. 270 and 274), and the carving of the acanthus on the cabriole is in subtle relief, as opposed to the flatter work of Massachusetts and the stringy acanthus which is characteristic of New York.

Charleston was the only Southern city with a school of cabinetmaking in the Chippendale period. The development of Baltimore came after the Revolution, and in Virginia and North Carolina plantation life produced the itinerant cabinetmaker. Charleston became important early in the eighteenth century, and the patronage of furniture makers was sufficient to encourage a local style. Fortunes were made in rice and indigo, and rich planters built fine houses in town to enjoy urban life and to escape the heat of the lowlands. But unfortunately the amount of Charleston furniture that has survived the fatalities of war, earthquake, fire, and change in fashion is small. What there is left of it is aristocratic, sophisticated, and more closely related in style to English furniture than other American work. The chest-on-chest in No. 309 is close to its English prototype. This form was a popular one, and Charleston inventories sometimes indicate as many as four such chests in a single house. Generally these pieces have a flat top over a fret-carved frieze. Many Charleston pieces show the same design of fret (No. 240), which is called the "Elfe fret" although on documentary evidence none can be traced definitely. However, Elfe's account book (1769-1775) records work done for all the prominent families, and pieces that have come down in these families which show strong relationship in design are reasonably considered to be his work. Mahogany was more frequently used than walnut. The former came by sea from the West Indies, Cuba, and Honduras, and was probably more easily obtained than walnut, which did not grow in coastal Carolina. Local cypress was sometimes used for entire pieces, but was generally reserved for use as a secondary wood, and its presence is accepted as an indication of probable Charleston origin.

While the foregoing represent the main centers of regional styles, others are recognized. In the work of the Dunlap family New Hampshire had a provincial version of Queen Anne which lingered on in the Chippendale period. This is represented by No. 307. Distinctive characteristics are found in Maryland (No. 267) and Kentucky (Nos. 496 and 524). These and other regional variations will repay more study than has been given to them up to the present time.[36]

PENNSYLVANIA-GERMAN FURNITURE. Although the subject of Pennsylvania-German furniture is not related to the Chippendale style, the period of the finest pieces (the second half of the eighteenth century) coincides with it, and for this reason a few examples are introduced in this chapter.

Pennsylvania-German furniture appears to be older than it is because it preserves the forms and ornament of German and Swiss work of the seventeenth and early eighteenth centuries. Traditional designs are apparent in scrolled-back chairs (No. 291), dower chests of painted tulipwood (Nos. 292 and 293), dressers and cupboards of walnut, oak, or yellow pine (No. 320), wardrobes with painted decoration or wax inlay (Nos. 404 and 405) and other utilitarian and decorative pieces.

Outside influence was scarcely felt in the farming communities of the Mennonites, Moravians, Dunkers, Amish, and Lutherans who settled southeastern Pennsylvania. These groups began to arrive from Europe in 1683 to take advantage of the freedom offered by William Penn, and for more than a century an influx from the Rhineland and Switzerland swelled the population of Bucks, Berks, Lancaster, Dauphin, Montgomery, and Lehigh Counties.

During the period of prosperity which followed the Revolution, cabinetmaker and clockmaker, decorative painter, iron caster and potter created a folk art which was a memory picture of what they had left in the homeland. Since it was based on memory rather than actual examples, which were few among the settlers, the decorative motifs are refreshingly transformed.

Favorite of all motifs was the tulip, which was used in Germany as long ago as the mid-sixteenth century, possibly earlier. Second to it is the heart, which was painted on chests, pierced in chair-backs, wrought in iron trivets, embroidered on samplers, and depicted on birth and marriage certificates. Designs also include the pomegranate, paired birds, vase of flowers, heraldic unicorns, figures of horsemen, geometric stars, and other motifs suggested by flowers and animals.

A certain amount of English influence is apparent in furniture forms, but while this is generally slight there is an important exception to this in the work of John Bachman of Lancaster, the most important member of the Bachman family of cabinetmakers. In his work (No. 335) the Philadelphia Chippendale style is interpreted in an individual manner.

WINDSOR CHAIRS. Early windsors belong chronologically in the 1760-1800 period and are therefore illustrated in this chapter (Nos. 284-290). Their development however, was quite independent of the new fashions and belongs to the tradition of the turner. The Philadelphia area was the first to produce windsor chairs, probably as early as 1725, but it would be hazardous to date an example before the middle of the century, and they did not come into general use before 1760. Most of the earliest existing windsors were made in the later 1700s. After 1800 they began to show the influence of Sheraton design, as in No. 464, and the best period ended about 1825.

There are six basic windsor types, named according to the style of back: comb-back, bow-back (sack-back, hoop-back), fan-back, low-back (horseshoe-shaped back), loop-back, and New England armchair. The finest of the last-named was the armchair with a continuous arm and back, which took great skill to make. Addition of a small shelf produced the writing-arm windsor, and when a drawer was added under the shelf, or under the seat, the windsor became a chair and desk in one.

Except for the pins, windsors were made of unseasoned wood, and a firm construction resulted from the contraction of the wood as it dried. The seat, usually saddle-shaped and thicker than found on the English windsor, was generally made of pine, and the legs were turned from maple, chestnut, birch, or ash. For the spindles and hoops (which were steamed) ash, hickory, and oak were used. A few other woods were found adaptable. Windsors were almost always painted. Green was the favorite color, but red and yellow, and sometimes black, were also used. Windsors were often advertised as garden chairs. Innkeepers found their sturdy construction an advantage, and they were also used in public buildings, such as the State House in Philadelphia (see No. 290).

The eighteenth-century New England windsor with the loop-back has much in common with the English windsor of the same period. This can be seen from the evidence of eighteenth-century prints. The English windsor with a pierced central splat came later. Another influence in the development of the American windsor seems to have come from Germany. Homer Eaton Keyes, in his remarks on "Unusual German Windsor Chairs" in *Antiques,* July 1936, illustrated a German painting of 1739 showing turned chairs with spindles and raked legs, one of which had an eared comb and another a low back. These are characteristics of the Pennsylvania windsors which may have a German origin. However there was a mingling of styles as the making of windsors spread from Philadelphia to many centers along the Atlantic coast, in New England, New York, and the South.

# Makers

*Thomas Affleck* (1740-1795), born in Scotland, arrived in Philadelphia in 1763. The furniture he made for Governor John Penn at Lansdowne and for his town house included outstanding examples in the Chinese Chippendale style. Affleck worked for many prominent families, including the Hollingsworths, Pembertons, and Fishers. Hornor's *Blue Book of Philadelphia Furniture* illustrates many documented examples. Affleck was a Loyalist and was banished to Virginia in 1777, but upon resuming work in Philadelphia he was well patronized. In 1794, the year before his death, he made furniture for Congress Hall. (No. 256. See also 248, 255, 264, 317, 369.)

*Gilbert Ash* (1717-1785) was listed as Freeman and joiner in New York in 1748. He had established himself in Wall Street by 1756, and in 1759 advertised "the Shop joiner or Cabinet Business." A last advertisement, 1763, mentions "Chairs, Mahogany and Black Walnut, Mahogany Tea Tables and Dining Tables . . ." Attributed to him on the basis of labeled and signed work are the chairs made for Sir William Johnson (1717-1774) of Johnson Hall (Johnstown, New York). Two of these are at the Winterthur Museum, and one is in the Garvan Collection at Yale University. These examples show his characteristic chair-back of interlaced scrolls enclosing a diamond. Cross-hatched lambrequins on the knee of the cabriole leg are also characteristic. (No. 260.)

*John Bachman* (1746-1829), born in Switzerland, came to Pennsylvania in 1766 a trained cabinetmaker. He worked in Lampeter Township, Lancaster County. His highly individual interpretation of the Chippendale style is distinguished by florid carving. Four succeeding generations of the family were cabinetmakers. (No. 335.)

*Thomas Burling,* Freeman of New York in 1769; advertised 1772-1775. He left New York during the Revolution, but in 1785 announced in an advertisement that he had "returned to this city and resumed his former calling, at the sign of the Chair . . . in Beekman-Street." (*New-York Packet,* January 24.) The advertisement also supplied the information that he had been apprenticed to Samuel Prince. In 1791 he was joined by his son, and the last advertisement, in 1796, mentions "a large assortment of the best Mahogany furniture . . ." A labeled wardrobe by Burling belongs to the New-York Historical Society. Other labeled pieces, a slope-front desk and desk and bookcase (*Antiques,* May 1936), show the stiffly gadrooned skirt which is typical of New York.

*Benjamin Burnham* (active 1769-1773), Colchester, Connecticut. The mystery regarding the history of the maker of the desk signed by Benjamin Burnham, 1769, in the Metropolitan Museum, was cleared up by Houghton Bulkeley in the Connecticut Historical Society *Bulletin,* July 1958, and in "Benjamin Burnham of Colchester, Cabinetmaker," *Antiques,* July 1959. He is no longer to be confused with Benjamin Burnham, innkeeper, of Norwich. The cabinetmaker, who may have been working in Colchester in 1769, left for England in 1773, and no further record of him has been found. His unusual blockfront desk in the Metropolitan Museum, signed and dated 1769, has an interior with twenty-nine small drawers arranged in sloping tiers. The inscription states that he had served his time in Philadelphia.

*Aaron Chapin* (1753-1838) worked in East Windsor and Hartford, Connecticut. He was apprenticed to his second cousin, Eliphalet Chapin, and was with him until he moved to Hartford in 1783. Aaron's work cannot be distinguished from that of his cousin. However, a fine Hepplewhite sideboard that he made for Frederick Robbins in 1804 is documented by a bill. (Nos. 486 and 512.)

*Eliphalet (or Eliphelet) Chapin* (1741-1807) worked in Philadelphia before establishing himself in East Windsor, where he was active by 1771 and until 1795. In a simplified Philadelphia style he made cherry high chests and desks and bookcases with latticework in scrolled pediments and pierced quatrefoil cartouche finials. A chair with pierced, scrolled splat crossed by a large X-shaped fret is attributed to him. (Nos. 261, 314, 331, 434.)

*John Cogswell* (active 1769, died 1818) held Boston town offices from 1778 to 1809. A signed and dated chest-on-chest (illustrated in *Antiques,* April 1952, in "John Cogswell, Cabinetmaker," by Joseph Downs) establishes him as the maker of Boston's finest bombé case pieces of rococo design. (No. 329.)

*Dunlap.* A family of New Hampshire cabinetmakers of this name worked in Chester and Salisbury, but little biographical information is available. Their work in curly maple represents a late expression of the Queen Anne style. Tall case pieces on small cabriole legs with pad foot, and flat tops crowned with a broad gallery of carved basketwork are characteristic. Their date is uncertain, but they were probably active in the late eighteenth and early nineteenth centuries. (No. 307.)

*Thomas Elfe* (active 1747-1775). A Charleston cabinetmaker whose account book (1768-1775), owned by the Charleston Library Society records about fifteen hundred pieces made for Charleston families. Frets are frequently mentioned, such as "double chest of drawers with a fret around" and "mahogany bookcase pediment head with a frett" (E. Milby Burton, *Thomas Elfe, Charleston Cabinetmaker,* Charleston Museum Leaflet, No. 25). Many pieces, showing the same "Elfe fret," are attributed to him on the basis of ownership in Charleston families for whom he is known to have worked. He also made "French chairs" (open-arm chairs). (Nos. 240, 309, 338.)

*John Elliott Sr.* (1713-1791), born in England, arrived in Philadelphia in 1753. Although he is known for furniture made for Edward Shippen, Jr., and Charles Norris, he is remembered chiefly as a maker of looking glasses. Since his label states that he imported and sold English looking glasses, a label alone is not proof that the mirror on which it appears is American. However, Downs says in *American Furniture* (No. 254) that there is evidence that some of the labeled mirrors were made in Philadelphia. Typical Elliott types are three: (1) Queen Anne design with a scrolled cresting enclosing a pierced gilded shell; (2) architectural looking glass with a broken-scrolled pediment; (3) plain fretwork design without carving or gilding. (Nos. 340 and 341.)

*John Folwell* (active 1762, died 1780). This Philadelphia maker followed a plate in Chippendale's *Director* while designing the pediment of his case for the orrery by David Rittenhouse, now in the University of Pennsylvania. In 1775 he was soliciting subscriptions for an American counterpart of the *Director,* to be called *The Gentleman and Cabinet-Maker's Assistant,* which was never published.

*Benjamin Frothingham* (1734-1809) was active by 1756 and worked with his father in Milk Street, Boston. During the Revolution he was a major of artillery and a friend of George Washington's. Ten of his labeled or signed pieces are known in the Queen Anne, Chippendale, and Hepplewhite styles. The labeled desk in the 1930 Flayderman sale showed an address in Charlestown; it represents a typical combination of blocking and oxbow (reverse-serpentine) construction which he repeated on chests-on-chests and desks and bookcases with arched-panel doors. (See "Major Benjamin Frothingham, Cabinetmaker," by Mabel M. Swan, *Antiques,* November 1952, and "Frothingham and the Question of Attributions," by Helen Comstock, *Antiques,* June 1953.) (No. 304.)

*James Gillingham* (1736-1781), a Philadelphia chairmaker and cabinetmaker well known for labeled chairs with a trefoil in the splat at the Metropolitan Museum and in the Mitchel Taradash collection. The design is based on Chippendale's *Director,* 1754 edition. In 1768 he dissolved partnership with Henry Clifton and moved to a shop in Second Street. This address appears on his label. A number of chairs are attributed to him (see No. 268), and others which are similar are said to be of "Gillingham type."

*John Goddard* (1723-1785) was active in Newport from the 1740s after having gone to sea. He was the son-in-law of Job Townsend, and with him and John and Edmund Townsend he brought the Newport blockfront-and-shell style to its full development. A documented tea table for Jabez Bowen at the Winterthur Museum and an inscribed secretary (Carpenter, *Arts and Crafts of Newport,* No. 43) are important pieces. A pierced claw foot is found on the Bowen table and is frequently cited as a basis for attribution. However, it was doubtless used by others in the Townsend-Goddard family. (No. 394.)

*Jonathan Gostelowe* (1745-1795) was a late exponent of the Chippendale style in Philadelphia. He is known for chests of drawers of serpentine form with fluted, canted corners and ogee bracket foot. A labeled example by him is in the Philadelphia Museum. (No. 294.)

*Adam Hains* (born 1768, working to about 1815) used the Chippendale style in Philadelphia after the Revolution and is best known for breakfast tables of pembroke type with shaped leaves and arched cross-stretcher. (Downs, *American Furniture,* No. 314.)

*Joseph Hosmer* (1735-1821) of Concord, Massachusetts, was a lieutenant of Minute Men in the Battle of Concord. He is known for cherry case pieces of individual style including the "Old Manse highboy" made for the grandfather of Ralph Waldo Emerson and now in the Winterthur Museum.

*Samuel Prince* (died 1778) advertised in New York between 1772 and 1776. Thomas Burling, his apprentice, described this cabinetmaker in an advertisement of 1785 as "a conspicuous character in his way and esteemed one of the best workmen in this city." Prince's case pieces are of straight form and have gadrooning across the skirt. They stand on square-cut, rather squat but well carved claw-and-ball feet. Several examples of a triangular pedimented desk and bookcase have a fret-carved frieze. (Nos. 327, 334.)

*Benjamin Randolph* (active c.1760-1790). Receipt books (1763-1777) of this Philadelphia maker are at the Winterthur Museum. His trade card, 1770, engraved by J. Smither, reproduces designs from the *Director*. Of all the Philadelphia cabinetmakers, Randolph shows the most advanced treatment of the rococo elements in the Chippendale style. He is most famous for the six *sample* chairs which descended in his wife's family. An armchair from this group and a side chair are in the Philadelphia Museum of Art, and the four remaining, all side chairs, are at the Winterthur Museum, Colonial Williamsburg, the Garvan Collection at the Yale University Art Gallery, and the collection formed by the late Henry W. Erving of Hartford, Connecticut. (Nos. 269, 275, 276.)

*Aaron Roberts* (1758-1831), New Britain, Connecticut. Although no signed, labeled, or documented pieces by this cabinetmaker exist, there are many records of him as a maker. The existence of many pieces of individual character found in the region, have caused an extensive group of case pieces to be assigned to his name. They are chiefly in cherry. Distinguishing characteristics include an elongated, applied shell below the center finial; applied dentils on the cornice; a carved quatrefoil on the scrolls terminating the pediment; two small notches in the pediment opening, which is likely to be beaded; incised outlines around the carved fan; and intaglio carving of geometric type on the cabriole leg. (No. 306.)

*William Savery* (1721-1788), Philadelphia. This cabinet- and chair-maker, active from the 1740s, worked first in the Queen Anne style. A labeled lowboy at the Van Cortlandt house in New York first established his identity, and since then about twenty labeled pieces have increased his reputation for furniture of high quality. An intaglio leaf carved on the knee of the cabriole is characteristic. A labeled side chair at Colonial Williamsburg has a Chippendale bowed cresting and Queen Anne vase-shaped splat, pad foot and flat, shaped stretcher. (No. 176.)

*Jonathan Shoemaker* (active by 1757, died 1793), a Philadelphia exponent of the rococo style, whose work is distinguished by fine carving. An armchair and card table which came down in his family are illustrated in Hornor's *Blue Book of Philadelphia Furniture,* Plates 157 and 158. (No. 245.)

*Simeon Skillin and Sons*. Pediment figures and ship figureheads were the specialty of this Boston family of six carvers. The most important members are Simeon, Sr. (1716-1778), and sons John (1746-1800) and Simeon, Jr. (1757-1806). A desk and bookcase made for Captain Moses Brown at the Beverly Historical Society has a bust of Milton. The most famous example of their work is the carving on the chest-on-chest by Stephen Badlam, made for Elias Hasket Derby of Salem in 1793, now in the Garvan Collection at the Yale University Art Gallery.

*Job Townsend* (1699-1765) worked at Newport on Easton's Point. He was one of a Quaker family of cabinetmakers[37] who, with the Goddards, developed the Newport blockfront-and-shell furniture. Twenty members of these two families through three generations supplied the Redwood, Wanton, Bowen, and other Newport families with furniture from the Queen

Anne to the Empire style. Job's labeled desk and bookcase in the Rhode Island School of Design (No. 201) marks the beginning of Newport shell-carved furniture. (No. 325.)

*John Townsend* (1732-1809), son of Job's brother Christopher (also a maker of furniture), was among the leading members of the Townsend-Goddard cabinetmakers. Documented pieces by him are known, including a labeled table at the Winterthur Museum, and a signed clock, chest of drawers, and card table at the Metropolitan Museum. It was formerly thought that John Townsend had worked in Norwich and Middletown, Connecticut, from 1777 to 1780 and to have influenced the development of Connecticut blockfront, but records were discovered which placed him continuously in Newport.[38] (Nos. 298, 361.)

*Daniel Trotter* (1747-1800), Philadelphia, worked in the Chippendale and classic revival styles. He was the partner of Ephraim Haines and was known for an individual type of pierced ladder-back chair. (No. 282.)

*Thomas Tufft* (active before 1772, died 1788), Philadelphia. In 1773 Tufft succeeded to the Second Street shop of James Gillingham. He worked for the Logans of Stenton, and for the Morris, Norris, and Powel families. Furniture made by him in 1779 for Richard Edwards, of Burlington County, New Jersey (illustrated in *Antiques,* October 1948), shows refinement in handling the rococo style. (Nos. 270, 374.)

## *Chart:* Chippendale, 1775–1790

**NEW FORMS**
Breakfront bookcase; blockfront chest of drawers; knee-hole chest of drawers; serpentine-back sofa; kettle stand; china table; pembroke table.

**PRINCIPAL WOODS**
Mahogany: *Santo Domingan:* dark, heavy, close-grained. *Cuban:* close-grained, brown in color; did not darken; finely figured. *Honduras* (baywood, from Bay of Honduras): open grain; crotch wood of best quality used for veneering; inferior quality, reddish, used for drawer linings. Walnut; maple; cherry.

**DECORATIVE TECHNIQUES**
Carving, parcel gilding, veneering.

**DESIGN**
Chairs have pierced splat and bowed cresting, with cabriole leg ending in claw-and-ball foot (No. 244). Marlborough leg, about 1770, may be plain (No. 248) or with block (No. 348). Rarities include hairy-paw foot (No. 274); scrolled toe (No. 275); Newport pierced claw and ball (No. 315). Gothic lancet arch and trefoil in chair backs (No. 270). Case pieces continue to have broken-scrolled pediment (No. 336); new are cyma-scrolled, paneled doors (No. 329); blockfront construction (No. 297); blockfront-and-shell (No. 298); bombé shape (No. 323). Carved shell continues an important motif (No. 310), becoming a fan in New England (No. 304), where it is generally accompanied by corkscrew finials. New carved motifs include Gothic frets as a motif for a frieze (No. 308); Chinese frets (No. 377); pierced Chinese fretwork (No. 371); the rococo cabochon (No. 270); pierced cartouche finial (No. 336); tattered acanthus (No. 369); floral garlands (No. 265).

## English Background

**NEW FORMS**
Fitted work table, 1770s.

Sofa table, a long pembroke, about 1780.
Sideboard in first form, originated by Robert Adam (1728-1792) in 1770s, consisted of side table flanked by pedestals; later was joined in one piece and given cupboard sections at sides; designer of final form unknown; in use in 1780s.

**NEW DESIGNS**
The classical revival in furniture design evident in furnishings for Osterley and Syon House in 1760s by Robert Adam. Slender, tapering, reeded leg introduced. Ornament from antique style (carved, inlaid, or painted), including anthemion, paterae, and festoons of husks.

**TECHNIQUES**
Inlay, caning, and japanning revived, 1760s.
Painted furniture by Angelica Kauffmann and Pergolesi, 1770s, 1780s.
Satinwood popular, 1765-1800.

**PUBLICATIONS**
Isaac Ware, *Complete Body of Architecture,* 2nd ed., 1756.
Sir William Chambers, *Designs of Chinese Buildings . . .,* 1757.
Abraham Swan, *Designs in Architecture,* 1757.
William and John Halfpenny, *The Modern Builder's Assistant,* 1757.
Robert Dossie, *Handmaid to the Arts,* 1758.
Ince and Mayhew, *Universal System of Household Furniture,* 1759-1762.
Thomas Chippendale, *The Gentleman and Cabinet-Maker's Director,* 1st ed., 1754; 2nd, 1755; 3rd, 1762.
Robert Adam, *Ruins of Spalatro* (modern spelling; Spalato), 1764.
Robert Manwaring, *Cabinet and Chair-Maker's Real Friend and Companion,* 1765.
Robert and James Adam, *Works in Architecture,* issued in sets, 1773-1778. A second volume, 1779; third, 1822.
George Hepplewhite, *Cabinet-Maker and Upholsterer's Guide,* 1788.
*Cabinet-Maker's London Book of Prices,* with plates by Thomas Shearer, Hepplewhite and others, 1788.

235

**235.** Mahogany bed with foot-posts showing the stop-fluting frequently found in Newport work. It was made about 1750-1770. The claw-and-ball foot of the cabriole leg has Newport's oval ball and extended talon. The scalloped pattern of the valance and skirt of antique red silk damask is based on an eighteenth-century design. Around 1750, when houses were more easily heated, bed hangings were omitted from the foot of the bed. Foot-posts were exposed and treated more decoratively, while head-posts were often plain. (*No. 1, Carpenter,* Arts and Crafts of Newport. *Rhode Island School of Design.*)

**236.** Connecticut bed of cherry, dating between 1770-1785, with foot-posts ending in a square Chinese Chippendale leg (called a Marlborough leg in Philadelphia). It is fluted and chamfered, and has a double-tiered base. The bed hangings with blue *chinoiserie* design are of antique French copperplate-printed cotton. The eighteenth-century spread is of blue silk damask. (*No. 7, Downs,* American Furniture. *H. F. du Pont Winterthur Museum.*)

236

**237.** Four-post bed painted blue, with fluted footposts and headposts of unbroken line (pencil posts). The headboard is shaped in cyma scrolls. The bed hangings, valance, and spread are of copperplate-printed English linen dated 1761. The design is printed in red. (*Brooklyn Museum.*)

**238.** Low-post bed, made of mahogany, about 1760, with claw-and-ball foot, and acanthus carved on the knee. Carved heads are terminals on the footposts. Low-post beds of the eighteenth century are extremely scarce and may have been intended for summer use. The blue and white coverlet and ruffle are of French resist-dyed linen. (See No. 139.) (*Brush-Everard House, Colonial Williamsburg.*)

**239**

**239.** Breakfront mahogany bookcase with original brasses, probably. made in New England about 1770-1780. A Chinese fret is carved on the frieze and there is a dentil course on the narrow cornice. The center drawer opens to a writing section, the drawer front falling forward to rest on slides. This piece was among the family furnishings in the Warner House, Portsmouth, New Hampshire. built in 1716 by Archibald Macphaedris and occupied by his descendants until 1931. American breakfront bookcases in the Chippendale style are rare. (*John S. Walton.*)

**240.** Breakfront mahogany bookcase attributed to Thomas Elfe (active 1747-1775) of Charleston, South Carolina. The center section, which has a broken triangular pediment, has a frieze showing the Elfe fret (a looped design suggesting horizontal figure eights), found also on Nos. 309 and 338. The presence of cypress in the interior suggests a Charleston origin. Doors of the lower section have mitred panels of crotch mahogany veneer inset with quatrefoil panels of flame grain outlined in stringing. (*Collection of Frank L. Horton.*)

**240**

**241**

**242**

**243**

**241.** Spice cabinet of walnut with arched-panel door of the Queen Anne period and ogee-bracket foot, made in Pennsylvania in the mid-1700s. A lock protects the contents of the interior, which is divided into nests of small drawers for sugar and spices. This piece stood in the parlor or dining room and was designed to harmonize with other furnishings. Such cabinets were in use in Pennsylvania and New Jersey in the Philadelphia region through the eighteenth century and vary little in design. (*Collection, Mrs. Alfred P. Bissell, Jr.*)

**242.** Spice cabinet made in Pennsylvania about 1760. It is of walnut with an inlay of light-toned woods showing a geometrized floral pattern surrounded by a herringbone border; a circular band in the center encloses the initials *L L*. The inlay is typical of Chester County. (See Nos. 139, 178, 197.) (*David Stockwell.*)

**243.** Southern cellaret made of walnut, with hard yellow southern pine used as the secondary wood. It consists of a cabinet section on a stand containing a drawer, and a mixing slide which pulls out at right. The front is carved with scrolls encircling the initial of the original owner. It has straight tapering legs, pierced corner brackets, and an arched stretcher. The cellaret, which provided locked storage for wines and liquors, was frequently made in the South, rarely in the North. (See Nos. 141, 418.) (*Hammond-Harwood House, Annapolis.*)

245

244

**244.** Philadelphia mahogany armchair (1760-1775) with claw-and-ball foot, voluted cresting rail enclosing shell and foliage. A rare daisy motif is carved on the splats. The contoured armrests end in a deeply carved scroll and have concave supports of Queen Anne type which were sometimes retained on Philadelphia Chippendale chairs. On the knee there is a punchwork background for the carving of shell and leafage. The pierced splat has the vase form of the earlier, solid splat. (*Ex Coll. Louis E. Brooks. Henry Ford Museum.*)

**245.** Philadelphia mahogany armchair, made about 1775 by Jonathan Shoemaker (active 1757-1793). The chair is said to have been made for a British officer stationed in Philadelphia who was recalled at the outbreak of the Revolution. It remained in the Shoemaker family until recent years. The full enrichment of the Chippendale chair is seen in the carving of acanthus, shell, and floral motifs which appear even on the arms and knuckles as well as on the bottom of the splat with its spiral-gadrooned base. The arm supports have the deep serpentine curve typical of Philadelphia. The plain, rounded rear leg (stump leg) was used repeatedly. Fluted uprights and shell on the seat frame are often seen on finer Philadelphia chairs. (*Philadelphia Museum of Art.*)

**246.** Massachusetts mahogany armchair made about 1765-1775 with molded straight leg, leaf-carved bracket, and rectangular cross-stretcher. The rear leg, slanting inward and tapering to a square foot, follows English design. A Gothic arch makes an inconspicuous appearance above the deep loop in the strapwork splat. The back, with uprights and serpentine cresting rail, although broad, is designed with a characteristic New England slenderness. (*Metropolitan Museum of Art.*)

246

**247**

**248**

**249**

**247.** New York mahogany armchair made about 1765-1775. It was originally owned by Stephen Van Rensselaer, seventh patroon of Rensselaerswyck. The broad ruffle and tassel on the splat and eagle's-head terminal on the arms are New York motifs based on English design (George II) but used in heavier form in New York. The stiff gadrooning on the seat frame, stringy acanthus on the knee, and square claw and ball indicate the New York chairmaker. (*No. 52, Downs, American Furniture, H. F. du Pont Winterthur Museum.*)

**248.** Philadelphia mahogany armchair made about 1765-1775 and attributed to Thomas Affleck (active 1763-1795). Marlborough legs are carved with Chinese fretwork on paneled insets, a variant of one of two patterns used by Affleck and illustrated in Hornor's *Blue Book of Philadelphia Furniture,* Plates 258, 259, 260. (See No. 253 for other type.) The cartouche-and-strapwork splat with serpentine cresting rail is a faithful repetition of an English design used in Philadelphia. (*Ex Coll. Louis E. Brooks. Henry Ford Museum.*)

**249.** Newport easy chair of mahogany made about 1750-1760. It has a voluted shell on the knee and a webbed claw extending well over the ball. Vertically rolled arms are typical of New England (also of New York) in contrast to Philadelphia's horizontal roll. The block-and-spindle stretcher of Queen Anne design was used in New England in the Chippendale period. (*Hunter House, Newport; Preservation Society of Newport County.*)

**250.** New York mahogany easy chair made about 1760-1775. The chair is broad and capacious, and has sturdy cabriole legs set far apart and vertically rolled arms. In the center of the broadly spreading acanthus is a small triangular area of punchwork, a forerunner of the cross-hatched lambrequin frequently used in New York. The claw-and-ball foot with its squared outline is characteristic of the area. (*No. 84, Downs, American Furniture. H. F. du Pont Winterthur Museum.*)

**250**

**251**

**251.** Philadelphia mahogany easy chair made about 1760-1775. The cabriole legs end in a claw and ball on the front and in a pad foot at rear. The placing of the front legs, close together, is different from that of the New York chair (No. 250) and is typical of Philadelphia. The scrolled arm ending in a horizontal roll is found on English chairs of the late 1600s and was popular in Philadelphia throughout the Chippendale period. The chair came from a direct descendant of the family of the cabinetmaker, Benjamin Randolph, and may be his work. (*Henry Ford Museum.*)

**252.** Philadelphia mahogany easy chair made about 1775-1785. It has a Marlborough leg with a blocked foot and cross-stretcher. The wings, broken at the armrest, indicate the approach of a new style in easy chairs, which was developed further in the Hepplewhite period (No. 421). Use of the straight leg in Chippendale furniture was suggested by Chinese styles drawn by Sir William Chambers on his trip to China in the 1740s. The blocked foot on the straight leg was peculiar to Philadelphia. (*Henry Ford Museum.*)

**252**

**253.** Philadelphia upholstered mahogany open-arm chair, with double serpentine back. It was made about 1765 and is possibly the work of Thomas Affleck. The Marlborough leg ending in a blocked foot has a paneled inset of husks and strapwork carved in relief. The design is similar to a set owned by Governor John Penn and is one of two related types used by Affleck between 1764 and 1766 (see No. 248). These upholstered chairs with open arms (based on the French *fauteuil*) were called "French chairs" by Chippendale. (*Colonial Williamsburg.*)

**253**

**254**

*delphia Furniture*). Also to be noted among examples of this rare type is the pair, apparently identical to this, which was in the Reginald M. Lewis sale in 1961. The design of the back is similar to that of the Speaker's Chair, No. 256. (*William Rockhill Nelson Gallery of Art and Atkins Museum.*)

**256**. Speaker's Chair, among the furnishings made by Thomas Affleck for Congress Hall. From 1790 to 1799 the seat of government was in Philadelphia, where the State House, today Independence Hall, was used by the Congress. Payment was made to Affleck in 1794, the year before his death. This resembles Affleck's Supreme Court chairs, as seen in the ropemolding between a bead-and-reel on legs and arms. The design of the back, however, is not like that of the chairs of the chief justice and associate justice (Hornor, plates 298 and 299) but is like the John Penn chairs and No. 255. It is not known just where this historic chair was used in Congress Hall, but it was purchased as a "Speaker's Chair" by Dr. Thomas Chalkly James (1766-1835) from the State House furnishings, presumably after Harrisburg became the capital of Pennsylvania in 1812. (*Plate 263, Hornor,* Blue Book of Philadelphia Furniture. *Reginald M. Lewis sale, 1961. Henry Ford Museum.*)

**254**. Upholstered open-arm chair of mahogany, with cypress in frame; made about 1770. The presence of cypress suggests a Charleston origin, and this sophisticated chair could have been made only in a thriving center of cabinetmaking. The straight leg is molded, the arm support fluted, ending in a carved rosette. "French chairs" are mentioned in the account book of Thomas Elfe, kept from 1768 to 1775. (*Collection of Frank L. Horton.*)

**255**. Philadelphia upholstered side chair attributed to Thomas Affleck; the channel-molded Marlborough leg is carved on the outside with egg-and-dart motif and rests on a low, spreading foot. The scrolled brackets are carved in a leaf design. It was made about 1765-1775. Affleck made similar chairs for Governor John Penn (plate 262, Hornor, *Blue Book of Phila-*

**255**

**256**

**257.** New York mahogany corner chair, made about 1760-1780. The carving on back is rare on a corner chair. The shell on the knee of the front leg ends in a floral pendant which is also unusual. The scrolled splats are pierced with a heart design, and the arm supports are formed in an S-curve which complements the line of the cabriole legs. The motif carved on the back — acanthus, pendent husk, and rococo rockwork — resembles the design on the cresting rail of the Van Rensselaer family chairs, No. 247. (*Bayou Bend Collection, Houston.*)

**258.** Massachusetts side chair, from a set of eight mahogany chairs and settee (No. 350), made about 1760 and originally owned by the Sanford family. The type is often called a "Salem chair" because many have descended in Salem families, but it was also made elsewhere. The splat design was a familiar one on English chairs of the mid-1700s and variations are shown on several plates in Manwaring's *Cabinet and Chair-Maker's . . . Companion.* The turned-back talon and the retention of the Queen Anne block-and-spindle stretcher on a Chippendale chair are typical of Massachusetts. (*Bayou Bend Collection, Houston.*)

**259.** New York mahogany side chair upholstered over the seat rail. It was made about 1770, and was originally in the home of Samuel Verplanck (1739-1820) on Wall Street. This chair, with its ruffled scrolls and Gothic tracery, is a further modification of the Manwaring design (see No. 258). The tapering rear leg, broadened at the end, is found on many New York chairs. Unusual points are the general delicacy of design, stop-fluted slender uprights, and the sensitively formed claw-and-ball foot. (*Metropolitan Museum of Art.*)

**260.** New York mahogany side chair with diamond splat. It is attributed to Gilbert Ash (active 1748-1763) because of similarity to a chair signed by him and dated *1756* (No. 76, *New York State Furniture*, Metropolitan Museum of Art, 1934). This English design, antedating Chippendale's *Director*, was widely used in America. Typical of Gilbert Ash is the dependent leafage carved on the ears, but, in place of the cross-hatched lambrequin which he used on the knee, here there is a ruffled shell overlapping the seat frame. This English treatment is rarely seen on American chairs. (*Bayou Bend Collection, Houston.*)

257

258

259

260

**261**

**262**

**261.** Connecticut side chair attributed to Eliphalet Chapin of East Windsor (active by 1771). It is made of cherry and stained to imitate mahogany. The diamond splat is simpler than in the New York versions of the design (see No. 260). Evidence of Chapin's early sojourn in Philadelphia is recognizable in the form of the cresting rail with molded ears, the shaped seat frame, the stump rear leg, and the good proportions of the splat. The shell on the cresting rail is rendered stiffly and the cabriole leg is ridged, as was often the case in Connecticut work. (*Los Angeles County Museum.*)

**262.** New York tassel-back side chair of mahogany, made about 1765-1780. The George II tassel motif was popular in New York (No. 247) and is used here with unusual delicacy. The chair is not typical in other respects — the carving of the claw and ball would suggest Philadelphia, the inward curve of rear legs is in Massachusetts style, but the cabriole's wide acanthus with lambrequin, suggests that it was made in New York. (*No. 145, Downs,* American Furniture. *H. F. du Pont Winterthur Museum.*)

**263.** Philadelphia tassel-back side chair of mahogany, made about 1760-1780. Compared to New York, the carving in this example has more refinement. The stop-fluted uprights, gadrooned base-molding of the splat, and handsomely scrolled ears of the cresting rail, which centers a sculpturesque shell, represent the sophistication of Philadelphia. Carving was done for the chairmaker by specialists who worked for the trade in general. (*Ex Coll. Louis E. Brooks. Henry Ford Museum.*)

**264.** Philadelphia mahogany side chair with pierced vase-shaped splat and shell-carved ears on the cresting rail. The chair was made about 1770-1780 and is attributed to Thomas Affleck. The corners of the seat frame are covered by a carved shell extending upward from the cabriole — an English design noted in Nos. 260 and 265. On the cabriole is a carved C-scroll with tattered acanthus and floral pendant. The applied shell in center of the shaped seat completes the lavish ornament. (*Pendleton Collection, Rhode Island School of Design.*)

**263**

**265.** Philadelphia mahogany side chair, one of a set made for the Lambert family about 1770-1780, and formerly in the Reifsnyder Collection. The same type of treatment of the juncture of cabriole and seat frame is seen in No. 264. Garlanded uprights and shaped border of the seat frame are richly carved. The design combines naturalistic floral forms and rococo ruffled acanthus and rockwork. Plate IX of the *Director*, 1762, gives a suggestion for pendent garlands such as these. (*No. 128, Downs, American Furniture. H. F. du Pont Winterthur Museum.*)

**266.** Ribbon-back mahogany chair, made in Maryland or Pennsylvania about 1760. The "ribband-back" chair was popular in England in mid-century, and Chippendale offered some imaginative suggestions in the *Director*. In America it appears in the Philadelphia area on chairs from Chester County and in New Jersey. A Maryland origin is likely for this chair, because of the splat design, the molded cresting rail and fanlike ornament, the heaviness of the uprights, and the ears of the cresting rail. These agree with the design of chairs that have come down in the family of Governor Bowie of Maryland. (*Gift of Mrs. J. Amory Haskell. Brooklyn Museum.*)

264

265

266

267

**267.** This Maryland mahogany side chair, made about 1770, is one of a set originally owned at Mount Clare, the home of Charles Carroll the Barrister. It has an elaborately pierced vase-shaped splat with pendent husks, a cresting rail with fringed acanthus, molded uprights, and straight legs. The great width of splat is characteristic of Maryland Chippendale chairs, which have the proportions, strength and grace of English types. (*Collection of Miss Constance Petre. No. 109, Baltimore Furniture, 1947. Courtesy Baltimore Museum of Art.*)

268

269

**268.** Philadelphia mahogany side chair, made about 1770-1780. It is attributed to James Gillingham (1736-1781). The trefoil design in the splat, based on Chippendale's *Director,* 1754 edition, appears on labeled chairs by Gillingham in the Metropolitan Museum and in the Mitchel Taradash collection. (*Philadelphia Museum of Art.*)

**269.** Philadelphia mahogany side chair, attributed to Benjamin Randolph (active 1760-1778). A labeled chair in the Karolik collection has the same back, and the acanthus-carved seat frame here is similar to one on a chair at the Win-

terthur Museum, also believed to have been made by Randolph. (*Garvan Collection, Yale University Art Gallery.*)

**270.** Philadelphia mahogany side chair. This is one of a pair made about 1760-1780 with the label of Thomas Tufft (active 1772-1788). The splat, with Gothic lancet arch and trefoil, is illustrated in the first edition of Chippendale's *Director,* Plate XIII. Tufft also used the design on straight-legged chairs for the Logan family. There is a rococo cabochon on the knee of the cabriole and in the center of the shaped seat frame. (*No. 134, Downs, American Furniture. H. F. du Pont Winterthur Museum.*)

270

271

**271.** Philadelphia Chippendale side chair of mahogany, made about 1765-1785. Such a facile blend of Gothic, Chinese, and rococo motifs is rare in American work. The trefoil and quatrefoil in the splat and the fretwork on seat rail, legs, and uprights are Gothic; the suggestion of a pagoda crest on the back rail is Chinese; and the twisting leaf motifs are rococo. Paneled insets with fret carving were used by Thomas Affleck, which has suggested a possible attribution to this Philadelphia cabinetmaker. The chair is obviously by a master craftsman, but there is no exact parallel to it in Affleck's work. (*Reginald M. Lewis sale, 1961. Henry Ford Museum.*)

272

273

**272.** Massachusetts mahogany side chair, made about 1760-1780. The Gothic arch, used sparingly in New England, is introduced here in the traditional vase-shaped splat. Characteristic of New England are the grace of the tapering, beaded upright, the refinement of the bow-shaped cresting rail ending in small, leaf-carved ears, the block-and-spindle stretcher; and particularly the form of the claw-and-ball foot with the turned-back talon. (*Metropolitan Museum of Art.*)

**273.** New York side chair of mahogany. The Gothic arch appears here in the splat of a provincial-type chair probably made in the lower Hudson River Valley between 1760 and 1780. There is stiff gadrooning across the front of the seat frame, and the foot has the square claw and ball. This belongs to a set which has descended in a New York State family. (*Van Cortlandt Manor, Sleepy Hollow Restorations.*)

**274.** Philadelphia mahogany side chair, made about 1760-1780. It has a Gothic splat, a rococo cabochon on the knee, and a hairy paw foot. The latter was used on only the finest Philadelphia furniture. Randolph finished two of the *sample* chairs in this manner. Here it appears on a chair with exceptionally rich carving. The upholstery over the seat frame is confined by a narrow skirt. (*Metropolitan Museum of Art.*)

275

274

**275.** Philadelphia side chair. This is one of the six *sample* chairs[39] attributed to Benjamin Randolph (active 1760-1778). The scrolled French toe, rare in American work, appears on this and two others of the group. With one exception, all are richly carved. Spiral gadrooning on the narrow seat frame unites with the deeply carved, plumelike acanthus bracket of the cabriole leg, which is carved with a cabochon on the knee. The back is a free interpretation of one of the three designs on Plate XII in the *Director*, 1754. (*Colonial Williamsburg.*)

276

277

**276.** Philadelphia mahogany side chair, one of a pair, attributed to Benjamin Randolph (active 1760-1778). It is rare to find a Chinese lattice in the splat of an American chair. The design is shown on Plate XII (left) of Chippendale's *Director*, 1754. The spiral gadrooning, rococo leaf-carving on the knee, scrolled toe and a leaf-bordered cresting rail are noteworthy. (*David Stockwell.*)

**277.** A New York side chair of walnut, made about 1760-1780. It comes from the Thompson family of Brooklyn and Long Island. This Chippendale design, based on the third edition of the *Director* (1762), was used only in New York. There is a small Gothic device in the center of a pierced splat. The tapering rear leg and stiff gadrooning are New York characteristics. (*Ex Coll. Mrs. J. Insley Blair. Museum of the City of New York.*)

**278.** Southern side chair of mahogany, made between 1770 and 1780, and originally at Blandfield, the home of the Beverley family in Essex County, Virginia. A vertically barred splat with central ribbon or band uniting the bars was frequently used on Southern chairs, and this example displays particularly graceful treatment. (*Collection of Mr. and Mrs. W. Welby Beverley.*)

**279.** New York mahogany side chairs and card table made about 1770-1780. The chairs are similar to No. 277 but have straight legs and pierced brackets. This is the restored parlor of the home of Gerard and Cornelia Van Cortlandt Beekman, who in 1785 bought the seventeenth-century house of the Philipse family in what is now North Tarrytown. It was originally called Upper Mills to distinguish it from the Lower Mills, today Philipse Manor at Yonkers. During the Beekman ownership it became known as "Philipse Castle." The Beekmans added a new wing to the old house and during the recent restoration this part has been furnished to represent the period of their occupancy. (See also Nos. 504, 529, 577.) The family portraits are by Gilbert Stuart and John Wollaston. (*Philipsburg Manor, Upper Mills, Sleepy Hollow Restorations.*)

278

280 281 279

**280.** Massachusetts mahogany ladder-back chair, made about 1770-1790. In the mid-1700s there was a revival in England of the chair back composed of parallel bars. Although neither Chippendale nor Manwaring show this design, many chairmakers developed different styles of piercing both for lightness and decoration. This design was frequently used in Massachusetts. From the Revere-Little family, Boston. (*Ginsburg and Levy.*)

**281.** Philadelphia mahogany ladder-back chair, made about 1770-1790. It was originally owned by George Washington and is now in the dining room at Mount Vernon. It is believed to be part of the set of "two doz. strong, neat and plain but fashionable Table chairs" about which Washington wrote Bushrod Washington in 1783. This is the typical Philadelphia "pretzel-back" chair. (*Mount Vernon Ladies' Association.*)

**282.** Philadelphia ladder-back chair of mahogany, made about 1780-1790 and attributed to Daniel Trotter (1747-1800). The splat pierced in parallel curves centering a spray of feathers in a medallion is seen on Trotter's documented chairs for Stephen Girard.[40] It is now in the American Museum near Bath, England. *(Photograph: David Stockwell.)*

**283.** Maryland mahogany ladder-back chair, made about 1770-1780. Serpentine bars and cresting rail center a pierced honeysuckle (anthemion.) This represents the most elaborate form of the American ladder-back chair. It was originally in the Brice House, Annapolis, Maryland. *(No. 117, Baltimore Furniture, 1947. Baltimore Museum of Art.)*

**284.** "A Windsor chair may be defined as a stick-leg chair, with a spindle back topped by a bent bow or comb," wrote Wallace Nutting in *Antiques*, February 1922.[41] This bow-back (hoop-back) windsor armchair with oak spindles, pine seat and maple legs and stretcher was made about 1750-1775. *(Metropolitan Museum of Art.)*

For general remarks on windsor chairs see introductory text.

**285.** New England writing-arm windsor chair with old green paint, made in Connecticut about 1780-1800. The light turnings and pronounced rake of the legs characterize the New England windsor. The foot is cone-shaped. (*Shelburne Museum.*)

**286.** New England comb-back armchair made about 1780-1800. The form is created by the addition of a comb to a low-back windsor. This has well-turned vase sections in arm supports and legs and has a deep saddle seat. (*Shelburne Museum.*)

**287.** At center is a New England armchair with continuous arm and back. It was made by Ebenezer Tracy (1744-1803) or Lisbon, Connecticut.[42] This has Tracy's turning of spindles tapering from the center and boldly turned, long-necked vase sections in the legs. Tracy, whose stamp is found on a number of excellent windsors, made seats of chestnut, spindles of hickory, legs of maple, and bows and stretchers of oak. (See also No. 463.) At left is a child's bow-back (sack-back or hoop-back) chair, at right a child's chair with continuous arm and back made in the late 1700s. (*Old Sturbridge Village.*)

286

287

**288.** New York and New England windsors in a restored tavern. At front is a loop-back windsor resembling those by Dewitt of Kingston. The brace-back on the other side of the table is probably a New York chair, and the fan-backs at right were made in New England. In the center is an eighteenth-century Hudson Valley hutch table with shoe feet; there are also sawbuck tables of country type, and an early eighteenth-century Hudson Valley dresser of unpainted pine. This is the restored ferry-house barroom at Van Cortlandt Manor, Croton, New York. (*Sleepy Hollow Restorations.*)

**289.** Philadelphia comb-back windsor armchair of hickory, oak, gumwood, and maple, made about 1750-1780. The Philadelphia windsor has a special form of ball foot, sometimes called the blunt-arrow foot. Above the pointed ball the leg continues with a cylindrical section followed by a vase, the legs being deeply raked. The cresting rail ends in a spiral. This chair has the brace-back construction. (*Art Institute of Chicago.*)

**290.** Independence Hall windsor, a Philadelphia bow-back windsor made by Francis Trumble, who is recorded as having supplied windsors for the State House (Independence Hall) from 1775 to 1778.[43] It is therefore possible that this chair may have been used by a Signer of the Declaration of Independence. So far, it is the only known surviving chair of the group made by Trumble. When Harrisburg became the capital in 1812 the windsors were taken there but were sold at auction about 1814. It descended in the family of the original purchaser and has now been returned to Independence Hall. (*Independence National Historical Park, Philadelphia.*)

**291.** Pennsylvania-German room, with stucco ceiling recalling the style of the German Renaissance. This comes from a house at Wernersville, near Reading, built in 1755. Side chairs have scrolled and heart-pierced backs, plank seats and raked legs. The armchairs show English influence in the use of vase-shaped splat and vertically slatted backs. Upholstered chairs are meagerly padded and have abbreviated wings. The wardrobe, or *schrank*, was made in 1768, and the tall clock is signed by Jacob Graff of Lancaster, working around 1750. The sawbuck table has crossed, scrolled supports. (See also Nos. 320, 404, 405.) (*Kershner Parlor, H. F. du Pont Winterthur Museum.*)

290

291

**292**

**293**

**292.** This Pennsylvania-German dower chest of tulipwood and yellow pine with painted decoration is typical of Berks County, where it was made about 1780. On a brown ground with white panels is a design of horsemen and rampant unicorns in red and black, accompanied by paired birds, conventionalized pomegranates, and vases of flowers. (*Metropolitan Museum of Art.*)

**293.** Pennsylvania-German dower chest signed and dated, *Christian Selzer 1784*. Rectangular panels are typical of Dauphin County, where Christian Selzer (1749-1831) was the principal decorator of chests. The wood is pine and the painted decoration on a red ground with off-white panels is in black, red, green, tan, and brown. (*Henry Ford Museum.*)

**294**

**294.** Serpentine chest of drawers in mahogany with the label of Jonathan Gostelowe of Philadelphia (active 1765-1793). Typical of Gostelowe are the broad, canted corners, which here are fluted, and the molded ogee bracket, which conforms to the canting. The top is similarly shaped. The drawer fronts are finished with a cockbead, and the ormolu mounts are in rococo style. The curving structural line typical of French rococo was sparingly used in England and America. Its most frequent appearance in America is on the chest of drawers. (*Philadelphia Museum of Art.*)

**295.** Massachusetts reverse serpentine, or oxbow, chest of drawers made of mahogany, about 1760. It has a straight bracket foot with the curving form carried down into the bracket. Original Chippendale brass mounts have an elaborately scrolled back plate. In contrast to No. 294, the cockbead is on the framework around the drawers. This method of construction was followed much longer in America than in England, where it went out of style in mid-century. (*Lent by Mrs. Eliot Alden to the Los Angeles County Museum.*)

**296.** This bombé (kettle-base) chest of drawers of mahogany was made in Massachusetts about 1760, and has a finely carved scallop shell in the center of the skirt. The bombé form was a specialty with Massachusetts cabinetmakers. It was seldom used in England, and is more often seen in Continental work. A desirable type is represented here, with sides of drawers conforming to the curves. Some bombé pieces have straight drawer sides within a curving framework. (*Bayou Bend Collection, Houston.*)

**296**                                     **295**

**297.** Massachusetts blockfront chest of drawers of mahogany made about 1760-1780. Blockfront furniture was made chiefly in Massachusetts, Rhode Island, Connecticut, and New York. In Massachusetts and New York the blocking extends uninterruptedly up to the top, while on Rhode Island and Connecticut pieces the blocking terminates in a large shell. (*Ex Coll. Louis E. Brooks. Henry Ford Museum.*)

**298.** Labeled Newport mahogany blockfront-and-shell chest of drawers made about 1765, by John Townsend (1732-1809). The forms of the shells, alternating relief and intaglio, are subtly rendered in Newport carving. Here the intaglio shell has the serrated outline of the later style. (See No. 221 for the early type.) At the center of each is a small palmette. It is not known which members of the Townsend-Goddard cabinetmakers were responsible for the carving. The small spiral scroll on the foot is found only on Newport work, although approximated by No. 299. (*Metropolitan Museum of Art.*)

**299.** Connecticut blockfront-and-shell chest of drawers made of mahogany about 1770-1790. This belongs to a small group of Connecticut chests of drawers which come close to the Newport style. Another is shown in No. 300, and a third is in the Frederick K. Barbour collection. The identity of the cabinetmakers who developed the Connecticut blockfront has not yet been discovered. (*Bayou Bend Collection, Houston.*)

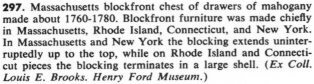

**300.** This cherry blockfront-and-shell chest of drawers, made about 1770-1790, is another example of the finest Connecticut work. It resembles No. 299 in the pliant forms of the shells but has the cabriole leg and claw-and-ball foot, and three drawers instead of four. Scrolled brackets, which conform to the blocking, are more gracefully designed than in most Connecticut work, and the foot is more skillfully carved. (*Ex Coll. Reginald M. Lewis. Henry Ford Museum.*)

**301.** Chest of drawers on frame, with claw-and-ball feet, made in the Valley of Virginia in the late 1700s. Walnut is used with hard yellow southern pine in the interior. The edges of the drawers are lip-molded, and the foot is finely carved. Development of the Shenandoah River Valley was active after the Revolution, and well-made furniture, sometimes showing Maryland influence, has been found there. (*Collection of Mr. and Mrs. G. Dallas Coons.*)

**302.** New York dressing chest of drawers of mahogany, made about 1770. This is a very rare form in America, but well known in England in the mid-1700s. A labeled dressing chest by Samuel Prince of New York (advertised in *Antiques,* July 1946) is of the same design, with a writing slide above a fitted drawer. There is also the same combination of mirror and bookrest which folds into the drawer. The style of gadrooning on the base is found in the work of Prince. This chest was originally owned by Dirck Lefferts, a New York merchant. (*Brooklyn Museum.*)

301

302

303

**303.** Cherry dressing chest ("gentleman's chest") from Culpepper County, Virginia, made in the late 1700s. The top drawer is fitted much like that of No. 302, and has a writing slide and mirror in addition to compartments for cosmetics and brushes. The upper part has shelves and drawers. The pierced gallery, carved fretwork frieze, stop-fluted pilasters, and shaped, fielded panel make this one of the outstanding pieces of Southern furniture to come to light. (*Berkeley Plantation, home of Mr. and Mrs. Malcolm Jamieson.*)

304

305

**304.** Mahogany chest-on-chest, made about 1760-1780 and attributed to Benjamin Frothingham of Boston and Charlestown (active 1756-1809). The oxbow-blocked lower section is the same as that on the key piece in Frothingham's work, the labeled desk from the Flayderman sale of 1930 (*Antiques*, December 1928, p. 537, and November 1952, p. 395). The floral rosettes resemble those on a labeled chest-on-chest belonging to John P. Kinsey. The dependent leafage, rare in American work, is found on a few Boston pieces. (*Henry Ford Museum.*)

**305.** Newport chest-on-chest of mahogany made about 1760-1780 by the Townsend-Goddard cabinetmakers. It has nine-lobed shells on the lower section, a bonnet-top closed at the back, and paneling in Newport style on the face of the pediment. Typical also are the fluted urn finials, the many-petaled rosettes, and the blocked ogee bracket with a spiral at foot. Newport chests-on-chests are less frequently seen than highboys. A few are blocked in both sections. (*Lent by Norman Herreshoff to the Rhode Island School of Design.*)

**306.** Connecticut cherry chest-on-chest made about 1780-1790. No documented pieces by Aaron Roberts (1758-1831) have yet been discovered, but furniture from the region of New Britain, Connecticut, where Roberts worked, has highly individual details attributed to him. Some of these, seen here, include rope-twisted columns, an elongated shell on the beaded pediment, two small notches in the opening of the pediment, an incised border around fans, and "pinwheels." Also characteristic is the deep point on the tall ogee bracket. Undoubtedly the abbreviated central finial originally matched the others. (*Collection of Mr. and Mrs. Frederick K. Barbour.*)

308

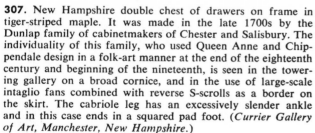

307

**307.** New Hampshire double chest of drawers on frame in tiger-striped maple. It was made in the late 1700s by the Dunlap family of cabinetmakers of Chester and Salisbury. The individuality of this family, who used Queen Anne and Chippendale design in a folk-art manner at the end of the eighteenth century and beginning of the nineteenth, is seen in the towering gallery on a broad cornice, and in the use of large-scale intaglio fans combined with reverse S-scrolls as a border on the skirt. The cabriole leg has an excessively slender ankle and in this case ends in a squared pad foot. (*Currier Gallery of Art, Manchester, New Hampshire.*)

**308.** Philadelphia chest-on-chest of mahogany, made about 1760-1780. The Chippendale pediment received its finest form on Philadelphia case pieces. Here an expertly carved basket-of-flowers finial is seen in the center of the pierced lattice pediment. Scrolls, breaking like waves in a swirl of acanthus, give this design both linear and three-dimensional power. The frieze has a carved fret of a type which Chippendale called Gothic. Inset quarter columns are typical of Philadelphia. (*Philadelphia Museum of Art.*)

**309.** Charleston chest-on-chest of mahogany, made about 1770. It is attributed to Thomas Elfe (active 1747-1775) because the design of the carved fret on the frieze appears on many pieces from Charleston families named in this maker's account book. Canted corners of the upper section also show the "Elfe fret." The proportions of the Charleston chest-on-chest, which was a popular form in the region, are close to those of the English tallboy. The piece belonged to Colonel William Washington, a kinsman of George Washington. (*Heyward-Washington House, Charleston Museum.*)

309

**310.** Philadelphia mahogany high chest or highboy, made about 1765-1780. Philadelphia enriched the basic Queen Anne form of the highboy with carved rococo ornament of the highest order. The pierced cabochon finial suggests the work of a London-trained carver. Entirely rococo in feeling is the all-over design on the face of the pediment — a flowing scroll-work of acanthus treated with a freedom and breadth rarely seen in American work but closely resembling Irish Chippendale.[44] This influence may possibly be explained by the large proportion of Irish among early settlers. (*Gift of Mrs. J. Insley Blair, New-York Historical Society.*)

310

312

**311.** The Wharton-Lisle mahogany highboy, made about 1765-1775, is one of the masterpieces of Philadelphia furniture. It was made for Joseph Wharton and designed in scale for a room in his home, Walnut Grove. During the British occupancy of the city in 1778, it was in the town house of Charles Wharton on Second Street, where it was struck by a rifle shot fired by a British soldier. The pierced cartouche finial is formed of acanthus leaves. A lattice pediment is light in effect. (*Plate 174, Hornor,* Blue Book of Philadelphia Furniture. *Bayou Bend Collection, Houston.*)

**312.** The Howe family highboy, or high chest, of mahogany, made about 1765-1775. The carved panel on the lower drawer illustrates Aesop's fable of the fox and grapes. This is one of seven known Philadelphia pieces illustrating designs based on the fables.[45] The vase-of-flowers finials are carved with masterful naturalism. Flower garlands on the chamfered corners are reminiscent of the treatment on the uprights of Philadelphia chairs (No. 265). (*Philadelphia Museum of Art.*)

**313**

**314**

**315**

313. Philadelphia high chest or highboy of mahogany, with basket-of-flowers finial and pierced lattice pediment. It was made about 1765-1775. An exceptional detail is the pierced acanthus skirt. This daring open-work pattern has a spontaneous freedom of outline which even the Philadelphia carver did not often attempt. The pediment is so like that on the chest-on-chest, No. 308 that it suggests the possibility of its having been made for the same room. (*Smithsonian Institution.*)

314. Connecticut cherry high chest attributed to Eliphalet Chapin of East Windsor (active 1771-1795). It may have been made about 1780-1790. Chapin's early sojourn in Philadelphia resulted in this adaptation of Philadelphia's scrolled top, lattice pediment, and inset quarter columns. The missing centerpiece may have been his pierced quatrefoil cartouche, which is a simplified version of one of Philadelphia's more elaborate forms. Carved fans have the precise quality of Connecticut work. (*Garvan Collection, Yale University Art Gallery.*)

315. Newport high chest of mahogany, made about 1760-1770 by the Townsend-Goddard cabinetmakers. The highboy with closed bonnet-top was a favorite one in Newport, but no two examples are exactly alike. This one has the prized detail of a pierced claw to be compared with the tea table John Goddard made for Jabez Bowen, while the work of Job Townsend is suggested by the type of shell with its edge firmly confined in the segment of an arch (see No. 201). The fluted, double-tiered finial is more elaborate than usual. This highboy was once owned by the Bartol family of Boston. (*Bayou Bend Collection, Houston.*)

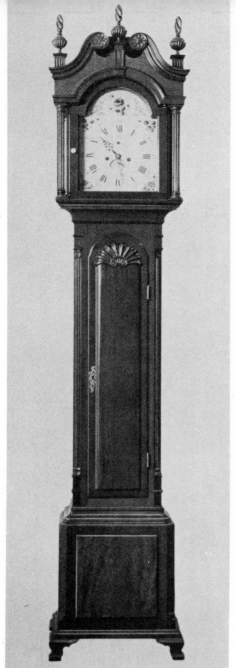

**317**

**316**

**316.** Newport tall clock in a mahogany case made by the Townsend-Goddard cabinetmakers about 1765-1775, with an English movement engraved *Wilson*. The nine-lobed shell, fluted-urn finials, and scrolls ending in rosettes represent the finest type of Newport work. The pediment is closed as on Newport highboys. (*Karolik Collection, Museum of Fine Arts, Boston.*)

**317.** Philadelphia tall clock made about 1765-1775 by David Rittenhouse (1732-1796) of Norriton (Norristown) and Philadelphia, in a mahogany case, by Thomas Affleck (active 1763-1795). The vase-of-flowers finial and pierced-lattice pediment are finely carved. This piece, along with other furniture made by Affleck, was originally owned by Levi Hollingsworth and has descended in the family. A letter from Mrs. Hollingsworth called this clock "the last made by the celebrated David Rittenhouse." (*Collection of Mrs. W. Logan MacCoy.*)

**318.** Bracket clocks were seldom made in America. This one from New York is signed by Charles Geddes, who advertised in 1773 as "clock and watchmaker and finisher from London." The case is veneered in walnut and the handle, finials, and feet are brass. The dial and leafage in the spandrels are also of brass. The bracket clock might also stand on a table or mantel. (*Henry Ford Museum.*)

**318**

319 A

319 B

**319.** Connecticut corner cupboard from a house built in Oakville Center in 1776. Removal of later paint has disclosed the original red and green color. Carved on a matted ground in the center of the domed top is a grapevine pattern, a motif found on many Connecticut case pieces. Semi-engaged columns support a concave shell which, with keystone and cornice, provided architectural interest in the interior. Basically this resembles the Queen Anne corner cupboard (No. 189), but it is more elaborate. (*Ex Coll. Mrs. Arthur G. Camp. Courtesy John S. Walton.*)

**320.** Pennsylvania-German walnut cupboard or dresser, made in the second half of the 1700s. The large cupboard in two sections was the dominating piece in the Pennsylvania-German interior, as the press cupboard was in the seventeenth-century New England hall. The upper section served for choice pieces of sgraffito and slipware, the lower section for linens and utensils. A broad cornice is reminiscent of the seventeenth-century kas. The influence of English design, transmitted through Philadelphia, is evident in the inset quarter columns, while the presence of glazed doors indicates the second half of the century. (*Gift of Titus C. Geesey. Philadelphia Museum of Art.*)

320

**321**

**322**

**323**

**321.** This slope-front desk of mahogany, with white pine used as the secondary wood, was made in Massachusetts about 1760. Drawer blockings are cut from solid mahogany. The unusual hairy-paw foot is found only occasionally in Massachusetts, and was reserved for exceptionally fine pieces. There are blocked drawers on two tiers in the writing compartment, with two sets of concave drawers at the sides. (*Karolik Collection, Museum of Fine Arts, Boston.*)

**322.** Massachusetts slope-front desk of mahogany and pine, with a reverse-serpentine (oxbow) front and original brasses. It was probably made in Boston or Salem, about 1770. The ogee-bracket foot ends in the Massachusetts claw-and-ball foot with turned-back talon. There is a carved central pendant on the base and the interior has an unusual amount of carving, with fans and sunburst and spiral-fluted columns. (*Collection of Mr. and Mrs. T. B. Christopher.*)

**323.** Massachusetts desk of bombé (kettle-base) form, made about 1760-1770. This is the finest type of bombé (see also Nos. 296 and 329), in which the drawer sides follow the curve of the case instead of being straight within a shaped framework. The fretted outlines of the ogee-bracket and pendant are unusually elaborate. The wood is heavy Santo Domingan mahogany. (*Karolik Collection, Museum of Fine Arts, Boston.*)

**324.** Newport mahogany slope-front desk of blockfront-and-shell construction, made about 1760-1770 by the Townsend-Goddard cabinetmakers. The unusual feet with abbreviated brackets ending in scrolls resemble those on a chest of drawers in the Karolik Collection, and the desk is like it in having three drawers instead of the usual four. (*Bayou Bend Collection, Houston.*)

**324**

**325 A**

**325 B**

**326**

**327**

**325.** Newport slope-front desk of mahogany made about 1760. It is attributed to Job Townsend (1699-1765) because it has the same detail of construction (a wooden bolt inside the top drawer) used on a secretary with his label. Plain desks of this type are thought to have been made for export to the South and the West Indies. (*No. 45, Carpenter,* Arts and Crafts of Newport. *New-York Historical Society.*)

**326.** Connecticut desk of cherry made about 1780. The well carved foot is outstanding. In Connecticut work, the claw and ball are apt to be crudely carved. The desk has inset quarter columns, which frequently appear on Connecticut and Philadelphia pieces. Document drawers and the door to the central compartment make decorative use of simple fluting. (*Collection of Mr. and Mrs. Frederick K. Barbour.*)

**327.** New York slope-front mahogany desk, made c. 1775, which is attributed to Samuel Prince (active 1772-1776). It has an ogee-bracket foot ending in New York's compressed claw and ball. The leaf carving on the bracket is similar to the design on the Hewlett family desk (*Antiques,* January, 1934) and on the great secretary, No. 334, both of which are attributed to Prince. The desk once belonged to President Ulysses S. Grant, and within the writing compartment is a cupboard door with mirror panel framed in braid allegedly from Grant's uniform. Back of it is an open compartment with a small drawer below. This whole section slides out to reveal drawers marked *Medals, Gold Coins, Silver Coins, Brass Knobs.* (*Henry Ford Museum.*)

**328**

**329**

**330**

**328.** Massachusetts blockfront desk and bookcase (secretary) of mahogany made about 1760-1780. Tall proportions are typical of Massachusetts, as is the somewhat flat blocking of the lower section. The fret-carved frieze, dentil course on cornice and broken, triangular pediment produce a rich effect with restrained means. Fluted pilasters frame the rectangular doors, which have fielded panels of crotch mahogany. The same division in fielded panels is seen on the lid of the desk section. (*Essex Institute.*)

**329.** Massachusetts bombé desk and bookcase of flame-grained Santo Domingan mahogany, made about 1770-1780. This is one of the most highly developed expressions of the rococo style in Boston. It is unusually small, similar to one of serpentine and bombé construction at the Winterthur Museum, considered possibly the work of John Cogswell. Mirror panels are inset in carved and gilt framework formed of ogee scrolls. The fluted pilasters have Ionic capitals. In the center of the broken triangular pediment is an urn with twisted flame finial. This secretary belonged originally to William Greenleaf, sheriff of Cambridge, who had charge of furnishing the headquarters of Washington in the old Vassall (later Craigie) mansion in Cambridge in 1775. (*Bayou Bend Collection, Houston.*)

**330.** Newport desk and bookcase of mahogany, made about 1760-1770 by the Townsend-Goddard cabinetmakers. The thirteen-lobed shells, closed bonnet-top with raised paneling on the pediment (see No. 305), fluted-urn finials, and stop-fluted inset quarter columns are typical Newport details. The interior has three blocked drawers in the cabinet and three carved shells in the writing compartment. About ten of the blockfront-and-shell secretaries are known. This descended in the family of John Taylor Gilman (1753-1828), governor of New Hampshire. (*Bayou Bend Collection, Houston.*)

**331**

**331.** Connecticut desk and bookcase of cherry, made about 1770-1790 and attributed to Eliphalet Chapin of East Windsor or his cousin, Aaron. The pierced lattice pediment and inset quarter columns show the Philadelphia influence in Chapin work. The fluted plinth under the central finial is a Chapin characteristic. (See No. 314.) Capitals, bases, and stop-fluting, all of brass, give elegance to this secretary, which belonged to Caleb Strong (1745-1819), governor of Massachusetts, who lived near East Windsor. *(Old Deerfield.)*

**332.** New Hampshire maple desk and bookcase, with tiger-stripe maple on the lid and paneled doors. The desk section of the secretary has a reverse-serpentine or oxbow front, a closed bonnet-top, corkscrew finials, a fan-carved pendant on the base, and claw-and-ball feet on blocked ogee brackets. The inscription *Walter Edge Gilmanton* may be that of the owner or of an unrecorded maker named Edge who lived in Gilmanton. *(Currier Gallery of Art.)*

**333.** Desk and bookcase of mahogany and tulipwood, made about 1760 in New York. The front feet have boldly knuckled claws grasping a compressed ball, and there are bracket-feet in the rear. Rich detail is provided by carving on the inner edge of the molded paneled doors, which have incurved corners. Characteristic of New York case pieces is the flat top. This secretary belonged to Dr. John Bard (1716-1799). *(Collection of Mr. and Mrs. John Walden Myer. Photograph: Museum of the City of New York.)*

**332**

**333**

**334.** This, one of the finest New York secretaries known, was probably made by Samuel Prince, who was active from 1772 to 1776, when he advertised. He died in 1778. It is of mahogany, with tulipwood and pine as secondary woods. Occasionally the pitch-pediment appears in New York work, but the flat top (see No. 333) was usual. The pediment has a Chinese carved fret on the frieze, and there is a Chinese motif on the door of the writing compartment. A labeled secretary of similar design is known but does not have the acanthus carving on the bracket. Glazed doors, formed of small pieces of glass held together by narrow mahogany astragals, were not as common in American Chippendale furniture as they were later. (*No. 224, Downs,* American Furniture, *H. F. du Pont Winterthur Museum.*)

**335.** Pennsylvania walnut desk and bookcase, attributed to John Bachman (1746-1829) of Lancaster County. This Swiss-born cabinetmaker who was long miscalled Jacob Bachman, settled in Lampeter Township in 1766. He was influenced by the Philadelphia Chippendale style, but employed it with originality, as seen here in the large-scale sunflowers which end the scrolls of the pediment, in the tall proportions of the twisted-flame finials, and in his novel use of flames on the columns on the document drawers. The date of this piece may be between 1770 and 1790. (*Collection of Mr. and Mrs. T. B. Christopher.*)

**336.** Philadelphia desk and bookcase of mahogany, made about 1760-1770. The fully developed rococo style is represented by the pierced cartouche finial and the pierced shell on the pediment. The arched-panel doors of the Queen Anne style often appear in the Chippendale period. This secretary descended in the family of Caspar Wistar (1696-1752), who founded the glassmaking industry in southern New Jersey. (*Philadelphia Museum of Art.*)

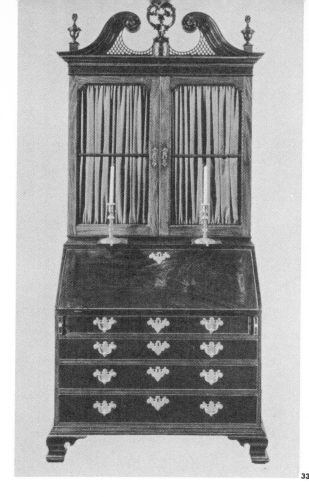

337

338

**337.** This Philadelphia mahogany desk and bookcase was made about 1760-1780 for the Wharton family, owners of the Wharton-Lisle highboy (No. 311), and is one of the master-pieces of Philadelphia furniture-making. A pierced cartouche finial rests on a rosette-carved plinth, and the broad, erect scrolls of the pediment end in whorls of leafage above grace-ful lattice work. Adding to the over-all richness are flame finials, a carved fret on the frieze, and an egg-and-dart band-ing around the glazed doors. (*Plate 201, Hornor,* Blue Book of Philadelphia Furniture. *Reginald M. Lewis sale, 1961. Henry Ford Museum.*)

**338.** Charleston desk and bookcase of mahogany with a cy-press interior, made about 1760-1770. The carved "Elfe fret" associates this piece with Thomas Elfe, the leading Charleston cabinetmaker (see also Nos. 240 and 309). Stop-fluted pilasters have Ionic capitals, and in the center of the broken triangular pediment is an unusual large scallop-shell finial. The cockbead used on the drawer fronts rather than on the framework fol-lows contemporary English practice. (*Collection of Frank L. Horton.*)

339

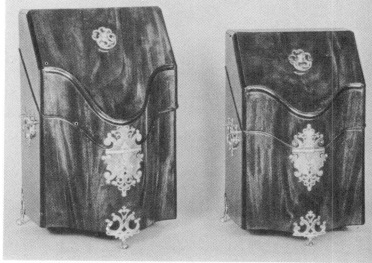

**339.** These mahogany knife cases with silver mounts descended for generations in the Stuyvesant family. They were made in New York about 1770, and have mounts made by Lewis Fueter, who was then working with his father, Daniel Chris-tian Fueter, a leading New York silversmith. Although knife cases were used by the well-to-do, most examples were im-ported shagreen cases. In 1788, a New York advertisement read: "Black table cases, with knives, forks, and spoons com-pleat." American cases are of the utmost rarity although they were advertised by cabinetmakers, such as Joseph Adam Fleming (in 1785), Gifford and Scotland (in 1791), and Fenwick Lyell (in 1799), who had "knife cases made to con-tain any Number of Knives, forks, or spoons." (*Metropolitan Musuem of Art.*)

**340**

**341**

**342**

**340.** Mahogany looking glass with the label of John Elliott (1713-1791). The presence of Elliott's third type of label, which he used from 1768 to 1776, makes it possible to determine the decade in which this example was made. The fretwork mirror in the Queen Anne style, with scrolled outline, continued to be produced in the Chippendale period. Although Elliott, the most important Philadelphia maker, sold imported mirrors as well as his own, this one is considered to be his work. (*Philadelphia Museum of Art.*)

**341.** Mahogany looking glass or sconce, with original glass candle-arms, made about 1760-1770, possibly by John Elliott, who is known to have produced the type with scalloped cresting inset with a gilded shell. The central motif here is a feather design. The mirror was found in an eighteenth-century house on Maryland's Eastern Shore, where it hung for generations. Easy transportation by

water brought much Philadelphia furniture to the region. The design is based on an English parcel-gilt mirror, which was popular from 1720 to 1760. (*Collection of Mr. and Mrs. Sifford Pearre.*)

**342.** Looking glass of mahogany with gilt decoration. It was made about 1760-1775 and was originally owned in the family of Peter van Gaasbeek of New York, a major in the Continental Army and member of the Continental Congress. Like the preceding example, this one is unusual for its original candle-arms. The style represents a combination of elements of the fretwork mirror with scrolled outline (Nos. 340 and 341) and the architectural style with broken-scrolled pediment (No. 344). Its history indicates a probable New York origin. (*Collection of Mrs. Giles Whiting.*)

**343.** Philadelphia Chippendale carved and gilt rococo looking glass, made about 1765-1775. Small sections of glass

are joined by pine framework. This method of gaining greater size was evolved in England in the mid-1700s. Chippendale and other designers offered intricate patterns with Chinese and rococo ornament which the American maker never attempted. The nearest approach to these elaborate forms is seen in examples like this from Philadelphia. (*Metropolitan Museum of Art.*)

**344.** Mahogany and gesso looking glass with gilt moldings and phoenix finial, made about 1760-1790. This is the architectural mirror; based on a George II style. The scrolled pediment, crosseted corners, cornice molding, and frieze resemble architectural designs for the chimneybreast. In America this is sometimes called a Constitution mirror, but the reason is unknown. It has also been called a Martha Washington mirror, but the reason was not clear until its recent return to Mount Vernon after a long absence suggested an explanation. After

**343**

**344**

**345**

the death of Martha Washington it was inherited by her granddaughter, Martha Parke Custis, who became Mrs. Thomas Peter of Tudor Place, Georgetown, D.C. It remained in the Peter family and came back to Mount Vernon in 1957 as part of the G. Freeland Peter Collection. (*Courtesy Mount Vernon Ladies' Association.*)

**345.** Looking glass of walnut, with gilding and gesso, made in the late 1790s. A paper label on the back gives the name of an unrecorded maker: *Hosea Dugliss / Looking Glass / Manufacturer / 11 Chathem* [sic] *Row / Between Ann Street and / the Park Theater / New York.* As the Park Theater opened in 1798, the looking glass may have been made in the late eighteenth or early nineteenth century. Here the traditional architectural mirror shows Hepplewhite influence in the type of urn, floral sprays, and the Adamesque crossed palm branches. (*Reginald M. Lewis Sale, 1961. Henry Ford Museum.*)

346

347

**346.** New England settee of mahogany with maple frame and rear legs, made about 1765-1780. It has a triple-scrolled back, vertically rolled arms and out-flaring wings. The slender cabriole leg is carved with cabochon and leafage and ends in a well-formed Massachusetts claw-and-ball foot with oval ball and outstretched talon. The tapering square rear leg which broadens at the base is rather similar to a New York type and is occasionally seen in Massachusetts. (*Graves Collection, Metropolitan Museum.*)

**347.** Philadelphia serpentine-back mahogany sofa with horizontally rolled arms, cabriole front legs, and stump rear legs. It was made about 1765-1780. The unusual length of this great Philadelphia sofa gives a majestic sweep to the line of the reverse curve of the back. This sofa represents a later stage of the Chippendale style than No. 346, and is a supreme example of the skillful manner in which Philadelphia cabinetmakers always handled the curving line. (*Philadelphia Museum of Art.*)

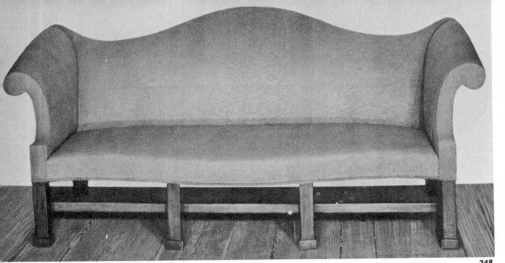

**348.** Philadelphia mahogany sofa with serpentine back, Marlborough leg, and blocked foot, made about 1770-1780. The horizontally rolled arms and serpentine line of the seat emphasize the bold curves which Philadelphia furniture often displays. Large sofas in the Chippendale style seem to have been made more frequently in Philadelphia than elsewhere. The upholstery here is red eighteenth-century moreen, a watered fabric. (*Brush-Everard House, Colonial Williamsburg.*)

348

**349.** New York mahogany serpentine-back sofa, made in the late 1700s. The spade foot on the tapering leg is a Hepplewhite innovation; otherwise the sofa is in characteristic Chippendale style. The rectangular stretcher is seen on other New York sofas. Upholstery is of French printed cotton with a design based on Guido Reni's fresco, *Aurora,* in the Rospigliosi Palace, Rome. (*Henry Ford Museum.*)

**350.** New England chair-back settee of mahogany, made about 1760-1775. It has the pierced vase splat of Manwaring type which appears on "Salem" chairs, and is one of a set with eight chairs (No. 258) that belonged to the Sanford family of New England. The block-and-spindle stretcher of the Queen Anne period was often retained in New England Chippendale furniture. The contoured, knuckled arm has incurved arm-supports, and the cabriole leg, with a flat-carved acanthus, ends in a conspicuously articulated version of the Massachusetts claw and ball. The chair-back settee, frequently made in England, is rare in America. (*Bayou Bend Collection, Houston.*)

349

350

**351.** Newport firescreen (polescreen) of mahogany with adjustable shield covered in eighteenth-century needlework. It was made about 1760-1775. Characteristic of Newport are the spiral fluting, carved on the pedestal, and the contracted, five-toed paw feet. A tea table with the same characteristics, shown in the loan exhibition of Newport furniture at Hunter House in 1953, was accompanied by the original bill from John Goddard. The firescreen of the Chippendale period had a larger shield than the Queen Anne type. Philadelphia may have produced more than New England, but the number of American examples is not large. (*Metropolitan Museum of Art.*)

**352.** Basin stand of mahogany, probably made by John Townsend between 1760 and 1775. The fluted pillars and five-toed paw foot distinguish it as Newport work. Vase-turnings support the molded rim, which holds a Chinese export porcelain basin. A matching ewer stands on the paneled shelf. The openings outlined with rings are for soap cups. Designs called "bason stands" were offered by Chippendale. (*No. 278, Downs,* American Furniture. *H. F. du Pont Winterthur Museum.*)

**353.** Massachusetts candlestand of mahogany, made about 1778. Tall candlestands for formal rooms were common in England, but are excessively rare in American furniture. Massachusetts characteristics are present in the elongated claw foot and the Corinthian capital on the column. The latter appears on pilasters of a few elaborately carved case pieces of the

351

354

352                                            353

region. The spiral reeding suggests the swirl carving on small New England tables and stands. An old inscription under the pedestal says it was the work of an English soldier captured at the Battle of Bennington in 1777 and made by him at Charlestown the following year. His English training would explain the unfamiliar motifs in the carving, the overlapping leaf on the knee, the parallel leaves around the rim, and the lotus-like canopy beneath it. (*No. 284, Downs,* American Furniture. *H. F. du Pont Winterthur Museum.*)

**354.** Newport mahogany candlestand made about 1760-1780. Although of a more usual form than No. 353, this is exceptional for the French scrolled toe, so seldom seen in American work. Randolph used it on three of the *sample* chairs and in Newport it was used on a card table now at the Winterthur Museum. The pedestal is handsomely proportioned and has the long vase section typical of Newport. (*Henry Ford Museum.*)

355

356

**355.** Philadelphia mahogany kettle stand of about 1770, with fretwork brackets and blocked Marlborough leg. There is a slide for the teacup. Kettle stands, as an auxiliary to the tea table, were seldom made in America although widely used in England. Most of those surviving come from New England, particularly Newport, while Philadelphia is represented by very few. (*Plate 284, Hornor, Blue Book of Philadelphia Furniture. Collection of Dr. William S. Serri.*)

**356.** Newport mahogany stand with fluted legs and pierced brackets, made by the Townsend-Goddard cabinetmakers about 1770-1790. This is of the kettle-stand type but, lacking the usual slide for the teacup, it may have been designed for occasional use and as a candlestand. The dished top is like that on a tea table. (*Rhode Island School of Design.*)

**357.** Mahogany stool upholstered over the seat frame, made about 1760-1780. The ridged cabriole leg and exaggerated knuckle on the claw-and-ball foot are similar to those on the New York center table, No. 372. Stools were never common in America, for here no rules existed for seating people according to their rank, with chairs considered an honored position and stools indicating lesser importance. Nor were stools used in sets as part of the decoration of a formal room, as they were in the larger English rooms. (*Shelburne Museum.*)

**358.** This Maryland window bench or stool of the Chippendale-Hepplewhite transition, which was made about 1780-1790, comes from the Ridgely family of Hampton. It is of mahogany, with tulipwood used as a secondary wood. This is a forerunner of the Hepplewhite window bench, but the heavier proportions of the straight tapering leg relate it to the Chippendale style. The rolled arms end in carved rosettes. Early examples are extremely rare. (*Collection of Mr. and Mrs. Sifford Pearre.*)

357

358

**359**. Mahogany breakfast table of pembroke type, made in Philadelphia about 1770-1790. The serpentine top has narrow scalloped leaves, and there is spiral gadrooning on the skirt. The molded straight legs are joined by a pierced cross-stretcher. The wide center represents a departure from the narrow centers found on dropleaf tables of the earlier types. According to Sheraton's *Cabinet Dictionary* (1803) the name Pembroke was that of the lady who first ordered one. Its purpose, he also wrote, "is for a gentleman or lady to breakfast on." (*William B. Goodwin Collection, Wadsworth Atheneum.*)

359

**360**. Mahogany breakfast table of pembroke type, made in Philadelphia about 1770-1790. The pierced cross-stretcher is flat, legs are fluted, and the skirt has spiral gadrooning. The curving lines of the pierced brackets lead naturally to the broader curves of the leaves. The design of the stretcher is based on a plate in Chippendale's *Director,* 1762. Omission of a drawer is unusual. Downs found a reference to a pembroke table in 1771 in the account book of a Philadelphia cabinet-maker, Reuben Haines, which was the earliest mention of it in America known to him. (*No. 312, Downs,* American Furniture. *H. F. du Pont Winterthur Museum.*)

**361**. Mahogany breakfast table of pembroke type made in Newport, about 1770-1790. It is attributed to John Townsend (1732-1809) on the basis of its similarity to a labeled table at the Winterthur Museum. The pierced Chinese fretwork on the cross-stretcher is also seen on two tables in private collections and on a kettle stand at Winterthur, in evidence of Newport's partiality for the geometric forms of Chinese Chippendale. (*Karolik Collection, Museum of Fine Arts, Boston.*)

**362**. This mahogany breakfast table of pembroke type, made in the late 1700s, was found in coastal North Carolina, where it may have been made. The flat cross-stretcher is a simplified version of the stretcher in No. 360. Chamfered legs ending in a blocked foot have been noted in other furniture from this region. The little-known makers of coastal North Carolina furniture deserve further study. (*Collection of Frank L. Horton.*)

360

361

362

363

364

365

**363**. Massachusetts card table of mahogany, made about 1760-1780, and once owned by John Hancock. Typical of Massachusetts is the straight, slender cabriole, the shallow apron, the restrained lines of the serpentine top. While fine carving and use of color or gilding sometimes distinguish Massachusetts furniture, its essential quality is expressed in terms of delicate outline. Square corners were suitable for the use of square-based silver candlesticks. (*Henry Ford Museum.*)

**364**. Massachusetts card table of mahogany combining both Chippendale and Hepplewhite characteristics. It was made by David Poignand, who came to Boston from St. Helier, Isle of Jersey, in 1787. Chippendale is represented by the pierced brackets, molded legs, and fluted rim, and Hepplewhite by inlaid paterae and stringing. This piece and others by Poignand, including a secretary dated *1788*, were taken by his family to Kentucky and then to Missouri. (See No. 541.) The table, made probably in the 1790s, represents one of many examples showing how strong the Chippendale influence remained in America to the end of the century. (*City Art Museum, St. Louis.*)

366

**365**. Newport card table with a blister-mahogany top, made by the Townsend-Goddard cabinetmakers about 1760-1770. The top opens to a cupboard section for playing cards and counters, a construction found on other Newport examples. The cabriole leg is carved with Newport's palmette and acanthus characteristically executed in relief combined with intaglio. An undercut, pierced claw suggests John Goddard but appears too on other pieces made by the Townsend-Goddard family. (*No. 63, Carpenter,* Arts and Crafts of Newport. *Bayou Bend Collection, Houston.*)

**366**. Newport mahogany card table, made about 1780-1790. This outstanding example by the Townsend-Goddard cabinetmakers has a serpentine top, squared corners, stop-fluted legs, pierced fretwork brackets, and fluted rim. The design was favored by these makers and is one of three main types of card tables illustrated in Carpenter's *Arts and Crafts of Newport.* (*Bayou Bend Collection, Houston.*)

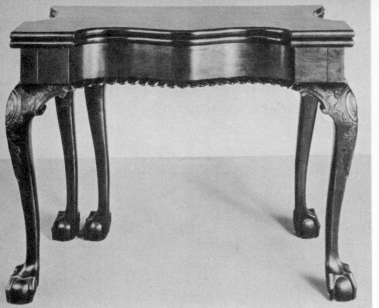

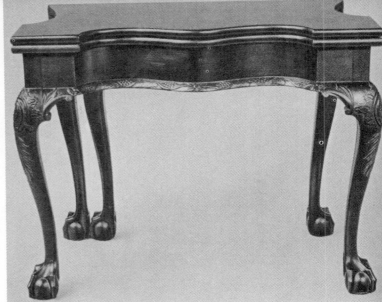

367   368

**367.** New York mahogany card table, made about 1765. Characteristic of the New York card table are the five legs, pronounced serpentine form, and an apron bordered with heavy gadrooning. Typical too are the C-scrolled brackets on the legs, and the rococo C-scrolls and streamers of acanthus carved on the knee. This example comes from the Van Rensselaer Manor House near Albany. (*Metropolitan Museum of Art.*)

**368.** New York mahogany card table, made about 1770. It has the same New York characteristics seen in No. 367, but an unusual detail is the grapevine design carved on the molded edge of the apron. Occasionally this motif is found on New York tables. The claw-and-ball foot is a particularly fine example of the New York type. (*Pendleton Collection, Rhode Island School of Design.*)

**369.** Philadelphia card table of mahogany, made about 1765-1785. The turret ends are carved with a half-cartouche, and the cabriole leg with rococo cabochon and tattered acanthus. The apron has spiral gadrooning. This is one of the richest Philadelphia card tables known. It emphasizes the curved line,

369

as contrasted with the rectilinear lines of No. 370. Both card tables are associated with the same great craftsman, Thomas Affleck. This one is comparable in style and lavish carving to the pair Affleck made for Governor John Penn's Chestnut Street house, illustrated in Hornor's *Blue Book of Philadelphia Furniture*, Plate 235. (*Bayou Bend Collection, Houston.*)

**370.** Philadelphia card table of mahogany, made about 1765-1785. The vibrant spiral gadrooning on the skirt and carved guilloche on the folding top make this an exceptional example. The chamfered and blocked Marlborough legs have paneled insets with Gothic fretwork. In place of the usual drawer found on Philadelphia card tables, the drawer here is simulated, which provides an excuse for the handsome brass mounts. Since Thomas Affleck is known to have used somewhat similar fretwork (see No. 248), fine examples in this style are associated with his name. (*Reginald M. Lewis sale, 1961. Henry Ford Museum.*)

370

**371.** Mahogany card table, made about 1780 in Charleston, South Carolina. The skirt has a wide band of pierced fretwork designed like Chinese railing illustrated in eighteenth-century English pattern books. Such conspicuous use of Chinese Chippendale ornament is unusual in American furniture but occurs on a Charleston breakfast table originally owned by the Rutledge family of Hampton Plantation which is illustrated in *Antiques*, January 1952, p. 54. (*Henry Ford Museum*.)

371

372

**372.** New York center table of mahogany with a gray and white marble top and ridged cabriole leg. It was made about 1760. In the eighteenth century this would have been called a "slab table."[20] At first glance it appears to be designed as a side table, yet is finished in similar fashion on all sides and could be used away from the wall. There are occasional examples of the center table in the seventeenth and eighteenth centuries, but the type did not become popular until after 1800 (No. 562). Downs calls attention to New York traits here in the "ruffling of short cyma curves" on the skirt and the exaggerated knuckles on the feet. (*No. 355, Downs,* American Furniture. *H. F. du Pont Winterthur Museum.*)

373

**373.** Mahogany china table which originally belonged to Francis Borland, a Boston Tory. It was probably made in Massachusetts about 1765-1775. Three other tables of similar type, with a gallery (designed to protect a display of china) and an arched cross-stretcher, have a New England background which suggests that they originated there. These include the Barrett Wendell table (Lockwood, *Colonial Furniture in America*, Vol. II, Fig. 738), one at the Warner House, Portsmouth, New Hampshire, and a third from another Portsmouth family. These tend to belie Myers' attribution of No. 653, Girl Scouts Loan Exhibition, formerly owned by Howard Reifsnyder, to Philadelphia. (*Bayou Bend Collection, Houston*.)

374.                                                 375

**374.** Philadelphia mahogany dressing table or lowboy, made about 1770-1780 by Thomas Tufft (active before 1772 to 1788). Usually the Philadelphia lowboy has a more elaborate apron which dips down in the center, but this rarer type has a rectangular outline. The short cyma scrolls of the skirt are finished with a beaded edge. (*Philadelphia Museum of Art.*)

**375.** Philadelphia mahogany dressing table, with original brasses. On the drawer is a carved intaglio shell, and on the apron an elaborate version of a rococo shell, surrounded by incised acanthus scrolls. This lowboy was owned by Sarah Williams Longstreth (1781-1848) of Barclay Hall, Philadelphia, but it was made for the preceding generation, probably about 1770-1780. (*Ginsburg and Levy.*)

**376.** An elaborate Philadelphia mahogany dressing table or lowboy, with carved inset columns. The original brasses combine Chinese and rococo design. On the drawer front the rococo style transforms and amplifies a traditional shell and leaf design. On the apron, acanthus streamers frame a ruffle-like shell. This matches a highboy in the same collection. Both were made in 1769 for the parents of the beautiful Rebecca Gratz, the original of Walter Scott's Rebecca in *Ivanhoe*. (*No. 333, Downs,* American Furniture. *H. F. du Pont Winterthur Museum.*)

376

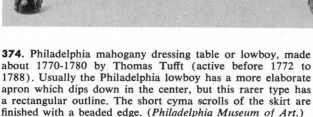

377

**377.** This richly carved dressing table or lowboy of Santo Domingan mahogany was made in Philadelphia about 1760-1780. It has Chinese fretwork on the frieze, naturalistic floral pendants on the inset columns, and a rococo leaflike design framing the figure of a swan. The swan was probably inspired by Aesop. Other Philadelphia pieces of the same type (see No. 312) illustrate the fables of the fox and grapes, the two pigeons, and other subjects from Aesop.[45] (*Karolik Collection, Museum of Fine Arts, Boston.*)

378

379

**378.** Connecticut dressing table or lowboy of cherry, made about 1780-1790. There are Connecticut characteristics in the wide overhang of the top, the stiffly carved intaglio shell on the drawer, and the flat-carved tulip on the cabriole leg. The precisely carved scallop shells and heart motif are also found on Connecticut pieces. (*Vermont House, Shelburne Museum.*)

**379.** Southern lowboy, made in the Valley of Virginia in the late 1700s. The top and upper part are of mahogany, the legs are cherry, and the interior is tulipwood. Cherry was frequently used in Virginia. The Shenandoah Valley, actively settled after the Revolution, produced furniture of sound craftsmanship. This piece reverts to the early form of dressing table with a single tier of drawers. The C-scroll of the bracket merges with the cabriole leg, which ends in a flattened claw-and-ball foot. (*Collection of Frank L. Horton.*)

380

381

**380.** Massachusetts kneehole dressing table, or chest of drawers, of blockfront construction with a gilt fan on cupboard door. The kneehole dressing table seems to have been more popular in New England than the lowboy dressing table. The use of gilding with mahogany (parcel-gilding) in the Chippendale period is occasionally found in this region, where a taste for colorful decoration was established by the painted and japanned pieces of the early 1700s. This was made in Massachusetts about 1760-1780. (*Luke Vincent Lockwood sale, 1954, Parke-Bernet Galleries.*)

**381.** Newport mahogany kneehole dressing table, or chest of drawers, in typical blockfront-and-shell construction made about 1760-1780 by the Townsend-Goddard cabinetmakers. The two convex shells and two intaglio make this a particularly splendid example. These eleven-lobed shells attract a lively play of light over the regularly undulating curves. The total effect is unlike that of any other regional style, although it was imitated in Connecticut. (*On loan from the George Burford Lorimer Collection. Brooklyn Museum.*)

**382**

**383**

**383.** Mahogany dropleaf table of "handkerchief" type, with triangular dropleaf, made in Pennsylvania about 1760. This form was designed to stand in a corner when not in use. The simplified design, with a top formed of only two sections and a single pivoting leg, was made all along the Atlantic coast. The deep apron seen here is said to be characteristic of the middle colonies. (*No. 309, Downs,* American Furniture. *H. F. du Pont Winterthur Museum.*)

**384.** New York dropleaf dining table with eight legs and an oval top, made about 1770. Although the square-cornered dining table made its appearance in the Chippendale period, the oval form of the early 1700s was retained on many American Chippendale examples. With its rich carving of New York's linear acanthus and a fine claw-and-ball foot, this is a great example of the dining-room table which preceded the extension tables of the Hepplewhite period (Nos. 565, 567). (*Metropolitan Museum of Art.*)

**384**

385

**385.** Massachusetts mahogany side table with a white marble top having rounded corners. Most unusual is the large scale of the pierced fretwork. This Gothic fret is one of three which Chippendale offered in the third edition of the *Director,* 1762, Plate CXCVI. The regional characteristics of Massachusetts are seen in the slender cabriole and the delicate talons, with those on the side turned back. The table was made about 1760-1775. (*No. 356, Downs.* American Furniture. *H. F. du Pont Winterthur Museum.*)

**386.** Newport side table of about 1770-1790 with a D-shaped marble top. It descended in the Bowen family of Providence. The mark *I P* on the under side of the marble may refer to Joseph Proud, a cabinetmaker who was working in Newport about 1762. The tapering legs have two flutes, which suggest the approach of the Hepplewhite style. Pierced brackets are similar to those in Goddard-Townsend work. The cross-stretcher seems a concession to the delicacy of the legs. (*Bayou Bend Collection, Houston.*)

**387.** New York mahogany side table with a gray marble top, made about 1760-1780. Here is an example of the influence of Chinese straight-leg design known from Sir William Chambers' drawings of Oriental furniture published in 1757. Chippendale offered a version of this design as a sideboard table in all three editions of his *Director.* It was widely used in both England and America. The gouge carving and molded legs were the contribution of the New York cabinetmaker. (*No. 363, Downs,* American Furniture. *H. F. du Pont Winterthur Museum.*)

**388.** Philadelphia half-round side table of serpentine form with a King-of-Prussia marble top. The skirt is elaborately carved with an incised border composed of scroll, shell, and ruffle. This joins with a diapered cartouche above the cabriole leg, in a manner suggesting comparison with the card table No. 369, which may be associated with Affleck. On the leg, scrolled brackets frame a long, slender acanthus. The date of this exceptional table is about 1760-1780. (*Bayou Bend Collection, Houston.*)

386

387   388

389

389. Mahogany side table, with marble top made about 1760-1780. This Philadelphia masterpiece is unusual for the carved fretwork on a convex molding. The familiar interlace of a figure eight imposed on a square is interrupted by a floral cartouche. Below it are a narrow Gothic fret and, completing the elaborate design, a spiral gadroon and flute, finished with an acanthus pendant. (*Metropolitan Museum of Art.*)

390. This Philadelphia marble-top side table was made about 1765, and originally belonged to the Fisher family of the Cliffs. The serpentine front and incurved sides are joined by turret ends. At the center of the severely plain skirt, which emphasizes the pattern of the mahogany, is a tablet carved with a two-handled urn. Unusual in American work is the contrast of a plain surface of the wood with a single, large-scale ornament. (*Plate 205, Hornor,* Blue Book of Philadelphia Furniture. *Bayou Bend Collection, Houston.*)

391. Spider gateleg table, made in New York about 1760. The spider-leg table,[46] with its slender turnings, was an English adaptation of the heavier gateleg table of the early 1700s. The gateleg was usually made of walnut, the spider-leg of mahogany. Hardness of mahogany made the extremely slender turnings possible. The type was seldom made in America, and those which have been discovered can be traced to New York. Another example was in the exhibition, "Furniture by New York Cabinetmakers," at the Museum of the City of New York in 1956, and one from the Livingston–Van Rensselaer heirlooms at Cherry Hill is in the Albany Institute of History and Art. (*Shelburne Museum.*)

390

391

**392**

**393**

**394**

**392.** Newport mahogany tea table, made about 1760-1780 by the Townsend-Goddard cabinetmakers. This rectangular table is of strikingly simple form. It has a dished top and indented corners, a ridged cabriole leg, scrolled brackets, and a molded apron or skirt. The pierced claw, known to have been used by John Goddard (1723-1785), suggests the possibility that this sensitively carved example may have been his work. The pad foot and slipper foot are more often seen on Newport tea tables. (*Bayou Bend Collection, Houston.*)

**393.** "Buttress" type mahogany tea table with scalloped apron and top, made in Massachusetts, probably Boston, about 1760-1780. The molded concave rim is cut from solid wood. This scalloped form (a great test of the cabinetmaker's skill) provided individual places for the pieces in the tea service. Few examples exist, and these have slight variations in detail. Others are in the Winterthur Museum and the Karolik collection. (*Ex Coll. Louis E. Brooks. Bayou Bend Collection, Houston.*)

**394.** Newport mahogany tea table, with dished top and cyma-curved frame, made about 1760. The ridged cabriole leg is carved with a palmette-and-leaf design in relief and intaglio. The table is attributed to John Goddard (1723-1785) because of its close similarity to the documented table that he made for Jabez Bowen in 1763. It does not have the latter table's pierced claw, but has the same foot seen on a table for which Goddard billed Captain Anthony Low, in 1755. (*Bayou Bend Collection, Houston.*)

**395.** The rare Philadelphia mahogany tea table in this drawing room is one of a pair, made about 1760-1780. It is of rectangular form and has a dished top with a double-beaded molding and gadrooned apron. With it are a New England bombé secretary made for the Banning family of Newport, an architectural mirror with phoenix finial, and a New York Sheraton sofa by Duncan Phyfe. (*Home of Mr. and Mrs. Mitchel Taradash.*)

**396.** Newport tripod tea table of mahogany with swirl-fluted column and pad feet, made about 1770-1780. The tripod tea table was not as highly favored in Newport as the rectangular type. This one belonged to Solomon Southwick, editor of the Newport *Mercury*, and is now in the collection of the Newport Historical Society. It is seen here in the Hunter House, where it was in the loan exhibition of 1953. Chairs are of the Queen Anne – Chippendale transition with pierced-vase splats. The Newport clock has a silvered dial. (*Photograph: Preservation Society of Newport County.*)

**397.** This mahogany tripod tea table with a dished top was probably made in Massachusetts about 1760-1780 and comes from the Jeremiah Lee House (1768) at Marblehead. Throughout New England the tripod tea table remained something of a rarity, and was much simpler in ornament than the Philadelphia table. The baluster section is less undulating and the tripod base somewhat heavier. However, the slender talons of what Downs called a "rat claw" are sensitively carved. (*Ginsburg and Levy.*)

397

**398.** Connecticut tripod tea table with a tilt-top, of cherry, made about 1780-1790. A tapering fluted column rises above a carved bowl. The dentil on the block is repeated in smaller scale at the top of the column. The slender, gracefully curved legs end in a simplified claw and ball. Connecticut tripod tables are rarer than other New England examples. (*Collection of Mr. and Mrs. Frederick K. Barbour.*)

**399.** New York State tripod tea table of small size with a piecrust edge and birdcage attachment. It is of mahogany and was made about 1760-1780. The plain, vase-shaped column is long in proportion and the legs are somewhat low. A New York trait is seen in the square line of the web of the talon. It is also seen on a tripod table which belonged to the Van Rensselaer family at Cherry Hill, now at the Albany Institute of History and Art. (*Norvin H. Green sale, 1950, Parke-Bernet Galleries.*)

**400.** Philadelphia tripod tea table of mahogany, made about 1760-1780. In Philadelphia this was one of the most popular forms, and carving was lavished upon it. A characteristic baluster was developed, with a somewhat flattened ball. This example is carved even on the base of the column, a position usually left bare. The table is somewhat similar to the Stevenson and Cadwalader tables illustrated in Hornor's *Blue Book of Philadelphia Furniture.* (*Bayou Bend Collection, Houston.*)

399

400

401 A

401 B

402

**402.** Philadelphia tripod tea table of Santo Domingan mahogany, made about 1760-1780. This superb example of the Philadelphia piecrust table has a flattened, richly carved ball below a fluted column. The arch of the leg is C-scrolled, the base of the shaft is shaped and carved, and the knee has an inverted shell above a rippling acanthus. (*Karolik Collection, Museum of Fine Arts, Boston.*)

**403.** Mahogany writing table, made in Philadelphia about 1770-1790. Chippendale's "library table," or pedestal desk, never became an accepted American type. This example is unusual, and it differs from the English equivalent in the design of the pedestal sections, which here do not extend to the floor. Massive proportions are sustained throughout. The Marlborough legs with paneled insets are so broadly chamfered on the inside that a five-sided leg has been created. Alternating gadroon and flute finish the sides as well as the recessed center, for this table was intended to be seen from every angle. Other points of interest are the boldly contoured serpentine front which almost suggests block-front construction, the arched center with an incised diaper on the spandrels, and the shaped top with lunetted corners. (*Metropolitan Museum of Art.*)

**401 (A).** Philadelphia tripod tea table, mahogany with birdcage attachment and piecrust edge, made about 1760-1780. Typical of Philadelphia is the fluted column rising from a carved urn. This is a richly carved table of perfect proportions. There is a bold thrust in the design of the cabriole, which is carved with a broad acanthus leaf. (*Teina Baumstone.*)

**401 (B).** Another view of 401. The piecrust edge is composed of reversed scrolls and segments of a circle, a form which English silversmiths developed on salvers in the 1730s. The cabinetmakers adopted it in the 1740s, when the tripod table was a new form in England.

403

**404.** A Pennsylvania-German wardrobe or *schrank,* dated *1779* and probably made in Lancaster County. It bears the name of the owner, *Georg Huber,* of whom nothing further is known. This is a fine example of dowry furniture, in which linens and embroideries were displayed at a wedding. The decoration in wax inlay was executed with beeswax and white lead, rubbed into incised lines.[47] The swastika of good luck and the symbolic crown of bliss appear on fielded panels. An unusual vine-scroll enclosing tulips, carnations, and other flowers rising from vases forms the border. Pieces of this type preserve the style of the late seventeenth and early eighteenth centuries. (*Philadelphia Museum of Art.*)

**405.** Wardrobe or *schrank* of tulipwood with painted decoration, probably made in Lancaster County about 1790. This is later than No. 404, and has small fielded panels and ogee-bracket feet. The ground is blue-green, the moldings red, and the off-white panels decorated with polychrome flowers typical of Pennsylvania-German folk art. The drawers have graining in tans and greens and a superimposed vine pattern in black; the base molding and feet are dark brown. There are shelves for linens on the left and wooden pegs on the right for clothing. Other examples of Pennsylvania-German furniture are shown in Nos. 291-293 and 320. (*Henry Ford Museum.*)

404

405

**406.** This room, representing the early classical period, contains a Sheraton mahogany field or tent bed of the late 1700s with reeded posts. English printed cotton hangings fall from the arched tester in graduated folds, with sides held taut by heavy tassels. The small Sheraton tables, on slender reeded legs, are inlaid with satinwood. Hepplewhite details are seen in the tapering of the sofa legs and the shield-back of the armchair. The room contains portraits, plaques, and medallions of Benjamin Franklin, and a Sheraton mirror with American Eagle finial has a portrait of him on the frieze. (*Franklin Room, H. F. du Pont Winterthur Museum.*)

# 4. Classical Period

## 1790-1830

There was no single classical style between 1790 and 1830. Rather this was a classical period in which Greco-Roman furniture and ornament inspired a logical sequence of developments in furniture design and interior decoration. After 1760 in Europe, in reaction to rococo curves and pseudo-Chinese and Gothic ornament, new furniture was given straight lines and rectangular forms. A fresh selection of classical motifs that appeared in wall decoration and on furniture was combined with already familiar classical ornament, which was continued in lighter scale. As a further development, in the 1790s actual forms of Greco-Roman and Egyptian furniture were adapted to modern use. About 1820, forms and ornament became heavier.

In France the classical period is represented by the Louis XVI style (1760-1790), Directoire (1790-1800), Empire (1800-1820), and Restauration (1820-1830). The last is named for the restoration of the monarchy (1814-1830) under Charles X. In England the same development is seen in the Adam style (1765-1785), Hepplewhite-Sheraton styles (1785-1800), and Regency style (1800-1830). The political Regency ended in 1820 when the Prince Regent became George IV, but the name continues to apply to the style. Finally, classical design survived into the Victorian period.

EUROPE: 1760-1790. New designs in furniture were the outcome of interest in the ruins of antiquity, shared alike by scholars, writers, collectors, architects, and artists. Accidental discoveries at Herculaneum in the early 1700s aroused great interest and were followed by sporadic excavations. In 1716 the Comte de Caylus saw Ephesus in Asia Minor, and in the 1730s was assembling the great collection of Egyptian, Etruscan, Greek, and Roman art (today in the Bibliothèque Nationale in Paris) which he was to describe in 1752 in his *Recueil d'antiquités.* In 1754, in Rome, the German scholar and founder of scientific archaeology, Johann Joachim Winckelmann (1717-1768), began his crusade for a deeper understanding of Greek and Roman art with a book which had an English translation the following year as *Thoughts on the Imitation of Greek Works.* His great contribution, *History of the Arts of Antiquity,* came in 1764 and *Unknown Monuments of Antiquity* in 1767.

In 1749, the younger brother of Madame de Pompadour, who later became Marquis de Marigny and *surintendant des bâtiments,* was sent by her to study the new excavations at Pompeii, which had begun the preceding year. With him were Nicolas Cochin, engraver and designer of ceremonies and spectacles for the French court, and the architect Soufflot, who on his return designed the Pantheon in Paris.

About 1757 the artist Louis-Joseph Le Lorrain was asked by the collector Lalive de Jully to design the ebony furniture for his study (today in the Musée Condé at Chantilly) which, with its straight lines, is the forerunner of the Louis XVI furniture by Leleu, Saunier, Reisener, and other *ébénistes* of the 1760s.

There were similar developments in England. In 1753, Robert Wood published his *Ruins of Palmyra,* and the following year young Robert Adam (1728-1792) set out for Italy to study architecture. During his travels he saw the palace of Diocletian in Dalmatia and later published his *Ruins . . . at Spalatro* (1764). This followed by two years the *Antiquities of Athens* by Stuart and Revett. The Duke of Hamilton's great collection of Greek and Roman vases was catalogued by P. F. d'Hancarville in 1766-1767. Finally, in 1769 the designers[48] were inspired by the finely detailed plates of the Italian artist Piranesi, which showed Etruscan, Egyptian, Greek, and Roman ornament. These appeared in *Diverse maniere d' adornare i camini,* which was immediately issued in French and English translations.

In Italy Robert Adam had examined the remains of the lately uncovered houses of Pompeii with their fragmentary but delicately painted wall decorations which occasionally showed designs of Roman furniture. And in Rome, Adam was impressed by the mural decorations of Raphael, who had also been influenced by classic ornament when he painted the frescoes in the Vatican. The work of the great Renaissance architect Palladio, who had influenced so many preceding English architects, also made a deep impression on Adam. He recorded architectural details at Hadrian's villa and also among other ancient monuments in Rome itself. His conclusion was that earlier use of classical ornament, by William Kent and others in the first half of the eighteenth century, had been too heavy, and he gave a new direction to English architectural and interior design with a classical style of his own.

The style that bears Adam's name first appeared in the 1760s, when he designed furniture for Syon House and Osterley as part of the architectural remodeling he had undertaken there. Along with the familiar patera, Greek key, and guilloche were new cameo-like medallions and an unfamiliar type of urn form with an ovoid body tapering to a spreading foot. The anthemion, said to represent the Greek honeysuckle, but more like a perforated palm leaf, was also new. Adam's manner of stringing small husks in slender festoons had so much delicacy that this age-old motif became transformed in relief decoration on walls and ceilings. Straight lines replaced serpentine curves; carving was discarded in favor of flat surfaces inlaid with marquetry or painted with classical figures. Furniture legs were tapered, and either were square in section, ending in a spade foot, or were turned, fluted, and reeded. Pilasters and light moldings emphasized structural lines. Case pieces in the Adam style are rectangular, but a semicircular plan is used for side tables and commodes. A new furniture form, the sideboard, was developed from Adam's use of a side table with flanking pedestals supporting urns. Eventually these were combined in a single piece of furniture.

Light-toned satinwood from the West Indies and from the Orient was used as solid wood or in veneered panels. It was often combined with harewood, which was native sycamore dyed a light greenish gray.

The Adam style was adapted for a wider public by Hepplewhite's *Guide* (1788). Hepplewhite favored the straight, tapering leg, square in section, and emphasized inlay. The decorative motifs he chose included drapery swags, medallions, wheat ears and Prince-of-Wales feathers. Hepplewhite did not dispense entirely with serpentine forms. A simplified rococo style, called French Hepplewhite, was long fashionable in England. Even on straight-leg chairs he used shield, heart-shape and oval backs.

Sheraton's *Drawing-Book* (1791-1794) offers a later interpretation of the Adam style, but Sheraton was also an observer of the work of Henry Holland (1746-1806), the architect who remodeled Carlton House in 1784 for the Prince of Wales. Holland was greatly influenced by the later phase of the Louis XVI style as represented by Beneman and Weisweiler. He had the restraint which Adam frequently lacked and favored the square lines which Sheraton adopted in designing chair-backs, mirrors, and sofas. Other Sheraton details are the turned, reeded leg, and the addition of elongated projecting columns at the corners of chests of drawers and on other pieces where they ran to the full height (a favorite treatment of Weisweiler which Holland adopted). Chairs had backs composed of vertical bars, or bars forming a trellis, or a drapery-and-urn center in a superimposed panel.

EUROPE: 1790-1820. Although Adam's style anticipated developments of the Regency period, other architects and designers carried them to conclusion in a spirit of reaction to Adam's ornate manner. However, Adam had already made use of the tripod, candelabrum, and Roman altar before Holland, Sheraton, and Hope used a wider selection of Greco-Roman and Egyptian furniture forms. They were influenced in this by the example of France, but Holland and Hope pursued their own study of antiquity independently as well. Holland sent a member of his staff, Charles Heathcote Tatham, to Rome in 1794 to make drawings of antique furniture for him. He made use of Tatham's sketches in designing furniture for Carlton House and later at Southill (1797). Tatham's drawings eventually became available to other designers through the publication of his *Etchings of Ancient Ornamental Architecture* (1799).

Thomas Hope (1769-1831) was a wealthy amateur architect who spent eight years in Egypt, Sicily, and the Near East and formed a collection of antique art. As a setting for his collections he designed furniture for his home, Deepdene, in Surrey, and for his house in London. Hope's book, *Household Furniture and Interior Decoration* (1807), illustrated this furniture. It was not well received at the time but has become increasingly important to the modern student in representing the height of the Regency style. It was not, however, the first publication of Regency furniture designs; Sheraton's second book, his *Cabinet Dictionary* (1803), was the first. Later came Sheraton's *Encyclopaedia* (1805), which he did not live to finish. George Smith's *Collection of Designs for Household Furniture* was published in 1808, the year following Hope's book, but some of the plates are dated as early as 1804. Smith's plates show his familiarity with French fashions. Since his publication played a part in popularizing the new classical forms, he is of interest to the student, although his designs run to extreme forms and are lacking in taste. Surviving furniture of the Regency period, however, is distinguished in line and shows French inspiration to the extent that it was once called English Empire.

French classicism of the 1790s, as represented by the architect Dugourc at Bagatelle, developed into the Directoire style and culminated in the work of Napoleon's architects, Percier and Fontaine. Charles Percier (1764-1838) and Pierre Fontaine (1762-1853) had both studied at the Academy in Rome between 1785 and 1789. In the early 1790s Fontaine was working as an obscure designer in London. In 1794 he returned to France to become Percier's partner in designing scenery for the Opéra. Thus began an association which was to last until 1814, uniting the efforts of a gifted designer, Percier, with the talents of an administrator and engineer, Fontaine. They were becoming known as fashionable interior decorators in Paris before the decade was out. Under their direction, L. M. Berthault, Percier's pupil, carried out designs in the Greek style for the bedroom of Madame Récamier. Immediately after this they remodeled Malmaison for the future Empress Josephine (1799). A summary of their work appeared under the title of *Recueil de décorations intérieures* (first published in 1801; 2nd edition, 1812). The illustrations in the *Recueil* and in Hope's *Household Furniture* have much in common. Hope wrote that he hoped his own book might compare favorably "with that publication which at present appears in Paris on a similar subject, described by an artist of my acquaintance, Percier . . ."

Among the new forms of the 1790s in France and England was a chair of flowing lines suggested by the Greek *klismos,* as seen on ancient vase paintings and grave monuments. A continuous line unites the seat rail and uprights, and flows into the incurved ("saber") leg. Chairs following the Greek original have a wide top rail projecting beyond the uprights, and those based on Egyptian lines have a rolled-over back. Next to the klismos in importance was the curule chair with a cross-base support suggested by the seat of the Roman magistrate. During the same period, an upswinging line ending in a roll was given to the arms of the sofa. Tables appeared with supports in the form of monopodia — the ancient design with an animal leg surmounted by an animal head, generally in a lion form.

Decoration consisted mainly of reeding, metal inlay, and ormolu mounts; the latter were in the form of wreaths, trophies, classic deities, griffins, swans, and medallions. Large plain surfaces became fashionable after Percier and Fontaine introduced furniture of this type at Malmaison in 1799, and ormolu mounts added both an effective decoration in relief and a practical one, for carving was costly by comparison.

Egyptian motifs had already been used on Louis XVI furniture and on pieces designed by Henry Holland, but they came into renewed favor following Napoleon's Egyptian campaign (1798-1802). Baron Vivant-Denon was on Napoleon's staff of archaeologists, and his book *Voyage dans la Basse et Haute Egypte,* published in 1802, supplied furniture designers with useful new source material. The winged figure, the sphinx, the animal foreleg, and various combinations of human and animal forms on furniture of cubical lines were inspired by Egyptian design.

The Directoire style flowed into Empire without a break. When Napoleon was crowned emperor in 1804 he made Percier and Fontaine his official architects and decorators. All the elements implicit in the earlier style were amplified to express the concept of imperial grandeur. A seat with a gondola back was introduced, suggesting an ancient throne. Case pieces became heavier and rested directly on the floor. The Empire bed had head and foot boards of equal height and was of much heavier construction than the Roman original shown in Pompeian wall paintings. Sometimes it had voluted ends and sometimes it curved in gondola line to become the "sleigh" bed. The lion's paw, and winged lion's paw, which appeared as supports on furniture of state soon supported console tables and sofas in the fashionable interior.

EUROPE: 1820-1830. The inevitable demand for something new resulted, after 1815, in changes within the classic framework. These are seen in increased scale of furniture, and heavier ornament, rather than in anything fundamentally new. Changes in fashions can be traced in two serial publications, Ackermann's *Repository of the Arts* in England and the Mésangère *Album* in France. As both included handsomely engraved plates of fashionable furniture, they constitute the best year-by-year record. Among English design books used at the time were George Smith's *Guide* (1826) and the *Complete Decorator* of the brothers Nicholson (1828). Heavy twist turning is characteristic of the period. A large, cone-shaped foot, based on a Roman type, was used on sofas. Columns at the sides of case pieces, supporting a projecting top, are seen repeatedly. The winged lion's-paw foot, exaggerated cornucopia arm, and heavy spirals are everywhere in evidence.

In the Regency period in England, Gothic and Oriental sources were explored as a phase of the cult of the picturesque. This was the period of the castellated mansion, the Indian villa, and the *cottage orné* among country houses. The most famous example of the Oriental style is the Brighton Pavilion, which was remodeled for the Prince of Wales in 1815 by John Nash with interior decoration by Frederick Crace. This aspect of the Regency style did not affect America until the Victorian period.

TERMINOLOGY OF AMERICAN STYLES. Furniture styles in America are usually identified by a mixture of English and French names. This is admittedly not satisfactory but since they are familiar they are used here:

Hepplewhite, 1790-1810.

Sheraton, 1800-1810.

Empire, 1810-1820.

    Late Sheraton, 1815-1820, as an aspect of Empire.

    Late Empire, 1820-1830.

The dates are, of course, approximate. Adam, as a style name, is seldom used, because the first expression of classical influence came to America in interpretations of the Adam style by Hepplewhite and Sheraton. Hepplewhite furniture is characterized by straight, tapering legs square in section; emphasis on inlay; serpentine lines; Adamesque urn finials; the flaring bracket foot on chests of drawers. Chairs have shield-shaped, heart-shaped, or oval backs.

Sheraton furniture has the tapering reeded leg; square backs on chairs and sofas; convex ends on case pieces; projecting sections and projecting colonnettes. Hepplewhite and Sheraton characteristics are often intermingled, even at their source in the design books.

Empire is represented by the klismos chair with incurved leg (known as early as the Directoire period in France); the curule chair; the rolled back, or else projecting top rails, on chairs; winged and caryatid supports; upswinging arms on sofas; lion's-paw foot; Egyptian dog's-paw foot; lyre splats and supports. Gondola lines are seen in the "sleigh" bed.

Late Sheraton is, broadly speaking, Empire, but expresses a shade of difference. With emphasis on twist turning and spiral arms, it stands between Empire and late Empire. While the source may be traced to Sheraton's later designs, it is a mistake to associate his name with only two phases of the classical period, early and late. As already noted, he was the first to publish designs in the Regency style (synonymous with Empire where England is concerned).

Late Empire introduces nothing new. The twist turning, which was widely used in the Regency period, became heavier, and forms in general were more massive. The lion's-paw foot and winged lion's paw, heavy spirals, heavy pedestals on tables, are characteristic. Late Empire has a successor in the Victorian period, which is called Victorian classical later in this book.

There are other style names for this period which have much to commend them on occasion. The most important of these is Federal, a name which has significance in suggesting the presence of American characteristics in furniture made during the first years of our Federal government. Added justification is given to the name by the fact that the style period coincides approximately with the existence of the Federal party (ending with the administration of John Quincy Adams, 1824-1828). American furniture of the Federal period has its own character, being simple in contrast to the more sophisticated European work. Federal may be used appropriately for American furniture in the Hepplewhite and Sheraton styles, 1790-1810, and for the early work of Duncan Phyfe, but since the name in itself gives no hint of design sources, the French and English names are used here. However, on the chart preceding the illustrations, the Federal period is shown as a chronological framework for the familiar style names.

Another justifiable term is Phyfe style, for Duncan Phyfe worked in so individual a manner, and inspired so many imitators, that he may rightly be credited with evolving a style of his own. Tables with vase pedestals and tripod supports, "cloverleaf" table tops, paw feet, the "saber" leg, curule supports, the carved waterleaf, and thunderbolts, the lyre or cornucopia in splats of chairs are some of the characteristics of the Phyfe style.

In specific instances other terms such as Adam, Directoire, and Regency can be useful in bringing out the design source of a particular piece of furniture. Some students would even have us use Regency far more frequently in describing American work. Nancy McClelland's book on Duncan Phyfe published in 1939 associates Phyfe's work closely with Regency, and there is justification for this, since American work is closer to English work than to French, except in the case of Lannuier. There seems, however, insufficient reason for making a drastic change in accepted terminology since from the 1790s France enjoyed the dominant role as the leader of fashion, so that Empire, even in relation to American work, is a logical term.

AMERICA: 1790-1810. While the new "classic" furniture styles were being introduced to America in the late 1700s, the Chippendale influence remained strong. Hepplewhite inlay was added to already familiar forms (No. 465), and the flaring bracket foot typical of Hepplewhite was used on case pieces with a Chippendale broken-scrolled pediment (No. 486). Chair-backs gradually became shield-shaped and narrower, the projecting "ears" on the cresting rail were dropped, and finally the central design was separated from the seat rail. The so-called "transition chair" represents the beginning of this process (No. 422). Pure Chippendale forms were made even after 1800, such as the sofa of 1812 by Adam S. Coe of Providence which is at the Winterthur Museum.

After the Revolution, American contact with Europe was renewed, and emigration brought English, Scottish, and Irish cabinetmakers to New York, Philadelphia, and Baltimore. Some of them were already working in the new styles. *The Cabinet-Maker's London Book of Prices* (1788), which contained Thomas Shearer's plates of sideboards, and the London price book for 1793, both of which showed the Adam straight-leg style, were soon in circulation, in addition to Hepplewhite's *Guide* and Sheraton's *Drawing-Book*.

Of the old forms, the highboy and lowboy disappeared, but the chest-on-chest was seen once more in two resplendent examples, the Lemon-McIntire chest-on-chest of the Karolik collection (No. 471), and the very similar Badlam-Skillin example in the Garvan Collection at the Yale University Art Gallery. Both pieces combine Chippendale and Adam design in the spirit of Hepplewhite.

A fashionable new piece designed for the parlor was the semicircular commode (No. 470). In New England a Sheraton dressing chest of drawers with attached mirror (No. 472) was a new form. This was the forerunner of the Victorian bureau. A fitted dressing chest with hinged, box lid was occasionally made (No. 571). The chest of drawers with projecting small columns at the sides (No. 469) and a swell front was a popular Sheraton form.

The tambour desk (No. 490) to some extent replaced the slope-front type, and secretaries frequently had cylinder closings (No. 494). A breakfront bookcase or cabinet with a writing compartment, called a "Salem secretary," was a specialty in New England (No. 415). The breakfront construction, although never common, was used more frequently now than in the Chippendale period.

Chairmakers displayed an almost equal preference for Hepplewhite shield- and heart-back forms (Nos. 424 and 430) and Sheraton square-back designs (No. 441). Occasionally seen were painted oval-back chairs (No. 436), which belonged in the most luxurious class of furnishings.

The most important new furniture form of the period was the sideboard. As a rule, the term Hepplewhite is given to the sideboard with square or concave ends, a recessed center, and square, tapering legs (No. 510), while Sheraton is reserved for the convex-end or kidney-shaped sideboard with turned, reeded legs (No. 517). Many sideboards combine characteristics of both styles (Nos. 512, 521). In Baltimore and the South the huntboard was a regional type; it is a high sideboard table with shallow body (No. 580).

Among tables, the work table (No. 592) was new. This was designed with the varied requirements of the needleworker in mind, and was sometimes equipped with a pouch of some fine fabric attached to a sliding frame under the lower drawer. The pembroke table (No. 576) was made in greater numbers than in the Chippendale period. It had rounded leaves, and opened to an oval top. Side tables in Sheraton style were sometimes made with rounded ends and projecting centers (No. 581), or they were semicircular in the Hepplewhite style (No. 583).

The sectional dining table was a great rarity in the Chippendale period, but now it was commonly used. It was made either in two sections, each with a circular end and drop-leaf (No. 565), or in three sections including a center dropleaf table and a pair of semicircular tables (No. 567). The latter could be used as side tables when the full extension was not required for dining.

Looking glasses in the Hepplewhite style were pedimented and ornamented with urn and floral sprays (No. 500). Sheraton examples (No. 503) had a flat top and a painted glass panel showing a landscape or some other ornamental design under a cornice adorned with balls.

An original American design appeared among the clocks of the period. This was the banjo clock, which Simon Willard patented in 1802 (No. 479).

Although foreign influence came chiefly from England, rare examples based directly on the Louis XVI style are seen in the Philadelphia chairs and matching sofa illustrated in Nos. 420 and 526.

AMERICA: 1810-1820. The changes in American furniture design[49] which reflected the Directoire and Empire influence transmitted, as a rule, by English Regency were first seen in New York. The new developments had relatively little effect on the popularity of Hepplewhite and Sheraton in Boston, Salem, Philadelphia and Baltimore.

In 1795, when Duncan Phyfe established himself on Partition Street, New York, he was working in the Hepplewhite and Sheraton styles. A few years later he turned to new fashions, which he may have found in Sheraton's *Cabinet Dictionary* (1803), the first published examples of Regency designs. Among these were the klismos or Greek chair and other classic forms based on the French Directoire style. By 1807 Phyfe was using the saber leg on chairs made for William Bayard of New York, now at the Winterthur Museum. Then came his adoption of the klismos chair, with the continuous line of back and seat rail flowing into the incurved leg. This became a popular form with many makers working in the Phyfe style (No. 452). The Roman curule or cross-base chair (No 454) and Grecian couch with scrolled arm and low foot (No. 533) also represent the Empire style in America around 1810. To about the same period belong the chairs with lyre splat (No. 453), and structural forms such as the Egyptian animal foreleg and paw foot, to which Phyfe gave special distinction (No. 412).

Phyfe had many imitators, and to distinguish his work from that of an able rival is difficult. Occasionally a piece which has many indications of Phyfe's work supplies evidence that it is by another maker (No. 559).

A direct link with the French Louis XVI and Empire styles is seen in the work of the French-born Charles-Honoré Lannuier. It was formerly thought that he arrived in America in the 1790s and so could not have been familiar with the developing Empire style, but it is now known that he did not arrive until 1803, which would have allowed him to observe the work of Percier and Fontaine before his departure. The year of his arrival was first published in "Lannuier in the President's House" by Lorraine Waxman Pearce, *Antiques,* January 1962, where his labeled *guéridon,* a unique example in American work, is illustrated. In Lannuier's furniture for the Van Rensselaer family there are striking Empire examples (Nos. 410, 560, 585), while his early work in the Louis XVI style is handsomely represented at Winterthur. His training and versatility were of a high order, but his influence was cut short by his early death in 1819.

While Empire and Regency influences transformed a great amount of American furniture, basic Sheraton forms were also continued in this period. The dressing chest of drawers with attached mirror was becoming a well-established type in New England (Nos. 473-475). The sideboard in both Sheraton and Empire forms had gradually deepening cupboards which approached the floor (Nos. 524, 525).

Gradually a new amplitude of form became apparent, as in the heavier reeding on the turned leg (No. 594) and the larger type of vase pedestal (No. 595).

**VI.** Among the choice examples of New England Hepplewhite and Sheraton furniture in the drawing room of this New York apartment is a sofa with carving attributed to Samuel McIntire. *(Mrs. Giles Whiting.)*

199

*The Dinner Party.* By Henry Sargent (1770-1845). *(Museum of Fine Arts, Boston.)*

In this dining room of the Federal period is a Sheraton sideboard with reeded legs and recessed front. The Hepplewhite extension table has been lengthened by dropleaf end sections. The cellaret at the left has a hinged top showing that it was for storage of bottles and not a wine cistern like No. 419.

Detail of Hepplewhite shield-back chair with carving attributed to Samuel McIntire of Salem, 1790-1800. *(Henry Ford Museum.)*

*Above left:* Detail of Sheraton arm-chair, No. 439. *(Karolik Collection, Museum of Fine Arts, Boston.)*

*Left:* Detail of Salem Hepplewhite sofa with grape carving attributed to Mc-Intire, 1790-1800. *(Karolik Collection, Museum of Fine Arts, Boston.)*

*Lady with a Harp, a portrait of Eliza Ridgely.* By Thomas Sully (1783-1872). *(National Gallery of Art. Gift of Maud M. Vetlesen.)*

Costume in the Greek style was worn at the time Empire furniture was in fashion. The music stool, which is almost concealed by Miss Ridgely's draperies, has a heavy classical column on a quadrangular base supported by paw feet. This was painted about 1818 when furniture forms were becoming heavier.

201

**VII.** The Red Room at the White House is an Empire parlor, with furniture by Lannuier (see No. 589), and sofas which belonged to Nellie Custis and Dolly Madison. *(Courtesy of The White House.)*

202

AMERICA: 1820-1830. In all the previous periods, American styles were generally from ten to twenty years behind European fashions but in the 1820s new publications reached America almost immediately, and the change was quickly apparent. American furniture after 1820 has the heavier forms currently in style in England and France. Large columns, as shown in Smith's *Guide,* were now used at the sides of case pieces (No. 498) or became supports on tables (No. 563). The winged lion's-paw foot was frequently used on sofas. A variant of this motif, in which a leafy bracket replaces the wing, is seen in No. 537. The bulbous turned foot, evolved from a Roman form, had been introduced by 1820 (No. 413). Pronounced spirals are conspicuous (No. 561). The pedestal support became still heavier (No. 569). Stenciling, first introduced about 1815, was often used in place of metal mounts and was handled so effectively that it became an attractive element in American furniture decoration (No. 536). Graining was also skillfully executed (No. 563).

The "fancy" chair was advertised in New York as early as 1796. This was a Sheraton chair of light construction with painted or japanned decoration. Many examples survive from the early nineteenth century (Nos. 459 and 460). Eventually it had a pleasing interpretation, through mass production, in the Hitchcock chair (No. 461). This, with its stencil decoration of flower and fruit designs, was known all over the country and was made not only by Lambert Hitchcock at Hitchcocksville, Connecticut, but in other parts of New England, in New York, and elsewhere.

There is a suggestion of the coming rococo revival in the curving line of the sofa, No. 538, made about 1825. However, the classical influence is still dominant here, and remains so in furniture design throughout the 1820s.

REGIONAL TRAITS. Local characteristics became less pronounced in the classical period, due to improvements in travel and communications. Nevertheless, distinctions are still to be seen. New England furniture continued to display slender lines and a general delicacy of form. Reeded legs were perilously frail (No. 494). A light cross-stretcher was retained as a support for the tapering leg of the Hepplewhite chair (No. 425). This detail was not generally seen in examples from New York and Philadelphia. Contrast of light and dark tones in finely patterned satin-wood or bird's-eye maple with banding of mahogany is seen on New England pieces (No. 493). The bowfront chest of drawers (No. 466) was frequently made, and the heart-shaped back was often used on Hepplewhite chairs (No. 430). The Martha Washington chair, known by this name at the time, was a New England type (No. 438). Salem chairs of shield-back form often had a large urn in the splat joined to the outside of the shield by slender swags of carved drapery (No. 426), and the rear legs were designed with an inward curve near the base. Sheraton dressing chests with attached mirrors (No. 472) and "Salem secretaries" (No. 415) are New England types from the Boston-Salem area.

Rhode Island chairs of the Chippendale-Hepplewhite transition period (No. 433) have the *kylix* in the splat instead of the usual urn. The kylix is the Greek tazza-like dish which Adam often used as a motif for a tablet on a frieze. It was seldom used in America outside Rhode Island, except in Salem, where Samuel McIntire left a drawing of it and also tangible evidence in a chair which is now in the Karolik Collection. Newport Hepplewhite card tables have a tapering geometric inlay on the leg surmounted by small rectangular panels called book or tambour inlay (No. 549).

So many New York sideboards have inlaid quarter-fans (No. 510) that this detail has become associated with New York. However, it was used elsewhere, particularly in New Jersey (No. 511). New York Hepplewhite chairs frequently have a drapery motif with Prince-of-Wales feathers, but this also occasionally appears in New England examples (No. 425) and in Charleston work (No. 424).

Philadelphia's typical rendering of the urn-and-drapery-motif is found on the Sheraton square-backed chair (No. 442). Round-ended sideboards were also frequently made (Nos. 516 and 517).

The prosperity of Baltimore after the Revolution fostered the development of a regional style of cabinetmaking. Inlay of large ovals in mitred panels is typical of Baltimore (No. 513). Light-toned panels inset on tapering legs served as a background for a characteristic husk motif of such flower-like form that it is appropriately called the bellflower. Each petal is distinctly de-lineated, and the central one is the longest (No. 553). The use of *églomisé* glass panels with allegorical figures is found only in Baltimore furniture (No. 489).

Not enough is known of Charleston cabinetmaking to permit much characterization, but it is a safe conclusion that a considerable quantity of fine Hepplewhite and Sheraton furniture was made there. High-post beds with reeded foot posts were carved with a distinctive wheat-ear which is called "rice carving," and indeed the resemblance to rice is striking. Sideboards from the Charleston area are of six-legged type with D-shaped ends and inlaid ovals reminiscent of Baltimore (No. 515). A drapery-back chair with a long Charleston history (No. 424) shows close affinities with New York design, which may be explained by the large amount of New York furniture which was sent there.

FEDERAL AMERICA. The America which La Rochefoucauld-Liancourt visited in the 1790s and described in considerable detail[50] was energetically occupied in becoming a nation. Writings of foreign travelers are often consulted today because they offer the best first-hand accounts of life in America in the first decades following the Revolution. Awaiting better times in France, La Rochefoucauld came to America and traveled extensively along the Eastern seaboard. He de-scribes a ball in Philadelphia which was as elegant as any he had seen in Europe; notes, with-out condescension, the incredible manner in which strangers shared accommodations at an inn; and observes with interest methods of rice culture in South Carolina and the whaling industry in New Bedford.

Pavel P. Svinin's *Picturesque United States* gives a lively impression of life at the or-dinary level. Svinin, a young Russian artist of noble birth, pupil of the Academy of Fine Arts in St. Petersburg, was secretary to the consul-general in Philadelphia. The drawings in his book are possibly the earliest extensive group of American genre subjects. Svinin has portrayed dancers at an inn, passengers on a ferry boat, a Quaker family going to meeting, the patrons of an oyster seller near the Chestnut Street Theatre — all with a wealth of fascinating detail regarding architecture, interiors, dress, and customs.

In 1818, Baron Axel Klinkowström, a Swedish naval officer, wrote thoughtfully of Ameri-can ways and compared our manners, customs, and conduct of business with those he had known in Europe. Occasionally Klinkowström gives a glimpse of domestic life, as at the home of Mr. du Pont de Nemours in Delaware, or of an official occasion, such as Mrs. Monroe's re-ception at the President's House in Washington, where "the drawing rooms are not elegant but suitably and tastefully furnished." He also wrote of the luxurious conditions of travel on a Hudson River steamboat, with its red satin draperies, mahogany paneling, and well-carpeted floors and stairs.

204

HOMES OF THE FEDERAL PERIOD. The boxlike house of the late 1700s and early 1800s can be seen today in hundreds of New England towns. Sometimes it has an eaves balustrade, almost always it has an elliptical fanlight over the entrance, and perhaps a delicately designed Palladian window above.

Many historic houses of the period are open to the public. Among those in New England are the Moffatt-Ladd and Governor John Langdon houses in Portsmouth, New Hampshire; the Pingree and Peirce-Nichols houses (representing the work of Samuel McIntire) in Salem, Massachusetts; and the Harrison Gray Otis house in Boston, which is now the headquarters for the Society for the Preservation of New England Antiquities.

In Philadelphia's Fairmount Park there are Sweetbrier and Strawberry, representing the architecture of the 1790s, and in the Georgetown section of Washington, D.C., there is Dumbarton House which, although the exterior is Georgian (it was begun soon after the mid-eighteenth century), has classical interiors finished in 1805.

Design books and builder's guides such as those by W. and J. Pain, which were owned by Samuel McIntire, were mostly English. However, in 1797, Asher Benjamin (c. 1772-1845) published the *Country Builder's Assistant* in his native Greenfield, Massachusetts. This was the first truly American builder's guide, for John Norman's work, published in Philadelphia, though of earlier date, was simply a combination of material gathered from English sources. Benjamin had the definite purpose of adapting English styles for American use, and the result was of immeasurable help to the local carpenter. In the preface to one of his later works, the *American Builder's Companion,* he wrote that only one-third of a European guide was useful in America because of the difference in materials and also because American people had less money to spend on building. His designs were aimed at reducing costs and providing the builder with good basic plans and practical ornamental detail. Fortunately Benjamin made a tasteful selection of classic ornament and managed not to distort it in his process of simplification. He respected purity of form and noted that "attempts which have sometimes been made to compose fancy orders only spoiled the work." Benjamin eventually published seven guides, which went through forty-five editions. These presented the Adam style, then the Greek Revival, and kept up to date with other nineteenth-century developments.

While Benjamin was not the first American architect to be aware of the Adam style, he was first to make it widely known in this country. His own familiarity with it came through his contact with Charles Bulfinch, the Boston architect. Bulfinch went to England for two years, 1785-1787, and on his return built houses for Joseph Barrell and Thomas Russell in Charlestown. The work of Bulfinch exerted great influence on three gifted architects, Samuel McIntire in Salem, Alexander Parris of Boston (who worked in Portland, Maine), and Asher Benjamin in the Connecticut River Valley.

Furniture in the Hepplewhite and Sheraton styles and early examples of Empire were made for these new houses. Light forms and clean-cut lines were well adapted to the architecture of the interiors, which had delicate friezes, reeded pilasters, and ceilings with plaster work in the Adam style.

By the time the first wave of Empire influence had spent itself and the new heavier furniture began to be made, most American architects were working in the Greek Revival style. The change, heralded by Latrobe's Bank of Pennsylvania in 1798 (the first Greek Revival building in America) was apparent in domestic architecture in the second decade of the nineteenth century. The new fashion is to be seen in the Regency-style interiors of the Wickham-Valentine

205

house in Richmond, Virginia. Here the oval hall, the use of the Doric order, narrow moldings, and delicately gilded friezes probably represent the work of Robert Mills. In William Jay's houses in Savannah, Georgia, Adam details are amplified and used with new vigor. A fully-developed Greek Revival style, attributed to Minard Lafever, is to be seen at Bartow Mansion at Pelham Bay, New York. The cornices over the windows of this house are finished with acroteria, and a large-scale anthemion decorates the door frames. For such houses as these, the furniture of the Empire and late Empire periods was eminently suited.

# Makers

*Lemuel Adams* (active by 1792), Hartford, Connecticut. Adams was in partnership with Samuel Kneeland from 1792 to 1795. In 1796 he was paid for chairs, desks, and other furniture for the State House which was completed that year. In 1798 he advertised cherry furniture in the *Connecticut Courant.* (No. 427.)

*Adams and Todd,* Cambridge Street, Boston. Samuel Adams of Southacks Street and William Todd of Hingham had a brief partnership. They were listed in the directory in 1798. Todd died in 1800. A labeled card table (No. 548) shows expert workmanship in the Sheraton style.

*John Aitken* (active by 1775), Philadelphia; born in Scotland. He is well known for the desk he made for George Washington in 1797, now at Mount Vernon, and a set of Sheraton chairs represented by No. 449.

*Michael Allison* (active 1800-1845), New York. This cabinetmaker worked in Hepplewhite, Sheraton, and Empire styles. His work is comparable to that of Duncan Phyfe. (No. 559.)

*Elbert Anderson* (active 1789-1800), New York. He is possibly the maker of truncated shield-back chairs shown represented by No. 428. The labeled sideboard (No. 510) indicates a superior cabinetmaker.

*Nathaniel Appleton, Sr.* (active by 1803), Salem. Appleton's name appears in shipping lists of 1803 as an exporter of furniture. His work has occasionally been attributed to McIntire. A Hepplewhite secretary at the Essex Institute, Salem, is by this maker.

*Stephen Badlam* (1751-1815), of Dorchester, Massachusetts, worked for Elias Hasket Derby of Salem. Original bills are in the Derby papers at the Essex Institute. His chest-on-chest, with carving by Simeon and John Skillin (in the Garvan Collection), was made for Derby. Shield-back chairs in the Hepplewhite style, stamped or burned *S. Badlam,* are represented by No. 423.

*John Budd* (active 1817-1840), New York. His label states that he exported furniture to the South. His card table (No. 497) shows influence of Duncan Phyfe.

*Aaron Chapin* (1753-1838), of Hartford, was the second cousin of Eliphalet Chapin and worked with him at East Windsor, Connecticut, making pieces in the Chippendale style. After moving to Hartford in 1783, he did work that displays modification of the Hepplewhite style (No. 486). A documented Hepplewhite sideboard that he made for the Robbins family is shown in No. 512.

*Silas E. Cheney* (active 1799-1821), Litchfield, Connecticut. Hepplewhite sideboards by this maker have been identified from account books.

*Adam S. Coe* (1782-1862), Newport. An inscribed sofa that he made in 1812 is at the Winterthur Museum (No. 276, Downs, *American Furniture*). Coe was in partnership with Gideon Palmer about 1800.

*Henry Connelly* (1770-1826), of Philadelphia worked in Sheraton and Empire styles and made furniture for Stephen Girard after 1811. His work was compared with that of Ephraim Haines in the 1953 loan exhibition at the Philadelphia Museum. He is represented by the labeled kidney-shaped sideboard in No. 517 and the chair in No. 442.

*John Doggett* (1780-1857), of Roxbury, Massachusetts, was a cabinetmaker, carver, and gilder. He owned a furniture factory which employed many cabinetmakers, carvers, and decorative painters.

*John T. Dolan,* New York, is listed in the directory in 1811 and known for work in the Phyfe style. A labeled table is shown in No. 557.

*Matthew Egerton, Sr.* (died 1802), New Brunswick, New Jersey. Hepplewhite and Sheraton case pieces, especially sideboards, were his speciality.

*Matthew Egerton, Jr.,* worked at first with his father, but owned his own shop about 1785. He died in 1837. The sideboard in No. 511 has his label.

*John and Hugh Finlay* (active 1799-1833), Baltimore; specialists in painted furniture. Their Irish origin is noted by R. L. Raley in "Irish Influences in Baltimore Decorative Arts," *Antiques,* March 1961, while in an earlier article, "Interior Designs by Benjamin Henry Latrobe for the President's House," the same author shows that "a Mr. Finlay," probably John or Hugh, executed Latrobe's designs for President James Madison. These makers were also listed in the directories as Findlay and Finley. (No. 532.)

*Stephen Goddard* (1764-1804) and *Thomas Goddard* (1765-1858), Newport. These were the sons of John Goddard. A labeled piece by them, a half-round card table, is at Metropolitan Museum.

*John Gruez* (advertised 1819), of New York, was the successor to Lannuier, the chief exponent of the Louis XVI and Empire styles.

*Ephraim Haines* (1775 to after 1811), of Philadelphia, was apprenticed to Daniel Trotter, and in 1799 became his son-in-law and partner. He worked for Stephen Girard until 1811, after which he opened a mahogany yard. His work was in the 1953 Connelly-Haines exhibition at the Philadelphia Museum. Examples are shown in Nos. 445 and 516.

*Lambert Hitchcock* (1795-1852), of Hitchcocksville, Connecticut, established his chair factory in 1825, and mass-produced Sheraton "fancy" chairs with stenciled designs (No. 461). Partnership with Alford began in 1829, and in 1843, Hitchock founded a factory in Unionville, Connecticut. The "Hitchcock" chair was made in other parts of New England, and also in New York, Ohio, and elsewhere.

*William Hook* (1777-1867), of Salem, worked for Edmund Johnson and Jacob Sanderson. The dressing chest of drawers shown in No. 475 is attributed to Hook.

*Edmund Johnson* (active 1793-1811), of Salem, made fine furniture for export. A labeled Salem secretary is shown in No. 415.

*Kneeland and Adams* (in partnership 1792-1795), Hartford, Connecticut. The label of the firm of Samuel Kneeland and Lemuel Adams is in a Chippendale serpentine chest of drawers at the Winterthur Museum. These makers are best known for furniture for the Connecticut State House made in 1796, chiefly by Adams (see No. 427).

*Charles-Honoré Lannuier* (1779-1819), New York, arrived from France in 1803 and advertised in the *New-York Evening Post,* July 15. He is listed in the directory in 1805. The chairs he made in 1812 for the Common Council Room of New York's City Hall no longer exist. Furniture that he made for the Van Rensselaer family is shown in Nos. 410, 560, 585. The sofa table (No. 589) at the White House is attributed. Lannuier worked in the Louis XVI and Empire styles, making use of fine ormolu mounts and carving and gilding. See Lorraine Waxman, "The Lannuier Brothers, Cabinetmakers," *Antiques,* August 1957; and Lorraine Waxman Pearce, "Lannuier in the President's House," *Antiques,* January 1962.

*William Lemon* (active 1796), Salem. McIntire billed Elias Hasket Derby for the chest-on-chest illustrated in No. 471 as a "case Drawers made by Mr. Lemon." Although little known, this craftsman did excellent work.

*Samuel McIntire* (1757-1811) was Salem's leading architect and carver. He is known as the architect of the Pingree and Peirce-Nichols houses and for his carving on furniture for the Derby family and other leading Salem merchants. His carving, which appears on furniture by other makers, is distinguished by individual motifs including a basket (or bowl) of fruit, cluster of grapes, cornucopia, wheat sheaf, and alternating flutes and rosettes. A matted background formed with a star-shaped punch was used by McIntire but also by other Salem carvers. He was succeeded by his son, *Samuel Field McIntire* (1780-1819). See Dean A. Fales, Jr., "McIntire Furniture," from *Samuel McIntire, A Bicentennial Symposium,* Essex Institute, Salem, 1957. Known work is represented by No. 471 and attributions by Nos. 426, 444, 528, 540.

*Mills and Deming,* of New York (listed in the directory 1793-1798), are known for an elaborately inlaid labeled sideboard for Governor Oliver Wolcott of Connecticut. Their work in the Sheraton style is comparable to the early work of Phyfe. A labeled tambour secretary was No. 85 in the exhibition, "Furniture by New York Cabinetmakers," Museum of the City of New York, 1956-1957.

*Duncan Phyfe* (1768-1854) came to America from Scotland in 1783 or 1784. He settled in Albany but was listed in the New York directory in 1792. In 1795 he moved to Partition Street (later called Fulton Street), where he maintained the most fashionable cabinetmaking shop in New York. As he did not retire until 1847, his work represents all phases of the classical style, from Hepplewhite and Sheraton to Empire and Victorian. His "cloverleaf" tables with vase pedestals and brass paw feet, and chairs and sofas with incurved or "saber" legs and reeded frames, are so distinctive as to represent a style of their own. The Phyfe style was copied so closely by others that identification is often difficult. Allison's marked card table (No. 559), if not thus identified, could well be attributed to Phyfe on stylistic grounds. Known works are seen in Nos. 412, 413, 451, 453, 454, 491. The following are attributed: Nos. 406, 509, 525, 533, 534, 558, 570, 591.

*David Poignand* (active 1788), Boston. He came from St. Helier, on the Isle of Jersey and later moved to Kentucky. A secretary dated *1788* and other pieces (Nos. 364, 541) are in the City Art Museum, St. Louis.

*Thomas Renshaw* of Baltimore (listed in the directory, 1814-1815) was the maker (with John Barnhart) of a labeled settee in the Baltimore Museum of Art which is accompanied by a pair of matching "fancy" chairs represented by No. 458.

*Elijah Sanderson* (1752-1825) and *Jacob Sanderson* (1758-1810), Salem. These brothers worked together between 1779 and 1820. Their shop employed many workmen, and furniture was made for export. A Sheraton bed at the Pingree house, Salem, is by Jacob Sanderson. See Mabel M. Swan, *Samuel McIntire, Carver, and The Sandersons* (1934).

*John Seymour* (about 1738-1818), Boston. He arrived in 1785 in Portland, Maine, from Axminster, Devonshire, England, accompanied by his family, including a son, *Thomas,* who worked with him. Seymour was already a highly trained cabinetmaker. The family moved to Boston about 1794, and he and his son worked as cabinetmakers in Creek Lane until 1803. In

1804 Thomas opened the Boston Furniture Warehouse, where the two continued in association. John Seymour was probably active until 1816. No distinction can be made between the work of father and son. Their furniture is characterized by excellent craftsmanship, fine dovetailing, the use of patterned satinwood and bird's-eye maple veneers, inlaid tambour shutters, ivory key escutcheons, and "Seymour blue" (a greenish blue) on interiors. There are only four labeled or documented works but over two hundred attributions have been made on the basis of style.[51] *John and Thomas Seymour* by Vernon C. Stoneman (1959), the major work on these makers, is copiously illustrated. No. 470 is a documented example and No. 490 seems undoubtedly to be their work. Other attributions include Nos. 416, 419, 472, 473, 518, 520, 522, 543, 544, 556, 592.

*Thomas Seymour* (1771-1848), Boston. See *John Seymour*. Thomas was listed as a cabinetmaker until 1826. He worked with James Cogswell, son of John Cogswell, from about 1809 until 1812; he also did work for Stephen Badlam. The painter John Ritto Penniman was employed by Thomas Seymour to decorate the commode, No. 470.

*John Shaw* (1745-1829) of Annapolis, Maryland, was born in Glasgow and came to the Colonies at an unknown date as a trained craftsman. He made furniture for the House of Delegates, later the State House, but is best known for Hepplewhite case pieces with pierced, scrolled pediments and shallow sideboards inlaid with ovals and conch shells. (No. 514.)

*Joseph Short* (1771-1819), Newburyport, Massachusetts. His label states that he made "Martha Washington chairs." These were in the Hepplewhite style.

*Slover and Taylor,* New York (in partnership 1802-1804). A half-daisy carved on the panel of the cresting rail of Sheraton chairs and sofas (No. 530) is associated with this firm. They were formerly miscalled Stover and Taylor. The discovery of the correct name was reported by Phelps Warren in "Setting the Record Straight," *Antiques,* October 1961.

*Stitcher and Clemmens,* Baltimore, are listed in the directory, 1804. A labeled Hepplewhite secretary inlaid with simulated fretwork, made by these cabinetmakers, was No. 76 in the Baltimore Furniture Loan Exhibition of 1947. On the basis of this, the case of a tall clock (No. 481) has been tentatively attributed to them.

*John Townsend* (1732-1809), Newport. Although known chiefly for work in blockfront-and-shell construction (No. 298), he also made pieces in the Hepplewhite style. Of two card tables with his label in the 1953 loan exhibition of Newport furniture, one is illustrated in No. 549.

*Holmes Weaver* (1769-1848), Newport, worked in the Hepplewhite style. Several labeled pieces have borders of crossbanded veneer, as seen on the labeled card table illustrated in Carpenter's *Arts and Crafts of Newport.*

*William Wilmerding* (active 1785-1794), New York. This looking-glass maker came to New York from Germany in 1783 and opened a store in Maiden Lane about 1785. In 1795 he visited Germany and on his return was listed only as a merchant, so that labeled mirrors can be dated with reasonable certainty before 1795. (No. 499.)

# *Chart:* Classical Period, 1790–1830

**NEW FORMS**

Hepplewhite, Sheraton styles: semicircular commode; dressing chest of drawers with attached mirror; tambour desk; convex mirror; sideboard; sectional dining table; work table.

Empire Style: *klismos* (or Greek) chair; curule chair (Roman) with cross-base; Grecian couch; "sleigh" bed; mirror-back pier table.

Late Empire Style: cornucopia-arm sofa; wardrobe.

**PRINCIPAL WOODS**

Hepplewhite, Sheraton styles: mahogany, satinwood, bird's-eye maple.

Empire style: mahogany, rosewood.

Late Empire style: mahogany, rosewood.

**DECORATIVE TECHNIQUES**

*Early Federal, 1790-1810*

Hepplewhite, Sheraton styles: carving; inlay; *églomisé* panels; painting, japanning, tambour construction, veneering.

*Mid-Federal, 1810-1820*

Empire style: carving; caning; ormolu mounts; painting, gilding, stenciling (c. 1815).

*Late Federal, 1820-1830*

Late Empire style: carving; stenciling; graining.

**DESIGN**

*Early Federal, 1790-1810*

Hepplewhite, Sheraton styles:

Hepplewhite square, tapering leg (No. 431).

Sheraton turned, reeded leg (No. 439).

Chairs: Shield-back (No. 424). Heart-back (No. 430). Oval-back (No. 436). Square-back (No. 441).

Adamesque urn (No. 471).

Bellflower (husk) (No. 554).

Colonnettes on case pieces (No. 523).

Eagle inlay (No. 484).

Feather motif (No. 436).

Wheat-ears (No. 423).

*Mid-Federal, 1810-1820*

Empire Style:

Lyre back (No. 453).

Cross-base (curule) support (No. 454).

Winged supports (No. 587).

"Saber" leg (No. 533).

Dog's-paw foot (No. 412).

Lion's-paw foot (No. 586).

Dolphin foot (No. 587).

Spirally rolled arm (No. 533).

*Late Federal, 1820-1830*

Late Empire Style:

Columns supporting projecting top (No. 498).

Exaggerated cornucopia motif (No. 538).

Heavy vase pedestal (No. 569).

Lion's-paw foot with leaf bracket (No. 537).

## European Background

**LATE 1700s**

*France:* Directoire style (1793-1804) represented by chairs and sofas with flowing curves; tables supported by winged figures and monopodia. Percier and Fontaine design furniture for Malmaison, 1799.

*England:* Regency style has expression in work of Henry Holland (1746-1806), at Carlton House (1784) and Southill (1795); shows influence of Louis XVI and Directoire, also classic sources in drawings which Charles H. Tatham made for him in Rome, 1784-1786.

**PUBLICATIONS**

George Hepplewhite, *Cabinet-Maker and Upholsterer's Guide,* 1788.

*Cabinet-Maker's London Book of Prices,* (with Thomas Shearer's designs for sideboards), 1788.

Thomas Sheraton, *Cabinet-Maker and Upholsterer's Drawing Book,* 1791-1794.

**EARLY 1800s**

*France:* Empire of Napoleon 1804-1813; Percier and Fontaine are Napoleon's official architects; Egyptian designs popularized by Napoleon's campaign on the Nile, 1798-1802.

*England:* Regency of Prince of Wales, 1811-1820; Thomas Hope (1769-1831), amateur architect, designs furniture using altar and candelabrum forms, Greek klismos and Roman curule chairs; favors monopodia support, tripod tables, Egyptian motifs.

**PUBLICATIONS**

Percier and Fontaine, *Recueil de décorations intérieures,* 1st ed., 1801.

Vivant-Denon, *Voyage dans la Basse et Haute Egypte,* 1802.

Sheraton, *Cabinet Dictionary,* 1803.

Hope, *Household Furniture and Interior Decoration,* 1807.

George Smith, *Collection of Designs for Household Furniture,* 1808.

*London Chair-Makers and Carvers' Book of Prices,* 1808.

**SERIALS**

Pierre la Mésangère. *Meubles et objets de goût,* 1802-1830.

Rudolph Ackermann, *Repository of the Arts,* 1809-1829.

**1815-1830**

*France:* Restoration of Bourbon monarchy under Charles X, 1814-1830; Restauration style in furniture marked by massive forms and coarse ornament as illustrated in plates from Mésangère's *Meubles et objets de goût.*

*England:* Reign of George IV, 1820-1830; Gothic revival, with furniture designs by Augustus Charles Pugin and his son, Augustus Welby N. Pugin, architect of Houses of Parliament; Oriental revival, introducing Turkish, Indian, and Chinese designs. The Chinese taste has outstanding representation at Brighton Pavilion, remodeled for the Prince of Wales in 1815 by John Nash, with furniture designed by Frederick Crace.

**PUBLICATIONS**

Henry Moses, *Designs of Modern Costume* (with drawings of furniture in style of Hope), 1823.

George Smith, *Cabinet-Makers and Upholsterers' Guide,* 1826-1828.

Peter and Michael Angelo Nicholson, *The Practical Cabinet-Maker, Upholsterer and Complete Decorator,* 1828.

**407.** Sheraton high-post mahogany bed attributed to Duncan Phyfe (1768-1854) and made probably between 1795 and 1800. The mahogany cornice has a painted floral border in shades of tan and light brown, interrupted by tablets showing eagles holding drapery. The reeding on the foot posts encloses delicately carved wheat-ears. A square leg tapers to a blocked foot. (*Gift of Doctors C. Ray and Winifred Hope Franklin. Museum of the City of New York.*)

**408.** Sheraton mahogany bed with reeded posts and carving attributed to Samuel McIntire (1757-1811). It was made about 1795 for Parker Cleaveland of Rowley, Massachusetts. The design for the festooned canopy and skirt was taken from Hepplewhite's *Guide*, 1788. The printed cotton reproduces a French *toile de Jouy* of classical design, of about 1800 by Oberkampf. (*Harrison Gray Otis House, Boston. Society for the Preservation of New England Antiquities.*)

407

408

**409.** Sheraton high-post bed painted white with gilt ornament. It belonged to Joseph C. Yates (1768-1837), who was quartermaster general under General Philip Schuyler, and later governor of New York. The matching settee and cane-seated chair belong to the same set, and there are two gold and white dressing tables in similar style. American painted furniture of the Hepplewhite-Sheraton period is generally represented by Sheraton "fancy" chairs and decorative cornices. It is rarely seen in such varied and sophisticated forms as here. Green and white striped satin in canopy and hangings adds to the effect. (*Gold and White Room, H. F. du Pont Winterthur Museum.*)

**410.** This Empire mahogany "sleigh bed" with dolphin feet, bearing the label of Charles-Honoré Lannuier (1779-1819), has elaborate ormolu mounts on veneered panels of satinwood. A medallion showing the head of Hypnos (sleep) among poppy sprays, and other mounts in the form of griffins, stars, and river gods, apparently originated in Paris. This use of Parisian mounts may be unique. The bed was part of a set owned by Stephen Van Rensselaer IV and Harriet Elizabeth Bayard, who were married in 1817. It was once in the Van Rensselaer Manor House at Watervliet. The couple moved there after the death of Stephen III, "the Patroon," in 1839. Photographs taken in the 1870s show pieces from the set in the drawing room and bridal room. After Mrs. Van Rensselaer's death in 1875 the house was closed and its furnishings divided among her sons and daughters, whose descendants presented to the Albany Institute the bed, card tables (No. 560), pier tables (No. 585), and two *encoignures*. A work table is now at the Winterthur Museum (No. 492). (*Albany Institute of History and Art.*)

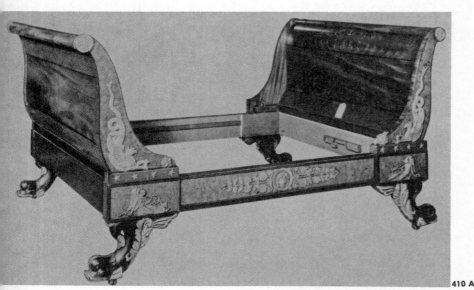

410 A

410 B

409

**411.** The Empire bed was intended for a position along a wall instead of at right angles to it. The tent-like hangings at the side are suspended from a crown. A chair of *klismos* type with rolled back and cornucopia splat has incurved legs ending in dog's-paw feet. The furniture here is from New York; the bed may have been made by Lannuier. (*Empire Bedroom, H.F. du Pont Winterthur Museum.*)

**412.** This Empire mahogany window bench with lyre splat and dog's-paw feet was made possibly about 1810-1815 by Duncan Phyfe. Accompanying it are thirteen chairs from the same set, made by Duncan Phyfe, for William Livingston, governor of New Jersey. The bench has been frequently exhibited and illustrated. It was shown in the Girl Scouts Loan Exhibition in 1929, illustrated in McClelland, *Duncan Phyfe and the English Regency,* and exhibited in "Furniture by New York Cabinet-makers," Museum of the City of New York, 1956-1957. (*Collection of Mrs. Andrew Varick Stout. Photograph: Museum of the City of New York.*)

**413.** Empire window bench, or ottoman, of rosewood, one of a pair signed by Duncan Phyfe. It was made about 1820. Decoration in gold leaf includes the anthemion, rosette, palmette, and spiral acanthus. Corner posts are in the form of acroteria, and the turned feet are based on a Roman type. The red silk damask squab and upholstery over the frame is the original material, bound with gold galloon. This is an interesting early example of the ottoman, which became popular in the Victorian period. It was introduced in the Regency period in England, when Turkish furnishings were fashionable. The name ottoman was given to the form about 1810. (*Gift of Mrs. J. Amory Haskell. Brooklyn Museum.*)

**414.** Hepplewhite inlaid mahogany breakfront bookcase with cypress interior, made about 1790. It was owned by Judge John Bee Holmes, recorder of the City of Charleston, South Carolina, at the time of Washington's visit in 1791. This is one of the great examples of Charleston cabinetmaking. It stands nine feet high, and is crowned with a floral finial on a double-scrolled pediment. Below the bookcase a fall-front drawer opens to a writing compartment. The serpentine lower section has cupboard doors veneered with panels of crotch mahogany outlined in scrolled stringing. (*Heyward-Washington House, Charleston Museum.*)

415

416

**415.** Sheraton breakfront cabinet and desk ("Salem secretary") of mahogany and satinwood, with writing section behind upper drawer front. It bears the label of Edmund Johnson, who worked in Salem between 1793 and 1811. The inlaid ovals are characteristic of Johnson's work. A similar piece is illustrated in Vol. I of Lockwood's *Colonial Furniture in America*. (*Henry Ford Museum.*)

**416.** Hepplewhite mahogany cabinet or bookcase, made about 1795-1810, with a type of inlay associated with the Seymours. Great care obviously went into the selection of the flame-patterned crotch mahogany framed in a double row of mitred crossbanding in the doors of the lower section. Satinwood stringing outlines the drawer panels and the frieze on the cornice. This supports a coved molding surmounted by the thumbprint, or lunette, inlay which is associated with the Seymours, but used also by other makers in the Boston area. (*Collection of Mrs. Giles Whiting.*)

**417.** The Hepplewhite inlaid mahogany cabinet (No. 416) is seen here in its own setting. The drawing room contains many masterpieces of American furniture, mainly Hepplewhite but also Queen Anne and Chippendale pieces. Among them are Hepplewhite Martha Washington chairs, New England pembroke and semicircular tables, a Salem sofa (back of the pembroke) with carving attributed to McIntire, and Rhode Island shield-back side chairs. Hepplewhite polescreens, with shield-shaped embroidered panels, stand on either side of an Adam mantel which has a fluted frieze and plaque showing an Adam urn and spiral acanthus. (*Apartment of Mrs. Giles Whiting.*)

**419**

**418**

**418.** Cellaret in Hepplewhite style, probably made in Virginia about 1790-1810. It is of walnut, with hard yellow pine[11] used as secondary wood. Stringing and simple geometric devices are inlaid in light-toned wood. There is a drawer for cutlery, and the interior of the storage space, equipped with a lock, is divided into compartments for bottles. Cellarets, which are sometimes arranged with additional space for sugar and spices, represent an important Southern furniture type, but are almost nonexistent elsewhere in the United States. The Southern cellaret is generally taller than its English prototype. (*Collection of Mr. and Mrs. Raymond C. Power.*)

**419.** This wine cooler in Hepplewhite style has lion-ring handles and is veneered with vertical bands of mahogany and satinwood enclosed in hoops of brass. The turned, reeded legs, fitted with brass casters, are capped with finely carved acanthus. The Derby family of Salem, Massachusetts, originally owned this elegant piece, which is attributed to John and Thomas Seymour of Boston and was made about 1795. This is sometimes called a cellaret, but a distinction should be made, the cellaret being for storage, the cooler for serving wine. (*Karolik Collection, Museum of Fine Arts, Boston.*)

**420**

**421**

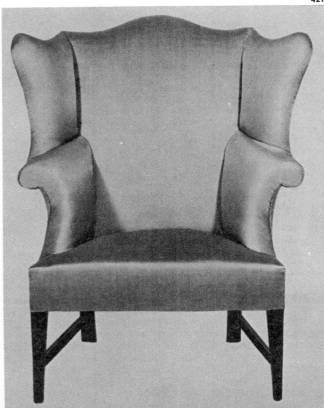

422

423

424

425

**420.** Philadelphia open-arm chair in the Louis XVI style, one of a set of twelve with a sofa (No. 526) which originally belonged to Edward Burd of Philadelphia and passed to Edward Shippen Burd. In time, its American origin was forgotten, and it passed as a French work through the auction room in New York in 1921. When it was sent to France and the Beauvais covering removed, its American construction was discovered. The set returned to America, and in 1929 was purchased by Fiske Kimball, then director of the Philadelphia Museum, for use at Lemon Hill in Fairmount Park, where it still forms part of the furnishings. The greenish-white paint with gold decoration is original; the modern lampas upholstery has an eighteenth-century pattern. (*Philadelphia Museum of Art.*)

**421.** This Baltimore Hepplewhite mahogany easy chair, made about 1790, is one of the finest American examples, and closely resembles the plate for an easy chair dated 1787 shown in Hepplewhite's *Guide.* Both have an exceptionally wide flare to the wings, diagonal rake to the arms, and serpentine line across the wings and top. The Hepplewhite easy chair has deeper wings than the Chippendale chair, and these are broken at the armrest. (*No. 66, Baltimore Furniture, 1947. Collection of Mr. and Mrs. James D. Harrison. Courtesy Baltimore Museum of Art.*)

**422.** Connecticut Chippendale-Hepplewhite transition side chair of cherry, with original haircloth upholstery fastened with nailheads. It was made about 1800. The type is associated with the

Hartford firm of Kneeland and Adams, but was made by others. The arching of the cresting rail and shaping of the uprights indicate the gradual approach of the shield-back. The urn in the splat is of Adam type. (*Connecticut Historical Society.*)

**423.** Hepplewhite carved mahogany shield-back chair with a die-stamp on the back rail, *S. Badlam,* for Stephen Badlam (1751-1815) of Dorchester, Massachusetts. The floral pendant carved on the stop-fluted leg seems to be characteristic of this maker. The shield, with pierced splat, has wheat-ears on the cresting over pendent husks. (*Ginsburg and Levy.*)

**424.** Hepplewhite shield-back mahogany armchair with drapery back. It is one of a pair from a set of twelve made about 1800 in Charleston for the Ball family. This drapery-back design was popular with American makers, particularly in New York, but used in much the same way in Charleston and New England (No. 425). Double festoons of drapery fall from rosettes against oval bars that rise from a segment of a rosette. The central motif is a variant of Hepplewhite's feather design. (*Collection of Frank L. Horton.*)

**425.** Hepplewhite shield-back mahogany side chair, probably made in Massachusetts, about 1790-1800. Although similar to No. 424, and to many New York chairs, it is lighter throughout. As on many New England chairs the stretcher is retained for strength. In crispness of line and delicacy of form the chair displays familiar New England characteristics. (*Garvan Collection, Yale University Art Gallery.*)

**426.** Hepplewhite shield-back mahogany side chair made about 1795, with carving attributed to Samuel McIntire. It was originally owned by Elias Hasket Derby.[52] The design is an almost literal version of Hepplewhite's *Guide* (Plate 2). The medial splat is an urn on a pedestal, supporting wheat-ears. Slender drapery swags unite it to the outer bars of the shield. The skill of McIntire is seen in the grapevine carved on the leg and the cluster of fruit at the base of the shield. (*Karolik Collection, Museum of Fine Arts, Boston.*)

**427.** Connecticut Senate chair of cherry in the Hepplewhite style made by Lemuel Adams. The chairs, tables, and other furniture for the State House, for which Adams was paid £105/6 in 1796, included twenty-two chairs for the Senate Chamber. Thirteen of these have been returned to their original position in the State House, which since 1960 has been maintained as a public museum in charge of the Connecticut Historical Society. The State House, designed by Charles Bulfinch, was completed in 1796. (*Connecticut Historical Society.*)

**428.** This Hepplewhite shield-back side chair with truncated shield, of mahogany with satinwood and ebony inlay, was made about 1795. The type, with horizontal top rail, is often associated with Elbert Anderson, who worked in New York about 1789-1800. The rake of the legs and slight thickening at the base suggest Anderson's labeled card table, which was in the Norvin H. Green sale in 1950. Truncated shield-back chairs which belonged to Alexander Hamilton are in the collection of C. K. Davis. Similar chairs have turned up in the Albany region and seem to have been a New York type. (*Metropolitan Museum of Art.*)

**429.** Baltimore shield-back mahogany chair in Hepplewhite-Sheraton style, from a set made for Charles Carroll of Carrollton (1737-1832), "Last of the Signers." This design combines details from two plates in Sheraton's *Drawing Book.* The five feathers and festoons of drapery suggest Hepplewhite, but were in common use at the time. The chair is carved with a bellflower (husk) on the center splat, acanthus leaves at the base, and bellflower pendants on two sides of the legs. As in New England, the Baltimore chair often has an inset cross-stretcher. (*No. 58, Baltimore Furniture, 1947. On loan from Mrs. Dorothea Harper Pennington Nelson to the Baltimore Museum of Art.*)

**430**

**431**

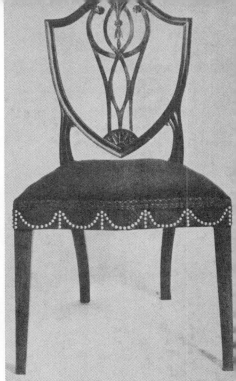
**432**

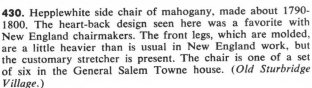

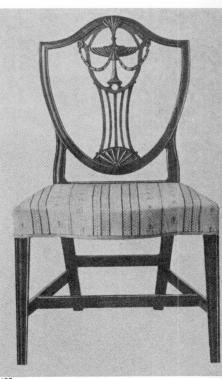
**433**

**430.** Hepplewhite side chair of mahogany, made about 1790-1800. The heart-back design seen here was a favorite with New England chairmakers. The front legs, which are molded, are a little heavier than is usual in New England work, but the customary stretcher is present. The chair is one of a set of six in the General Salem Towne house. (*Old Sturbridge Village.*)

**431.** Hepplewhite heart-back mahogany side chair, one of a pair, made in New York probably about 1790, and once owned by Robert Fulton. The chair has carved bellflower pendants on two sides of the legs (unusual in New York), floral carving on the back, undulating supports for the shield, and spade feet on the tapering straight legs. (*Collection of Doctors C. Ray and Winifred Hope Franklin. Photograph: Museum of the City of New York.*)

**432.** The design for this Hepplewhite shield-back mahogany chair appears in Hepplewhite's *Guide* (Plate 4, 3rd ed.). It was made in Salem about 1790-1800, and represents a lighter form of the pierced, scrolled splat which had been known from the early Georgian period. This splat was retained in Chippendale chair designs and can be seen in Manwaring types (see Nos. 172 and 258). The curve of the rear legs is often noted on Salem chairs. (*Essex Institute.*)

**433.** Hepplewhite shield-back mahogany side chair, made about 1790-1800. This is the typical "Rhode Island chair." One of Adam's favorite motifs, the *kylix*, a Greek footed dish, in an oval with festoons, decorates the splat. The motif was occasionally used in Salem. Samuel McIntire's drawing of it is in the Essex Institute, and his chair (No. 102 of the Karolik Collection) bears a striking resemblance to this but has a fruit basket at the base of the splat. (*Karolik Collection, Museum of Fine Arts, Boston.*)

434

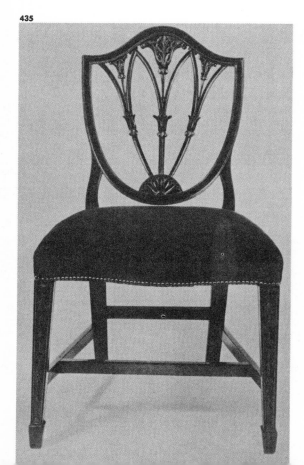

435

**434.** A pair of Hepplewhite upholstered side chairs, made in New England about 1790, is seen at the fireplace of this neoclassic parlor from the home of Oliver Phelps in Suffield, Connecticut, remodeled in the 1790s. At the left is a Hartford side chair with the same general design of splat seen in No. 427. A Connecticut cherry shield-back chair, with five converging bars, stands in front of a Connecticut cherry secretary with lattice pediment and eagle inlay, probably the work of Eliphalet Chapin (1741-1807) of East Windsor. The French wallpaper of about 1790 has a stamp thought to be that of Réveillon. (*Federal Parlor, H. F. du Pont Winterthur Museum.*)

**435.** The rounded shield of this Baltimore Hepplewhite mahogany chair has molded bars springing from a rosette segment and forming a pattern of intersecting ovals which enclose carved acanthus leaves. On the inset panels of the tapering legs are long bellflower (husk) pendants held by half-rosettes. It was made about 1790-1800, and came originally from The Oaks (now Dumbarton Oaks), in Georgetown, D.C., the home of William Hammond Dorsey (1764-1818). (*No. 59, Baltimore Furniture, 1947. Collection of the Maryland Historical Society. Photograph: Baltimore Museum of Art.*)

**436.** Philadelphia Hepplewhite oval-back side chair painted in a bowknot-and-ostrich-plume design in polychrome on a frame of beech. It is one of the set of twenty-four oval-back chairs ordered by Elias Hasket Derby in 1796 through Joseph Anthony and Company of Philadelphia.[52, 53] Three variants appear in this set, which is now widely scattered. Resemblance to English painted chairs suggests an English-trained decorator. In quality they are unsurpassed in American painted furniture. (*Karolik Collection, Museum of Fine Arts, Boston.*)

**437.** Hepplewhite oval-back mahogany side chair, made in Baltimore about 1790-1800. The back with curving pierced splats, was based on an English type and was used in America only by Baltimore chairmakers. Narrow inlay at the bottom of the rail, a bellflower pendant inlaid on the central splat, and carving on the others contribute to the rich effect. (*No. 54, Baltimore Furniture, 1947. Collection of Mrs. Frederick Leiter. Courtesy Baltimore Museum of Art.*)

436

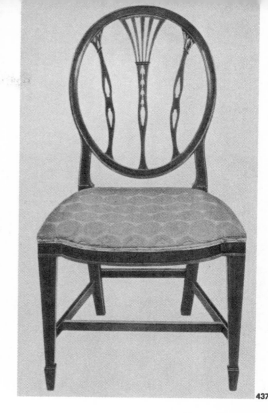

437

**438.** Sheraton Martha Washington mahogany chair made in New England about 1790-1810. The vase-shaped, reeded arm support is a continuation of the turned leg, which has a carved acanthus capping. The Martha Washington chair was known by this name in the eighteenth century. The label of Joseph Short (1771-1818) of Newburyport states that he "also makes Martha Washington chairs." A tall-backed open-arm chair had been made since the early 1700s (No. 145). Joseph Short's chair was of Hepplewhite type, with straight tapering legs and incurved supports for the arms. The Hepplewhite type is represented by the chair in No. 577. (*Henry Ford Museum.*)

**439.** One of a unique pair of Sheraton upholstered mahogany armchairs made about 1795, which has descended in the family of Elias Hasket Derby[52] and has been attributed by most authorities to John and Thomas Seymour of Boston. The design of the arm is like that on some Sheraton sofas but is not often seen on chairs (see No. 440). It is not a recognized English type, although Sheraton offers such a treatment in the *Cabinet Dictionary* (1803). The sloping arm is met by a projecting reeded baluster which is a continuation of the turned and reeded leg. The rosette carvings on the corner blocks and acanthus cappings on the legs are of the highest order. (*Karolik Collection, Museum of Fine Arts, Boston.*)

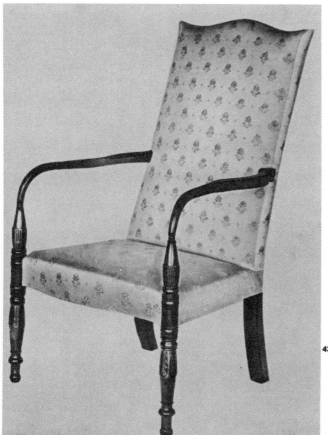

438

439

**440.** Boston State House chair made about 1800, shortly after the completion of the State House, which was designed by Bulfinch. This mahogany chair is upholstered in crimson leather. It shows Regency influence and, through the English interpretation, that of the gondola-like French *fauteuil de bureau* with the back continuing as sides of the chair. This was a French type of the 1790s which was assimilated in the Regency style. (*Norvin H. Green sale, 1950. Henry Ford Museum.*)

**441.** This square-back New York Sheraton mahogany armchair, one of a pair made about 1790-1810, is nearly identical to a design in the Appendix of Sheraton's *Drawing Book* (1791-1794). Here the urn is pierced. The use of the feather motif and tapering straight leg associated with Hepplewhite is characteristic of some Sheraton designs. This urn-and-drapery back was frequently used by New York chairmakers. (*Karolik Collection, Museum of Fine Arts, Boston.*)

**442.** This Sheraton mahogany armchair, made about 1800, is attributed to Henry Connelly (1770-1826). This form of urn-and-drapery back was popular in Philadelphia. It is here used on a chair which has a distinctive type of cylindrical spade foot tapering smoothly to the base which is also found on Connelly's labeled sideboard (No. 517). The sideboard provides a basis for attributing pieces with this detail to him. The design of the back resembles a plate in Sheraton's *Drawing Book* which was familiar to Connelly and his contemporaries through publication in the Philadelphia *Journeyman Cabinet and Chairmakers' Book of Prices*, 1795. (*Art Institute of Chicago.*)

**443.** Sheraton trellis-back armchair of mahogany, probably made in Salem about 1790-1800. With the introduction of the square-back came a number of new devices for providing a back support using light members. The geometric trellis-back was very frequently used. Carved rosettes decorate the top rail and intersections of the bars, which have bead moldings. (*Karolik Collection, Museum of Fine Arts, Boston.*)

**444.** Salem Sheraton mahogany side chair, made about 1790-1810, with carving attributed to Samuel McIntire. A geometric pattern formed by intersecting arches entirely fills the back. The center of the cresting rail has a tablet carved with

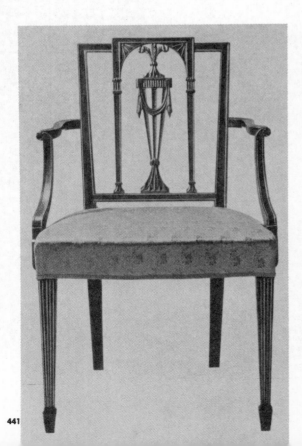

**443**

**444**

**445**

McIntire's favorite motif — a basket of fruit. (He also used it on the base of the chest-on-chest, No. 471.) The chair is upholstered in leather over the seat frame with a festoon of nailheads. (*Henry Ford Museum.*)

**445.** Philadelphia Sheraton bar-back armchair of mahogany, attributed to Ephraim Haines (1775 to after 1811). It may have been made about 1800. Except for the terminals of the arms, it is similar to the ebony chairs made by Haines for Stephen Girard in 1806-1807 which were in the Connelly-Haines Exhibition in Philadelphia in 1953. The Girard chairs show the same bulbous foot which provides a basis for attributions to Haines, whose work is otherwise so much like Connelly's (No. 446). (*Henry Ford Museum.*)

**446.** Philadelphia Sheraton mahogany bar-back side chair, attributed to Henry Connelly and made in the early 1800s. Both Connelly and Haines used a carved bulbous turning showing an "oak-leaf" type of acanthus, but each had his own manner of designing the foot (No. 442; also Nos. 516 and 517). This was first demonstrated in the Philadelphia Museum's loan exhibition in 1953. (*Philadelphia Museum of Art.*)

**446**

447                                        448

**447.** Baltimore Sheraton mahogany armchair made about 1800-1810. The drapery-back design is related to Plate 6 in Hepplewhite's *Guide* (3rd ed.), but on account of the square back it is classified as Sheraton. Carving of the bowknot in the arch has exceptional freedom, the drapery swags are crisp, and the central splat in the form of a plinth, supporting an octagonal medallion carved with a rosette, is fine in proportion. On the front leg, a carved cuff takes the place of the inlaid cuff usually seen on Baltimore chairs. (*Reginald M. Lewis sale, 1961. Henry Ford Museum.*)

**448.** Baltimore Sheraton mahogany armchair from a set of two armchairs and six side chairs, made about 1790-1810. The design is based on plate 34 of Sheraton's *Drawing Book* (3rd ed.). The inlay of a shaded leaf in the diamond in the splat is combined with delicately carved rosettes, fluting, and leafage. A Philadelphia origin has also been suggested for the chairs, but the exceptional richness of inlay and carving, which is close to English work, supports an attribution to Baltimore. (*Collection of Frank L. Horton.*)

**449.** Sheraton mahogany side chair by John Aitken, who was active in Philadelphia after 1775. It is one of a set of twelve made for George Washington.

The set was included in the two dozen chairs for which, along with two sideboards, Aitken received the sum of $402.20 in 1797, according to an entry in Washington's account book. Aitken also made the secretary and writing chair now at Mount Vernon. This chair, used by Washington in his new banquet hall, is among a number of pieces that passed to Nellie Custis Lewis, becoming part of the Lewis family heirlooms which were purchased by Act of Congress in 1878. (*Smithsonian Institution.*)

**450.** Sheraton side chair of mahogany and satinwood attributed to John and

Thomas Seymour of Boston, and probably made about 1795-1810. Matching chairs, apparently from a set, include pairs in the Karolik, Bayou Bend, and Winterthur collections. At Winterthur there are also a matching twelve-leg settee with a back composed of five chair-backs, and a smaller settee with two. The incurved leg and rolled-back cresting show classic influence. Emphasis on handsomely patterned satinwood inlays and the style of carving has led to an attribution to the Seymours, although unlike their work in its response to the Directoire style. (*Reginald M. Lewis sale, 1961. Henry Ford Museum.*)

449                                        450

**451.** New York mahogany armchair with reeded frame, made by Duncan Phyfe about 1800-1810 for William Bayard of New York. The Sheraton design represents a step toward the Greek chair with rolled back and outward curve of the back rest. Bowknot and darts are carved on the top rail. The straight, turned and reeded leg of Sheraton type ends in the long slender bulbous foot which is typical of Phyfe. (*Ex Coll. Mrs. J. Insley Blair. Museum of the City of New York.*)

**452.** New York mahogany side chair of klismos form, made about 1810. The design shows Directoire influence and represents the beginning of the Empire style in America. This type of chair was introduced by Phyfe but is seen here in the work of an unidentified maker. The source is the Greek chair with incurved leg and with seat rail and upright in unbroken line. The rolled back was used on Egyptian chairs as well as in Greco-Roman furniture. This Phyfe-type klismos is closer to English Regency than French Directoire. (*J. K. Byard sale, 1960. Parke-Bernet Galleries.*)

**453.** New York mahogany side chair in the Empire style made by Duncan Phyfe about 1810-1820. It is one of a set of twelve which belonged to Charles Ludlow, aide-de-camp to General George Washington. Five more are in the Metropolitan Museum. This, like No. 452, is the klismos type and has the Empire lyre motif, which Phyfe alternated with an eagle or cornucopias in the splat. The incurved or "saber" leg is crisply carved with the Phyfe waterleaf. (*Plate 267, McClelland,* Duncan Phyfe and the *English Regency. Henry Ford Museum.*)

451

452

453

454

**454.** New York mahogany side chair of curule design in the Empire style, made by Duncan Phyfe for the Pearsall family of New York about 1810-1820. The source is the Roman magistrate's folding stool. This type was made in both England and France. The *London Chair-Makers and Carvers' Book of Prices* for 1810, which was doubtless known to American chairmakers, lists "Grecian cross Fronts." (*Museum of the City of New York.*)

**455.** Woodlawn was the home of Nellie Custis, adopted daughter of George Washington, and of Lawrence Lewis, his nephew, who were married in 1799. These late Sheraton maple chairs of klismos form around the mahogany dining table belonged originally to the Lewises and it is believed they were made in the large workshop that Duncan Phyfe maintained in New York. Phyfe gave special attention to orders from the South. Similar chairs are in the Telfair Academy and in Charleston. With their twist reeding, cane panels, and scrolled armrests, they may be dated about 1815-1820. (*Woodlawn Plantation, Mount Vernon, Virginia. National Trust for Historic Preservation.*)

455

**456.** New York mahogany armchair in Empire style showing English Regency influence in further developing the klismos form. The chair was made about 1810 by John Hewitt (1777-1857), who was born and trained in England. Hewitt came to New York about 1800 and was engaged in exporting to the South, where a partner represented him in Savannah. He was the grandfather of the Misses Hewitt who founded the Museum for the Arts of Decoration at Cooper Union, New York City. This chair has carved scrolls holding the tablet in the splat. The back rail is paneled. (*Cooper Union Museum.*)

**457.** This Empire side chair of mahogany with gilt ruffled carving on the edge of the seat frame and elaborate stencil decoration was probably made in New York about 1810-1820. It is in pseudo-klismos style with a broken line at the seat rail and leg, but the Greek klismos is followed in the back rest which projects beyond the uprights. The horizontal splat is composed of harps supporting a tablet. On some examples of Empire and late Empire furniture stencil decoration took the place of metal mounts. New York was responsible for some of the finest stenciling. (*H. F. du Pont Winterthur Museum.*)

457

**459**

**458**

**460**

**458.** One of a pair of Sheraton "fancy" chairs made about 1815 in Baltimore by Thomas Renshaw and decorated by John Barnhart. A matching four-chair-back settee in the museum's collection has an inscription giving the names of both, with Barnhart as "Ornamenter." The "fancy" chair, which was known by this name in the eighteenth century, was of light construction and had painted decoration. Here the landscape medallion, notched border, and drapery swags are in polychrome and gilt on a cream-colored ground. The tablet below the seat is an unusual detail. (*Baltimore Museum of Art.*)

**459.** Sheraton "fancy" chairs made in New England about 1815-1820, forerunners of the Hitchcock chair. They are from an original set of six used on *Cleopatra's Barge,* a luxurious yacht owned by George Crowninshield of Salem. Background is in bottle green and gold, and each has a different landscape panel. Stretcher bars are joined with gilt balls, and stenciled leaves decorate the tops of the daintily turned legs, which rest on ball feet. The artist may have been Samuel Bartoll (c. 1765-1835), who worked in Salem from 1814. (*Peabody Museum, Salem.*)

**460.** New York Sheraton "fancy" chair, made about 1820. It is of maple and beech and has a black and gold stenciled decoration and metal mounts. This example may be the work of Thomas Ash who, according to Longworth's *Directory,* succeeded to the chair manufactory of his father, William Ash, at 33 John Street in 1815. William Ash was the son of Gilbert Ash (1716-1785), New York's leading eighteenth-century chairmaker. The spirally scrolled armrest is usual on chairs of this period. (*Metropolitan Museum of Art.*)

**461.** Hitchcock chair of maple and hickory painted black. It was made between 1825 and 1828 and on the seat rail is the mark *L. Hitchcock, Hitchcocksville, Conn. Warrented.* The turned top rail and wide splat have a stenciled design of fruit and leaves, and the uprights are decorated with arrows. The legs are turned and the rush seat is painted gray. Lambert Hitchcock's factory, established in 1825, marketed chairs all over the country, but the type was produced by other makers in New England (including Seymour Watrous of Hartford and William Moore, Jr., of Barkhamsted, Connecticut), and in New York, Ohio, and other states. The mark on this chair was used between 1825 and 1828, but from 1829 to 1843 the mark was *Hitchcock, Alford & Co. Warrented.* Chairs marked *Lambert Hitchcock, Unionville, Connecticut,* were made after 1843. (*Henry Ford Museum.*)

**461**

**462.** Boston rocker of about 1835, made of maple and pine and painted black. It has a bowed back and is stenciled with flowers and leaves on the top rail and on the front roll of the grained seat. The tall-backed New England windsor rocking chair was the forerunner of the widely used Boston rocker, which appeared in New England about 1825. According to Dyer and Fraser, in *The Rocking Chair — An American Institution* (1928), there is no proof that the style originated in Boston. Lambert Hitchcock manufactured it, and so did many unknown American chairmakers. This chair has the usual shaping of the seat, rolled up in back and rolled over in front, a design suited to mass production. The popularity of the Boston rocker has possibly taken it into more American homes than any other type of chair. (*Henry Ford Museum.*)

**462**

**463.** Windsor chair made about 1800 by Ebenezer B. Tracy (1744-1803), of Lisbon (part of Norwich), Connecticut. Under the seat is the brand *EB:TRACY*. Oak was used for the bow and stretchers, maple for the legs, and hickory for the spindles. Turnings are of early bamboo type, a simplification of vase-turning combined with grooving common after 1800 but also seen on eighteenth-century examples. The original flower-embossed black leather places this in the rare group of upholstered windsors.[54] (For earlier work by Tracy see No. 287.) (*Los Angeles County Museum.*)

**464.** New England Sheraton windsor armchair, with pine seat and maple legs, made about 1800. The influence of Sheraton square-backed chairs affected windsor-chair design. The curve of the bow, which was one of the finest elements of New England design, was superseded by a straight line. The raked back has double cross rails. (For earlier examples see Nos. 284-290.) (*Shelburne Museum.*)

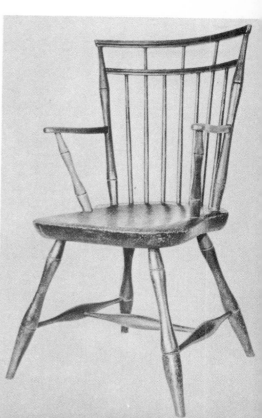

**463**                                                            **464**

465

466

**465.** Chippendale-Hepplewhite bowfront mahogany chest of drawers from New Britain, Connecticut, made about 1790. The elaborate Hepplewhite inlay of quarter fans and stringing on the drawer fronts, and book, or tambour, inlay on the stiles above interlaced ovals and tapering pendants, is combined with a Chippendale-style ogee-bracket foot. Transition pieces combining Chippendale and Hepplewhite design are not infrequent. (*George Dudley Seymour Collection. Connecticut Historical Society.*)

**466.** Hepplewhite bowfront chest of drawers with bracket feet, from Portsmouth, New Hampshire. It was made about 1790-1800 and is of birch, veneered with flame-patterned crotch satinwood and mahogany crossbanding. The apparent division of the drawer fronts has been achieved by alternation of vertical and horizontal grain. Contrast of light and dark wood is typical of New England. (*Henry Ford Museum.*)

**467.** Hepplewhite mahogany and satinwood chest of drawers with French bracket foot, made in New England about 1790-1800. The serpentine form, which had been popular with American cabinetmakers in the Chippendale period (Nos. 294, 295), was retained in the Hepplewhite style. New England cabinetmakers made frequent use of West Indian satinwood, which has plume-like patterns in the grain. (*Garvan Collection, Yale University Art Gallery.*)

467

468

469

**468.** Hepplewhite inlaid mahogany serpentine chest of drawers, probably made in Norfolk or southeastern Virginia, about 1800. It has a shaped apron and flaring French foot. The four drawers, with beaded edge, are veneered in flame-patterned crotch mahogany banded in triple stringing. The interior woods, tulipwood (tulip poplar) and hard yellow pine indicate Southern origin. The serpentine chest of drawers was a favorite in the South and often had a shaped apron. (*Collection of Frank L. Horton.*)

**469.** Salem Sheraton swell-front chest of drawers of mahogany, made about 1810-1815. The carving is attributed to Samuel McIntire. Projecting colonettes are not often as richly carved as here. McIntire's grapevine forms a spiral on a star-punched ground, and the unusual border on the top of the chest resembles a carved counterpart of thumbprint inlay. This chest of drawers formerly belonged to the early collec-

tor, Dwight Blaney of Boston, many of whose pieces were illustrated by Lockwood and Nutting. (*Collection of Richard Blaney.*)

**470.** Sheraton chest of drawers, or commode, of semi-elliptical form, made in Boston and billed in 1809 by Thomas Seymour to Elizabeth Derby, daughter of Elias Hasket Derby of Salem.[52] Mahogany, satinwood, bird's-eye maple and rosewood are combined in one of the richest examples of Boston furniture. Projecting colonnettes in Sheraton style have carved floral motifs (rare in Seymour work) at the top, and end in brass paw feet at the bottom. The sides, simulating drawer fronts, are actually cupboard doors which swing open. The lion-mask handles are original. Seymour's bill, owned by the museum, shows that John Ritto Penniman of Boston painted the fine shell decoration on top. (*Karolik Collection, Museum of Fine Arts, Boston.*)

470 B

470 A

**471.** Hepplewhite mahogany chest-on-chest by William Lemon with carving by Samuel McIntire, made in Salem in 1796. This key piece in Samuel McIntire's work shows typical motifs of bowl of fruit, basket of fruit, grape cluster, cornucopia, floral festoons, and alternating rosettes and flutes. In basic form, the chest represents the Chippendale style modified by Hepplewhite, but the rich ornament is McIntire's. Adam-type urn finials stand on a low broken triangular pediment over a frieze carved with *putti* bearing floral festoons. Among the McIntire papers at the Essex Institute is McIntire's bill to Madame Elizabeth Derby (wife of Elias Hasket Derby[52]), October 22, 1796, which identifies it in his charge for carving "a case of drawers by Mr. Lemon." The chest-on-chest has a close counterpart in the Garvan collection in the slightly earlier, and simpler, example by Stephen Badlam with carving by the Skillin brothers made for Elias Hasket Derby in 1793. Both are crowned with the figure of Victory. (*Karolik Collection, Museum of Fine Arts, Boston.*)

**472.** This Sheraton dressing chest of drawers with attached mirror, of mahogany and bird's-eye maple, was made in New England about 1800-1810. The mirror, in S-scrolled frame, has a painted decoration, and the reeded legs, ending in button feet, are continued as projecting columns. This is one of a small group of dressing chests with attached mirrors usually attributed to John and Thomas Seymour, who were working together in Boston between 1794 and 1816. The thumbprint inlay, considered a mark of Seymour workmanship, and the details of turning and use of patterned veneers form the basis of this attribution which has been generally accepted. However, the publication by Richard H. Randall, Jr.,[51] of labeled works, including similar dressing chests by other makers of the Boston area, suggests that further study may be required. (*Museum of Fine Arts, Boston.*)

**473.** This Sheraton dressing chest of drawers of mahogany inlaid with bird's-eye maple and satinwood is the most elaborate example from the Boston-Salem area. The combination of carving, painting, and veneering is unparalleled. The dressing chest, made about 1800, was originally in the Elias Hasket Derby mansion in Salem and was given by Elizabeth Derby West to her daughter, Elizabeth West Landers, of Oak Hill, Peabody, where it remained until 1896. It has been variously attributed to McIntire and to the Seymours, but, as in the case of the preceding (No. 472) its origin may require further investigation. (*Pingree House, Salem. Collection of the Essex Institute.*)

**474.** Hepplewhite dressing chest of drawers, with an oval mirror held by obelisk-shaped supports with urn finials. It is of mahogany inlaid with quarter fans and stringings, and has a French bracket foot. This example has a long history of ownership in Salem, and the shaping of the feet and skirt suggest local workmanship of about 1790-1800. (*Collection of Mr. and Mrs. Dean A. Fales, Jr.*)

**475.** Sheraton mahogany bowfront dressing chest of drawers with dressing glass, made in Salem by William Hook (1777-1867). The heavier scrolls and legs indicate a date after 1815, and this is substantiated by information supplied in the will of the donor, George Rea Curwen, that it was made in 1818. In his article, "Salem Furniture Makers," in *Antiques*, April 1934, Fiske Kimball pointed out that since Curwen probably knew Hook, and since Curwen kept careful records of his early furniture, the attribution of this piece to Hook was a strong one. (*Essex Institute.*)

473

474

875

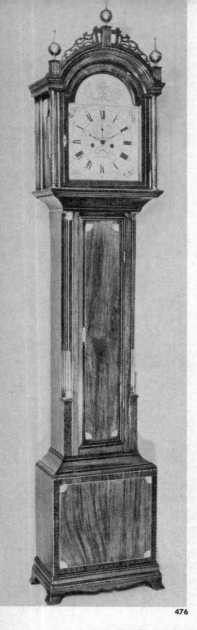

476

477

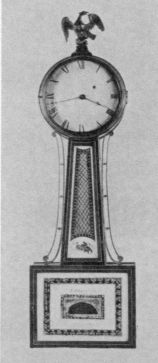

478

479

**476.** Tall clock by Simon Willard (1753-1848) of Grafton and Roxbury, Massachusetts. It was made about 1796 and has Willard's first printed label (the rarer of the two he used) printed by J. and Joseph N. Russell of Boston. This is one of his "common eight-day clocks with very elegant faces and mahogany cases, price from 50 to 60 dollars." Willard is known for an extraordinary variety and number of clocks — not only tall clocks, but shelf, wall, gallery, and steeple clocks as well. The Hepplewhite case by an unknown cabinetmaker is in the usual style for Willard clocks and has inlay of quarter fans and rope banding, brass reeding on the inset columns, and fretwork cresting with brass finials. (*Collection of Mr. and Mrs. T. B. Christopher.*)

**477.** Clock by Aaron Willard (1757-1844), brother of Simon Willard and next to him in importance in a distinguished family of clockmakers. He worked in Grafton and Roxbury before establishing himself in Boston in the 1790s. Aaron had a long career there as a clockmaker and is especially known for Massachusetts shelf clocks. This tall clock has his printed label and was made about 1800-1810. Cases for Willard clocks seem to be the work of one cabinetmaker, varying slightly in details. The extreme delicacy and almost calligraphic quality of the fretwork places this in a slightly later category than No. 476. (*Garvan Collection, Yale University Art Gallery.*)

**478.** This case-on-case wall clock by Simon Willard (1753-1848), signed *Willard / Grafton,* is one of about twenty-five known thirty-hour timepieces which seem to have been experimental models in the development of the banjo clock.[55] All are of this rectangular form and have a distinctive kidney-shaped framework door in front of the dial. A bell, which can be seen over the movement, is struck once on the hour by a hammer actuated by a pin on the hour wheel. (*Metropolitan Museum of Art.*)

**479.** Banjo clock by Simon Willard, marked *S. Willard's Patent;* Roxbury, about 1805. In 1802 Willard secured a patent for what he called an "improved timepiece," a wall clock with brass works which, like the more expensive tall clock, would run for eight days. The smaller case could not contain a striking mechanism but justified itself in the attractiveness of its design with highly polished metal fittings and decorative glass panels. It became an essential addition to the Federal parlor and was widely pirated by other makers. (*Old Sturbridge Village.*)

**480.** Tall clock in a Hepplewhite case, possibly made in Delaware about 1800. The initials of the original owners on the scrolled pediment, *I C/D,* are executed in ivory. The lightness of the Hepplewhite form is fully realized in the delicate, flaring bracket feet. Mahogany panels with incurved corners and arched top have maple borders, and the design has an effective division on the center section which gives additional lightness and sparkle to the whole. Particolored stars on the hood are in maple and ebony. (*Henry Ford Museum.*)

**481.** Tall clock made in Baltimore by Charles Tinges, who was listed in the directories from 1787 to 1816. The elaborately inlaid Hepplewhite mahogany case has a pierced and scrolled pediment and vine inlay on the hood. The simulated fretwork of interlaced semicircles on the frieze resembles this treatment on a labeled secretary by Stitcher and Clemmens of Baltimore. (*No. 91, Baltimore Furniture, 1947. Owned by the Maryland Historical Society. Photograph: Baltimore Museum of Art.*)

**482.** Girandole clock made about 1815 by Lemuel Curtis (1790-1857) of Concord, Massachusetts. Curtis, who was born in Boston and worked in Concord about 1814-1818, moved later to Burlington, Vermont. He is best known as the maker of this exceedingly rare type of wall clock, which many consider the most beautiful American clock. Its distinctive feature is a painted convex panel, suggesting the fashionable convex or girandole mirrors of the period, with frames set with gilt balls. The panels, which were generally painted by Benjamin Curtis, are frequently of allegorical subjects, but this shows an unidentified street scene. (*Old Sturbridge Village.*)

**483.** "Pillar and scroll" clock by Eli Terry (1772-1852) of Plymouth, Connecticut. It was made about 1817 and is one of the very rare early examples of the Connecticut shelf clock. Terry, who had begun to make wood-movement tall clocks at Plymouth in the early 1800s, began to experiment with shelf clocks in 1814, and a few years later introduced this type with a decorative case having columns at the side and a scrolled pediment. It was manufactured in quantity until 1840. (*Old Sturbridge Village.*)

480

481

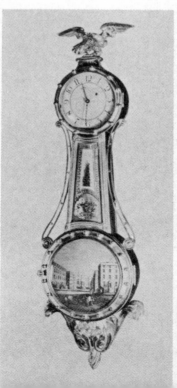

482

483

484

485

**484.** Baltimore Hepplewhite slope-front desk of inlaid mahogany, made about 1800. This type of desk, originating in the late 1600s (see Nos. 94, 95), has survived through all periods. In the Hepplewhite style, it has a French bracket foot and shaped skirt. Although it is generally inlaid, seldom does it have such superb workmanship as seen here. The eagle, standing on the globe, with shield of stripes and bars on his breast, a streamer marked with stars in his beak, is rendered with the freedom of a pen drawing. (*No. 70, Baltimore Furniture, 1947. Collection of Mr. and Mrs. Charles F. Stein, Jr. Courtesy Baltimore Museum of Art.*)

**485.** Hepplewhite slope-front desk of inlaid mahogany, made in Massachusetts. It has the label of Ezekiel Brigham of Grafton and the date, February 1816. In the early 1800s many examples of this type were made in both the large and small centers of cabinetmaking. It represents the sound workmanship and good design which were at the command of many obscure craftsmen, such as the unrecorded Brigham, and has the basic good points of more elegant desks such as No. 484. (*Old Sturbridge Village.*)

**486.** Connecticut cherry desk and bookcase or secretary; it is attributed to Aaron Chapin (1753-1838), of Hartford. The drawer front opens on a quadrant and the writing section slides forward. Chippendale design is here modified by Hepplewhite in the bracket foot. The pierced cartouche finial and pierced pediment have Chapin characteristics, although the pediment is not in the usual lattice, but is formed of graceful, leafy scrolls. The history of this secretary[56] traces it to the home of the Robbins family of Rocky Hill, for whom Aaron made a documented sideboard (No. 512). The secretary may have been made about 1800. (*Connecticut Historical Society.*)

**487.** Hepplewhite lady's desk of mahogany with secondary woods tulip poplar (tulipwood) and hard yellow pine. It was probably made in southeastern Virginia about 1800. A small desk made in two sections, perhaps for portability, was popular in the South for a long period beginning in the early 1700s. This desk has deep drawers, and the depth of frame gives it pleasing proportions. (*Collection of Frank L. Horton.*)

486

**488.** Sheraton desk with folding top, delicately reeded legs, and bail handles for carrying. It is made of mahogany and has crotch-satinwood panels on the face and crossbanding of bird's-eye maple on top. In the long drawer one of the small inner drawers is fitted for writing accessories. Writing boxes, for which separate stands were made, were known both in imported and American examples.[57] The more utilitarian writing box used by sea captains, army officers, and traveling merchants is here transformed by workmanship of jewel-like perfection which suggests that this example was intended to be a lady's desk. (*Karolik Collection. Museum of Fine Arts, Boston.*)

**487**

**489**

**488**

**489.** Baltimore Sheraton lady's writing desk of mahogany and satinwood with *églomisé* glass panels showing figural decorations of a type peculiar to Baltimore.[58] It was made about 1800 and has a cylinder closing. A writing slide, with adjustable reading stand, pulls forward. On the cabinet doors, left and right, are "Temperance" and "Justice." Religious figures decorate the gallery of the shelf. Originally this desk belonged to the Harris family of Mount Mill (later called Bloomingdale) on Maryland's Eastern Shore. (*No. 77*, Baltimore Furniture, *1947. Metropolitan Museum of Art.*)

**490.** Hepplewhite inlaid tambour desk of mahogany, holly, and satinwood with ring handles enclosing Bilston enamels. It is attributed to John and Thomas Seymour of Boston and was made about 1795-1810. This is almost identical to the tambour desk at the Winterthur Museum with the label *John Seymour & Son,* and belongs to a small group of which others are in the Karolik Collection and at the Henry Ford Museum. These vary only in minute details, and it seems unquestionable that all are the work of the Seymours. While tambour closings appear on English furniture, the exact prototype of the American Hepplewhite tambour desk is not found there. The suggestion has been made that they show the influence of the French *bonheur du jour* with tambour *cartonnier,* of the Louis XVI period.[59] (*Bayou Bend Collection, Houston.*)

**490**

**491.** New York mahogany butler's desk in the Empire style by Duncan Phyfe, with matched panels of flame pattern in crossbanded panels. The sections are separated by fluted columns ending in rosettes. It was made about 1815-1820 as part of the wedding furniture of Sophia Miles and George Belden. The simple cubic proportions are those which Percier and Fontaine gave to French Empire furniture. The desk is illustrated in McClelland's *Duncan Phyfe and the English Regency.* Pl. 250. (*Collection of Mrs. Giles Whiting.*)

**492.** Empire furnishings of the 1815-1825 period include an inlaid mahogany desk with cylinder closing and gallery top. This is related to the Louis XVI *bureau à cylindre,* a form which was late in reaching America, although the cylinder closing was used on a few Sheraton secretaries (No. 494). The work table at right, labeled by Charles-Honoré Lannuier, with Empire lyre supports and lion's-paw feet, is from a set formerly in the Van Rensselaer Manor House (see Nos. 410, 560, 585). The painted and gilded side chair has an anthemion splat. (*Empire Hall, H. F. du Pont Winterthur Museum.*)

491

492

**493**

**494**

**493.** Sheraton desk and bookcase or secretary, of inlaid mahogany, made about 1800-1810. Typical of Massachusetts is the crossbanding of mahogany interrupted with light-toned wood. This method of inlay may have been an attempt to suggest an exotic wood. A profile portrait of Washington appears on the brass knob handles and on the medallions supporting eagle finials. Glazing bars form a geometrical pattern of intersecting diamonds and ovals. Characteristic of New England's refinement of form are the delicately ringed, bulbous legs. (*H. F. du Pont Winterthur Museum.*)

**494.** Sheraton desk and bookcase, with cylinder closing, probably made in Boston or Salem, about 1790-1810. This type of secretary on tall legs, without tiers of drawers in the base, was made even more frequently in America than in England, and was particularly popular in New England. The cylinder closing shows French influence, and is rare. *Églomisé* panels[58] add a brilliant decoration of black, white, and gold. The severe simplicity of the design is counterbalanced by the use of handsomely figured mahogany. (*Karolik Collection, Museum of Fine Arts, Boston.*)

**495.** Baltimore Hepplewhite desk and bookcase of mahogany inlaid with light-toned woods. It was made about 1790-1800. The lower section is inlaid with ovals of flame-grain set in panels of matched diagonals. The shaded conch shell is a motif frequently seen in Baltimore work, and the festooned drapery in the cabinet section is copied from Sheraton's *Drawing Book.* Chinese export porcelain, English luster, and other ceramics may be seen on the shelves. This secretary stands in the Benkard Room in the American Wing, a parlor from the home of Mrs. Harry Horton Benkard at Oyster Bay, Long Island. After her death in 1945 it was presented to the museum by her friends, complete with paneling and all its furnishings, representing the taste of one of the most discriminating collectors of American furniture. (*Metropolitan Museum of Art.*)

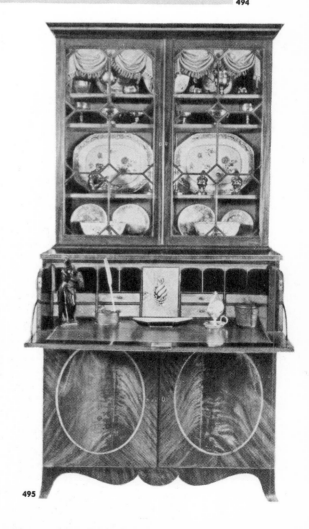

**495**

496

497

498

**496.** Desk and bookcase of cherry, with crossbanding, stringing, and geometrical inlay in light-toned wood. It was made about 1790-1800 and is attributed by tradition to a cabinetmaker known only by the name Josiah, whose work, chiefly in cherry in the Hepplewhite style, has been found in Green County, Kentucky. The suggestion has been made that he was Joseph Sayre, mentioned as Joe Sayre, which in the South would have been pronounced "Joe Si-yah."[60] Sayre came as a trained cabinetmaker from New England, was working in Louisville in 1779, and was in Green County in 1801. (*Collection of Mrs. Lucian D. Nelson.*)

**497.** Late Sheraton writing table of mahogany with fruitwood interior and the label of John Budd (who worked in New York between 1817 and 1840). His label, dated May 1817, carries the address of No. 118 Fulton Street and states, *Orders from southern ports immediately attended to* . . . Brass inlay, twist turning (of which this is a restrained example), and the stretcher shelf show the influence of the English Regency style. Twist turning became a distinctive feature of American furniture about 1815. (*Museum of the City of New York.*)

**498.** This New York Empire fall-front desk with mahogany veneer was made about 1820 and originally belonged to DeWitt Clinton, governor of New York, 1817-1821, 1825-1828. The form is derived from the French *secretaire à abattant*. The late Empire style is represented by the columnar supports under a projecting section. The small cabinet columns which frame a shelf above two tiers of drawers relieve the austerity of the design. Ormolu mounts in the form of Corinthian capitals and bases decorate the pilasters. (*Museum of the City of New York.*)

**499.** Chippendale-Hepplewhite looking glass, with a mahogany frame, gilt scrolls, and phoenix crest, made by William Wilmerding. The original bill of sale reads, "bot from William Wilmerding in New York, August 15, 1794 for £ 8:0:0 by Jacob Everson." This is a Chippendale type (actually of George II origin; see No. 344) but as a dated example of 1794 it is shown here to represent the persistence of the Chippendale style and its modification under classical influence. The simplified entablature has a delicate beaded oval gilt ornament in the Adam manner. It is typical of labeled mirrors by the German-born Wilmerding which, as they have turned up only in the New York area, may safely be accepted as his work and not those he imported.[61] (*Collection of Henry A. Wilmerding. Photograph: Museum of the City of New York.*)

**500.** Hepplewhite looking glass of mahogany with gilt gesso and wire ornament, and an ebony and holly inlay. The Hepplewhite looking glass has a scrolled pediment of greater delicacy than the Chippendale form (No. 499) and here the scrolls rise almost vertically to frame an Adam urn holding wired flowers and ears of wheat. The eagle of the Great Seal is inlaid with such a careful distribution of the fifteen stars that the mirror may perhaps be dated before 1796 when the sixteenth state, Tennessee, was admitted. The number of stars, however, cannot always be considered an indication of date. The *églomisé* panel[58] showing a landscape is somewhat rare on a Hepplewhite mirror, although it almost always appears on Sheraton examples. (*Ex Coll. Louis E. Brooks. Henry Ford Museum.*)

**501.** Chippendale-Hepplewhite dressing glass, of mahogany, birch, and white pine, with gilt gesso. It was probably made in the Boston area about 1790. The Chippendale rococo crest and block-front construction are harmonized here with the Hepplewhite serpentine line and lightness of design. Oval mirrors became fashionable in the late 1700s. Standing on a serpentine chest of drawers, such a dressing glass completed the Hepplewhite equivalent to the Sheraton dressing chest of drawers with attached mirror (No. 472). (*Henry Ford Museum.*)

**502.** Hepplewhite looking glass, made in New England about 1800-1810. By working with a composition known as "French putty," and with wires and gilding, the looking-glass maker created pleasing designs with a light, airy effect. Here acanthus spirals form a graceful cresting terminating in a ewer with wired flowers. There is a beaded inner molding, as is usual in glasses of this date, and an outer molding of husks alternating with berries. An acanthus pendant embodies the delicacy of Adam ornament. (*Karolik Collection, Museum of Fine Arts, Boston.*)

499

500

501

502

**503.** New York Sheraton looking glass of pine with an *églomisé* glass panel[58] having a landscape design and surmounted by three urns in the Adam style. The date is about 1790-1800. Although this type, the tabernacle mirror, was made long after 1800, the earlier date is indicated by the columns, which were later replaced by twisted rope moldings. The gilded ornament of gesso and wire consists of bouquets of wheat ears and flowers. The Sheraton looking glass has a flat cornice, and a molding studded with gilt balls which became progressively larger after 1800. (*Ex Coll. Mrs. J. Insley Blair. Museum of the City of New York.*)

**504.** This is the restored Beekman parlor at Philipsburg Manor, Upper Mills, in North Tarrytown, New York. The Sheraton looking glass with chains and gilt balls was probably made in New York State. Many like it have been found in houses along the Hudson River. Note the similarity of the frame to No. 508. The piano, with painted floral decoration, is by John Geib and Company of New York. Cream-colored satin window hangings lined in yellow and finished with blue and white ball fringe were copied from a primitive painting of an interior in "country classical" style. In 1785 this seventeenth-century home of the Philipse family was purchased by Gerard and Cornelia Van Cortlandt Beekman, who added a new wing. While this parlor was being restored[62] the inventory of the estate of Cornelia Beekman in 1822 was of help in selecting similar furnishings. (See also Nos. 279, 529, 577.) (*Sleepy Hollow Restorations.*)

503

504

505

506

507

**505.** Sheraton oval looking glass of pine and gilt gesso, with an eagle finial and entwined dolphins at the base. It was made about 1800-1810 in the Boston area and originally belonged to the Derby family of Salem. The slightly heavier ornamentation of the early 1800s is seen here in the modeling of the acanthus leaves of the cresting, the treatment of the Prince-of-Wales feathers supporting the eagle, and the rope molding in the frame. However, the intertwined dolphins are modeled with delicacy. This large Sheraton looking glass is over six feet in height and was obviously designed for a high-ceiled room. where it may have hung over a commode or console table. (*Garvan Collection, Yale University Art Gallery.*)

**506.** Girandole in the form of a convex mirror with gilt candle arms and an inner reed-molded frame simulating ebony. It was made probably in Boston, about 1800-1810. The wood is pine. The carved eagle, in black and gold, is placed on a rockery between dolphins. From his beak hang festoons of gilt balls on slender chains. The brass candle arms with carved wood leafage have cut-glass *bobèches* and faceted pendants. Convex mirrors, introduced into England from France in the late 1700s, became the most popular form in the Empire period. It is customary to call all convex mirrors girandoles whether or not they have candle arms, but the term was originally used for any wall light with sections of mirror glass. (*Karolik Collection, Museum of Fine Arts, Boston.*)

**507.** Sheraton overmantel gilt mirror in the Peirce-Nichols house at Salem. According to family tradition it was designed by Samuel McIntire, and it is said to have been made in France. It is constructed in three sections joined by reeded columns wreathed in laurel. Crossed palm branches, festoons of drapery, trophies, and flattened acanthus are elements of Adam design. McIntire remodeled the eastern part of Jerathmeel Peirce's house in preparation for the marriage of the latter's daughter, Sally, to George Nichols in 1801. This mirror was part of the new interior. (*Peirce-Nichols House, Salem. Essex Institute.*)

**508.** Late Sheraton looking glass with gilt frame and *églomisé* panels[58] in blue and gold, made about 1815. Among the vignettes is a view of the Dutch Church at Albany (demolished in 1806) as engraved by Henry W. Snyder. A towering crest with the customary eagle and festoons of balls is enlivened with military emblems. Although of unusual height — over seven feet — its style and craftsmanship are typical of the Albany Federal looking glass. It descended in an Albany family, and was presented to the Institute by Catherine Gansevoort Lansing (Mrs. Abraham Lansing), granddaughter of Gen. Peter Gansevoort. (*Albany Institute of History and Art.*)

508

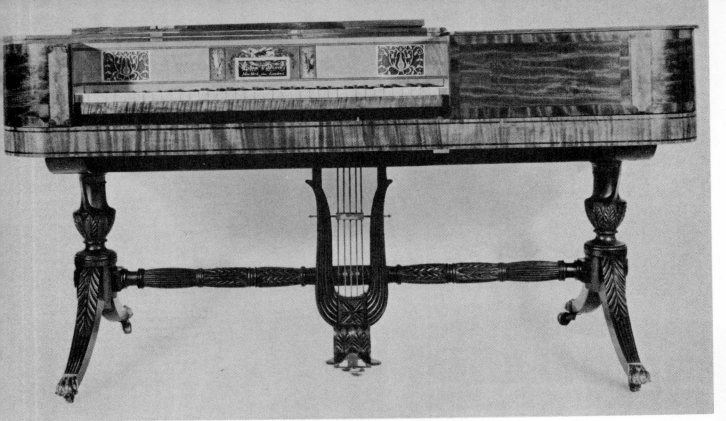

**509**

**510**

**509.** Piano case with mahogany and satinwood veneer, made about 1810-1820 and attributed to Duncan Phyfe. The instrument is by Gibson and Davis (active 1801-1820), the back panel bearing the inscription *Gibson & Davis, New York from London*. The lyre-shaped pedal is in the Empire style, while the vase pedestals and reeded stretcher represent a continuation of Sheraton motifs with bolder accent. This piano was formerly in the collection of Mrs. J. Insley Blair. (*Bayou Bend Collection, Houston.*)

**510.** New York Hepplewhite sideboard of inlaid mahogany, made about 1790-1795. It has the label of Elbert Anderson (engraved by Cornelius Tiebout), giving his address in Maiden Lane where he worked from 1789 to about 1796. The serpentine sideboard, with recessed section under the central drawer, square ends, and incurved side cupboards, was a popular type in New York and its vicinity. Inlaid quarter-fans, widely used elsewhere, appear almost invariably on New York examples. Inner legs set diagonally are also characteristic. (*Norvin H. Green sale, 1950, Parke-Bernet Galleries.*)

**511.** New Jersey Hepplewhite sideboard of inlaid mahogany, made about 1790-1800. It bears the label of Matthew Egerton, Jr., who, after working with his father, established his own shop about 1785. Egerton's first label was of octagonal form; his second (used on this sideboard) was oval with a scalloped edge. The Egertons were best known for their sideboards, which have many New York characteristics such as are seen in No. 510. Comparison with the

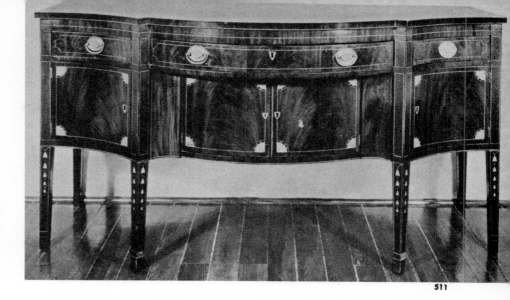

small sideboard by Egerton at the Philadelphia Museum shows the same type of bellflower and inlaid cuffs on the legs. (*John S. Walton.*)

**512.** Connecticut eight-legged sideboard made by Aaron Chapin of Hartford for Frederick Robbins of Rocky Hill. It is of serpentine form, with convex ends. A bill dated November 22, 1804, makes this the only documented piece by Aaron Chapin, except for utilitarian cases at the Connecticut Historical Society. Most of his work is in cherry; unexpectedly, this is of mahogany, with veneer of finely patterned flame grain. Emphasis is placed on the linked ovals forming long pendants on the legs, a detail often noted on Connecticut case pieces. (*Wadsworth Atheneum.*)

511

512

513

**513.** Baltimore mahogany sideboard made about 1790-1810. The bowfront design brings it closer to Sheraton than Hepplewhite, but no sharp line can be drawn between these two styles. A Baltimore origin is indicated by the many ovals in the mitred panels, given emphasis by broad, light-toned, crossbanded borders. Typical of Baltimore are the bellflowers with long central petals, and the cuffs of satinwood inlay around the sharply tapering legs. Laurel and acacia are also used in this inlay. (*Garvan Collection, Yale University Art Gallery.*)

**514.** Annapolis mahogany sideboard in Hepplewhite style attributed to John Shaw (1745-1829) and made about 1790-1800. The shallow body and broad center section, the inlaid ovals in wide crossbanding, and the unusual rounding of the spade foot closely resemble the labeled sideboard in the Baltimore Museum. These pieces could be compared in the 1947 Loan Exhibition at the Baltimore Museum. The line inlay of rectangles with incurved corners, and the panel with a lobed top on the leg, exactly agree with the labeled piece. Shaded inlay of shells in ovals is often seen on furniture of the Annapolis-Baltimore area. (*Collection of Mrs. F. F. Beirne.*)

514

515

516

517

**515.** South Carolina sideboard in Sheraton-Hepplewhite style with D-shaped ends and curly maple inlay, made about 1800. The wood is mahogany with interior of tulip poplar (tulipwood) and hard yellow pine. Ovals are outlined in triple stringing, the panels have quarter-fans, and the legs have the "crow-foot" bellflower. Sideboards with convex ends and inlaid ovals outlined by stringing (as compared with Baltimore's wide crossbanding around the ovals) are typical of South Carolina, but not all examples are as fine. It belonged originally to Joseph Alston, governor of South Carolina (husband of Theodosia Burr), and was once on his estate near Georgetown. (*Collection of Frank L. Horton.*)

**516.** Philadelphia Sheraton kidney-shaped sideboard of mahogany, with carved and reeded legs. It is attributed to Ephraim Haines (1775 to after 1811) and was made about 1800. The design resembles the labeled sideboard (No. 517) by Henry Connelly. These Philadelphia cabinetmakers worked in so similar a style that it has been difficult to distinguish their work. The Connelly-Haines loan exhibition at the Philadelphia Museum in 1953 showed that Haines used a bulbous tapering foot (seen here), a characteristic found on his documented furniture for Stephen Girard. (*Collection of Mr. and Mrs. T. B. Christopher.*)

**517.** Philadelphia kidney-shaped Sheraton mahogany sideboard, made about 1800 by Henry Connelly. This labeled sideboard, and also the card table, made for Henry Hollingsworth, are the key pieces in identifying Connelly's work, showing his use of the cylindrically tapering spade foot. (See also No. 446.) (*Philadelphia Museum of Art.*)

518

**518.** Boston Sheraton mahogany and bird's-eye maple sideboard with tiered top, made about 1800-1810. An attribution has been made by Hipkiss in *Eighteenth-Century American Arts* to John and Thomas Seymour. The hollow front appears to have been advocated by Sheraton for a practical reason. In his *Encyclopaedia* (1805), he states that "the hollow front will sometimes secure the butler from the jostles of the other servants." (*Karolik Collection, Museum of Fine Arts, Boston.*)

**519.** Federal dining room in the restored Barrett house at New Ipswich, New Hampshire. The Sheraton tiered sideboard, originally in the house, resembles No. 518. Salem drapery-back chairs are used at the dining table, which is set with Chinese export porcelain decorated with sepia landscape medallions and borders touched with Indian red. The French scenic wallpaper, *Les Jardins Français,* is in shades of green, blue, and soft gray. The house was built for Charles Barrett (1773-1836) and his bride by the former's father, about the time of their marriage in 1800. (*Society for the Preservation of New England Antiquities.*)

519

**520.** Boston Sheraton sideboard of mahogany, inlaid with maple, attributed to John and Thomas Seymour; made about 1800. The shutters are composed of alternating strips of mahogany and light-toned, striped maple, and the keyhole escutcheons are inlaid in ivory. Pilasters which similate fluting by means of inlay have carved ovals above. There are unusual square corner blocks above the reeded legs where turnings usually appear. Most Seymour straight-fronted sideboards have the graceful pendant on the skirt. The design shows striking similarity to the sideboard belonging to Mrs. Andrew Varick Stout (No. 81, Stoneman, *John and Thomas Seymour*), recognized as a Seymour masterpiece. (*Asa Stebbins House, Old Deerfield.*)

**520**

**521.** Sheraton four-legged sideboard of inlaid mahogany, with southern hard yellow pine interior. It was made in the South about 1800 and was found in western North Carolina. Vine inlay and floral urn are characteristic of the Valley of Virginia, and show a relationship to Pennsylvania-German design. The sideboard is now at Wilton in Richmond, Virginia. (*Courtesy of the Colonial Dames of America in the State of Virginia.*)

**522.** Sheraton bowfront mahogany sideboard with butler's drawer, attributed to John and Thomas Seymour; made about 1800-1810. Turnings, inlay, and use of "Seymour blue" in the interior suggest the attribution. The gray marble is unusual. Marble tops were often used on side tables, but seldom on sideboards. The deep central drawer front, opening on quadrants, gives access to the writing compartment, which is typical of the "butler's desk." *Los Angeles County Museum.*)

**523.** Small Sheraton carved mahogany sideboard, made in Salem, probably about 1800. The brass handles are stamped with a profile of Benjamin Franklin. At the sides are projecting colonnettes forming an extension of the leg, a frequent Sheraton feature. The reeded legs have the slender, tapering, bulbous foot found in Salem work, the columns are wreathed with carved grapevine on a punched ground but not in a manner to suggest McIntire's work.[63] Small sideboards which could be conveniently placed between windows were well liked in New England. (*Karolik Collection, Museum of Fine Arts, Boston.*)

52

52

523

524

525

**524.** Kentucky Sheraton inlaid cherry sideboard with shaped front and arched center section. It was made about 1810. The end compartments are blocked, and small cupboards are recessed under the swelled center drawer. A number of sideboards of the type have been found in the vicinity of Frankfort. It is typical of the large, deep-ended sideboard made in the South, with slender Sheraton style turnings, which preceded the fully developed Empire sideboard. (*The Speed Art Museum, Louisville, Kentucky.*)

**525.** New York Empire mahogany sideboard of about 1820, attributed to Duncan Phyfe. The use of large plain surfaces, the lion's-paw foot, and engaged classic columns are typical of the Empire style. The stepped board at the back has carved pineapple finials. Tambour shutters close the center section. An Irish eighteenth-century cut-glass compote stands between French gilt-bronze candelabra of about 1810. (*Henry Ford Museum.*)

**526.** Philadelphia sofa of about 1790 in Louis XVI style. It has original greenish-white paint with gold decoration and is upholstered in modern lampas copying an eighteenth-century pattern. In the Federal period, close ties with France affected American taste. Washington, Jefferson, Adams, and Monroe purchased French furniture, seen today at Mount Vernon, Monticello, the Adams home in Quincy, and the James Monroe Law Office at Fredericksburg.[64] However, there is only occasional evidence of direct influence of the Louis XVI style on American furniture design, and this sofa and matching chairs (No. 420) are rare. The rectangular form, straight lines, and slender turned straight leg typify French neoclassic furniture. (*Philadelphia Museum of Art.*)

526

527

528

**527.** Though curves were discarded by Robert Adam, they are often characteristic of Adam's interpreter, Hepplewhite, as represented in the "French Hepplewhite" style. This is more often seen in English than American furniture. The Hepplewhite sofa with continuous arm and serpentine back is rare in American work, but seems to have been made in Baltimore. This example in mahogany inlaid with ovals (the casters are missing) was made there about 1790-1800, and was originally owned by Brian Philpot (1750-1812), who had it made for the parlor of his summer home in Worthington Valley. The relationship to an Irish type has been convincingly demonstrated by R. L. Raley.[65] (*Collection of Mrs. Harry R. Slack, Jr. On loan at the Baltimore Museum of Art.*)

**528.** Salem Sheraton sofa of mahogany, made about 1800. The carved basket of fruit with sprays of laurel, drapery swags, and roses, and the top rail carved with fluting and rosettes, indicate the work of Samuel McIntire. The star-punched ground is also typical but not in itself an indication of his hand.[63] The design, based on Plate 35 of Sheraton's *Drawing Book,* also appears on other Salem sofas with carving attributed to McIntire. One of these, with an eagle on the center tablet, is in the Winterthur Museum. More typical, however, is a back with fruit or flowers as here. The laurel sprays are unusual, but occur on the sofa in the Karolik collection. (*Bayou Bend Collection, Houston.*)

**529.** New York inlaid mahogany sofa in the Hepplewhite style, made about 1790 for the Livingston family. The straight top rail is inlaid with Hepplewhite's feather motif and drapery swags. Especially graceful are the outward-flaring arms ending in inlaid rosettes. Appropriately, this sofa, originally owned in the lower Hudson Valley, is now part of the furnishings in the restored Beekman parlor (see also Nos. 279, 504, and 577), at Philipsburg Manor, Upper Mills, in North Tarrytown. (*Sleepy Hollow Restorations.*)

529

530

**530.** New York Sheraton carved mahogany sofa, attributed to Slover and Taylor, who were in partnership between 1802 and 1804. A half-daisy carved on the tablet on the top rail associates this with a group of Sheraton chairs which had fragmentary labels, a composite of which was long misread as Stover and Taylor. Phelps Warren has called attention to Longworth's *New-York Directory* for 1802-1804 which lists "Slover, (Abraham A.) & Taylor" at 94 Broad Street.[66] Several sofas, as well as chairs, with this distinctive half-daisy are known to exist. (*Sleepy Hollow Restorations.*)

**531.** Parlor at Woodlawn, the restored home of Lawrence and Nellie Custis Lewis (see also No. 455). In the group in front of the Adam fireplace is a Sheraton sofa of a type much favored in the Boston area. It was made about 1800, and has a slightly rounded back and top rail inlaid with maple. The projecting armrests unite with the vase-turning, which is a continuation of the leg. The late Sheraton armchair painted in cream color is a New England piece, and so is the Sheraton maple work table, probably made in Salem. The tea table represents the Queen Anne period. Bristol vases on the mantel shelf were originally owned by Nellie Custis, whose portrait, a copy of a Stuart, hangs above them. (*Woodlawn Plantation, Mount Vernon, Virginia. National Trust for Historic Preservation.*)

531

**532.** This Baltimore Sheraton painted settee is from a set of thirteen pieces believed to have been made in 1805 by John and Hugh Finlay (or Findlay) for John B. Morris (1785-1874). They have descended in his family with traditional ascription to the Finlays, who were "fancy" chair makers, coachmakers, and decorators of Irish origin.[65] In 1803 the couple were in partnership but John had been advertising since 1799. The perfection of the painting is indicative of foreign training. Decoration, mainly in black and gold, consists of scenic medallions, tablets with quiver and arrows, floral sprays, and paterae. The medallions depict views of estates of the Carroll family. Shown here are Homewood (left) and Mount Clare (right). (*Collection of Mrs. Edward Venable and Mrs. Herbert de Roth, on loan to the Baltimore Museum of Art.*)

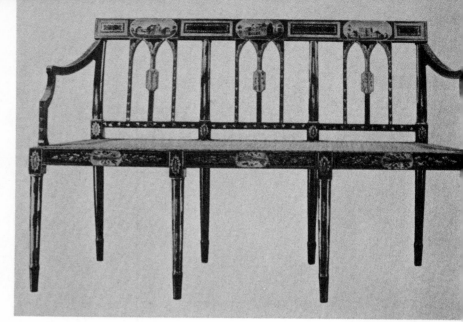

532

533

**533.** New York Empire mahogany couch, made about 1810. It is attributed to Duncan Phyfe (1768-1854). The spirally rolled ends are of unequal height, and the reeded frame has "saber" legs ending in brass paw feet. The form of the Roman *triclinium* (banquet couch), used by Thomas Hope and modified by Sheraton, inspired this design which had long-continuing popularity. A later example is shown in No. 535. Sheraton called this couch a "Grecian squab" (*Cabinet Dictionary*, 1803). It is at present called a Récamier couch, but actually Madame Récamier's couch, as shown in David's portrait of her in the Louvre, has equal ends and straight legs. (*Henry Ford Museum.*)

**534.** New York Empire sofa of mahogany and cane, with brass paw feet, attributed to Duncan Phyfe. It was made about 1810-1820. The line of the reeded cross-bars flows into the arm with an uninterrupted sweep. This type of construction is related to the chairs made by Phyfe for the Pearsall family of New York (No. 454). The X-shaped support was suggested by the folding stool of the Roman magistrate. Cornucopias, wheat sheafs, and a bowknot between festoons of drapery are carved in low relief. Caning, an English revival along with japanning toward the end of the eighteenth century, was seen again in American furniture around 1800. (*Karolik Collection, Museum of Fine Arts, Boston.*)

534

**535.** This late Empire couch, of bird's-eye maple and cane, made about 1820, shows the continued popularity of Sheraton's "Grecian squab" (No. 533). Later developments are seen in the heavy ring turning on the seat frame, and in the exaggerated scrolls on the foot and back. Spirals and scrolls grew progressively heavier in the 1820s and 1830s. (Nos. 561, 602, 606). (*Philadelphia Museum of Art.*)

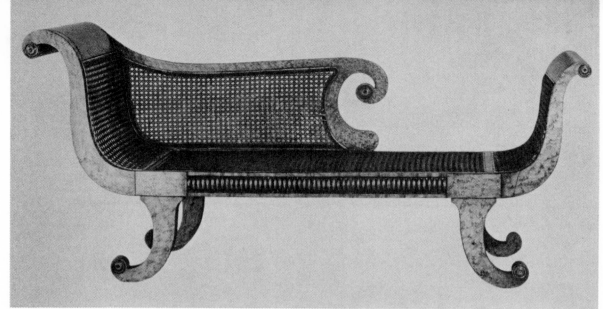

535

536

**536.** New York late Empire couch with rush seat, made about 1820. The ground is painted red, and gilt-stenciled ornamentation is used with metal mounts. This couch and No. 535 would have been used with a long cushion, or squab. Stenciled decoration made an appearance about 1815, and represents one of the most attractive features of late Empire furniture in America. (*Brooklyn Museum.*)

**537.** Late Empire mahogany sofa with stenciled decoration, made about 1820 for the Verplanck family of New York. It probably originated in the workshop of Duncan Phyfe (1768-1854). The elaborate design of spiral acanthus, eagles, cornucopias, and anthemion, shows the high order of stenciling which was done in New York. (See also Nos. 457 and 538.) The Empire winged lion's-paw foot is seen in a variant used on many late Empire sofas. A leafy bracket takes the place of an eagle's wing. (*Gift of Mrs. Bayard Verplanck. Metropolitan Museum of Art.*)

537

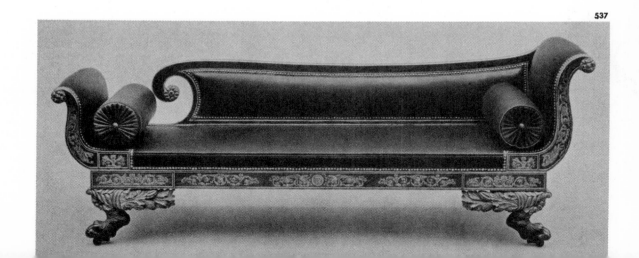

538.

538. Late-Empire mahogany sofa with stenciled decoration, probably made in New York about 1825-1830. The design shows the anthemion, cornucopias, and acanthus as used in No. 537, but the form is heavier. The fruit-filled cornucopia which ends in a broad curve illustrates the popular cornucopia arm of late Empire sofas. In the outline of the foot and back there is a suggestion of the rococo revival which was to flower in the following decade. The rounded top over the cornucopia is the "hammer end" sometimes seen on sofas of the 1830s. (*Garvan Collection, Yale University Art Gallery.*)

539. Salem mahogany candlestand in Sheraton style, made about 1800-1810. The swelling, reeded shaft with leaf-carved vase pedestal is three feet in height. The incurved legs are beaded and carved with strings of husks. Tall stands of pedestal form were favored by Robert Adam. They are rare in America, having been made for luxurious interiors. (*Essex Institute.*)

540. Hepplewhite mahogany urn stand, made about 1795, with carving attributed to Samuel McIntire. The design of this unique stand, which is only two feet, six inches in height, is based on a tall candlestand in Hepplewhite's *Guide*. The shaft is wreathed with McIntire's characteristic grapevine, and the acanthus, paterae, flutes, and beaded edge on the galleried top are almost as delicate and precise as the work of a jeweler. Since it has descended in the family of Elias Hasket Derby,[52] this stand is assumed to have been among the furnishings of the mansion which McIntire designed for him. (*Karolik Collection, Museum of Fine Arts, Boston.*)

541. Hepplewhite tilt-top stand of inlaid mahogany by David Poignand, who was working in Boston in 1788. The Hepplewhite stand has the "snake" foot of the Queen Anne period (No. 209), but the shaft is no longer pyriform in shape but has become an Adamesque urn. Small tables served many useful purposes. As a stand for candles they were indispensable. (*City Art Museum, St. Louis.*)

542. Mahogany candlestand, probably made in the Boston-Salem area about 1800-1810. The Sheraton tripod stand is characterized by a convex foot of great delicacy. Here flame-grained satinwood is inlaid in an oval on an eight-sided top crossbanded in wood of a darker tone. The vase section is stop-fluted and inlaid with bone, the base with paired quarter-fans. Apparent simplicity is belied by the unobtrusive detail, which shows the craftsman's skill. (*Henry Ford Museum.*)

543. Sheraton tambour basin stand of mahogany inlaid with satinwood stringing. The panels on the stiles are of curly maple. This stand, attributed to John and Thomas Seymour, was made about 1800. It was designed for a corner and has a shaped stretcher which serves as a small shelf for the ewer. The circular opening for a porcelain basin (Chinese export porcelain was frequently used) is flanked by removable mahogany bowls. The slightly incurved legs suggest the influence of the curving form of the Greek chair which was fashionable at the same period. (*Karolik Collection, Museum of Fine Arts, Boston.*)

539

540

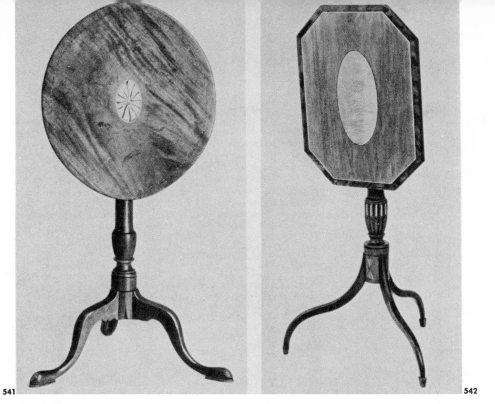

541

542

545

546

**544.** Sheraton mahogany bedside stand with a gray marble top, made about 1800-1810. The inlays are of satinwood and rosewood. Among details which suggest attribution to the Seymours are the thumbprint, or lunette, inlay on the base, the blue-green interior of the cabinet section, the shutter alternating light and dark wood (mahogany and curly maple), and inlay simulating pilasters. (*Karolik Collection, Museum of Fine Arts, Boston.*)

**545.** Chippendale-Hepplewhite mahogany candlestand and polescreen with dropleaf shelf, made about 1790 by Thomas Hodgkins for Jacob Sanderson (1758-1810) of Salem. This rare example might have been included in the Chippendale section because of the design of the shaft, but its oval shield is in the Hepplewhite style. The form with a shelf was not often made. A Chippendale example with adjustable shelf is at Winterthur. (The same museum has one in Queen Anne style with a stationary shelf and panel. See No. 209.) The shelf with a dropleaf is a later and apparently an American innovation. It appears here. (*Essex Institute.*)

**546.** Sheraton candlestand and polescreen of mahogany, probably made in New England about 1790. The eight-sided shield is shaped like Sheraton tilt-top tables, and the tripod base offers a graceful example of the Sheraton convex foot. Greater slenderness and delicacy of form distinguish this from the slightly earlier Salem example seen in No. 545. Like it, this also has a hinged shelf for the candlestick. (*Norvin H. Green sale, 1950, Parke-Bernet Galleries.*)

543

544

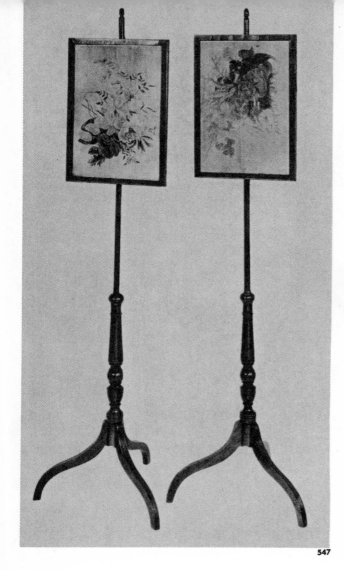

547

548

**547.** A pair of mahogany Sheraton polescreens, with floral prints in the panels, made about 1800-1810. Where the Chippendale polescreen had a wide shield and was of moderate height (No. 351), the Sheraton and Hepplewhite screens were tall, and had small shields. When rectangular, they are banner-like in effect. These two show fine detail in the delicate turning of the vase pedestals, in the reeding of the legs, and in the stringing of satinwood on the borders of the frames. Paintings, prints, and embroideries on satin were generally framed on these screens. (*Henry Ford Museum.*)

549

**548.** Sheraton card table of mahogany and satinwood, with tapering reeded legs. It has the fragmentary label of Adams and Todd and was probably made about 1798, when these cabinetmakers were listed in the directory. Samuel Adams and William Todd (died 1800) were in partnership on Cambridge Street. The thumbprint, or lunette, inlay which is seen on this table is frequently taken as a mark of Seymour workmanship when finely executed. From this evidence, the same type of inlay was ably used by some of their contemporaries.[51] The satinwood panels and finely proportioned reeded legs indicate that sophistication of design and refinement of detail are to be found in work by lesser-known cabinetmakers around 1800 in the Boston area. (*Old Deerfield.*)

**549.** This Hepplewhite card table of mahogany with inlay of shaded holly was made about 1790 and is one of a pair from an original set of four with label of John Townsend (1721-1809). It was originally owned by Colonel John Cooke and was included in the Flayderman sale in 1930. The serpentine table inlaid with a patera on the skirt is a characteristic Hepplewhite form. Geometric pendants (on two sides of the legs) surmounted by a tambour (or book) inlay are in the Newport manner. Tapering legs have inlaid cuffs. Townsend, who worked formerly in the Chippendale blockfront-and-shell style (No. 298) made furniture of Hepplewhite design late in his career. (*William Rockhill Nelson Gallery of Art and Atkins Museum.*)

**550** **551**

**550.** New England inlaid mahogany card table in the Sheraton-Hepplewhite style. Eighteen stars in the oval with eagle and shield are carefully indicated, which suggests a date between 1812 and 1816. The Sheraton rounded or D-shaped ends and the Hepplewhite tapering leg are combined here in a piece with New England characteristics in the acutely tapering foot, type of eagle medallion, and geometric satinwood and ebony inlays. (*Garvan Collection, Yale University Art Gallery.*)

**551.** Baltimore mahogany card table with a Sheraton kidney-shaped top and Hepplewhite tapering legs, made about 1800-1810. The satinwood tablet is inlaid with a shaded conch shell and breaking wave, a motif seen on furniture by John Shaw (such as the secretary he made for John Randall of Annapolis) but also used by others in the Annapolis-Baltimore area. A tapering leg with greater emphasis on the inside of the taper is a further characteristic detail of the Baltimore region. (*Collection of Mr. and Mrs. Sifford Pearre.*)

**552**

**553**

**552.** Salem Hepplewhite circular card table, probably made about 1800. As there is no baize lining, the polished surface of flame-patterned mahogany can be admired on both sides of the top. The husks-and-rosette motif on the legs is identical to the carving on a chair owned by Elias Hasket Derby which is attributed to Samuel McIntire and is in the Karolik Collection. The treatment of the inlaid semicircle with a "shell" in shaded inlay on top of the table, is like that on the Derby card tables, also attributed to McIntire, and, although simpler, is enclosed in the same "barber pole" or rope inlay. Hepplewhite suggested a circular form for card tables in his *Guide*. (*Collection of Mr. and Mrs. T. B. Christopher.*)

**553.** Baltimore Hepplewhite circular card table of inlaid mahogany. It was made in 1796 as a wedding present to Mr. and Mrs. George Coulston of Baltimore, and has since remained in the family. Indicative of the region are the long "tear-drop" panels of light-toned wood inlaid with bellflower pendants. The narrow geometric inlay, with broad striations of light and dark, is found on other Baltimore furniture. (*No. 2, Baltimore Furniture, 1947. Collection of Mr. and Mrs. Alexander Stewart. Courtesy Baltimore Museum of Art.*)

554

555

**554.** Baltimore mahogany card table in Sheraton-Hepplewhite style, with unusually rich carving and inlay. It was made about 1790-1810 and is from a widely scattered set (see also No. 429) which displays marked Baltimore characteristics. Among these are the long bellflower (husk) pendants suspended from half-rosettes carved on two sides of the legs, and the large inlaid ovals on the skirt outlined in wide banding. (*No. 7, Baltimore Furniture, 1947. Collection of Mr. and Mrs. Harry B. Dille-hunt, Jr. Courtesy Baltimore Museum of Art.*)

**555.** This Charleston Hepplewhite card table of mahogany, in-laid with satinwood, was made in the early 1800s. The inlay of a basket of flowers and broad floral scrolls on the skirt, and the floral vine pendants held by a four-petaled flower on the legs, represent Charleston's manner of defining design by actu-ally engraving on the surface of the wood, thus enhancing the linear quality of the inlay. The flower forms are remarkable for their naturalism. (*Henry Ford Museum.*)

**556.** Boston Sheraton card table of mahogany and satinwood, possibly the work of John and Thomas Seymour (1794-1816). It has reeded legs ending in tapering feet, and turned rings on the posts. The finely patterned satinwood panels are cross-banded in mahogany. The thumbprint, or lunette, inlay on the skirt and vertical face of the shaped top is finely executed here, resembling the work of the Seymours, although other skillful Boston makers used it. (See No. 548.) (*Philadelphia Museum.*)

556

557

**557.** New York labeled card table in the Sheraton style with characteristic "cloverleaf" top in rare five-lobed form. The label of John T. Dolan, one of Phyfe's contemporaries, gives the address 30 Beekman Street, at which he is listed in the directory only in 1811. The Sheraton style was popular in New York, where Phyfe was making furniture with the reeded leg and slender bulbous foot. This inspired numerous imitators. In basic form this table is like Phyfe's table from Mrs. J. Insley Blair's collection (No. 99, *Furniture by New York Cabinet-makers,* 1956). (*Museum of the City of New York.*)

**558**

**559**

**560**

**558.** New York card table in Duncan Phyfe style, one of a rare pair in satinwood, made about 1800-1810. The maker is not known, and an attribution to Phyfe was suggested by Hipkiss. Phyfe introduced this type (based on Sheraton designs), with the result that similar card tables with vase pedestal and incurved leg are frequently attributed to him unless other origin (as in the case of No. 559) can be proved. The "cloverleaf" top and the waterleaf carved on the leg are also important elements in the Phyfe-style card table. This illustrates his initial step in the direction of basic classic forms. (*Karolik Collection, Museum of Fine Arts, Boston.*)

**559.** New York mahogany card table, made about 1800-1810. It has a vase pedestal, tripod base ending in brass paw feet, a "cloverleaf" top, and the stamp of Michael Allison, who was active between 1800 and 1845. The design, execution of carving and reeding, and choice of waterleaf and drapery festoons as decoration all suggest the work of Phyfe so strongly that were it not for this stamp an attribution to Phyfe would have seemed reasonable. (*Henry Ford Museum.*)

**560.** New York Empire card table of mahogany with gilding, ormolu mounts, and wire inlay. This is one of a pair from the Van Rensselaer Manor House near Albany, and has the label of Charles-Honoré Lannuier. It belonged to a set (see also Nos. 410 and 585) made for Stephen Van Rensselaer IV and his wife Harriet Elizabeth Bayard presumably about 1817. They took the furniture at a later date to the Manor house, which became theirs in 1839. Typical of Empire design are the winged supports, lion's-paw feet, use of gilding, and the fine ormolu (gilt bronze) mounts which were probably made in Paris where Lannuier's brother was an *ébéniste*.[67] (See also No. 586.) (*Albany Institute of History and Art.*)

**561.** Late Empire mahogany and rosewood card table with stenciled decoration, made in Philadelphia about 1820-1830. It belonged to Commodore Samuel Woodhouse, U.S.N., who was in the War of 1812. Supports resting on a platform, either single columns or clustered, are typical of the Empire style. The design here is coarser than earlier examples. Heavy scrolls and spirals, seen on the skirt, are characteristics of furniture design after 1820 and in the early Victorian period (No. 606). (*Metropolitan Museum of Art.*)

**561**

562

**562.** The center table assumed its dominant role when it became fashionable to arrange furniture away from the walls.[68] In this room is an Empire version of the "pillar and claw" table with a massive center column and four incurved legs with brass paw feet. These tables, often used for cards, were called "loo tables." The design goes back to a table introduced by Georges Jacob in Paris in the 1790s, adopted by Thomas Hope and popularized by George Smith. Near the table is a modified klismos chair (see No. 457). The mirror-back pier table and round tea table have column-supports and lion's-paw feet. Empire fashions are represented by the convex mirror, eagle bracket, the cut-glass and bronze chandelier hung with faceted drops and prisms, and French porcelains with portraits of American heroes. A French ormolu clock stands on a mantel supported by marble caryatid figures from a Greek Revival Albany house built about 1830. (*Empire Parlor, H. F. du Pont Winterthur Museum.*)

**563.** New York center table of mahogany grained to imitate rosewood. It was made about 1820-1825 and was originally owned by the Schermerhorn family. The column supports, platform base, and leaf-bracketed paw feet are typical late Empire details. Stenciled decoration was often used in America as a substitute for fine ormolu, and the design of rosette, leaf scrolls, and palmette is skillfully executed. A similar example, a tea table, is shown in No. 562. (*Cooper Union Museum.*)

**563**

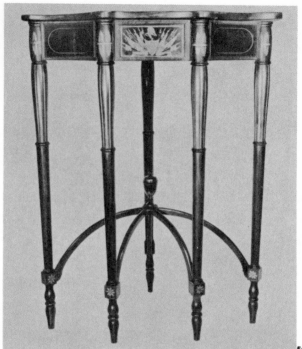

**564**

**564.** Baltimore Sheraton corner table of mahogany with inlay and gilt decoration. It has a marble top and an *églomisé* glass panel displaying military emblems executed in gold and light blue. The tops of the turned legs are striped in gold. An arched stretcher curves upward to an urn finial from blocks decorated with gilt rosettes. This rare table, an equivalent of the French *encoignure*, was probably used in a dining room. (*No. 31, Baltimore Furniture, 1947. Maryland Historical Society Collection. Photograph: Baltimore Museum of Art.*)

**565.** Baltimore Hepplewhite mahogany dining table, made about 1800-1810. Regional characteristics are recognized in the eagle medallions and tear-drop panels of light-toned wood inlaid with bellflower pendants in darker wood (see No. 553). Also frequently noted in Baltimore furniture is the narrow geometric inlay of light and dark wood, used in rectangles with incurved corners on the skirt and as a band on the lower edge. This simplest form of oval dining table is composed of two semicircular sections with drop leaves. (*No. 47, Baltimore Furniture, 1947. Collection of Mrs. Reginald M. Lewis. Courtesy Baltimore Museum of Art.*)

**566.** Empire three-part mahogany dining table with pedestal supports. It was made about 1810-1820 by Duncan Phyfe for William Gaston of New Jersey, who took it to Savannah, Georgia. (See McClelland, *Duncan Phyfe and the English Regency,* plate 262; Cornelius, *Furniture Masterpieces of Duncan Phyfe,* plate XLI.) The Phyfe design of clustered columns on a platform supported by incurved legs was the next step (after the vase pedestal) in the development of the classical style. In introducing it he came closer to English Regency than to French Empire design. A structural improvement in these dining tables was the use of brass clips to join the sections together. (*Norvin H. Green sale, 1950, Parke-Bernet Galleries.*)

**565**

**566**

567

567. This is one of the great Georgian interiors of America, designed by William Buckland between 1770 and 1774 for Matthias Hammond of Annapolis. The Hepplewhite inlaid mahogany dining table from Baltimore is composed of a drop-leaf center section and two semicircular ends. This table, the Chippendale chairs, and the Baltimore Hepplewhite sideboard with swell front and oval inlays were all part of the original furnishings of the house. The cellaret, partly seen at the left and illustrated in detail in No. 243, is one of the pieces acquired for its restoration. The portraits are of relatives of the Hammond family, painted by Charles Willson Peale. (Hammond-Harwood House Association, Annapolis.)

568. This green and ivory dining room, with a wealth of Adam detail in the mantelpiece, lintels, and cornices, is in a Boston house designed in 1795, probably by Charles Bulfinch, for Harrison Gray Otis (1765-1848), a leader of the Federal party and mayor of Boston. The New England early-nineteenth-century Sheraton table was originally owned by the family of

William Sumner Appleton, founder of the society which now owns the house. Two main supports composed of four hinged legs open outward to hold the fully extended mahogany top. This was one of the methods of increasing the length of the dining table before the advent of the telescope frame. Also in the room are Sheraton square-back chairs with urn splats and a Sheraton bowfront sideboard of Massachusetts origin. (Harrison Gray Otis House, Society for the Preservation of New England Antiquities.)

569. Late Empire three-pedestal dining table of mahogany, made about 1820-1830. Heavy vase pillars carved with acanthus rest on platforms supported by incurved legs ending in brass paw feet. The very large vase pillars are indicative of the late Empire style, in which existing forms were made heavier. The slender clustered columns of the table, No. 566, gave way to this form after 1820. (Mrs. J. Amory Haskell sale, Part VI, 1945, Parke-Bernet Galleries.)

568

569

**570**

**571**

**570.** Sheraton drawing table of mahogany, made about 1800-1810. It is one of the rare forms and is attributed to Duncan Phyfe. The table is constructed with a fifth leg which swings out to support the top when folded back to provide a rectangular surface. There is a working drawer at the end, and a simulated drawer on the front. This piece belonged to Louis Guerineau Myers, whose interest in Phyfe led to a special Duncan Phyfe section in the 1929 Girl Scouts Loan Exhibition in New York, in which this table, lent anonymously, was No. 781. It is very like Phyfe's small folding-lid desk, No. 772 in the same catalogue. (*Mrs. J. Insley Blair sale, 1954, Parke-Bernet Galleries.*)

**571.** Hepplewhite cherry dressing table with folding box lid, possibly made in Connecticut about 1800. Dressing tables with fitted top, easel mirror, and small drawers for cosmetics and accessories were illustrated in Hepplewhite's *Guide* (1788) as "Ladies Dressing Tables." The design was seldom made in America. This example, with its many drawers and compartments, its arched and beaded center, and slender legs fitted with cup casters, was obviously the work of a competent craftsman. The popular name "Beau Brummel(l)" is meaningless, as the form antedates the dominance of the sartorially elegant Beau Brummell. (*Old Deerfield.*)

**572.** A rare New York harlequin table of mahogany, crossbanded and inlaid with satinwood stringing. This table, in Sheraton style, made about 1800-1810, is possibly unique in American work. The two end compartments drop down within the frame, the lid closes, and the fifth leg pivots on a gate to one side, giving the piece the appearance of a side table. A "Harlequin Pembroke Table" is illustrated in Sheraton's *Drawing Book* (1791-1794) as suitable for a lady's writing and breakfast table. It is so

named, he writes, "for no other reason but because, in exhibitions of that sort, there is generally a great deal of machinery introduced in the scenery." This refers to the complicated mechanical features of the raising and lowering by means of weights, shown in detail on Sheraton's plate. (*Collection of Mrs. Louis J. Appell.*)

**573.** "Musical glasses" in an original late Sheraton table probably made in Baltimore, about 1825-1830. The table

has a folding box-lid, with crossbanding of mahogany. Drawer fronts are simulated. The large-scale vase pedestal and massive reeding are typical of the 1820s. A more exact date is given with the original *Instructions for the Grand Harmonicon invented and patented by Francis Hopkinson Smith of Virginia,* published in Baltimore by J. D. Troy, 1826. This set of musical glasses belonged to Josiah Bayly (1769-1846), Dorchester County, attorney general of Maryland. (*Maryland Historical Society.*)

**572**

**573**

**574.** A New England Hepplewhite pembroke is used here as a tea table. Contributing to the impression of comfort in a prosperous rural home about the year 1800 are the Worcester blue and gold tea set, the New England Hepplewhite heart-back chair, and the Martha Washington armchair. These pieces belonged to General Salem Towne (1746-1825), first owner of the house built in 1796 at Charlton, Massachusetts, which was moved to Old Sturbridge Village.[69] The table has rounded leaves which open to form the popular oval top of the period. (See Nos. 359-362 for Chippendale pembrokes.) A modest geometric inlay suggests the work of a well-trained rural craftsman familiar with city fashions. (*General Salem Towne House, Old Sturbridge Village.*)

**575.** Connecticut pembroke table of inlaid cherry, made about 1790-1800. The Chippendale influence still shows here in the scalloped leaves and pierced brackets, but the slender tapering legs and general delicacy of proportions classify it as a Hepplewhite example. The table represents a harmonious transitional form, of which Connecticut makers were masters. (*Collection of Mr. and Mrs. Frederick K. Barbour.*)

According to Hepplewhite, pembrokes might be square or oval, and both Hepplewhite and Sheraton offered designs for extravagant ornamentation. *The Dictionary of English Furniture* mentions an elaborate example which belonged to the Royal Household. Jane Austen's heroines used them as dining and tea tables, and the novelist's mother kept her valuables in the locked drawer of a pembroke table. They were also used as work tables. American pembroke tables of this period are generally inlaid.

**576.** Charleston Hepplewhite pembroke table of mahogany inlaid with holly and ebony. The secondary woods are tulip poplar (tulipwood), hard yellow pine, and cypress. The last strongly suggests a Charleston origin. The unusually large husk pendants are engraved on their outer edges, so that the use of incised lines on inlaid detail (see No. 555) again indicates the craftsmanship of Charleston. (*Collection of Frank L. Horton.*)

**577.** The Hepplewhite mahogany pembroke table in this parlor (see also Nos. 279, 504, 529) was probably made in the New York area. The inlaid leaf medallion on the stiles is a regional feature. Also seen here are a kettle-on-stand and a condiment dish, both of rare eighteenth-century China-Trade enamel. The New England Martha Washington chair, made about 1790, is of cherry, covered with striped apricot brocade. The type is Hepplewhite but a lingering Chippendale influence is seen in the heaviness of the legs. (No. 438 shows the Sheraton form.) The Wollaston portrait is of Margaret Philipse, a cousin of Cornelia Van Cortlandt Beekman. (*Philipsburg Manor, Upper Mills. Sleepy Hollow Restorations.*)

577

**578.** Hepplewhite pembroke gaming table of mahogany inlaid with satinwood and unidentified woods; made about 1790-1800. The tulipwood interior indicates Baltimore origin, an attribution also suggested by the broad satinwood banding and emphasis on the taper on the inside of the leg. This is a rare, possibly unique, example. (*Collection of Mr. and Mrs. Sifford Pearre.*)

**579.** Open view of table No. 578, showing the reversible top inlaid for chess, and the well inlaid for backgammon. Similar English tables are known and the example suggests the work of some English, Irish, or Scottish cabinetmaker. Many of them settled in Baltimore.

**580.** Baltimore hunt board of inlaid mahogany made about 1790-1810. It is in Hepplewhite style, with inlaid ovals on the stiles, bellflower pendants on the legs, and a skirt divided into three sections. Each has a center panel of choice grain inset in figured veneer and outlined in stringing. The top and the vertical face are crossbanded in mahogany. Below the light-toned cuff the feet are of darker wood in the Baltimore manner. The hunt board is a distinctively Southern form of sideboard table with tall legs. This unusually long example was shown in the Baltimore Furniture Loan Exhibition of 1947. (*Collection of Mrs. Clarence Miles. Courtesy Baltimore Museum of Art.*)

**581.** Baltimore Sheraton side or pier table of mahogany and satinwood, made about 1790-1800. The design is in the Appendix to Sheraton's *Drawing Book* (1791-1794), even to the exact form of the "stretcher rails," as Sheraton called them. The ornament, however, with its combination of inlays, is entirely in the Baltimore style. The floral panel is the same (in reverse) as on the Paca family table (No. 15, *Baltimore Furniture*). The large bellflowers suspended from a four-petaled flower are the same as on the table in the Garvan collection (No.

16, *Baltimore Furniture*). The flower pots and six-petaled blossoms complete the elaborate decoration. (*Collection of Mr. and Mrs. Sifford Pearre.*)

**582.** Detail of the top of table No. 581. The design is faithful to Sheraton and has D-shaped ends and projecting front, while the "stretcher rails" contain a small, semicircular shelf. The crossbanded top is formed of radiating bands of satinwood converging on a segment of an oval containing a shaded shell design similar to that on No. 514. Sheraton believed that the pier table should be treated solely as an ornament under a pier glass, but seldom does an American table so completely fulfill this concept.

**583.** Baltimore Hepplewhite semicircular side table of inlaid mahogany, made about 1790-1800. It has eagle medallions on the stiles, bellflower pendants with well-articulated petals, and a skirt with panels of crotch mahogany outlined in satinwood inlay. The marble top indicates its use as a serving table. The looking glass, possibly made in Baltimore about 1790, is typical of the Hepplewhite style with floral urn in composition ornament and an inlaid oval on the pediment of a frame which retains the broken scroll and pendant leafage of the earlier style (No. 344). (*Art Institute of Chicago.*)

580

583

581

582

**584**

**585**

**584.** New York mahogany side table with canted corners, reeded legs, and plain tablet on the skirt. It was designed by the architect John McComb (1763-1853) for the house he built in 1798 at 317 Washington Street. This formed part of a set for his dining room, but the table appears to have been made about 1810-1815. McComb, with Joseph Mangin, designed New York's City Hall (1803-1812) which shows Louis XVI influence, and he seems to have been equally inspired by Percier and Fontaine's Empire furniture, with plain surfaces of polished wood. The swelling form of the reeded leg seen here is the first indication of the late Sheraton style. The casters with ornamental cuffs of foliate design are not like any others observed on furniture of the period. (*New-York Historical Society.*)

**585.** New York Empire side or pier table of carved and gilt mahogany with mirror back, ormolu mounts, and wire inlay. It is one of a pair bearing the label of Charles-Honoré Lannuier, and comes from the Van Rensselaer Manor House. This is part of the same set described in Nos. 410, 560. Carved and gilt supports, half swan, half fish, represent the Egyptian ingredient in Empire design. The extraordinary mounts on this set, unsurpassed on American furniture, undoubtedly came from Paris. The lyres on the canted corners flank a central medallion with paired cornucopias, Greek honeysuckle, and flower clusters, with strawberry leaf terminals. (*Albany Institute of History and Art.*)

**586**

**586.** New York Empire pier table of rosewood with mirror back, lion's-paw foot, ormolu mounts, wire inlay, and white marble top. It was made about 1815 and has the label of Charles-Honoré Lannuier. Lannuier varied his supports, using caryatids, winged figures, and animal forms (Nos. 560 and 585), and brought the use of sculpture on American Empire furniture to its finest development. A pair similar to this belonged to Nathaniel Prime of No. 1 Broadway and is now in the Museum of the City of New York. The beginning of the vogue of the white marble top is represented here. (*Metropolitan Museum of Art.*)

**587**

588

**587.** New York Empire mirror-back pier table of rosewood, with gilt winged supports and dolphin feet. It was made about 1815 and is attributed to Charles-Honoré Lannuier. The supports are like those on the labeled card table, No. 560, and similar dolphin feet are seen on the labeled bed, No. 410. The table was originally owned by the Pierrepont family of Brooklyn, and was shown in the Metropolitan Museum's Greek Revival exhibition in 1943. The columns on plinths and the broad, plain frieze, sparingly embellished with metal mounts, contribute to an over-all design which shows the influence of Percier and Fontaine's Empire style. (*Brooklyn Museum.*)

**588.** Late Empire furniture from the Randall mansion in Cortland, New York, decorates this hall at Fountain Elms.[70] The rosewood table (about 1830) with marble top and columns, has stenciled decorations of the finest type. It was probably made in the workshop of Duncan Phyfe. The conical foot is in the French Restauration style. A pair of stenciled "fancy" chairs are of pseudo-klismos form, with the straight leg instead of the early curve (No. 452). The back rests project over the uprights in the Greek manner, and the splats are painted with pairs of griffins. The gilt pier glass has the label of Isaac Platt of New York. The portraits are by Ezra Ames (1768-1836). (*Fountain Elms, Munson-Williams-Proctor Institute, Utica.*)

589

**589.** New York mahogany sofa table with gilt winged supports and twist-turned stretchers, made about 1815. Attribution is made to Charles-Honoré Lannuier because of the table's similarity to labeled pieces such as No. 560, and to the Ames labeled console which was in the New York State furniture exhibition at the Metropolitan Museum in 1934. In his *Drawing Book*, Sheraton wrote that sofa tables "are those used before a sofa," and he included an illustration to show them in position. They represent a larger form of pembroke, and were intended for ladies while engaged in needlework, writing, or reading. Although frequently made in England, they very seldom appear in American work. In 1961 this table was selected for the White House by the Fine Arts Committee, with Mrs. John F. Kennedy as honorary chairman. It is now in the Red Room with other pieces by Lannuier, including a labeled *guéridon*.[71] See color plate VII. (*Courtesy of The White House.*)

**590.** New York mahogany tripod table with carved paw feet. It is in late Sheraton style and was made about 1815-1820, possibly in the workshop of Duncan Phyfe. The tripod table gradually acquired a heavier pillar, with a reeded columnar section in place of Phyfe's earlier vase pedestal. The reeded incurved legs end in paw feet, which are heavier than in Phyfe's early work. The canted corners, seen also on other tables of about 1815 (Nos. 584 and 589), indicate the passing of the long-fashionable oval top. Small tripod tables were used chiefly as candlestands and tea tables. (*Los Angeles County Museum.*)

**591.** Lady's work table, made about 1800-1810 and attributed to Duncan Phyfe. The body is partly reeded to simulate a tambour closing. Reeding also appears on the vase pedestal and on the incurved legs which end in brass paw feet. This mahogany tripod work table represents Phyfe's early use of classical design based on Sheraton. The rounded ends contain small trays, and there is a writing slide. One of the drawer fronts is simulated above a work drawer. (*Karolik Collection, Museum of Fine Arts, Boston.*)

590

591

**592.** Lady's work table, in the Sheraton style. It was made in Boston about 1800, and is attributed to John and Thomas Seymour because of the lunette or thumbprint inlay on the top and bottom edges, the fine dovetailing, and the lavish use of veneered panels. The top is of crotch mahogany; the reeded legs, which represent the slenderness of form prized in New England furniture, are of mahogany; and the body glows with the mellow golden tone of the maple panels. Three apparent drawer fronts mask a single drawer and add to the decorative effect. The legs, continued as turnings on the canted corners, produce the lines of the projecting colonnette found on Sheraton furniture of many types. There are few American work tables which so closely approach the elegance of the English equivalent. (*Karolik Collection, Museum of Fine Arts, Boston.*)

**593.** Hepplewhite work table made about 1790-1800. It is of mahogany inlaid with satinwood. The unusual recessed front with concave drawers repeating the line of the shaped top gives this simple piece distinction. The proportions are fine, and the tall slender legs have dark cuffs bordered in stringing which, with the long ovals inlaid on the stiles, suggest a Baltimore origin. It may have been used as an occasional table or for sewing. However, the drawers are not fitted for needlework, and there are no trays or pouch, which in the case of Nos. 591 and 592 indicated a specific use. (*Luke Vincent Lockwood sale, 1954, Parke-Bernet Galleries.*)

593

592

**594.** This mahogany work table in the Sheraton style, probably made in Salem about 1815, is of a later type than No. 592. Comparison of the reeding of the leg and the turning of the foot on these two examples shows the emergence of much heavier forms. The same designs were followed but on a different scale. The rosette and leaf, a motif often found on tablets in Sheraton designs where it is carved on a flat surface, has been adapted here to a rounded form and is more exaggerated in size. This new aspect is to be traced to contemporary English fashions. (*Essex Institute.*)

**595.** Late Sheraton work table with slide. It is of mahogany and bird's-eye maple, and was made in New York about 1815. Rich carving appears in the form of acanthus on the vase pedestal and in the rippling waterleaf on the four incurving legs. The carved paw feet end in finely articulated claws. This table could have originated only in the shop of a superior cabinetmaker such as Phyfe or Allison. The convex edge of the top is crossbanded, and the curly maple veneered panel has a crossbanded frame with indented, mitred corners. (*Collection of Mrs. Giles Whiting.*)

The "lady's work table" which Sheraton offered in the *Drawing Book* was a small object of great elegance and luxury, obviously not intended for more than the lightest form of "fancy needlework," an occupation for the drawing room and parlor. The fitted work table was a new form introduced about 1770 in England, reaching America in the late 1700s. It was not made with such elaborate inlays and painted decoration in America, although these modes of decoration were employed, and there were many which prove that the best efforts of the cabinetmaker were concentrated upon them.

594

595

596

597

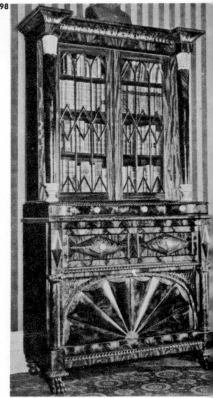

598

**596.** Library at Fountain Elms, Utica.[70] This house, in Tuscan villa style, was built in 1850 after designs by the Albany architect William J. Woollett, Jr., for Alfred Munson, who presented it to his daughter on her marriage to James Watson Williams. It was restored in 1961 with 1830-1850 furnishings, including a labeled secretary by Anthony Querville. The mantel of white marble with brown and black marbleizing came from another house in the area. The bookcase (left) is one of a pair with twist-reeded columns made in the 1840s for the Gothic cottage at Nicholas Biddle's Andalusia on the Delaware River. The table cover, important in Victorian decoration, has a floral design in raised work. Rococo armchairs are covered in black horsehair.

**597.** Carved and gilded mahogany desk and bookcase with paper label of Anthony Querville (active 1835-1849).[73] It was made in Philadelphia about 1835 and has been owned in Utica, New York, for over a century. Applied convex panels in the form of a fan on the base are capped with ash burl stained walnut; the interior of the writing section is bird's-eye maple. Late classical design is present in the semi-engaged columns, lion's-paw foot, acanthus, and anthemion, but the coved cornice, rippled moldings, and cut-glass knob handles are Victorian.

**598.** This closed view of the Querville secretary shown in No. 597 displays more fully the fine craftsmanship of this French-born cabinetmaker. The use of matched veneers of crotch mahogany remained in evidence at the opening of the Victorian period. Victorian inclination toward novelty is seen in the introduction of the convex diamond-shaped panels on the front of the writing section and on the stiles. (*Fountain Elms, Munson-Williams-Proctor Institute, Utica.*)

# 5. Early Victorian

## 1830-1870

ERA OF CHANGE. In the 1830s the many political and technological changes coincided with the emergence of a new middle class in Europe and an industrial aristocracy in America. Romanticism was the chief inspiration of art and literature, and it was natural that furniture and the decorative arts should be affected by the trends, inventions, and customs of the times.

In France the rich *bourgeoisie* were holding their material gains under an unpopular Louis Philippe, whom they had mistakenly accepted as a liberal. In 1832 the Reform Bill in England gave greater power to the rich middle class, and only to that class. In America, Jacksonian Democracy was so well established that the stanch Federalist Philip Hone was still expressing acute sorrow over the fact that the name of "the most patriotic party which ever existed should continue to be a term of reproach," in his *Diary* for June 18. Against this background of political ferment the mechanization of industry went forward, better transport became available, and new products found a ready market among the expanding population.

In America as in Europe, railroads were under construction. They started in the late 1820s, and were soon linking cities along the Atlantic coast and penetrating the interior. In 1832 the cornerstone of the Baltimore and Ohio was laid. In 1838 New York harbor welcomed the *Great Western* and *Sirius,* forerunners of the Atlantic passenger liners, which in the 1840s made European travelers of well-to-do Americans. In the United States, improvements in hotels made travel more agreeable. Boston's Tremont House was completed in 1829, and the architect, Isaiah Rogers, gave innkeeping an entirely new concept of comfort and splendor. Tremont House was followed by the Astor House in New York, in 1836, and other elegant hotels were built in the larger cities.

Long before midcentury the Greek style was challenged by the Gothic. A revolutionary step was taken in the 1830s when the architect Alexander J. Davis (1803-1892), a leader in the Greek Revival, started designing Gothic country houses. He found a sympathetic spirit in Andrew Jackson Downing (1815-1852), who referred to Greek Revival homes as "tasteless temples." This remarkable horticulturalist and scientist with a streak of poetry in his nature found the Gothic style fitted to his concept of beauty. He believed that "order and culture" could be established among men when they lived among "smiling lawns and tasteful cottages." When he built his new home at Newburgh on the Hudson River about 1840 he gave it Gothic-style octagonal towers, and there was a Gothic entrance between un-Gothic verandas. Downing advocated verandas, piazzas, balconies, and bay windows as means of increasing the enjoyment of nature as well as comfort and a sense of well being. His two books, *Cottage Residences* (1842) and *Architecture of Country Houses* (1850), advocate the use of historic styles not for their own sake but as a means of suggesting the individuality of the owner and of creating a suitable environment for the cultivation of the mind. His principles of landscape gardening, which gave art a tactful role in a quiet understatement of the picturesque, are seen in public parks today. Downing was killed when the steamboat *Henry Clay* burned in 1852, and his partner, Calvert Vaux, working with Frederick Law Olmsted, carried out his ideas in the landscaping of New York's Central Park in 1856.

By 1835 the Tuscan style had joined the Gothic in competing for favor. Architectural designs, supposedly suggested by the country houses of Italy, showed large, square towers, coupled windows, canopied verandas, and details borrowed from Greek and Gothic styles. These liberties represented an eclecticism in which the architects of the day gloried. After 1844 Downing and Davis, working in an unofficial partnership, designed houses in Tuscan style.

Furniture in the new homes of the 1830s and 1840s represented the era of change. Mechanized industry had much to offer in machine-woven carpets, textiles for upholstery and hangings, roller-printed wallpapers, pattern-molded glass, electroplated tableware, and statuettes. Mechanization made many new luxuries possible for the family of average means, but design lost the restraining guidance of tradition, and there occurred what is generally called the "decline in taste."

Furniture design was not immediately affected by the use of machinery, although the tendency was in that direction. There is a question how much the better grade of furniture in the early Victorian period was influenced by mechanization. Machinery in this field was not as revolutionary as that in the textile industry and in the making of ornamental accessories.

FURNITURE AND THE MACHINE. The circular saw came into increasing use between 1830 and 1850. It had been known in the eighteenth century, and there is occasional mention of its use in America in the early 1800s. *The Massachusetts Spy,* September 26, 1821, reports it as a novelty employed by the Shakers at Watervliet, New York. After 1830 the use of the circular saw was not unusual, and about midcentury it was widespread. Very fine cuts could be made with it, and veneers could be produced in much thinner and larger pieces. It was thus possible to use a veneer for an entire surface, covering a core of less expensive wood.

The use of the bandsaw developed more slowly, although an English patent for it had been granted in 1808. A satisfactory form was not found until about 1850, and improvements came still later. Perfected fret-cutting machinery was available in the 1850s, and wood-carving machines were demonstrated at the Crystal Palace exhibition in London in 1851. These were not in general use at the time, however. On November 17, 1857, a paper, "On the Conversion of

Wood by Machinery," was read by G. L. Molesworth before the Institute of Civil Engineers in England, in which he mentioned only the circular saw, bandsaw, and planing and mortising machines as in general use at the time. From this it would seem that design was not being affected to a decisive extent. Peter Floud called attention to this paper in the *Connoisseur Period Guide, Early Victorian,* 1958.

A step toward the assembly line was taken in some of the furniture-making shops through the distribution of labor, but such "factories" as those of Meeks and Belter in New York in the 1840s and 1850s were not factories in the modern sense. In these great workshops many trained cabinetmakers were employed along with other less skilled workmen. There were other craftsmen, such John Jelliff in Newark and John Needles in Baltimore, who continued to make furniture according to the old traditions. In 1861, however, "steam factories" for the making of furniture were mentioned as a new development; the Philadelphia architect Samuel Sloan (1815-1884), author of *Designs for Rural Buildings,* mentioned them. Machinery undoubtedly influenced the design of inexpensive furniture, and there was a growing market for this kind of product. John Hall's *Cabinet-Maker's Assistant* (1840) illustrated scrolled supports in monotonous repetition for every conceivable position, and these were well suited for cutting with a bandsaw. Hall's designs successfully fulfilled his intention to offer "an economical arrangement to save labor" and were addressed to the maker who wanted to produce furniture quickly and cheaply.

Machinery took an increasingly important place in the great new international exhibitions as inventors showed the wonders it could perform. A few far-seeing art critics warned of the harmful potentialities, but not before considerable aesthetic damage had been done in the field of design.

ERA OF REFORM. In certain ways the new preoccupation with machinery brought obvious advantages, but in the production of furnishings for the interior the increasing number of machines used for stamping, embossing, molding, die-sinking, plating, and all kinds of mechanical ornamentation began to alarm thoughtful people in England even before Morris and Eastlake reacted so strongly against it in the 1860s. Siegfried Giedion's *Mechanization Takes Command* (1948) offers an account of the many patents, from 1820 to 1850, which affected the decorative arts. Giedion also describes the resulting excesses, and the beginnings of reform.

An early voice on the subject was that of Henry Cole (1802-1883), whose pseudonym was Felix Summerly. He urged the right use of machinery, invented the term "art manufactures," and published a *Journal of Design* from 1848 to 1852. His ideas were shared by Owen Jones, whose *Grammar of Ornament* (1856) foreshadows the *art nouveau* of the end of the century. Cole's persistence was rewarded in the Great Exhibition at the Crystal Palace in 1851, for which he obtained the support of the Prince Consort and the Society of Arts. This was London's first international exhibition, and the excesses in which the manufacturers prided themselves were brought to light. An excellent impression of this can be gained from the catalogue prepared by Cole's co-worker, Matthew Digby Wyatt, *The Industrial Arts of the Nineteenth Century: Illustrations of the Choicest Specimens of the Exhibition of 1851.* Here unspoiled handcrafts of the Far East are illustrated with the blatant offerings of the Western market.

In the next decade the current of reform was directed by William Morris. His point of view was different, but he asked for a return to handwork and a new use of an earlier Gothic style. Charles Eastlake advocated honesty of design and sound construction, and his words were taken to heart in America when his *Hints on Household Taste* was published here in 1872. In the succeeding decades of the nineteenth century, designers, architects, and makers of taste were deeply interested in the relation of handcraft to the machine and in principles of design. Revivals continued, but there was a new element of self-expression, of concern with the present, which is evidence of a fresh start. The period 1870-1900 is a new period, closer in spirit to the reactionary twentieth century than to the Romantic decades when a link with tradition, slight though it was, united early Victorian design to the past.

The available literature on the subject of early Victorian furniture is fragmentary, and most of it is of an introductory nature.[72] The special character of this period has suggested a treatment which differs from that of earlier chapters, and the arrangement is based on distinctive styles and the use of materials rather than on furniture forms.

VICTORIAN CLASSICAL. The first indications of a Victorian style in America, as in England, can be seen in the mid-1830s as a modification of long-lived classical designs. France became interested in the Near East, in divans and experiments with upholstery, but for the time being England and America were more concerned with revivals. Historic ornament of other periods, Gothic, Elizabethan, Louis Quatorze, Renaissance, was selected for Romantic association. Styles were thought to be evocatory. Gothic was considered suitable for libraries and serious study; French styles provided the desired atmosphere for drawing rooms and polite conversation; the Elizabethan period had a chivalrous connotation. No chronology can be offered for the use of these and other styles, for most of them were in evidence at about the same time.

Victorian classical furniture does not differ greatly from the furniture of the 1820s, but it was still heavier in scale and carried more elaborate ornamentation. This can be seen by comparison of the late Empire sofa, No. 537, with the Victorian classical sofa, No. 602. The generously proportioned vase pedestal of the Empire dining table, No. 569, is surpassed by the still heavier pedestal of the table in the dining room shown in No. 599. The sideboard in this dining room illustrates a similar increase in the proportions of the columns over the Empire sideboard illustrated by No. 525.

GOTHIC. There were numerous adaptations of Gothic design in American Victorian furniture, although the style was not as popular as in England, where its historical and romantic significance had greater meaning. The Gothic style never completely died out in England. It had been revived between 1730 and 1770 by Kent, Batty Langley, and Chippendale, and at Walpole's Strawberry Hill. Toward the end of the century the landscape architects Lancelot (Capability) Brown and Humphrey Repton substituted for the formal garden an informal planting in which Gothic "ruins" were built. The cult of the picturesque attained greater importance in the Regency period, when it branched out into fanciful Oriental manifestations and pseudo-rustic architecture represented by the *cottage orné*. Repton's partner, John Nash (1752-1835), was especially influential in adapting the Gothic style to domestic architecture. The castellated country house, with drum tower, battlements, and machicolations, was more successful than a mere enumeration of such unlikely details on a small-scale dwelling would suggest.

The French *émigré* Augustus Charles Pugin, a scholarly writer on medieval architecture, had a profound interest in Gothic. He published designs for Gothic furniture in Ackermann's *Repository of the Arts*, which were collected in book form in 1827. His son, Augustus Welby Northmore Pugin, later associated with Sir Charles Barry in remodeling the Houses of Parlia-

**VIII.** This Victorian parlor at Fountain Elms, built in 1850 at Utica, New York, has furniture by John Henry Belter, Elijah Galusha, and Charles A. Baudouine. *(Munson-Williams-Proctor Institute.)*

279

*Above: Family Group.* By Frederick R. Spencer (1806-1875). *(Brooklyn Museum.)*

The Victorian classical style is represented by the exaggerated spiral arm on the sofa and the heaviness of the column and paw feet on the pedestal table. The painting is dated 1840.

*Right:* Cresting rail. Back of sofa by Belter, No. 637. *(Metropolitan Museum of Art.)*

280

ment, became a leader in Gothic Revival church architecture. He occasionally turned his attention to furniture, and in 1835 designed Gothic pieces while at work at Scarisbrick Hall near Manchester. This was the same year that his *Gothic Furniture in the Style of the Fifteenth Century* was published. The direct influence of the younger Pugin on furniture styles was not great, for his designs were not practical. Distorted versions of them, however, were contributed by such pedestrian designers as Henry Wood, who included Gothic designs in his *Furniture Decoration,* published about 1845. An earlier designer was George Smith, whose *Household Furniture* illustrated a Gothic state bed as early as 1808. Smith also introduced Gothic plates in his *Guide* of 1826. His pupil Robert Conner left England for New York, and in 1842 Conner's *Cabinet-Maker's Assistant* became the first book of Gothic designs to appear in America. The use of Gothic detail in American furniture had not waited for this, however. Smith's work was available, and so was J. C. Loudon's standard guide, the *Encyclopaedia of Cottage, Farm and Villa Architecture* (1833), which contained sections on furniture.

The Gothic style influenced American architecture considerably more than it did furniture design. As a rule, Gothic motifs were sparingly used. They can be seen in pointed arches on doors of case pieces (such as No. 605) or in carved detail on the table by Needles, No. 610. Tracery of the perpendicular style in the manner of Pugin appears on the corner whatnot, No. 618. Gothic lancet arches and crockets were used on the chair by A. J. Davis, No. 613. An anonymous book entitled *Gothic Album for Cabinetmakers,* published in Philadelphia in 1868, shows that interest in the style continued, although it became of secondary importance.

RENAISSANCE. The style called Renaissance was of uncertain source. It was in evidence in the Crystal Palace exhibitions in London in 1851 and in New York in 1853. As early as the mid-1830s "Cinque-Cento" and "French Renaissance" were included in pattern books, and this marks the beginning of the revival of sixteenth- and early seventeenth-century French architectural ornament. The style was in use in America in the 1850s and 1860s, and as late as the 1876 Centennial Exposition in Philadelphia, for which a Renaissance bedroom set was especially designed (No. 628). Reference to the style is to be found in *Architecture of Country Houses* (1850), where Downing mentions it as being currently in favor, along with Gothic, Grecian, Elizabethan, Romanesque, and French (rococo).

Typical Renaissance motifs include a crest, or rounded pediment enclosing a cartouche, and the use of consoles, as seen on the set mentioned (No. 628). Sculptured busts are also related to the design, as on the chair by John Jelliff (No. 625). It is to be noted that this example and the chair by Thomas Brooks (No. 626) have the characteristic tapering baluster leg which resembles the style used on early Louis XIV chairs. For some reason an acorn turning (Nos. 623 and 628) became associated with Renaissance motifs. Applied medallions are also considered typical, as in No. 629; this, however, shows an overlapping of the Elizabethan style (as used in England) in which carved medallions of fruit and game were added to sideboards. This provides an example of the confusion that attends an effort to separate the Victorian revivals.

ELIZABETHAN. Like the Gothic, the Victorian Elizabethan style was more widely followed in England than in America. The strapwork carving which marks the English style is not characteristic of American furniture, but both have an anachronistic detail which is to be seen in spiral-twist turning, actually to be found not on Elizabethan (or Tudor) work but on Charles II furniture of the second half of the seventeenth century. Smith's *Guide* of 1826 states that the

Elizabethans had chairs with "light spiral columns in the backs," and in 1845 Henry Wood illustrated twist turning as Elizabethan. An American example of its use is seen in a New York chair (No. 651), where the whole design shows a confusion with the English chair of the late 1600s. In furniture of simpler type the Elizabethan style is seen in spool-turnings on beds and stands, or applied split-turnings in the form of bobbins, knobs, and other lathe-turned forms on cottage furniture (No. 654).

ROCOCO. England and America shared the rococo style with the country representing the fountainhead of fashion — France. The style had a genuine quality lacking in the other revivals. Nineteenth-century rococo is a creation of its own time, yet is in harmony with eighteenth-century concepts of the curvilinear form. English and American work lacks the subtlety of Louis XV furniture, but is often distinguished by grace and vitality.

In the early 1830s the Victorian rococo style in England began as "Louis XIV," but this was late Louis XIV of about 1700. After a somewhat ponderous beginning, England took up the lighter forms which were in style in France. Although the rococo was supplanted in that country during the Second Empire, when the Empress Eugénie favored a return to Louis XVI designs, American design was not affected at once. Here the rococo style was fashionable by 1850 and remained so for several decades more.

The cabriole leg was reintroduced, but without the scroll toe or claw-and-ball foot of the eighteenth century. Instead, a short tapering cylinder was used (No. 640). The typical rear leg is not a cabriole, as in the Louis XV period, but a reverse curve with the convex section at the foot, producing a graceful form of great stability. The backs of chairs were made higher than in the original style.

The serpentine lines and S-scrolls of the original rococo were interpreted in a new manner with lacy borders of carved naturalistic fruit and flowers (No. 641). Swags of flowers and grapes are a typical adornment of the skirts of center tables (No. 645). Belter identified the Victorian rococo style primarily with his name, but it was also used with distinction by Elijah Galusha of Troy, New York, the Meeks firm and Charles Baudouine of New York, Daniel Pabst of Philadelphia, Seignouret and Mallard of New Orleans, and many other makers of lesser note.

MATERIALS. The favorite wood of the early Victorian period was figured tropical rosewood, especially liked for its fine pattern. Mahogany continued in use, and toward the end of the period black walnut became popular. Belter used stained oak for less expensive furniture, or other hard wood which was ebonized. Solid wood was used, although at first there was occasional use of veneered matched panels following the fashion of the preceding period. Veneers were, however, used in other ways. Belter used a laminating process in which thin strips of veneer were glued and pressed together and steamed in a mold to produce the curved forms he desired. Veneering was also used to give an expensive appearance to a cheaper piece of furniture.

Laminating was not Belter's invention. When applying for a patent (which he received in 1856) he stated that he realized the glueing together of thin veneers had been done before, but the unusual part of his method was the steaming in "cawls," or molds, which produced curving forms. The method proved so successful that his concaved chair-backs, serpentine bureaus, and triple-arched sofas have survived a century of use almost unscathed. Laminating, although patented by Belter, was imitated by Charles Baudouine, George Henkels, and others.

During this period, upholstered furniture became increasingly important and upholsterers rose to a dominant position as regents of style. The improvements in metal coil springs, made throughout the first half of the 1800s, and the fabrics produced by the new power looms led eventually to the development of all-upholstered furniture where no framework was visible. The French perfected this type, which had originally been inspired by the Orient and which suited the times when many other new comforts were becoming available. The French easy chairs (*confortables*), tabourets (*poufs*), and ottomans (*bornes*), set the style for England and America. In the 1840s and 1850s in America, frames of chairs were upholstered over the seat rail with comfortable cushioning held in place by tufting and buttons (No. 631), typical of the Victorian period, and backs of sofas in the *tête-à-tête* style were almost entirely covered (No. 630). Entirely upholstered furniture belongs to the period beginning about 1870.

Marble tops for center tables, *étagères,* and sideboards were the rule. In America white and colored Italian marbles were commonly used, as well as local white Tennessee marble.

A considerable amount of iron and brass furniture was made in America in the nineteenth century. An unusually early example originated in the Wood Foundry in Philadelphia. This cast-iron garden chair marked and dated *1807* was exhibited at the Philadelphia (then the Pennsylvania) Museum in the 1935 loan exhibition of authenticated Philadelphia furniture (see No. 112 of the catalogue). This is a notable exception, for examples even of the 1830s are rare (No. 661). But around 1850 and later the market was well supplied. The usual forms in metal were garden furniture and hat and umbrella stands for the hall (Nos. 659 and 660). These were made by firms specializing in architectural ironwork. About 1870, improvements in the making of wire resulted in designs combining iron and wirework for garden furniture (No. 662), and also for ornaments and elaborate flower stands. Brass furniture was shown in the international exhibitions of the mid-nineteenth century, but the use of this metal in American work occurred chiefly after the period which ends this book.

In spite of its fragility, papier-mâché was a favorite for very light chairs and tables in English and American Victorian rooms. So far as has been determined, little of this furniture was made in America, but a considerable quantity was imported from England (No. 664), where the firm of Jennens and Bettridge of Birmingham was a leading manufacturer.

NEW FORMS. The ottoman, at first a boxlike couch with cushions, or even no more than an upholstered bench (No. 413), assumed a circular form and a position in the center of the room. Sometimes it was made in sectional form, with arms dividing it into compartments. The center support might be crowned with a *jardinière,* as illustrated by Henry Wood in 1845. A circular ottoman made by Gottlieb Vollmer of Philadelphia in 1859 is at the White House.

The whatnot also began its existence during the Regency period. The name was first applied to it about 1810, when it was a small, rectangular stand with shelves, about the height of a side table, designed for a place against the wall. The whatnot in its Victorian form came into general use only in the 1840s, grew in height (No. 620), and in the 1850s was often designed for a corner (No. 618).

When made on a larger scale and combined with mirror panels and marble, the whatnot became an *étagère* (No. 622). This French name was introduced in the 1850s.

The balloon-back chair (No. 632) may be mentioned, although a change in pattern does not constitute a new form. The shape originated in the 1830s in England, was adopted in America around 1840, and remained important as long as the rococo style was followed. In America this was until about 1870. The design was evolved through the rounding off of the top rail of the klismos-type chair and the curving inward of the uprights. The rail joining the uprights was scrolled, and all other lines, including those of the cabriole leg and the seat rail, became free-flowing curves. This made the balloon-back chair one of the most attractive examples of the rococo style.

The single-end sofa is also preeminently Victorian. Typical examples have a high back at one end, tapering sharply away to the open end. (No. 636.) Another popular design, with chair-back ends and a low center, is illustrated in No. 630.

PATENT FURNITURE. Between 1850 and 1900 there was a great increase in the number of inventions of adjustable and convertible types of furniture. Patent furniture was not new in the nineteenth century; English examples from the preceding century exist, although they are very rare. Patent furniture represents an age-old preoccupation with furniture construction involving movement, seen in the Roman folding stool and the medieval revolving desk. The granting of patent to inventors, giving exclusive right of manufacture, began in England in the sixteenth century.

In nineteenth-century America the great upsurge of inventiveness in every phase of mechanics is represented by successive improvements in reclining chairs, swivel and tilting chairs, and other adjustable forms for home, office, travel, and professional use. An early reclining chair is illustrated by No. 658. Readers interested in this phase of furniture design will find an extensive account of it in Siegfried Giedion's *Mechanization Takes Command*.

VICTORIAN COLLECTIONS. Victorian furniture has not been collected in the systematic manner that characterizes the study of earlier American periods, and available material is widely scattered. However, there are a few notable collections in existence, and interest is increasing. In 1953 the Brooklyn Museum installed four nineteenth-century interiors under the supervision of Charles Nagel, who was then director. Three of these represent the period under consideration and are illustrated in Nos. 612, 627, 635. In the museum's "Victoriana" exhibition of 1960, arranged by Marvin D. Schwartz, curator of decorative arts, a first attempt was made to survey the arts of the period as a whole. Two of the furniture alcoves are illustrated here, Nos. 628 and 638.

One of the most extensive Victorian collections is to be found at the Henry Ford Museum and Greenfield Village at Dearborn, Michigan. Here decorative arts, craftwork, machinery, houses, shops, mills — in fact, everything relating to nineteenth-century life — are included in a comprehensive plan, originated by Henry Ford himself, to reproduce "American life as lived." In the decorative-arts galleries of the museum are many examples of the late classical and rococo phases of the Victorian style, including pieces by Belter from Lincoln's home in Springfield (Nos. 638-640).

Among historic house museums is Sunnyside, the home of Washington Irving at Irvington-on-Hudson, now under the care of Sleepy Hollow Restorations. Of great interest here are the furnishings Irving used between 1836, when he completed the remodeling of an old Dutch farmhouse, and 1859, the year of his death. These pieces are represented with others acquired for the restoration (Nos. 602, 603, 614, 654, 655, 656, 659, 660).

Fountain Elms, a Tuscan villa built in Utica, New York, in 1850 and restored in 1961 by the Munson-Williams-Proctor Institute, contains many furnishings from the Williams family, the original owners, and from other homes in the area. This carefully restored Victorian house has striking wallpapers and textiles reproducing authentic patterns of the period, and there are antique gas chandeliers and lamps to illustrate the lighting devices of a luxurious home. Fountain Elms was built in the years of prosperity following the opening of the Erie Canal, when there was a market upstate for fine furniture from New York, carpets from England, and wallpapers and porcelains from France. (Nos. 596, 599, 606-608, 622, 633, 644, 650.)

The South is fortunate in having many notable houses of the period with an impressive number of the original furnishings. Among the restored and publicly maintained Victorian houses are Rosalie in Natchez, owned by the Daughters of the American Revolution; Belle Meade in Nashville, maintained by the Association for the Preservation of Tennessee Antiquities; and the Hermitage near Nashville, home of Andrew Jackson, now under the care of The Ladies' Hermitage Association. In recent years the Campbell house in St. Louis, owned by the Campbell House Foundation, has been open to the public with original furnishings of 1850-1860 which are in an exceptional state of preservation.

# Makers

*Charles A. Baudouine* (active 1845-1900), New York. This successful rival of Belter's had a factory with two hundred employees, of whom seventy were trained cabinetmakers. In the introduction to the catalogue of the "Victoriana" exhibition at the Brooklyn Museum (1960), Marvin D. Schwartz supplies this information and also mentions Baudouine's unpublished notebook of reminiscences (now in the libary of the Winterthur Museum) which describes how he avoided infringement of Belter's patent by making laminations with a division down the center.

*John Henry Belter* (1804-1863), New York. Belter was born in Württemberg, Germany, and came to America as a trained cabinetmaker. He was active in New York from 1844 and his principal places of business were first at 552 Broadway, then at 722 Broadway. In 1858 he opened a factory on Third Avenue near 76th Street as the J. H. Belter and Company Cabinet Factory. Belter was the leading exponent of the rococo style, using wide lacework borders of naturalistically carved flowers and grapes combined with scrolls. A description of this maker's laminating process (patented 1856) is given in Joseph Downs' article in *Antiques,* September 1948: "Belter used thin layers of rosewood glued together, with the grain of each layer at right angles to the next. The number of layers varied from three to sixteen; however, the average was six to eight, and the total thickness usually measured less than an inch. These layers of wood were glued and pressed together, and steamed to take the required curves in a special matrix to give the parts their shape. The layers of veneer were then ready for carving." His later work is flatter and shows the use of interlacing bands. (Nos. 636-649.)

*Thomas Brooks* (1811-1887). This maker is listed in the Brooklyn directories from 1856 to 1876. He died in Dalton, Massachusetts. Brooks is known for work in the Renaissance style. (Nos. 626 and 627.)

*Elijah Galusha* (1804-1871), Troy, New York. Galusha moved to Troy about 1830 from his home in Shaftsbury, Vermont. He opened a cabinetmaker's shop and worked first in the Sheraton and Empire styles. Later he turned to the Victorian rococo and Renaissance styles, which he executed in rosewood and mahogany. His finely carved furniture, which rivals Belter's in quality, was prized throughout upstate New York. (Nos. 622 and 635.)

*John Jelliff* (1813-1893), Newark, New Jersey. Jelliff, who was active by 1836 and retired in 1890, was an excellent carver, and made furniture chiefly in walnut and rosewood, working in the traditions of the eighteenth-century cabinetmaker. Examples of his furniture may be seen at the Newark Museum and the New Jersey Historical Society. See Mary Elizabeth Mann, "The Corner Cupboard: John Jelliff, Cabinetmaker of Newark, New Jersey" *Antiques,* June 1946. (Nos. 625 and 634.)

*Prudent Mallard* (1809-1879), New Orleans. Mallard was born in Sèvres and trained in Paris. He came to New York, where he may have worked briefly with Phyfe before moving to New Orleans and opening a shop there in 1838. He is best known for large-scale furniture, such as armoires and great high-post beds called Victoria beds, with a half-canopy lined with silk or brocade. He worked in the rococo and Renaissance styles. See Maud O'Bryan Ronstrom, "Seignouret and Mallard, Cabinetmakers" *Antiques,* August 1944; and Felice Davis, "Victorian Cabinetmakers in America," *Antiques,* September 1943.

*Joseph Meeks and Sons* (originally listed in the directory as Joseph and Edward) (1797-1868), New York. This important firm, in existence for seventy-one years, had a "Manufactory of Cabinet Furniture" at 43 and 45 Broad Street. In 1833 they had Endicott and Swett print a colored lithograph illustrating over forty pieces of furniture they were ready to supply upon order (No. 665). This print represents the first American publication of complete designs for furniture, formerly shown only in details in cabinetmakers' price books. The designs show the large, plain surfaces, scroll supports, and projecting columns of French furniture of the 1820s. Many are based on "the French Taste" as illustrated in Smith's *Guide* of 1826. There is a possibility that Nos. 605 and 609 may be by Meeks.

*John Needles* (1786-1878), Baltimore. Needles is listed in the directories from 1812; he retired in 1853. His work is known through twenty or more labeled or documented pieces. Most of these are in walnut and rosewood. There is one example in mahogany (No. 610), and several maple pieces in the Empire style are recorded. He is known for work in the Sheraton and Victorian styles. See Charles F. Montgomery, "John Needles — Baltimore Cabinetmaker," *Antiques,* April 1954.

*Daniel Pabst,* mid-nineteenth century, Philadelphia. Pabst is known especially for his walnut case pieces. He worked in the rococo and Renaissance styles and is represented in the Philadelphia Museum of Art. (No. 629.)

*Anthony Quervelle* (working 1835-1849), Philadelphia. This competent and successful maker was born, and presumably trained, in France. According to his label on the secretary, No. 597, he had a "Cabinet and Sofa Manufactory, South Second Street, a few doors below Dock, Philadelphia." Querville is mentioned in Watson's *Annals of Philadelphia* as a man of wealth, worth over $75,000, who "made his money by steady industry."

*François Seignouret* (born 1768), leading cabinetmaker in New Orleans. Born in France, he came to New Orleans in 1815, and by 1822 had a furniture-making shop where he worked until 1853. Then he returned to Bordeaux, and his firm soon closed. His furniture, scarce and much sought after, includes armoires and a "Seignouret chair" of gondola form with open back and vertical splat. His work is distinguished by the use of beaded and rippled moldings. See Maud O'Bryan Ronstrom, "Seignouret and Mallard, Cabinetmakers," *Antiques,* August 1944; and Felice Davis, "Victorian Cabinetmakers in America," *Antiques,* September 1943.

*(See chart on page 311)*

**599.** In an Early Victorian dining room a stenciled mahogany table with heavy pedestals is in the last phase of the classical style. It was made for a Syracuse family in the 1830s, and probably originated in New York. Comparison with No. 569 in the style of the 1820s shows development of heavier forms. The New York State mahogany sideboard has twist-reeded columns with faceted sections reminiscent of "pineapple" carving. The Biedermeier (German) chairs and the English silver coffee urn and candelabra were owned by the Williams family. Red damask hangings came from the Joseph Bonaparte house at Bordentown, New Jersey. The gas chandelier was made about 1850 by Cornelius and Baker of Philadelphia. As the house originally had English carpets, a pattern of the 1840s, with a gold and brown mosaic on a green ground, was reproduced. This was woven by an English firm, a successor to one exporting to America in the 1840s. The flocked wallpaper in red and white is a reproduction of a type used in houses of the region. (*Fountain Elms, Munson-Williams-Proctor Institute.*)

599

600    601

602

603

**600.** New York dropleaf center table of carved mahogany with heavy vase pedestal made about 1830-1840. The lion's-paw foot is joined with an acanthus bracket directly to the base of the pedestal. The carving, although florid, is skillfully done. Shaped leaves are reminiscent of the "cloverleaf" on earlier New York tables (No. 557). Large dropleaf tables with a vase pedestal were made in great numbers at this period. A similar example, called a "breakfast table," appears as No. 24 in an 1833 advertisement of Joseph Meeks and Sons of New York. (See No. 665.) (*Henry Ford Museum.*)

**601.** New York pier or console table of mahogany with mirror back. It has a marble top and alabaster columns and was made about 1830. Gilt stenciling simulates metal mounts, and gilding appears on the Corinthian capitals and on the leaf brackets of the paw feet. This represents the late form of the mirror-back pier table, and, while it may be called Empire, it is included in this section because its style and proportions conform to early Victorian taste. Two versions of this style are illustrated (as Nos. 22 and 30) in the Meeks advertisement of 1833 (No. 665), which lists them as pier tables with either white marble or Egyptian marble tops. This table originally belonged to Mr. and Mrs. Edward Sands of 143 Cherry Street, later 18 East 23rd Street, New York. (*Museum of the City of New York.*)

**602.** Mahogany sofa with spiral ends, lion's-paw feet, and leaf bracket; upholstered in black horsehair. It was made about 1830-1840. Like the pier table No. 601, this sofa represents a style frequently described as Empire. But when compared to such late Empire examples seen in No. 537 and 538, the heaviness and magnified ornamental forms begin to express a new taste. This is one of the pieces acquired for the restoration of the home of Washington Irving, in which he lived from 1836 to 1859. (*Sunnyside. Irvington-on-Hudson. Sleepy Hollow Restorations.*)

**604**

**605**

**606**

**603.** This library or writing chair of mahogany is upholstered in crimson leather and has a drawer with a lock in the seat rail. It was originally owned by Washington Irving and is documented by a sketch (about 1840) by Daniel Huntington, which shows him sitting in it. The heavy, square tapering leg and rectangular lines are close to the French Restauration style (1820-1830). An unbroken line of back and armrest was characteristic of one type of French chair in the classical style from the Directoire period to rococo revival. (*Sunnyside. Sleepy Hollow Restorations.*)

**604.** New York library table of walnut, made c. 1842 for the home of Robert Kelly at 9 West 16th Street designed by Richard Upjohn (1802-1878). The architect, who was at the time engaged in remodeling Trinity Church (1839-1846), also designed a set of bookcases (No. 617), and selected the furniture seen in Nos. 630-632. The table has traditional late Sheraton details, such as a tapering fluted leg with vase turnings, but the heavier lines are in the Victorian taste. The break in the molded skirt indicates the presence of two drawers. Omission of hardware was no doubt a considered detail. (*Gift of Mrs. Erving C. Pruyn. Munson-Williams-Proctor Institute.*)

**605.** Stenciled mahogany wardrobe made in New York in the 1830s. Basically, this piece (with columns supporting a projecting top) is in the late classical style, but the pointed arches on the paneled doors show the new Victorian Gothic style. A similar arched-panel wardrobe appears in the 1833 advertisement of Joseph Meeks and Sons (No. 665), and it is possible that this well-made and expertly stenciled wardrobe is their work. The floral decoration suggests the treatment on japanned tin-plate of the period. (*Museum of the City of New York.*)

**606.** Japanned center table in black and gold, with oak base and mahogany top, probably made in New York about 1830-1840. This Victorian version of a classical pedestal table, incorporating Gothic, naturalistic, and Chinese design, represents what an English writer has called the "unfettered eclecticism" of the Victorian style. A scalloped skirt formed of ogee scrolls is decorated with flowers. The massive spiral, usually conspicuous in design in the 1830s, is seen here on the voluted base. The center column, which rests on a tripod supported by paw feet, is surrounded by a Gothic arcade. (*Fountain Elms, Munson-Williams-Proctor Institute.*)

**607.** The top of the black and gold japanned table (No. 606) is crowded with motifs borrowed from Chinese design. The bewildering detail is typically Victorian. The border of the table is composed of an alternating Gothic and Oriental diaper. Chinese motifs are of the traditional type, as old as the designs in Stalker and Parker's *Treatise of Japanning and Varnishing* (1688).

**607**

**609.** A New York mahogany breakfront bookcase and desk, believed to have been used by Andrew Jackson at the Hermitage. It was made about 1835, possibly by Joseph Meeks and Sons, whose 1833 advertisement (No. 665) shows a somewhat similar example, No. 20. The monopodia and brass paw feet are of Empire design. Victorian innovations are the arched Gothic panels (inset in flame-patterned mahogany), the lion heads designed as gargoyles, the cavetto molding (separating the sections) and the cut-glass knob handles. The desk section has a cylinder closing and a felt-covered writing surface which pulls forward for use. This piece was inherited by Rachel Jackson's nephew and remained in the family until 1924. (*Henry Ford Museum.*)

**610.** Sofa table, with drop leaves, made about 1857 by John Needles of Baltimore (active 1810-1853). This table, of basic Sheraton form, is said to be Gothic because of the crocketed ornament carved on the bases of the triple-column supports. Needles, a cabinetmaker working in traditions of craftsmanship of the eighteenth century, favored maple, but he also used mahogany (as here), walnut, and rosewood. The table was a presentation to his daughter on her marriage in 1857. (*Baltimore Museum of Art.*)

**611.** Mahogany extension dining table in mid-nineteenth-century Victorian Gothic style. It comes from the home of Robert Kelly, New York, built in 1842. The single pedestal is designed in two sections which open for the insertion of extra leaves. The pedestal has deeply inset lancet arches enclosing tracery and a base decorated with quatrefoils. The carved border on the skirt is a Victorian variant of gadrooning. (*Munson-Williams-Proctor Institute.*)

609

**608.** The japanned center table (No. 606) is seen again here in the library at Fountain Elms with furniture in the late classical, "Renaissance," and rococo styles. The writing table and tall-back Renaissance chair were Williams family pieces. The black and gilt gas chandelier was made about 1850 in Philadelphia. A design for the green velvet window hangings with green and gold tassels was found in a decorator's book of the mid-nineteenth century. Wallpapers were specially reproduced for the house; the one here is purple with a flocked stripe. The English looped-pile carpeting reproduces a black and brown medallion pattern of the 1840s. (*Fountain Elms, Munson-Williams-Proctor Institute.*)

610

611

608

612

**612.** The furnishings in this library-study are the original ones from the Saratoga home of Robert Milligan, built in 1853.[74] The mahogany veneer bookcase with Gothic arches was made by Henry Bruner of 396 Hudson Street, New York. A tall desk chair has lancet arches and quatrefoil in the back, and the corner whatnot (see also No. 618) has Gothic tracery supports for the shelves. Late Sheraton side chairs have Gothic backs. The pedestal desk, favored by Chippendale, was not made in America in the eighteenth century but appears here in Victorian form with applied carving in high relief showing a bow and quiver of arrows. Draperies suspended from crossed javelins and a lion's-skin rug introduce a fashionable Oriental note, and literary interests are indicated by plaster casts of busts of Byron and Scott by Sir Francis Chantry (1781-1842) on each side of the bookcase. (*Brooklyn Museum.*)

**613.** Oak side chair, designed by the architect A. J. Davis (1803-1892), and made in New York about 1830-1840. Gothic tracery in chamfered moldings defines the back, and on the top rail crockets (bunched leaves) are carved. Rustic furniture may have suggested the hoof feet. Davis, known for work in Greek Revival style in partnership with Ithiel Town, began to design Gothic Revival country houses in the 1830s. He became a leading exponent of the Gothic style, and at times worked in association with A. J. Downing. This chair was presented to the museum by the architect's son, Joseph B. Davis. (*Museum of the City of New York.*)

613

614

615

**614.** This mahogany side chair, with its original black horsehair upholstery in an impressed floral design, was used by Washington Irving as a dining-room chair at Sunnyside. It represents the conservative taste in Early Victorian furniture and style is based on late Sheraton. Solid wood and heavy uprights surround Gothic pointed arches, and the legs, with vase-turnings divided symmetrically by a ring, illustrate a Victorian modification unrelated to Sheraton design. (*Sunnyside, Sleepy Hollow Restorations.*)

**615.** Walnut side chair made about 1850. The Gothic arch, leading to a crocketed finial, is combined with baroque scrolls of the Renaissance style. The cresting, with flowers and fruit carved in the full round, shows the influence of the English naturalistic school of woodcarving, active about 1848-1860. Cabriole legs and a serpentine seat rail of rococo design complete this characteristic Victorian blend of styles. (*Henry Ford Museum.*)

616

**616.** Doll's dressing table in Gothic style, painted to imitate mahogany. Stained-glass roundels were the source of the pattern on the cupboard doors. The Gothic canopy over the mirror is draped in blue silk. This elaborate little piece was made about 1840-1850 and is as representative of its period as full-sized furniture. (*Sunnyside, Sleepy Hollow Restorations.*)

**617.** Walnut bookcase in Romanesque style made about 1842. It is from a large set once in the home of Robert Kelly, New York, and was designed by the architect, Richard Upjohn. Two have pediments (as here), three have flat tops, but only this one has a slope-front writing section. In *The Architecture of Country Houses*, 1850, A. J. Downing mentioned Romanesque in his list of current styles. The use of round arches, classic columns, and arcaded frieze has a genuine architectural quality which parallels A. W. N. Pugin's Gothic style in English furniture. Upjohn came from England in 1829 as a trained cabinet-maker and builder. (*Gift of Mrs. Erving C. Pruyn. Munson-Williams-Proctor Institute.*)

617

**618.** Mahogany corner whatnot in Gothic style with mirror doors, made about 1860. It is one of the original furnishings of the library-study in the Robert Milligan house at Saratoga (No. 612). The elaborate fretwork superstructure has Gothic tracery in the manner of Pugin's *Gothic Furniture* (1835). The combination of classic vase finials and Gothic tracery did not seem out of place to the Victorian designer. The whatnot (a stand with shelves about the height of a side table) was a Regency form, and the name was applied to it about 1810. After 1840 it became particularly popular, grew in height, and in the 1850s was generally made as a corner piece. (*Brooklyn Museum.*)

**619.** Renaissance style *étagère* of rosewood, made about 1850-1860. It has mirror doors and panels, applied turnings and baroque scrollwork. The word *étagère* was adopted from the French in the 1850s to denote a piece with a number of shelves, used for the display of ornaments. The *étagère* marks the final evolution of the whatnot from an incidental accessory to a major form. In more elaborate examples, such as No. 622, it is comparable to the court cupboard in the seventeenth-century room. (*Los Angeles County Museum.*)

**620.** Mahogany whatnot with fretwork rococo scrolls at the back of each shelf, and a pendant on the front. It was made about 1860-1870. Fret-cutting machinery, perfected in the 1850s, brought an increase in elaborately pierced ornament. Flat silhouette work was used wherever a place could be found to accommodate it. In the Brooklyn Museum's "Victoriana" exhibition, this whatnot was correctly used to display porcelains, wax flowers under a glass bell, sea shells, and other small objects that were indicative of the broad interests of the owner. (See No. 638.) (*Philadelphia Museum of Art.*)

**621.** *Étagère* of black walnut with mirror panels, made about 1860-1870. The arched cresting is in the Renaissance style, while the Gothic and rococo framework around the mirror panels displays the imagination as well as the eclecticism of the Victorian designer. A bracket in classical urn shape is placed so that a choice possession can be displayed to best advantage. Molded edges frame the mirror sections and the outer border. The height of this piece (more than seven feet) ensured it a dominating role in a Victorian parlor. (*Henry Ford Museum.*)

618

619

620

621

622

**623.** Walnut side chair with ebonizing and bleaching. A stamp on the rear seat rail reads: *Hunzinger N.Y. PAT March 30 1869.* The top rail has acorn turnings. In 1866 G. Hunzinger patented a design for a folding chair, of which there is an incomplete example in the Brooklyn Museum. In this chair and in No. 624 he has used a similar form of leg bracing. While neither is collapsible, they express his interest in the form. Hundreds of patents for folding chairs were taken out in the second half of the nineteenth century, perhaps to answer the need for occasional chairs that could be used outdoors or on the new verandas. This chair and No. 624 were originally in the Chadwick Villa at Newburgh, New York. (*Collection of Joseph T. Butler.*)

**624.** Side chair of walnut with ebonizing and bleaching. On the rear seat rail is the stamp: *Hunzinger N.Y. PAT March 30 1869.* The turnings on this chair and its companion, No. 623, are associated with the Renaissance style, but their design represents sheer fantasy. This is in keeping with later developments when designers worked more daringly. The chair is light and easily moved, and may have been designed to appeal to women. A chair without arms accommodated billowing skirts, and, although these were not so extreme as in 1860, they were still voluminous in 1870. (*Collection of Joseph T. Butler.*)

**622.** The rosewood *étagère* and pair of side chairs in this corner of the parlor at Fountain Elms, Utica,[70] were made by Elijah Galusha (1804-1871), the leading cabinetmaker in Troy, New York. He was working there by 1830. On the *étagère* are traditional leafage and scrolls. spiral gadrooning, and shell and acanthus, combined with entirely new naturalistic floral forms of more than usual delicacy for the Victorian period. The lower section has projecting corners supported by clustered columns divided in the center by graceful carved buds. The upholstered chairs with tufted backs have delicately carved floral crests. The dancing girl of marble by Thomas Crawford (1814-1857) stands in the niche, and is one of a pair on either side of the doorway to the dining room (No. 599). (*Fountain Elms, Munson-Williams-Proctor Institute.*)

623

624

**625.** Upholstered armchair of rosewood, made by John Jelliff (1813-1893) in Newark, New Jersey. The chair was part of a double set of parlor furniture made in the 1860s for John Laimbeer, Sr., of New York. Jelliff worked in eighteenth-century traditions, and refused to employ machinery. The classic heads on the arm supports are among the conglomerate motifs from Renaissance and baroque design which distinguish the Victorian Renaissance style. The tapering turned legs are typical. They vaguely suggest the trumpet turnings of the William and Mary period and the tapering baluster of early Louis XIV. Incised linear ornament became a feature of Victorian Renaissance furniture. (*Newark Museum.*)

**626.** Mahogany side chair made by Thomas Brooks (1811-1887), active in Brooklyn from 1856 until 1876. The turned, tapering legs with trumpet-like tops, the scrolling of the seat rail and uprights, and the triangular crest identify this as Renaissance, the style for which Brooks was especially known. Emphasis on upholstery and on the shape of the rear leg, a reverse curve, are common to many Victorian chairs. This one was made for Judge and Mrs. Nathaniel Holmes Clement of Brooklyn. It is seen again in the foreground of No. 627. (*Brooklyn Museum.*)

625

626

627

**628.** Bedroom set in walnut and walnut burl, consisting of a bed, bureau, and night stand. It was made by the Berkey and Gay Company and was exhibited in the Centennial Exposition in Philadelphia in 1876 and the "Victoriana" Exhibition at the Brooklyn Museum in 1960. The massive crests enclosing cartouches, the consoles at the sides, acorn turnings (see also No. 623) and decoration with incised lines (as in No. 625) are typical elements of the Renaissance style, of which this is a late example. (*Grand Rapids Public Museum. Photograph: Brooklyn Museum.*)

628

629

**627.** Victorian dressing room[74] of the 1860-1870 period. The mahogany bureau, armchair, and side chair by Thomas Brooks of 127-129 Fulton Street, Brooklyn, originally belonged to Judge and Mrs. Nathaniel Holmes Clement, parents of Arthur W. Clement, authority on American ceramics. The bureau has the typical Renaissance crest enclosing a cartouche. The chairs, upholstered in original blue damask, are accompanied by other pieces of the period — the marble-topped washstand, towel rack and shaving stand, ceramics, fancy work including Berlin woolwork, Parian ware, crocheted doilies and antimacassars, coal scuttle, and a gas chandelier. The mantel was a mid-nineteenth-century addition removed from the White House during alterations shortly after 1900. (*Brooklyn Museum.*)

**629.** Renaissance-style sideboard of red walnut made about 1870 by Daniel Pabst, who was working in Philadelphia during the second half of the nineteenth century. Shortly after 1850 sideboards began to be designed with rounded ends, and backs with a raised center became progressively higher. This example is in two stages and has a marble shelf. Typical of the second half of the century are applied panels in high relief showing naturalistic floral forms, or fish and game. Characteristic too is the base resting directly on the floor. The Renaissance style is seen in the use of the cartouche, console, and urns, to which are added Tudor bosses, faceted ornament, and imbrication. Stylized, naturalistic, and geometric forms are executed in high and low relief. (*Philadelphia Museum of Art.*)

**630.** White and gold sofa with mahogany framework, made in New York about 1845. It is part of a large rococo parlor set which includes a piano, center table, armchairs (No. 631), and side chairs (No. 632). The shaping of the back of the sofa, with chair-back ends and low center, was one of many Victorian experiments with the design of "sociables" and *tête-à-têtes*. Carved and painted furniture of formal and elegant type is rare in this period. It was originally selected for the New York home of Robert Kelly, by the architect Richard Upjohn. (See also Nos. 604 and 617.) (*Gift of Mrs. Erving C. Pruyn. Munson-Williams-Proctor Institute.*)

630

631

632

**631.** New York white and gold armchair with mahogany frame from the parlor set shown also in Nos. 630, 632. The cherry-colored silk damask is a reproduction of the original upholstery. The tendency to minimize framework in favor of upholstery is seen here at an early date (about 1845) for American work. Little of the back frame is visible, but there is a decorative pierced crest. The solidly upholstered back and sides, curving like a French gondola chair, have tufting secured with buttons. This typical Victorian fashion is seen in American furniture beginning in the 1840s. (*Munson-Williams-Proctor Institute.*)

**632.** Mahogany balloon-back side chair decorated in white and gold, from the parlor set illustrated in Nos. 630 and 631. The balloon-back chair is the most original contribution of the Victorian period (England and America) to chair design. It was developed from the klismos-type chair with projecting top rail and transverse splat (No. 457). Gradually the corners were rounded off and the uprights were curved inward in rococo fashion. At first a straight leg was retained, particularly for dining-room chairs, but the cabriole offered the logical completion to a design of flowing curves. The balloon-back chair was the most popular side chair of the mid-nineteenth century and remained a standard form until nearly 1870. (*Munson-Williams-Proctor Institute.*)

633

634

**633.** Lady's desk of rosewood with kingwood interior. It has matched panels on the drawer fronts, a mirror-back shelf with a pierced gallery, and floral urn finials. This superior example of cabinetmaking has the stamp of an unlisted New York maker, *F. W. Hutchins 475 Broadway*. It was made about 1850-1860. The pierced leaf-scrolls in the gallery, and the cabochon and leafage on the leg, are in traditional rococo style, although heavier than on the Louis XV *bonheur-de-jour* which was the prototype of this little desk. This form (with shelf above) is typical of the Victorian period. (*Fountain Elms, Munson-Williams-Proctor Institute.*)

**634.** Lady's writing cabinet of rosewood, made about 1850-1860 by John Jelliff (1813-1893) of Newark, New Jersey, for Mrs. Daniel McMurty (Mary Roff). Jelliff's fine carving is seen in the leafage, which is skillfully adjusted to scrolled forms. This Victorian rococo cabriole has an S-curve with fully rounded lines, a departure from eighteenth-century rococo, in which more emphasis was placed on the vertical form. The importance of the shelf in Victorian design is repeatedly demonstrated on desks, whatnots, sideboards, and bureaus. (*Newark Museum.*)

**635.** Parlor from the home of Robert Milligan, built in 1853 at Saratoga, New York, installed in 1953 in the Brooklyn Museum. It has many of the original decorations, including the rosewood furniture made by Elijah Galusha (1804-1871) of Troy, New York. The chairs and sofas are upholstered in yellow damask, a color repeated in the red and yellow damask draperies, which came from the Electus B. Lichfield mansion in Prospect Park near the museum. Galusha's work invites favorable comparison with that of John Henry Belter. His individuality is displayed in the delicacy of the floral ornament on the narrow framework surrounding the tufted upholstery, and in the design of the center table, with spiral gadrooning around a white marble top (see also No. 622). The legs of the table are more slender than those Belter used on similar pieces, and the lower part of the S-curve is emphasized to a greater degree. Contributing to the perfection of this Victorian parlor are the white marble mantel with great oval mirror in a vine-decked gilt frame, the tapestry-velvet floral carpet, fretted corner whatnot, and the crystal chandelier suspended from an elaborate plaster ceiling. (*Brooklyn Museum.*)

636

637

**636.** Laminated rosewood sofa in rococo style, made in New York about 1850 by John Henry Belter (1804-1863). The upholstery, with blue stripes and black swirls on an eggshell ground, is not original. Belter's lacy carving was done on molded layers (usually from six to eight) of rosewood which had been glued and pressed together under steam in a mold. Graceful scrolls united by vine tendrils follow the curve of the back to an arched cresting of flowers. The expert carving preserves a balance between stylization and naturalism. Belter's originality was unfailing. "It seems quite certain that Belter never repeated a design," wrote Joseph Downs in an article on Belter in *Antiques* (September 1948). The single-end sofa was a Victorian favorite. (*Cooper Union Museum.*)

**637.** This rosewood sofa is part of a parlor set attributed to John Henry Belter. The back and ends of Victorian sofas display a greater variety of design than those of any other period. As seen here, the conventional rectangular form was not abandoned, but the outlines were given rococo curves. The pierced back rail has a formal high crest suggestive of the Renaissance style. This sofa is like those of the early 1800s, the back curving into the arms without a break, and would appear to belong to Belter's early period. It was probably made a few years after 1844, when his name appeared in the New York directory. (*Metropolitan Museum of Art.*)

638

**638.** Rococo furniture as grouped in the Brooklyn Museum's "Victoriana" Exhibition (1960). The center table of laminated rosewood was made by John Henry Belter and was used by Abraham Lincoln about 1850-1860, at his home in Springfield, Illinois (*Henry Ford Museum*). The single-end rosewood sofa and matching side chair are from a set made by Belter for the Middlebrook family of Brooklyn about 1855 (*Brooklyn Museum*). A rosewood piano stool covered in dark blue velvet (*Chicago Historical Society*) and mahogany whatnot (*Philadelphia Museum of Art*), displaying sea shells, porcelains, and wax flowers in a vitrine, create a faithful impression of the Victorian parlor. The exhibition, which brought together ceramics, glass, silver, and paintings as well as furniture, was the first to survey the varied aspects of the period. (*Courtesy of the Brooklyn Museum.*)

**639.** Laminated rosewood couch made in New York about 1850-1860 by John Henry Belter. It is from a set of furniture used by Abraham Lincoln at Springfield (see Nos. 638 and 640). Belter's openwork border combines traditional leaf scrolls and naturalistic grape clusters and flowers. (*Henry Ford Museum.*)

**640.** Rosewood armchair and side chair from the set made by John Henry Belter and owned by Abraham Lincoln (see Nos. 638 and 639). The back of the side chair shows Belter's typical method of construction. Rosewood veneer covers the entire back, and this finely patterned, polished surface has a sufficient ornamental quality of its own. Both chairs also show Belter's individual manner of joining the back and arm to the base of the seat frame through the use of graceful scrolls. (*Henry Ford Museum.*)

**641.** Laminated rosewood sofa by John Henry Belter, covered in silk damask. It is part of a parlor set made between 1856 and 1861 for Mr. and Mrs. Carl Vietor of New York. The museum also owns an armchair, a child's armchair, and a center table (No. 645) from this set, which was made when Belter was at 552 Broadway, his address until 1857. An intricate flower, leaf, and grape pattern (he used these motifs frequently but in ever new combinations) is carved with such vitality and grace as to mark the highest development of the Belter style. Such lacy designs in high relief may be contrasted with his other work, in which interlacing bands carry the design (No. 648), or in which solid framework is used with little carving (No. 642). (*Gift of Mr. and Mrs. Ernest G. Vietor. Museum of the City of New York.*)

**639**

**640**

**641**

**642.** New York side chair of laminated rosewood upholstered in tan velvet, made about 1850-1860 by John Henry Belter. The long spirals of the molded back support a rounded top with a carved floral crest, and the rear legs show the Victorian use of a simple reverse curve to provide a slender yet stable support. Belter's furniture with plain framework shows even more clearly how masterfully he handled curving lines. (*Collection of Joseph T. Butler.*)

642

643

644

**643.** Slipper chair of laminated rosewood, upholstered in gold velvet, by John Henry Belter, about 1850-1860. The slipper chair (see No. 175), after being neglected for nearly a century, returned in the Victorian period as an important form. It was illustrated in English design books as a "prie-dieu" or "vesper" chair, usually with upholstery and a wide top. Belter gave the slipper chair with completely carved back some of his most striking openwork patterns. Here the grape clusters and leaves are borne by a trellis-work of scrolls which, despite their airy freedom, preserve the functional lines of splat, uprights, and cresting rail. Another example belongs to the Metropolitan Museum. (*Collection of Joseph T. Butler.*)

**644.** Victorian bedroom furnished in the rococo and classical style. The marble-topped rococo center table shows John Henry Belter's usual inventiveness in the carving of scrolls and flowers. An unusual side chair, with masks on the knee and cresting, is in Renaissance style. The high-post bed, veneered in patterned mahogany, has great square posts representing classical design in the 1830s, and a bronze-mounted chest of drawers shows French Empire design. In the corner is a balloon-back chair, the most popular and graceful Victorian side chair. The marble fireplace (from a house in Canandaigua, New York, built about 1845) is carved with masks and floral pendants and has a crocketed border around the usual arched opening. The hangings for the bed and windows are copied from originals in an 1847 house at Auburn, New York. Floral lattice wallpaper reproduces a French paper of the 1840s, and a medallion-patterned carpet woven in England represents the fashions of the same decade. (*Fountain Elms, Munson-Williams-Proctor Institute.*)

645

646

647

648

**645.** Labeled Belter rosewood table with mottled gray and pink marble top. The legs are joined by a scrolled saltire stretcher supporting a floral ornament. The table is part of a set (see No. 641) made for Mr. and Mrs. Carl Vietor between 1856 and 1861, and has a label: *J. H. Belter & Co. Factory Warehouse . . . 552 Broadway, Manufacturers of all kinds of fine furniture, New York.* While most Victorian tables were concealed under a cover, the richly carved marble-topped table was usually allowed to display its full splendor. (*No. 141,* Furniture by New York Cabinetmakers, *1956. Museum of the City of New York.*)

**646.** Rectangular center table of rosewood with marble top, belonging to a parlor set attributed to John Henry Belter (1804-1863). The design reverts almost entirely to the use of formal scrolls, and has only a touch of naturalistic floral carving. The broken scroll forming the cabriole leg, the shaping of the skirt, and the pierced fan at its center represent a logical development of baroque design. Delicacy of effect is achieved in the definition of the scrolls that form the leg, piercing of the skirt, and the pierced cartouche which takes the place of the usual bouquet of flowers on the saltire stretcher. (*Metropolitan Museum of Art.*)

**647.** Rosewood side chair of Belter type made about mid-century. The wide pierced vine-trellis border frames the upholstered back, and the crest is carved in a basket-of-roses design. The chair lacks the usual vibrant carving of Belter's work, but he may possibly have made it. The chair closely resembles a Metropolitan Museum example, which Joseph Downs suggested may represent Belter's early period (*Antiques,* September 1948). However, Belter had imitators, including Charles Baudouine of New York (No. 650). (*Brooklyn Museum.*)

**648.** Rosewood side chair with laminated back, made by John Henry Belter probably in the 1850s. New points are to be noted here. The front leg is no longer a cabriole but a reverse curve, complementing the convex form on the rear. Of great interest is the openwork back with an interlace of S-scrolls around a central diamond. This seems to have superseded Belter's use of lacy floral borders and preceded the simpler strapwork bands with incised lines which he used after 1860. This chair resembles No. 642, with curving lines contracted about midway on the back and swelling broadly toward the top, the whole concave in plan and having Belter's typical three-dimensional curves. The upholstery is modern. (*Cooper Union Museum.*)

**649.** Laminated rosewood bureau in the rococo style, made by John Henry Belter about 1860. Laminating was not original to this period, but Belter perfected and patented a new molding process in 1856. He used traditional ornament with originality and, more than any other American cabinetmaker, helped to create a representative Victorian style. The upper part of this bureau is rather mediocre, but the base is a distinguished expression of nineteenth-century baroque. (*Gift of Mrs. Ernest Vietor. Brooklyn Museum.*)

**650.** Rosewood card or side table with the mark of Charles A. Baudouine, active in New York between 1845 and 1900. It was purchased in 1852 by the Williams family of Fountain Elms. The table, baize-lined, is boldly shaped in rococo curves. The broken-scroll legs pivot outward to support the folding top. It is one of a pair which, when fitted together, form what the original bill of sale calls a "multiform table." (*Fountain Elms, Munson-Williams-Proctor Institute.*)

**651.** New York rosewood and mahogany Victorian side chair in so-called Elizabethan style, made about 1845. It comes from the Van Wyck family and has the original needlework seat by Mrs. Richard Van Wyck. Spiral-twist turning is used on the legs and uprights, and the latter are ornamented with urn finials. The pierced splat and arched crest form an interlacing leaf-scroll design suggestive of Daniel Marot. Chairs of this type, resembling English tall-backs of the James II and William and Mary periods, were for some reason thought to represent a Tudor style. (*Gift of Mrs. Henry deBevoise Schenck. Museum of the City of New York.*)

650

**652.** Rosewood slipper chair, about 1860, made by John Jelliff and originally owned by Moses Bigelow of Newark. The tall, narrow back and Marot-like splat, urn finials, and arched crest are like No. 651, but the turnings of the tapering legs and uprights are in Renaissance style. (*Gift of Mrs. Robert H. Southard. Newark Museum.*)

649

651

652

**653.** Bureau painted black and gold with a polychrome floral design. The piece is part of a bedroom set made about 1850 by Hart, Ware and Company of Philadelphia. The wood is poplar. Painted furniture was called "cottage furniture" and was considered suitable for use in country houses, the style and furnishing of which were of so much concern to A. J. Downing (*The Architecture of Country Houses*, 1850). The makers of painted furniture used traditional forms of the Hepplewhite and Sheraton period, and such examples may be considered a continuation of Sheraton "fancy" furniture. The flower patterns are rendered naturalistically in Victorian design. (*Philadelphia Museum of Art.*)

**654.** Painted bureau and side chair of about 1850 in the guest room at Sunnyside, New York. (See also Nos. 655 and 656.) The set, acquired for the restoration of Washington Irving's home, has a design of copper-colored scrolls and red and yellow flowers on a light green ground. Downing illustrates an almost identical set in his *Architecture of Country Houses.* The applied turnings represent a type of ball and spool turnings associated with the Elizabethan style which is nearly always found on cottage furniture. The old Brussels carpet is in shades of tan and light blue. (*Sunnyside, Sleepy Hollow Restorations.*)

653

654

**655.** Painted bed, table, and chair from the set in the guest room at Sunnyside, represented also by Nos. 654 and 656. The persistence of earlier styles is seen in the spiral ends of equal height on the bed, a survival of classical design. The light green ground color of the furniture is repeated in a lighter tone on the walls. The woodwork is a much paler green. Washington Irving purchased an old Dutch farmhouse on the Hudson in 1835 and remodeled it as Sunnyside, his home from 1836 until his death in 1859. The woodwork in this bedroom represents a simplified Greek Revival style. (*Sunnyside, Sleepy Hollow Restorations.*)

**656.** Light green painted side chair, one of the furnishings made about 1850 in the guest room at Sunnyside (see also Nos. 654 and 655). The late Sheraton form is still recognizable, although the broad, projecting back rest and the rail above the seat have been shaped and scalloped for the sake of novelty. (*Sunnyside, Sleepy Hollow Restorations.*)

**657.** This iron rocking chair of about 1850-1860, painted to imitate blond tortoise-shell, is believed to have been made by Peter Cooper (1791-1883) at his iron works at Trenton, New Jersey. The red cut velvet in which it is covered is not original but may be dated about 1880. The rocker represents an experiment in functional form. The chair is not dissimilar in shape to Michael Thonet's bentwood furniture imported from Austria in the mid-nineteenth century. Its lines were dictated, literally, by the laws of balance and movement. This chair is possibly unique and has an interesting association with a great philanthropist who was also an innovator in the use of structural iron-work in the building industry. (*Cooper Union Museum.*)

655

656

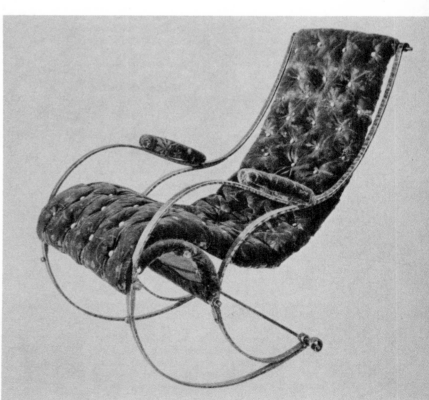

657

658    659

660    661

**658.** Patent reclining armchair of iron and wood with spring-based construction patented in 1849 by Thomas W. Warren. It was made by the American Chair Company of Troy, New York, manufacturer of reclining seats for railroad cars. As many patents remained on paper, this example of an executed design is of particular interest. It was represented in several variations at the Crystal Palace, London, in 1851. The chair has a cast-iron base and arms, with wood covering the arms. Wood is used entirely in the construction of the seat, and there is a tacking strip of wood around the edge of the back for securing the upholstery of cotton and wool velvet, applied over padding. The back of the chair is of sheet metal, japanned on the exterior. The design is in the rococo style, often used for cast-iron garden furniture of the period. The chair was first shown in the 1949 exhibition, "Designs for Modern Living," at the Detroit Institute of Arts, and in the "Victoriana" exhibition at the Brooklyn Museum in 1960. (*Collection of Edgar Kaufmann, Jr.*)

**659.** Cast-iron garden bench, made about 1850. It belonged to Washington Irving and is one of a pair manufactured at Cold Spring, New York, at the iron furnace of Irving's life-long friend, Gouverneur Kemble. This is the foundry where cannon were first successfully cast in the United States. Garden furniture of iron was made in imitation of wood furniture, often in the rococo style, and sometimes in rustic designs suggested by natural forms such as the branches of trees. Catalogues illustrating iron garden furniture began to appear in the 1840s. (*Sunnyside, Sleepy Hollow Restorations.*)

**660.** Cast-iron hat and umbrella stand, believed to have belonged to Washington Irving; made about 1840. Furniture for the hall and garden were the two main forms in cast iron, although an attempt was made to introduce other types for the interior. Very often the casting is of a fine type, for this was also the period of the cast-iron parlor stove, on which manufacturers spent much time and skill. Here rococo scrolls are ingeniously terminated as hooks, and the floral ornament has been carefully modeled and cast. (*Sunnyside, Sleepy Hollow Restorations.*)

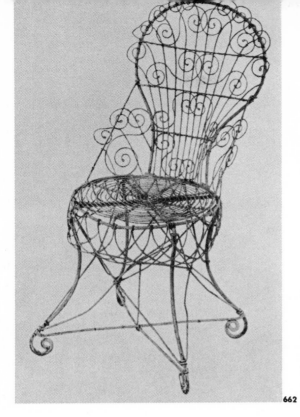

**662**

**663**

**661.** Cast-iron hot-air circulator with the mark of Stratton and Seymour of New York; made between 1837 and 1842. The figure of Hebe, cupbearer to the gods, is shown in a niche under an American eagle. Late classical ornament includes griffins, drapery festoons suspended over vases, paterae, and anthemion. In the directory for 1845 Robert M. Stratton was listed at 242 Water Street, with a "novelty iron works," and G. W. Seymour was selling stoves at 246 Water Street. This piece was shown in the Greek Revival Exhibition at the Metropolitan Museum in 1943. (*Cooper Union Museum. Photograph: Metropolitan Museum of Art.*)

**662.** Garden chair of about 1870 made of iron and wire, painted green. As a result of the improvement in wire making, manufacturers began to use it in the construction of iron furniture. Among the great variety of iron and wire garden ornaments were garden seats, trellises for vines, and stands for flower pots (both for indoors and outdoors), many of which were developed in elaborate lacy patterns. This garden seat translates the Victorian balloon-back chair into iron and wire and gives a new lightness as well as functional significance to the traditional scrollwork. (*Henry Ford Museum.*)

**663.** This cast-iron mantel clock of about 1865 has the mark of the American Clock Company, New York. It represents a combination of Gothic and classical design. A cast-iron "screen," with cusped arches and crocketed finials, classical figures, urns, and columns, conceals a wooden box which contains the mechanism. The background is painted black; the figures, urns, and raised leafage are green; the scrolls on the dome, the spires, and the steps are rust red; and the romantic landscape details are white. (*Henry Ford Museum.*)

**664.** Balloon-back side chair of papier-mâché encrusted with mother-of-pearl decoration. It was used in the home of Mr. and Mrs. Daniel H. Wickham at 71 West 11th Street, New York. Papier-mâché furniture was popular in the Victorian period, and this example, made about 1850, is illustrated to represent the type used in America, although it was probably manufactured in England. Papier-mâché furniture appears not to have been made in America to any extent. The best-known English firm producing movable furniture (in addition to small articles such as boxes and trays) was Jennens and Bettridge of Birmingham. They patented the use of mother-of-pearl in 1825 and of what was called "gem inlaying" in 1847. (*Museum of the City of New York.*)

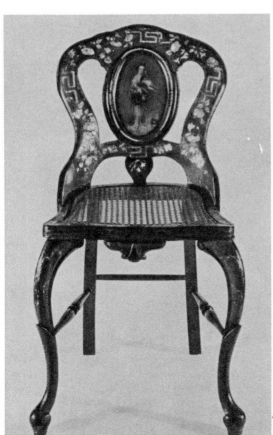

**664**

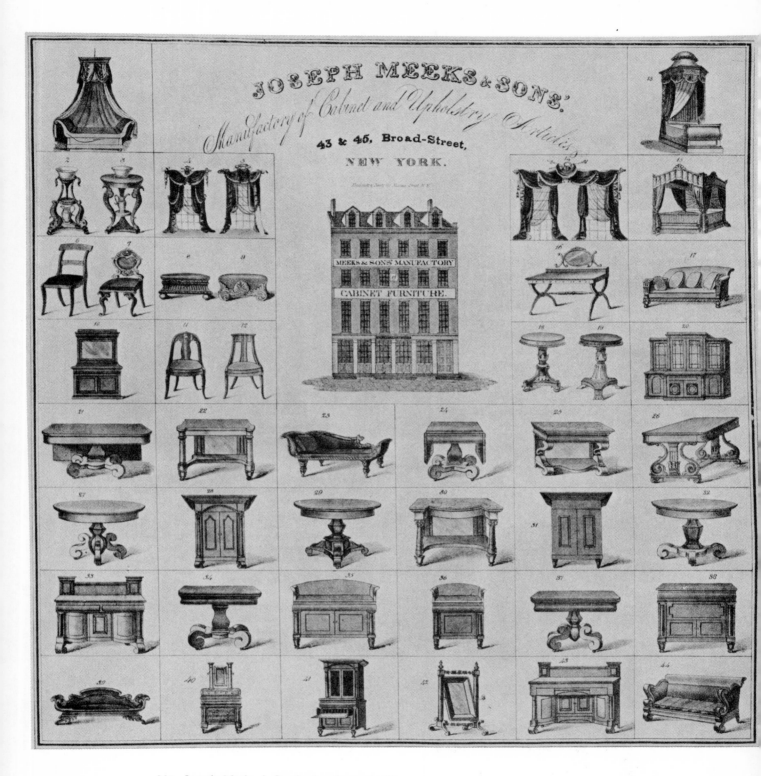

**665.** Joseph Meeks & Sons' advertisement, lithograph by Endicott & Swett, New York, 1833. This is the earliest publication in America of full-scale furniture designs. (*Metropolitan Museum of Art.*)

# Chart: Early Victorian, 1830–1870

NEW FORMS
Balloon-back chair; *étagère;* single-end sofa.

PRINCIPAL WOODS AND OTHER MATERIALS
Rosewood, mahogany, black walnut, iron, brass, papier-mâché.

DECORATIVE TECHNIQUES
Carving, painting, stenciling, japanning (occasional), laminating (although structural, this contributed to decorative effect), veneering of entire surface for costly appearance.

DESIGN
*Victorian classical, 1830-1850*
Heavy lion's-paw foot and leaf bracket (No. 602).
Large spirals (No. 606).
*Gothic, 1830-1860*
Arched panels (No. 612).
Fretwork tracery (No. 618).
*Rococo, 1850-1870*
Cabriole leg (No. 640).
Convex rear leg (No. 640).
Serpentine forms (No. 649).
Swags of roses and grapes (No. 645).
Saltire stretcher (No. 645).
*Renaissance, 1850-1870*
Crest enclosing cartouche (No. 629).
Consoles (No. 629).
Tapering baluster leg (No. 625).
Carved busts (No. 625).
*Elizabethan, 1840-1860*
Spiral twist turnings (No. 651).
Spool turnings (No. 654).

## European Background

### 1830s

*England: William IV, 1830-1837; Victoria crowned, 1837*
Louis Quatorze (early phase of rococo), Gothic, and Elizabethan designs appear in design books. Balloon-back chair appears about 1835; dominant to 1850. Papier-mâché furniture, 1830-1850; Tunbridge ware (mosaic of colored woods applied to boxes and small articles), 1830-1850. Pile carpets, looped, cut, from Kidderminster, Wilton, etc., from 1830s.
J. C. Loudon, *Encyclopaedia of Cottage, Farm and Villa Architecture*, 1833. A. W. N. Pugin, *Gothic Furniture in the Style of the Fifteenth Century*, 1835. Thomas King, *Cabinet Maker's Sketchbook*, c. 1835.
*France: Louis Philippe, 1830-1848*
Rococo style revived. Aimé Chenavard (1798-1838), cabinetmaker to the court. *Recueil de dessins de tapis, tapisseries et autres objets d'ameublement executés dans le manufacture de M. Chenavard*, 1833-1835.
Oriental influence expressed in new forms of upholstered furniture; upholstery over springs produces new type of heavily cushioned furniture; the *confortable* (easy chair), exhibited in 1834.

### 1840s
*England*
All-over upholstered furniture becomes popular: rococo style important, but Gothic, Elizabethan, Renaissance, Arabesque are current.
George Fildes, *Elizabethan Furniture*, 1844. Henry Wood, *A Series of Designs of Furniture Decoration*, c. 1845. Henry Whitaker, *Practical Cabinet-Maker*, 1847.
Moorish influence appears gradually after publication by Owen Jones of *Plans . . . of the Alhambra*, 1842.
*France: Second Republic, 1848-1852.*
Rococo becomes the dominant style in work of such Parisian cabinetmakers as Jeanselme, Fourdinois, Rinquet and Leprince, and others.
Continued experiments with upholstered furniture; a form of ottoman, the *borne*, given central position in the salon; the *pouf*, a large stool, introduced.

### 1850s
*England*
Naturalistic school of wood carving (1848-1860) responsible for addition of carved fruit, flowers, game, to furniture. Return to use of framework with upholstery; half-padded arms on chairs; sofas with swivel ends ("sociables," *tête-à-têtes*); high backs on sideboards.
Henry Lawford, *Cabinet of Practical, Useful and Decorative Furniture Designs*, 1855.
The Great Exhibition at the Crystal Palace, London, 1851; the "prestige" pieces (such as the "Kenilworth buffet") bring a reaction to excesses in design; Henry Cole, Digby Wyatt, and Owen Jones participate in reform.
Revival of inlay, boulle-work and marquetry under French influence, 1855, but effect is not general until 1870s.
Matthew Digby Wyatt. *Report on the Furniture at the Paris Exhibition of 1855*, 1856.
*France: Second Empire, Napoleon III and Eugénie, 1852-1870*
Paris exhibition, 1855, at which Louis XVI style is stressed; used by Eugénie in restoring St. Cloud, Compiègne, etc.; characterized by straight lines, inlay, ormolu, porcelain plaques.

### 1860s
*England*
William Morris urges return to handwork; firm of Morris, Marshall, Faulkner, and Company, "Fine Art Workmen in Painting, Carving, Furniture and the Metals," founded 1861; furniture designed for Morris by Burne-Jones and Rossetti shown in London exhibition, 1862.
Bruce Talbert, *Gothic Forms Applied to Furniture*, 1867; "Plank Gothic."
Charles Eastlake, *Hints on Household Taste*, 1868, preaches integrity of design, honesty in construction; uses seventeenth-century design.
*France*
Continued popularity of the *sièges de fantaisie* and all forms of upholstered furniture; the *fauteuil bébé* is a new form of gondola type, with very low back.
A. Sanguineti, *Ameublement au XIXᵉ Siècle*, 1863.

# Notes

## 1. JACOBEAN — WILLIAM AND MARY

1. The crafts of joiner and turner were highly specialized in England, not so much so in the Colonies. The turner shaped wood by cutting it with gouges and chisels while it revolved in a lathe operated by the foot. He was the maker of supports of vase shape or columnar outline, used on tables and cupboards by joiners, and was himself the maker of chairs consisting chiefly of turned members. In America these included Brewster, Carver, slat-back, and banister-back types.

The joiner used the mortice and tenon joint, employed in antiquity but not used in furniture of western Europe before the medieval period (although it is seen at prehistoric Stonehenge). A mortice is an opening in the upright or stile; a tenon is a projection on the horizontal member, the rail. The tenon is inserted in the mortice and a peg or dowel driven through the three layers of wood. After using this method of joining planks for several centuries, the joiner lightened construction through the invention of paneling. This called for the insertion of a thinner piece of wood in the stile-rail framework, in a groove made to receive it. The panel was held in position by pegs and was not glued, to allow for warping. This, called the framed-panel construction, was used in walls, doors, and in parts of furniture, such as chests, cupboards, wainscot chairs. It reduced weight and cost, and made decorative effects possible through geometric arrangement.

2. Inventories, particularly those describing contents by rooms, provide the most complete picture available of the furniture and other possessions of our ancestors. Especially valuable are the Probate Records of Essex County and Suffolk County, Massachusetts, since from the earliest days of settlement it was required that a full inventory accompany the filing of a will. For Virginia, the *Virginia Historical Index* (1934) edited by Earl Gregg Swem in invaluable. Luke Vincent Lockwood's *Colonial Furniture in America* (3rd ed. 1926) gives many references to inventories.

3. *Probate Records of Essex County. Massachusetts,* Vol. I, 1635-1664; Essex Institute, Salem, 1916; pp. 65-67.

4. Balusters are low columns or piers such as were employed by Italian Renaissance architects to support railings of staircases, balconies, and parapets. The design comes from Greek and Roman state candelabra composed of shapes borrowed from the column, funerary urn, and amphora (vase). Balusters were angular as well as curved, but we associate the word with curves in regard to furniture design because of the seventeenth-century style. The word also connotes bulk, because early seventeenth-century turnings were massive. Balusters are like large vases, but "vase-shape" in describing a turning is associated with the more slender forms of the late 1600s and early 1700s.

A spindle should taper symmetrically from the center, so the term "split spindle," in common use, is really a misnomer for a split baluster. The turned spindles in chair-backs and under armrests taper toward the ends.

5. Attributions to Thomas Dennis once grew to an unreasonable number — over sixty — based on a series of six articles by Dr. Irving P. Lyon, *Antiques,* November and December 1937 and February, April, June, and August 1938, in which fifty-nine pieces were assigned to him. In 1958 an exhibition of some of them was held in Ipswich, and the resulting study led to the conclusion that the greater part must represent other craftsmen in Ipswich and nearby towns in Essex County. These conclusions were summed up by Helen Park in "Thomas Dennis, Ipswich Joiner: a Re-examination," *Antiques,* July 1960. Definite suggestions regarding some of these heretofore unrecognized makers are contained in her second article, "The Seventeenth-Century Furniture of Essex County and Its Makers," *Antiques*, October 1960. The chair in No. 24 descended in the Dennis family and was presented by a collateral descendant in 1821 to the Essex County Historical Society, later the Essex Institute. The Dennis-type motifs are rendered so stiffly in comparison with other Dennis family pieces as to suggest the work of an apprentice or some other craftsman working in association with Dennis.

6. In Randle Holme's *Academy of Armory,* published in the reign of Charles II (though the manuscript is dated 1649), there is a description of "Things necessary for and belonging to a dineing Rome" in which chairs and stools of Turkey work or Russia leather are specified first, as evidently the most usual.

7. An English print, entitled "The Tea-Table," published by John Bowles in London about 1710, shows an interior with six ladies seated in tall-back chairs drinking tea around a large table.

8. Helen Comstock, "An Ipswich Account Book, 1707-1762," *Antiques,* September 1954.

9. The crown crest on an American chair is composed of leaves and scrolls but does not contain an actual crown supported by cherubs in what is called a "Boys and Crowns" crest on English chairs.

10. Similar chairs by John Gaines, which descended in his family, are illustrated in *Antiques,* September 1954, p. 190. On these chairs attributions to John Gaines of Portsmouth are based.

11. The yellow pine used so frequently as a secondary wood in Southern furniture, occasionally as a primary wood, may be the short-leaf (*Pinus echinata*), the long-leaf (*Pinus palustria*), or loblolly (*Pinus taeda*). Of these, *echinata* grows as far north as Pennsylvania and Long Island and is found in Pennsylvania furniture. It is frequently difficult to distinguish the Southern-grown pine, but in general the striations of light and dark show greater variation in tone and width compared to the pines of New England and the middle colonies. New England's yellow pine (*rigida*), which also grows as far south as Georgia, has dark striations which may be deceiving, but was seldom used in furniture. Southern-grown yellow pines have an almost purplish cast in the lines that mark the summer growth, and these are often broader than in northern wood, because of the concentration of resin. Because yellow pine is harder than white pine (both being softwoods), it is often called "hard pine." It is also sometimes called "heart pine" because the part employed in furniture may have been cut from the center of the log.

12. Houghton Bulkeley, "A Discovery on the Connecticut Chest," *Bulletin* of the Connecticut Historical Society, January 1958. Mr. Bulkeley traces the origin of the Connecticut or Sunflower chest probably to Peter Blin, active from about 1675 to 1725 in Wethersfield.

13. For an account of the Belding and Allis families as makers of Hadley chests, see Ethel Hall Bjerkoe's *The Cabinetmakers of America,* 1957.

14. Marvin D. Schwartz, "American Painted Furniture before the Classic Revival," *Antiques,* April 1956.

15. No exact prototype of the Guilford chest in English furniture has been discovered. American examples are comparatively rare. In the Acton Library, Old Saybrook, Connecticut, is a chest of this type which has been associated by Ethel Hall Bjerkoe in her *Cabinetmakers of America* possibly with Charles Gillim of Saybrook, a decorative painter and furniture maker who died in 1727. Her suggestion may provide the clue to the mystery of their origin.

16. This is the earliest form of the fully developed American high chest, of which the chest-on-frame (Nos. 57 and 58) was the short-lived forerunner.

17. Dr. Irving W. Lyon, *The Colonial Furniture of New England* (1924), Fig. 16.

18. John M. Graham II, "An Early Philadelphia Desk," *Antiques,* January 1960.

19. Because this table has the baluster supports and applied spindles as seen on court cupboards, the type is sometimes called a court-cupboard table, the assumption being that it was made as a matching piece to stand in the same room.

20. Mabel Munson Swan, "American Slab Tables," *Antiques,* January 1953.

21. This information is from Winslow Ames, "Swiss Export Table Tops," *Antiques,* July 1961.

## 2. QUEEN ANNE PERIOD

22. Sarah Kemble Knight, *The Private Journal of a Journey from Boston to New York, 1704.* Albany, 1865; re-issued Norwich, Connecticut, 1901; Boston, 1920.

23. *Dr. Alexander Hamilton's Itinerarium,* 1744; ed. by Albert Bushnell Hart. St. Louis, 1907, 1st. ed., limited. Best for the student is Carl Bridenbaugh's annotated edition published as *Gentleman's Progress,* The Institute of Early American History and Culture, Williamsburg, 1948.

24. David Stockwell, "Irish Influence in Pennsylvania Queen Anne Furniture," *Antiques,* March 1961. Irish prototypes are illustrated side by side with Philadelphia examples. Between fifteen hundred and two thousand Irish Quakers came to Pennsylvania in the early period. Among these were many craftsmen, as well as founders of leading families, such as Hollingsworth and Pemberton, who were patrons of cabinetmakers.

25. The definitive article on Robert Crosman is by Esther Stevens Fraser, "The Tantalizing Chests of Taunton," *Antiques,* April 1933.

26. Edith Gaines, "The Step-Top Highboy," *Antiques*, October 1957.

27. As a result of trade with the Far East and the importation of Oriental lacquer, European craftsmen of the seventeenth century developed an imitation of it which they called japanning. In place of the sap of the tree, *Rhus vernicifera*, used by the Oriental, they employed a varnish composed of seed-lac and spirits of wine. By means of this varnish, paint, whiting, and metal leaf (or metal dust) they decorated furniture in pseudo-Oriental designs. This was fashionable from the Charles II period until the mid-eighteenth century and continued to be made to some degree thereafter.

The American japanner simplified European methods. The English, like the Dutch from whom they learned most of their techniques, began with a gesso ground on oak or deal (pine), but the American used fine-grained maple, with pine for less important areas, and gesso was not required. He did not use varnish in his ground colors, nor did he employ the great variety of ground colors seen on European japanned furniture, but used a black background or "tortoise shell," made with vermilion and lampblack. After the ground was prepared, figures, buildings, animals — all parts to be executed in relief — were built up in layers of whiting and, when dry, polished. Then these relief sections and the landscape background, which was left flat, were painted in colored size. Metal leaf, or dust, was applied, and finally the whole was covered with clear varnish.

Designs were suggested by Oriental porcelains, delftware, Indian palampores, and examples of imported lacquer. Published designs were also followed, particularly those in Stalker's *Treatise of Japanning and Varnishing*, published in 1688.

Boston produced the greatest amount of American japanned furniture. The first advertisement of a japanner was that of Nehemiah Partridge in 1712, followed by William Randle's in 1715. The most important name in connection with the craft in Boston is that of Thomas Johnston (also spelled Johnson), who engraved a trade card (1732) showing his shop sign. On this sign are two winged cherubs' heads, and as these are conspicuous motifs on the Metropolitan Museum's highboy and lowboy, and on the highboy signed by the cabinetmaker John Pimm, now at Wintherthur, the trade card has been instrumental in the attribution of this work to Johnston. He was working until 1767.

In New York, Gerardus Duyckinck, father and son, advertised from 1736 to 1772, and there are a few records from Philadelphia.

For a general account of japanning, see Macquoid and Edwards, *Dictionary of English Furniture*; and Joseph Downs, "American Japanned Furniture," Metropolitan Museum *Bulletin*, March 1933 and July 1940. Much information on Boston japanners will be found in two articles by Esther Stevens Brazer: "A Pedigreed Lacquered Highboy," *Antiques*, May 1929, and "The Early Boston Japanners," *Antiques*, May 1943. Also see Mabel M. Swan, "The Johnstons and the Reas — Japanners," *Antiques*, May 1943.

28. Lockwood, *Colonial Furniture in America*, 1926, Vol. I, p. 179.

29. Any small table may have been used as a breakfast table; the term does not refer to style or design. That it was the custom from an early period to have breakfast in private at a small table is evident from sixteenth-century references to the "brekefaste borde" (*Dictionary of English Furniture*).

30. Concertina action and accordion construction are modern terms given to a method of constructing card tables in which the back part of the frame is hinged to fold inward. This was an alternate method to the use of the pivoting leg and was employed in England from the Queen Anne period until about 1765. It brought the four legs of the table to a corner position when extended, an advantage in seating the players. A diagram will be found in the *Dictionary of English Furniture*, under "Construction."

31. See Margaret E. White, "Further Notes on Early Furniture of New Jersey," *Antiques*, August 1960, where the dressing table (c. 1732) is illustrated on p. 138.

32. This dressing table is related in design to two high chests at Winterthur which are tentatively attributed to Maryland, illustrated in Downs, *American Furniture*, Nos. 192 and 199.

## 3. CHIPPENDALE PERIOD

33. Peter (Pehr) Kalm (1716-1778), a Finnish pupil of Linnaeus, came to America for the Swedish Academy of Sciences, but made many observations on life in general. He went from Philadelphia to Montreal, 1748-1751, and on his return published an account of his travels. This was translated into English (London, 1770-

1771) by J. R. Forster as *Travels into North America: Containing its Natural History, and a Circumstantial Account of Its Plantations . . .* In 1937 it was edited, with additions translated for the first time into English, by Adolph B. Benson as *The America of 1750: Peter Kalm's Travels in North America* (New York, Wilson Erickson Inc., 2 vols.).

34. Philip Vickers Fithian (1747-1776), a Princeton graduate of 1772, became tutor to the children of Councilor Robert Carter of Nomini Hall in Westmoreland County, Virginia. He was in Virginia for a year, then returned to fulfill his intention of becoming an ordained minister. As a chaplain in Washington's army, he died of exposure in camp. The *Journal* which he kept while in Virginia was copied, with his letters, by his brother Enoch in seven manuscript volumes. These eventually became the property of Princeton University which published an abridged version in 1900. In 1945 the manuscript was published in full by Colonial Williamsburg, as *Journal and Letters of Philip Vickers Fithian, 1773-1775: A Plantation Tutor of the Old Dominion*, edited and with an introduction by Hunter Dickinson Farish.

35. Chippendale's letter to Sir Rowland Winn of Nostell Priory, for which he made documented furniture, refers to designs he was making for Harewood House, his equally famous work. The letter, dated July 19, 1767, is quoted in an article by R. W. Symonds, "Chippendale Furniture at Nostell Priory," in *Country Life*, October 3, 1952, and contains the following: "As soon as I had got to Mr. Lascelles and looked over the whole of ye house I found that I should want a many designs. I knowing that I had time enough I went to York to do them . . . ."

36. Studies of lesser known regional types have so far been exploratory. In November 1947, *Antiques* published an issue devoted to Kentucky in which furniture is one of the important subjects. Paul H. Burroughs' *Southern Antiques* (1931) was the first book to be devoted to Southern furniture. The entire issue of *Antiques*, January 1952, formed the catalogue of the loan exhibition of Southern furniture sponsored by *Antiques* and Colonial Williamsburg, held at the Virginia Museum of Fine Arts, Richmond. Furniture from Tidewater Virginia, the Shenandoah Valley, North Carolina, Kentucky, and Georgia was shown, as well as a large group of Charleston furniture. The last has been treated in detail by E. Milby Burton in *Charleston Furniture, 1700-1825* (1955). New Jersey furniture was the subject of a special exhibition at the Newark Museum, recorded in a catalogue, *Early Furniture Made in New Jersey, 1690-1870* (1958). Margaret E. White, who arranged and catalogued the furniture, also wrote "Further Notes on Early Furniture of New Jersey," *Antiques*, August 1960.

37. The genealogy and history of the Townsend family was first presented in detail by Mabel M. Swan in "The Goddard and Townsend Joiners," *Antiques*, April and May 1946. Joseph Downs reviewed the findings of students since 1902 and discussed characteristics in "The Furniture of Goddard and Townsend," *Antiques*, December 1947. Many examples of their work will be found in *The Arts and Crafts of Newport* by Ralph E. Carpenter, Jr., 1954, a catalogue of the loan exhibition in Newport of the previous year.

38. For detailed information see Houghton Bulkeley, "John Townsend and Connecticut," *Bulletin*, Connecticut Historical Society, July 1960. Also "Collectors' Notes," *Antiques*, July 1961, p. 58, with information from Mabel M. Swan.

39. The *sample* chairs, five side chairs and an armchair, are very elaborate Philadelphia chairs which descended in the family of Benjamin Randolph's second wife and are assumed to have been made by him. They are called *sample* chairs because their richness of design seems to indicate that they were made as samples of his skill. They were at one time thought to be English, but their American origin is assured by the manner of their construction. The Philadelphia Museum of Art owns the armchair and one of the side chairs. The others are in the Winterthur Museum, the Garvan Collection at Yale University Art Gallery, and the collection formed by the late Henry W. Erving of Hartford.

40. Milo M. Naeve, "Daniel Trotter and His Ladder-Back Chairs," *Antiques*, November 1959.

41. *Antiques* has published a number of helpful articles on windsors: J. Stogdell Stokes, "The American Windsor Chair," April 1926; Karl E. Weston, "Windsor Chairs at Williams College," November 1944; Joe Kindig III, "Upholstered Windsors," July 1952; David Stockwell, "Windsors in Independence Hall," September 1952. Carl Drepperd's *Handbook of Antique Chairs* (1948) illustrates types through the early nineteenth century. Wallace Nutting's *A Windsor Handbook* (1917) has long been out of print, but its illustrations are in his *Furniture Treasury* (1926 and reprintings). See also Marvin D. Schwartz, "Windsor Chairs," in the *Concise Encyclopedia of American Antiques*, Vol. I (1958). A recent book is Thomas H. Ormsbee, *The Windsor Chair* (1962).

42. For Tracy's characteristic style see Ada R. Chase, "Ebenezer Tracy, Connecticut Chairmaker," *Antiques*, December 1936.

43. David Stockwell, "Windsors in Independence Hall," *Antiques*, September 1952. Francis Trumble, whose mark *FT* appears on this chair, is listed in the *Philadelphia Directory*, 1785, as "windsor chair maker." An entry in the records of the Cash Book of the Assembly shows that he was paid for twelve chairs in 1776.

44. Meyric R. Rogers, "Philadelphia via Dublin: Influences in Rococo Furniture," *Antiques*, March 1961.

45. David Stockwell, "Aesop's Fables on Philadelphia Furniture," *Antiques*, December 1951.

46. Benjamin Ginsburg, "An American Spider-Leg Table," *Antiques*, December 1934.

47. Frances Lichten, "A Masterpiece of Pennsylvania-German Furniture," *Antiques*, February 1960.

## 4. CLASSICAL PERIOD

48. Important design books of the period 1752-1830 relating to the classical style:

1725-1757. Comte de Caylus, *Recueil d'antiquités égyptiennes, étrusques, grecques, gauloises.*
1753. Robert Wood, *Ruins of Palmyra.*
1762. Stuart and Revett, *Antiquities of Athens:* final volume, 1830.
1766-1767. Catalogue of the Duke of Hamilton's vases by P. F. d'Hancarville.
1769. Piranesi, *Divers Manners of Ornamenting Chimneys.*
1773-1778. Robert and James Adam, *Works in Architecture;* Vol. 2, 1779; Vol. 3, 1822.
1788. George Hepplewhite, *Cabinet-Maker and Upholsterer's Guide.*
1788. *Cabinet-Maker's London Book of Prices,* with plates by Shearer and Hepplewhite and others.
1791-1794. Thomas Sheraton, *Cabinet-Maker and Upholsterer's Drawing-Book.*
1793. *The London Book of Prices* (style of Hepplewhite and Sheraton).
1797. Asher Benjamin, *Country Builder's Assistant.*
1801. Charles Percier and Pierre Fontaine, *Recueil de décorations intérieures,* 1st ed.
1802. Vivant-Denon, *Voyage dans la Basse et Haute Egypte.*
1802-1830. Pierre la Mésangère, *Meubles et objets de goût.*
1803. Thomas Sheraton, *Cabinet Dictionary.*
1805-1806. Sheraton, *Cabinet-Maker, Upholsterer, and General Artist's Encyclopaedia.*
1807. Thomas Hope, *Household Furniture and Interior Decoration.*
1808. George Smith, *Collection of Designs for Household Furniture.*
1808. *London Chair-Makers and Carvers' Book of Prices* (Regency designs).

1809-1829. Rudolph Ackerman, *Repository of the Arts.*
1826-1828. George Smith, *Cabinet-Makers and Upholsterers' Guide.*
1828. Peter and Michael Angelo Nicholson, *The Practical Cabinet-Maker, Upholsterer and Complete Decorator.*
1830. Asher Benjamin, *The Practical House Carpenter.*

49. Recommended for an account of the styles of the classical period in relation to American furniture design are the following articles in *Antiques:* Robert C. Smith, "Key Pieces of Federal Furniture," September 1957; "The Classical Style in France and England, 1800-1840," November 1958; and "Late Classical Furniture in the United States, 1820-1850," December 1958; Ruth Ralston, "The *Style Antique* in Furniture," May and October 1945.

50. The titles of this work and the two following which are mentioned for source material are:

La Rochefoucauld-Liancourt, F.A.F., Duc de, *Travels through the United States of North America, the Country of the Iroquois, and Upper Canada, in the Years 1795, 1796 and 1797, with an Authentic Account of Lower Canada,* London, 1799.
Avraham Yarmolinsky, *Picturesque United States of America, 1811, 1812, 1813, a Memoir on Paul Svinin,* New York, 1930.
Franklin D. Scott, *Baron Klinkowström's America 1818-1820,* Northwestern University Studies, Social Sciences Series Number Eight, 1952.

51. Publication in *Antiques,* February and April 1962, by Richard H. Randall, Jr., "Works of Boston Cabinetmakers, 1795-1825, Parts I and II," has called attention to labeled furniture by little-known makers in the Bos-

ton-Salem area, 1795-1825, which is similar to the work of the Seymours. This group displays types of inlay, stringing patterns, and details of turning considered identifying marks of Seymour craftsmanship. In these articles the following cabinetmakers are among those mentioned who are known for labeled or documented work:

Boston: Levi Ruggles, active from 1813; Elisha Learnard (Learned), active 1796-1821; Adams and Todd, 1798; Elisha Tucker, listed 1809-1810; and George Vannevar, 1823.

Salem: Thomas R. Williams, active 1804-1813; and William Hook, 1777-1867.

Charlestown: Archelaus Flint, active 1803-1814.

Lynn: Emery Moulton, active 1814.

52. Elias Hasket Derby (1739-1799), merchant, of Salem, further developed his family's trade with Europe and the Orient, made improvements in shipbuilding, and was able to lend money and give supplies during the Revolution. His wealth enabled him to subsidize the building of frigates for the new American Navy in 1798. The one-million-dollar fortune that he left was said to be the largest in America in the eighteenth century. To students of architecture and the decorative arts he is best known for his great mansion in Salem, designed by Samuel McIntire and completed in 1798. As it was too costly to maintain, it was pulled down some years after his death. Many superb examples of furniture are traced to his ownership, such as the chest-on-chest in the Garvan Collection, Yale University Art Gallery — the work of Stephen Badlam with carved figures by John and Simeon Skillin. Fifteen pieces in the Hepplewhite and Sheraton styles owned by him or his immediate family are now in the Karolik Collection, Museum of Fine Arts, Boston, and are illustrated in Hipkiss, *Eighteenth Century American Arts*.

Students are sometimes confused by the two Elizabeth Derbys mentioned in accounts with Samuel McIntire and with John Doggett. Mrs. Elizabeth Derby, for whom the chest-on-chest in No. 471, was made, was Elizabeth Crowninshield Derby, wife of Elias Hasket. This one died in 1799. The commode in No. 470 was billed by John Doggett to "Mrs. Elizabeth Derby" in 1809. This was the daughter of Elias Hasket and Elizabeth Crowninshield Derby, who married Nathaniel West and was divorced in 1806. After this she took the name of Mrs. Elizabeth Derby.

53. Mabel M. Swan, "Where Elias Hasket Derby Bought his Furniture," *Antiques*, November 1931, was the first publication of the history of this set of chairs.

54. Joe Kindig III, "Upholstered Windsors," *Antiques*, July 1952, illustrates a windsor chair, 1797, with label of John De Witt of New York, and upholsterer's label of William W. Galatian; it also quotes a 1793 Maryland advertisement for windsors with "seats neatly stuffed and covered with red, green, yellow, blue and black Morocco coloured leather . . ."

55. Lockwood Barr, "The Forerunner of the Willard Banjo," *Antiques*, March 1959.

56. Newton C. Brainard, "Chapin Secretary," *Bulletin*, Connecticut Historical Society, April 1958.

57. Ralph B. Little and W. Conway Price, "The Neglected Portable Writing Desk," *Antiques*, November 1941.

58. *Verre églomisé* is a form of painted glass with metal-foil backing executed in a technique which originated in France and was introduced into England in the late seventeenth century. It was used especially in the decoration of the border of the looking glass and showed designs in gold or silver on black, red or green grounds. The technique was again fashionable in the late eighteenth century and was often used on the panels of Sheraton mirrors and on the cases of wall and shelf clocks. Designs in black, white, and gold are frequently to be found.

59. Celia Jackson Otto, "The Secretary with the Tambour *Cartonnier*," *Antiques*, April 1960.

60. Mary James Leach, "Josiah . . . and Other Kentucky Cabinetmakers," *Antiques*, February 1954.

61. Joseph Downs, "Two Looking Glasses," *Antiques*, May 1946.

62. Robert G. Wheeler and Joseph T. Butler, "Furnishing Madam Beekman's Parlor at Philipsburg Manor, Upper Mills," *Antiques*, April 1959.

63. For an analysis of McIntire carving see Dean A. Fales, Jr., "McIntire Furniture," in *Samuel McIntire, a Bicentennial Symposium*, Essex Institute, 1957.

64. Celia Jackson Otto, "French Furniture for American Patriots," *Antiques*, April 1961.

65. R. L. Raley, "Irish Influences in Baltimore Decorative Arts, 1785-1815, *Antiques*, March 1961.

66. Phelps Warren, "Setting the Record Straight," *Antiques,* October 1961.

67. Lorraine Waxman, "The Lannuier Brothers, Cabinet-makers," *Antiques,* August 1957.

68. The Duc de la Rochefoucauld, visiting Osterley about 1810, commented on the manner of arranging furniture, "studiously *dérangés* about the fire places, and in the middle of rooms. . . . The apartments of a fashionable house look like an upholsterer's or cabinet-maker's shop."

69. Nina Fletcher Little, "The General Salem Towne House at Old Sturbridge Village," *Antiques,* April 1959. Mrs. Little gives not only the history of the house but an account of methods and policies which have shaped this historic house museum.

70. Richard B. K. McLanathan, "History in Houses: Fountain Elms in Utica, New York," *Antiques,* April 1961.

71. The labeled *guéridon* by Lannuier, of mahogany and satinwood with inlaid marble top, which descended in the Livingston family, is illustrated as the frontispiece to *Antiques,* January 1962, in connection with the publication of an article by Lorraine Waxman Pearce, "Lannuier in the President's House." For an account of original furnishings see R. L. Raley, "Interior Designs by Benjamin Henry Latrobe for the President's House," *Antiques,* June 1959; and Marie Kimball, "Original Furnishings of the White House," *Antiques,* July 1952.

## 5. EARLY VICTORIAN

72. A series of six articles in *Antiques* by Robert C. Smith, which has laid the groundwork for a better understanding of nineteenth-century styles, has frequently been consulted in preparing this text. Four relate to the period under review: "The Classical Style in France and England, 1800-1840," November 1958; "Late Classical Furniture in the United States, 1820-1850," December 1958; "Gothic and Elizabethan Revival Furniture, 1800-1850," March 1959; "Rococo Revival Furniture, 1850-1870," May 1959.

Other works which have proved especially helpful include: Marvin D. Schwartz, *Victoriana, a Catalogue of an Exhibition of the Arts of the Victorian Era in America,* The Brooklyn Museum, 1960; Marvin D. Schwartz, "Victorian Furniture," *Concise Encyclopedia of American Antiques,* Vol. I, 1958; Peter Floud, "Victorian Furniture," *Connoisseur Period Guides, Early Victorian,* 1958; Peter Floud, "Victorian Furniture," *Concise Encyclopedia of Antiques,* Vol. III, 1957; Bernard and Therle Hughes, *After the Regency,* 1952.

Articles in *Antiques*: Ruth Ralston, "Nineteenth-Century New York Interiors," June 1943; Felice Davis, "The Victorians and Their Furniture," June 1943; Felice Davis, "Victorian Cabinetmakers in America," September 1943; Maud O'Bryan Ronstrom, "Seignouret and Mallard, Cabinetmakers," August 1944; Ruth Ralston, "The *Style Antique* in Furniture," Part II, October 1945; Joseph Downs, "John Henry Belter and Company," September 1948; Charles Nagel, "Four Nineteenth-Century Interiors," December 1953; Charles F. Montgomery, "John Needles — Baltimore Cabinetmaker," April 1954.

American books mentioned: John Hall, *The Cabinet-Maker's Assistant,* Baltimore, 1840; Robert Conner, *The Cabinet-Maker's Assistant,* New York, 1842; A. J. Downing, *Cottage Residences,* New York, 1842, and *The Architecture of Country Houses,* 1850; Anon., *Gothic Album for Cabinet Makers,* Philadelphia 1868.

73. This labeled secretary by Quervelle was first illustrated in "Queries and Opinions," *Antiques,* November 1934. It has also been illustrated by Joseph Downs in *American Collector,* November 1943.

74. Charles Nagel, "Four Nineteenth-Century Interiors," *Antiques,* December 1953.

# Selected Bibliography

(Including a few references to architecture)

### GENERAL

Bjerkoe, Ethel Hall, *The Cabinetmakers of America.* Garden City, New York, 1957.

Bridenbaugh, Carl, *The Colonial Craftsman.* New York, 1950.

Brooklyn Museum, *Country Style.* Exhibition catalogue, 1956.

———, *Victoriana.* Exhibition catalogue, 1960.

Christensen, Erwin O., *The Index of American Design.* New York, 1950.

Comstock, Helen, ed., *The Concise Encyclopedia of American Antiques,* 2 vols., New York, 1958.

Cummings, Abbott Lowell, and Little, Nina Fletcher, *Bed Hangings, 1650-1850.* Society for the Preservation of New England Antiquities, Boston, 1961.

Downs, Joseph, *American Furniture, Queen Anne and Chippendale Periods.* New York, 1952.

———, *The China Trade and Its Influences.* Exhibition catalogue, Metropolitan Museum of Art, 1941.

———, *The Greek Revival in the United States.* Exhibition catalogue, Metropolitan Museum of Art, 1943.

———, H. F. du Pont Winterthur Museum special issue, *Antiques,* November 1951.

———, "Regional Characteristics of American Furniture," *Antiques,* June 1949.

Dyer, Walter A., and Fraser, Esther Stevens, *The Rocking Chair — an American Institution.* New York, 1928.

Drepperd, Carl, *Dictionary of Antiques.* Garden City, New York, 1953.

———, *Handbook of Antique Chairs.* Garden City, New York, 1948.

Eberlein, H. D., and Hubbard, C. v. D., *American Georgian Architecture.* Indiana University, 1952.

———, *Historic Houses of George-Town and Washington City.* Richmond, 1958.

Fales, Martha Gandy, "Looking Glasses Used in America," *Concise Encyclopedia of American Antiques, Vol. I.* New York, 1958.

Flayderman sale catalogue, "Collection of the Late Philip Flayderman," American Art Association – Anderson Galleries. New York, 1930.

Fraser, Esther Stevens, "Painted Furniture in America," *Antiques,* June and September 1924, January 1925.

*Girl Scouts Loan Exhibition Catalogue* (by Louis Guerineau Myers). New York, 1929.

Halsey, R. T. H.; Cornelius, C.O.; and Downs, J., *A Handbook of the American Wing.* Metropolitan Museum of Art, 7th ed., 1942.

Hamlin, Talbot, *Greek Revival Architecture in America.* New York, 1944.

Hinckley, F. Lewis, *A Directory of Antique Furniture.* New York, 1953.

———, *A Directory of the Historic Cabinet Woods.* New York, 1960.

Hipkiss, Edwin J., *The M. and M. Karolik Collection of Eighteenth Century American Arts.* Museum of Fine Arts, Boston, 1941.

Iverson, Marion Day, *The American Chair, 1630-1890.* New York, 1957.

Kettell, R. H., ed. *Early American Rooms.* Portland, Maine, 1936.

Kimball, Marie G., "Furnishings of Lansdowne, Governor Penn's Country Estate," *Antiques,* June 1931.

———, "Furnishing of Monticello," *Antiques,* November and December 1927.

———, "Furnishings of Solitude, the Country Estate of John Penn," *Antiques,* July 1931.

———, "More Jefferson Furniture Comes Home to Monticello," *Antiques,* July 1940.

———, "Original Furnishings of the White House," *Antiques,* July 1952 (reprinted from June and July 1929).

Lea, Zilla Rider, ed., *The Ornamented Chair.* Publication of the Esther Stevens Brazer Guild of the Historical Society of Early American Decoration, Rutland, Vermont, 1960.

Lichten, Frances, *Decorative Art of Victoria's Era.* New York, 1950.

Lockwood, L. V., *Colonial Furniture in America,* 2 vols., 3rd ed., New York, 1926, reprinted 1951.

Miller, Edgar G., Jr., *American Antique Furniture,* 2 vols. Baltimore, 1937; reprinted in New York, 1950.

Montgomery, Charles F., Florence, and Charles F., Jr., section on "Design and Decorative Arts of the Seventeenth and Eighteenth Centuries," *Arts of the United States,* ed. by William H. Pierson, Jr., and Martha Davidson. New York, 1960.

Morrison, Hugh, *Early American Architecture.* New York, 1952.

Morse, Frances Clary, *Furniture of the Olden Time.* New York, 1902.

Nagel, Charles, *American Furniture, 1650-1850.* New York, 1949.

Nutting, Wallace, *Furniture Treasury*, 3 vols. Framingham, Massachusetts, 1928-1933; reprinted New York, 1948, 1954.

———, *A Windsor Handbook*. Boston and Framingham, 1917.

Ormsbee, T. H., *Early American Furniture Makers*, New York, 1930.

———, *Field Guide to Early American Furniture*. Boston, 1951.

———, *Field Guide to American Victorian Furniture*. Boston, 1952.

———, *The Windsor Chair*. New York, 1962.

Pratt, Dorothy and Richard, *A Guide to Early American Homes — North* and *A Guide to Early American Homes — South*. New York, 1956.

———, *Second Treasury of Early American Homes*. New York, 1954.

Pratt, Richard, *Treasury of Early American Homes*. New York, 1949.

Ralston, Ruth, "Greek Revival Architecture," *Antiques*, February 1944.

———, "The *Style Antique* in Furniture," *Antiques*, May and October 1945.

Rogers, M. R., *American Interior Design*. New York, 1947.

Sack, Albert, *Fine Points of Furniture: Early American*, New York, 1950.

Schwartz, Marvin D., "American Furniture 1640-1840," "Victorian Furniture," and "Windsor Chairs," *Concise Encyclopedia of America Antiques*, ed. by Helen Comstock. New York, 1958.

Singleton, Esther, *Furniture of Our Forefathers*. New York, 1900; 4th ed., 1922.

Smith, Robert C., "The Classical Style in France and England, 1800-1840," *Antiques*, November 1958.

———, "The Eighteenth-Century House in America," *Antiques*, December 1954.

———, "Gothic and Elizabethan Revival Furniture, 1800-1850," *Antiques*, March 1959.

———, "Key Pieces of Federal Furniture," *Antiques*, September 1957.

———, "Late Classical Furniture in the United States, 1820-1850," *Antiques*, December 1958.

———, "Rococo Revival Furniture, 1850-1870," *Antiques*, May 1959.

Stokes, J. Stogdell, "The American Windsor Chair," *Antiques*, April 1926.

Sweeney, John A. H., "The Cabinetmaker in America," *Antiques*, October 1956.

Winchester, Alice, ed., *The Antiques Treasury of Furniture and Other Decorative Arts*, New York, 1959.

———, *Collectors and Collections*. New York, 1961.

———, *How to Know American Antiques*. New York, 1951.

———, *Living with Antiques*. New York, 1941.

Winterthur Corporation, *Accessions, Winterthur 1960*. Exhibition catalogue, Winterthur, Delaware.

## REGIONAL

### New England

Belknap, H. W., *The Artists and Craftsmen of Essex County, Massachusetts*. Privately printed, 1927.

Briggs, Martin S., *The Homes of the Pilgrim Fathers in England and America*. London and New York, 1932.

Chamberlain, Samuel, and Flynt, Henry N., *Frontier of Freedom (Old Deerfield)*. New York, 1952.

Comstock, Helen, "An Ipswich Account Book, 1707-1762" (John Gaines), *Antiques*, September 1954.

Cummings, Abbott Lowell, "Furnishing the Seventeenth-Century House," *Old-Time New England*, January-March 1956.

Dow, George F., *The Arts and Crafts in New England, 1704-1775*. Topsfield, Massachusetts, 1927.

———, "The Houses of the First Settlers in New England," *Antiques*, August 1930.

Essex Institute, *Samuel McIntire, a Bicentennial Symposium*. Salem, 1957.

Fales, Dean A., Jr., "McIntire Furniture," in Essex Institute's *Samuel McIntire, a Bicentennial Symposium*.

Fraser, Esther Stevens, "The Tantalizing Chests of Taunton," *Antiques*, April 1933.

Howe, Florence T., "Asher Benjamin, Country Builders' Assistant," *Antiques*, December 1941.

Kettell, R. H., *Pine Furniture of Early New England*. New York, 1929; reprinted 1952.

Kimball, Fiske, "The Estimate of McIntire," *Antiques*, January 1932.

———, "Furniture Carvings by Samuel McIntire," *Antiques*, November and December 1930; January, February, and March 1931.

———, "Furniture Carvings by Samuel Field McIntire," *Antiques*, February 1933.

———, "Salem Furniture Makers," *Antiques*, September 1933 (Nathaniel Appleton); December 1933 (Nehemiah Adams); April 1934 (William Hook).

———, "Salem Secretaries and Their Makers," *Antiques*, May 1933.

———, *Samuel McIntire (Mr.), Carver, the Architect of Salem*. Salem, 1940.

Little, Bertram K., "A McIntire Country House," *Antiques*, June 1953.

Little, Nina Fletcher, "Country Art in New England, 1790-1840" (booklet). Old Sturbridge, 1960.

———, "On Dating New England Houses" *Antiques,* March, April, May, and June 1945.

Luther, Reverend Clair Franklin, "The Hadley Chest," *Antiques,* October 1928.

———, *The Hadley Chest.* Hartford, 1935.

Lyon, Irving P., "The Oak Furniture of Ipswich, Massachusetts," *Antiques,* November and December 1937; February, April, June, and August 1938.

Lyon, Irving W., *The Colonial Furniture of New England.* Boston, 1891; 3rd ed., 1925.

Nutting, Wallace, *Furniture of the Pilgrim Century.* Framingham, Massachusetts, 1921 and 1924.

Park, Helen, "Thomas Dennis, Ipswich Joiner: a Reexamination," *Antiques,* July 1960.

———, "The Seventeenth-Century Furniture of Essex County and Its Makers," *Antiques,* October 1960.

Spinney, Frank O., "Country Furniture," *Antiques,* August 1953.

———, "Country Furniture," *Concise Encyclopedia of American Antiques,* Vol. I., New York, 1958.

Swan, Mabel M., "Coastwise Cargoes of Venture Furniture," *Antiques,* April 1949.

———, "Furniture Makers of Charlestown," *Antiques,* October 1944.

———, "General Stephen Badlam—Cabinet and Looking-Glass Maker," *Antiques,* May 1954.

———, "McIntire, Check and Countercheck," *Antiques,* February 1932.

———, "McIntire Vindicated," *Antiques,* October 1934.

———, "Major Benjamin Frothingham, Cabinetmaker," *Antiques,* November 1952.

———, "Newburyport Furnituremakers," *Antiques,* April 1945.

———, "A Revised Estimate of McIntire," *Antiques,* December 1931.

———, "Where Elias Hasket Derby Bought His Furniture," *Antiques,* November 1931.

### Boston

Brazer, Esther Stevens, "The Early Boston Japanners," *Antiques,* May 1943.

Downs, Joseph, "American Japanned Furniture," Metropolitan Museum *Bulletin,* March 1933 and July 1940; *Old-Time New England,* October 1937.

———, "John Cogswell, Cabinetmaker," *Antiques,* April 1952.

Randall, Richard H., Jr., "Works of Boston Cabinetmakers, 1795-1825," *Antiques,* February and April 1962.

Swan, Mabel M., "Boston's Carvers and Joiners," *Antiques,* March 1948.

———, "John Seymour and Son, Cabinetmakers," *Antiques,* October 1937.

Stoneman, Vernon C., *John and Thomas Seymour: Cabinetmakers in Boston.* Boston, 1959.

### Newport

Carpenter, Ralph E., Jr., *The Arts and Crafts of Newport, Rhode Island, 1640-1820.* Preservation Society of Newport County, 1954.

———, "Discoveries in Newport Furniture and Silver," *Antiques,* July 1955.

Downing, Antoinette F., and Scully, Vincent J., Jr., *The Architectural Heritage of Newport, Rhode Island, 1640-1915.* Cambridge, Massachusetts, 1952.

Downs, Joseph, "The Furniture of Goddard and Townsend," *Antiques,* December 1947.

Garrett, Wendell D., "The Newport Cabinetmakers: A Corrected Checklist," *Antiques,* June 1958.

Ralston, Ruth, "Holmes Weaver," *Antiques,* February 1942.

Swan, Mabel M., "The Goddard and Townsend Joiners," *Antiques,* April and May 1946.

### Connecticut

Barbour, F. K., *The Stature of Fine Connecticut Furniture.* Privately printed, 1959.

Bissell, Charles S., *Antique Furniture in Suffield, Connecticut, 1670-1835.* Connecticut Historical Society and Suffield Historical Society, 1956.

Bulkeley, Houghton, "Aaron Roberts, His Life and Times," Connecticut Historical Society *Bulletin,* April 1957.

———, "Benjamin Burnham of Colchester, Cabinetmaker," *Antiques,* July 1959, and Connecticut Historical Society *Bulletin,* July 1958.

———, *The Connecticut Antiquarian,* January 1958.

———, "John Townsend and Connecticut," Connecticut Historical Society *Bulletin,* July 1960.

Chase, Ada R., "Ebenezer Tracy, Connecticut Chairmaker," *Antiques,* December 1936.

Connecticut Historical Society, Hartford, *Connecticut Chairs in the Collection of the Connecticut Historical Society,* 1956; *George Dudley Seymour's Furniture Collection,* 1959.

Davis, Emily M., "Eliphelet Chapin," *Antiques,* April 1939.

Fraser, Esther Stevens, "Random Notes on Hitchcock and His Competitors," *Antiques,* August 1936.

Gaines, Edith, "The Step-Top Highboy," *Antiques,* October 1957.

Tercentenary Commission of the State of Connecticut, *Three Centuries of Connecticut Furniture*, Exhibition at the Morgan Memorial, Hartford, 1935.

Walcott, William Stuart, Jr., "Furniture of the Old Hartford State House, *Antiques*, July 1928.

————, "Isaac Tryon's Cherry Highboy," *Antiques*, August 1931.

Warren, W. L., "More about Painted Chests," Connecticut Historical Society *Bulletin*, January and April 1958.

## New York

Cornelius, Charles O., *Furniture Masterpieces of Duncan Phyfe*. New York, 1922.

Downs, Joseph, "Bartow Mansion," *Antiques*, April 1949.

————, "Furniture of the Hudson Valley," *Antiques*, July 1951.

————, "John Henry Belter and Company," *Antiques*, September 1948.

————, "Two Looking Glasses" (William Wilmerding), *Antiques*, May 1946.

Downs, Joseph and Ralston, Ruth, "Loan Exhibition of New York State Furniture," Metropolitan Museum of Art. 1934.

Ginsburg, Benjamin, "An American Spider-Leg Table," *Antiques*, December 1934.

————, "The Furniture of Albany's Cherry Hill," *Antiques*, June 1960.

————, "Some Observations on Pre-Revolutionary New York Furniture," *Antiques*, November 1956.

McClelland, Nancy, *Duncan Phyfe and the English Regency, 1795-1830*. New York, 1939.

Miller, V. Isabelle, "Furniture by New York Cabinetmakers, 1650-1860," a loan exhibition at the Museum of the City of New York, 1956.

Pearce, Lorraine Waxman, "Lannuier in the President's House," *Antiques*, January 1962.

Ralston, Ruth, "Ernest Hagen's Order Books," *Antiques*, December 1945.

————, "A New York Cabinetmaker's Reminiscences," *Antiques*, December 1943.

Susswein, Rita Gottesman, *The Arts and Crafts in New York, 1726-1776*. The New-York Historical Society *Collections*, 1938.

————, *The Arts and Crafts in New York, 1777-1799*. The New-York Historical Society, 1954.

Waxman, Lorraine, "The Lannuier Brothers, Cabinetmakers," *Antiques*, August 1957.

## New Jersey

Hornor, William M., Jr., "Three Generations of Cabinetmakers. I, Matthew Egerton; II, Matthew Egerton, Jr.,

and His Sons," *Antiques*, September–November 1928.

Naeve, Milo M., "New Jersey Furniture Exhibition at the Newark Museum," *The Art Quarterly*, Spring 1959.

White, Margaret E., *Early Furniture Made in New Jersey, 1690-1870*. Exhibition catalogue, Newark Museum, 1958.

————, "Some Early Furniture Makers of New Jersey," *Antiques*, October 1958.

————, "Further Notes on Early Furniture of New Jersey," *Antiques*, August 1960.

## Philadelphia

Brazer, Clarence, "Jonathan Gostelowe, Philadelphia Cabinet and Chair Maker," *Antiques*, June and August 1926.

Carson, Marian S., "Sheraton's Influence in Philadelphia" (Connelly and Haines), *Antiques*, April 1953.

Downs, Joseph, "Jonathan Gostelowe," Pennsylvania Museum *Bulletin*, March 1926.

————, "A Savery Chest," *Antiques*, February 1929.

Eberlein, H. D., and Hubbard, C. v. D., *Portrait of a Colonial City* (Philadelphia). Philadelphia, 1940.

Hornor, William M., Jr., *Blue Book, Philadelphia Furniture*. Philadelphia, 1935.

Naeve, Milo M., "Daniel Trotter and His Ladder-Back Chairs," *Antiques*, November 1959.

Philadelphia Museum of Art, "Henry Connelly and Ephraim Haines," *Bulletin*, Spring 1953.

Prime, Alfred Coxe, *The Arts and Crafts in Philadelphia, Maryland and South Carolina*. Vol. I, 1721-1785; Vol. II, 1786-1800. Walpole Society, 1932.

Reifsnyder sale. "The Collection of the Late Howard Reifsnyder," American Art Assn., New York, 1929.

Rice, Howard C., Jr., *The Rittenhouse Orrery*. Princeton University Library, 1954.

Rogers, Meyric R., "Philadelphia via Dublin: Influences in Rococo Furniture," *Antiques*, March 1961.

Stockwell, David, "Irish Influence in Pennsylvania Queen Anne Furniture," *Antiques*, March 1961.

Woodhouse, Samuel W., Jr., "Benjamin Randolph of Philadelphia," *Antiques*, May 1927.

————, "More about Benjamin Randolph," *Antiques*, January 1930.

————, "Thomas Tufft," *Antiques*, October 1927.

Williams, Carl M., "Adam Hains of Philadelphia," *Antiques*, May 1947.

————, "Thomas Tufft and His Furniture for Richard Edwards," *Antiques*, October 1948.

## Pennsylvania German

Fraser, Esther Stevens, "Pennsylvania Bride Boxes and Dower Chests," *Antiques*, July and August 1925.

———, "Pennsylvania German Dower Chests," *Antiques,* February, April, and June, 1927.

Kauffman, H. J., *Pennsylvania Dutch American Folk Art.* 1946.

Lichten, Frances, *Folk Art of Rural Pennsylvania.* New York, 1946.

———, *Folk Art Motifs of Pennsylvania.* New York, 1954.

Philadelphia Museum of Art, *Pennsylvania Dutch Folk Arts from the Geesey Collection and Others.* 1958.

Stoudt, J. J., *Pennsylvania Folk Art: An Interpretation.* 1948.

*Delaware*

Dorman, Charles G., "Delaware Cabinetmakers and Allied Artisans, 1655-1855," *Delaware History,* Wilmington, October 1960.

*Baltimore*

Baltimore Museum of Art, *Baltimore Furniture, 1760-1810,* Exhibition catalogue, 1947.

Beirne, Rosamond Randall, in collaboration with Stewart, Eleanor Pinkerton, "John Shaw, Cabinetmaker," *Antiques,* December 1960.

Montgomery, Charles F., "John Needles — Baltimore Cabinetmaker," *Antiques,* April 1954.

Pinkerton, Eleanor C., "Federal Furniture of Baltimore," *Antiques,* May 1940.

Raley, R. L., "Irish Influences in Baltimore Decorative Arts, 1785-1815," *Antiques,* March 1961.

*Southern*

*Antiques,* special issues: November 1947, Kentucky; January 1952, exhibition catalogue, *Southern Furniture, 1640-1820,* Virginia Museum, Richmond.

Burroughs, Paul H., *Southern Antiques.* Richmond, 1931.

Burton, E. Milby, *Charleston Furniture, 1700-1825.* Charleston, 1955.

———, "The Furniture of Charleston," *Antiques,* January 1952.

———, "Thomas Elfe, Charleston Cabinet-Maker," Charleston Museum Leaflet 25, 1952.

Chamberlain, Samuel and Narcissa, *Southern Interiors of Charleston, South Carolina.* New York, 1956.

Cohen, Hennig, *The South Carolina Gazette.* University of South Carolina, 1953.

Comstock, Helen, "Discoveries in Southern Furniture" (Mardun V. Eventon), *Antiques,* February 1954.

Dockstader, Mary Ralls, "Huntboards from Georgia," *Antiques,* September 1932.

———, "Simple Furniture of the Old South," *Antiques,* August 1931.

———, "Sugar Chests," *Antiques,* April 1934.

Leach, Mary James, "Josiah . . . and Other Kentucky Cabinetmakers," *Antiques,* February 1954.

Offutt, Eleanor Hume, "Kentucky Furniture. The Makers," *Antiques,* November 1947.

Ronstrom, Maud O'Bryan, "Seignouret and Mallard, Cabinetmakers," *Antiques,* August 1944.

Rose, Jennie Haskell, "Pre-Revolution Cabinetmakers of Charles Town," *Antiques,* April and May 1933.

———, "Thomas Elfe, Cabinetmaker, His Account Book," *Antiques,* April 1934.

*South Carolina Historical and Genealogical Magazine,* Vols. 35-42: "Account Book of Thomas Elfe, 1768-1775," printed in full.

Whiffen, Marcus, *The Eighteenth-Century Houses of Williamsburg.* New York and Williamsburg, 1960.

*Shaker*

Andrews, Edward D., *The Community Industries of the Shakers.* Handbook No. 15, New York State Museum, Albany, New York, 1932.

Andrews, Edward D., and Faith, *Shaker Furniture.* New Haven, 1937; reprinted, 1950.

———, "Craftsmanship of an American Religious Sect," *Antiques,* August 1928, April 1929.

Hopping, D. M. C., and Watland, Gerald R., "The Architecture of the Shakers," *Antiques,* October 1957.

CLOCKS

Chandlee, E. E., *Six Quaker Clockmakers.* Philadelphia, 1943.

Eckhardt, G. H., *Pennsylvania Clocks and Clockmakers.* New York, 1955.

Hoopes, P. R., *Connecticut Clockmakers of the Eighteenth Century.* Hartford and New York, 1930.

James, Arthur, *Chester County Clocks and Their Makers.* West Chester, Pennsylvania, 1947.

Palmer, Brooks, *The Book of American Clocks.* New York, 1950.

Willard, John Ware, *A History of Simon Willard, Inventor and Clockmaker.* Boston, 1911.

ENGLISH FURNITURE

Edwards, Ralph, and Jourdain, Margaret, *Georgian Cabinet Makers.* Revised ed., London, 1956.

Edwards, Ralph and Ramsey, L. G. G., eds., *Connoisseur Period Guides: Tudor, Stuart, Early Georgian, Late Georgian, Regency, Early Victorian,* 6 vols. London and New York, 1956-1958.

Fastnedge, Ralph, *English Furniture Styles from 1500 to 1830*. London, 1955.

Harris, John, *Regency Furniture Designs, 1803-1826*. London, 1960.

Jourdain, Margaret, *English Interior Decoration*. London, 1951.

Jourdain, M., and Rose, F., *English Furniture — the Georgian Period*. London, 1953.

Gloag, John, *English Furniture*. 4th ed., London, 1952.

Macquoid, Percy, and Edwards, Ralph, *Dictionary of English Furniture*, 3 vols., revised by Ralph Edwards, London, 1954.

Musgrave, Clifford, *Regency Furniture, 1800-1830*. London, 1961.

Ramsey, L. G. G., ed., *Connoisseur New Guides to the Decorative Arts. I. Antique English Furniture*. London and New York, 1961.

Roe, F. Gordon, *Victorian Furniture*. London, 1952.

Symonds, R. W., *English Furniture from Charles II to George II*. New York, 1929.

Ward-Jackson, Peter, *English Furniture Designs of the Eighteenth Century*. London, 1958.

Watson, F. J. B., *Southill, A Regency House*. London, 1951.

# ACKNOWLEDGMENTS

The realization of how deeply indebted I am to Alice Winchester has made it clear to me that this book would never have come into existence without her help. This has been extended over many years, at first in the form of the opportunities which she, editor of *Antiques* since 1938, has given me as a member of the staff since 1940. My interest in American furniture was stimulated by countless opportunities for study of special subjects and the visiting of collections in many parts of the country. Finally, in 1958, her encouragement led me to begin a book which I had been preparing to write for a number of years but otherwise would not have had the courage to attempt. As the work progressed she read most of the manuscript, and her analysis of my Chippendale and Classical sections led to a significant revision. I assume, however, responsibility for the final form.

The first two sections received a critical reading from John Askling, whose suggestions regarding the Jacobean and William and Mary periods provided me with helpful criteria for the remainder of the work.

As forty museum collections are represented, staff members have been repeatedly asked for information. For their patience and cooperation I thank them warmly. Repeated claim upon time and consideration call for particular acknowledgment of the help of Joseph T. Butler of Sleepy Hollow Restorations; Dean A. Fales, Jr., of the Essex Institute; Lillian Green of the Metropolitan Museum of Art; Thompson R. Harlow of the Connecticut Historical Society; Louis C. Madeira of the Philadelphia Museum of Art; Henry P. Maynard of the Wadsworth Atheneum; V. Isabelle Miller of the Museum of the City of New York; Milo M. Naeve of the Henry Francis du Pont Winterthur Museum; Gregor Norman-Wilcox of the Los Angeles County Museum; Robert H. Palmiter of the Munson-Williams-Proctor Institute; Richard H. Randall, Jr., of the Museum of Fine Arts, Boston; Norman S. Rice of the Albany Institute of History and Art; Marvin D. Schwartz of the Brooklyn Museum; Romaine Stec of the Baltimore Museum of Art; and C. Malcolm Watkins of the Smithsonian Institution.

Dr. Donald A. Shelley, director of the Henry Ford Museum and Greenfield Village, who has encouraged me in a study of regional aspects of American furniture, has shown continued interest in the progress of this book. For his confidence I thank him, and also members of his staff, Gerald G. Gibson and Katharine Hagler, for answering many questions about the collections.

The Baltimore Museum of Art has generously made available to me irreplaceable photographs taken at the time of the Baltimore Furniture Loan Exhibition of 1947 which have added supremely fine examples of Baltimore work to the illustrations. Colonial Williamsburg has opened its file of photographs for subjects taken during the loan exhibition of Southern furniture in 1952, thus enabling me to include the results of a study in which I had personally taken part as a member of the committee and feel continuing interest.

I am deeply grateful to Eleanor Pinkerton Stewart for help in securing some of the subjects from Baltimore and for her particularly cordial response to my appeal.

I am very much indebted to the many private collectors who have allowed me to include their possessions in this book. They have rounded out many aspects of the subject with unfamiliar examples, sometimes unpublished before. Miss Ima Hogg of Houston, Texas, has conferred a very great privilege in allowing me to illustrate so many pieces from the collection at Bayou Bend which she plans eventually to make a public one. Through the kindness of Frank L. Horton of Old Salem I am able to show examples in his private collection in which there are fine and rare pieces of Charleston and other Southern furniture.

Henry N. Flynt has made repeated efforts to secure at the last moment illustrations of much-desired examples which he has recently acquired for Old Deerfield.

Mary Vandegrift of the Parke-Bernet Galleries has been most cooperative in locating photographs from sales of important collections.

My thanks for photographs from dealers' files go to Teina Baumstone, Ginsburg & Levy, Israel

Sack, Inc., David Stockwell, and John S. Walton. I have derived much benefit through opportunities they have given me to examine closely the pieces in their galleries and have learned through their observations. I am especially indebted to Benjamin Ginsburg and Bernard Levy for information regarding some of the New York and New England furniture in this book.

When I acted as co-chairman of the loan exhibition of Southern furniture at Richmond in 1952 I had many preliminary conversations on the characteristics of Southern furniture with Joe Kindig, Jr., and much information from him and from Charles Navis while the committee of selection, of which both were members, were at work assembling the loans. This I recalled with gratitude while introducing subjects from the exhibition here.

Repeated help has been given by my associates at *Antiques*, Edith Gaines, Ruth Davidson, Barbara Snow, Dorothy Baltar, and Eta Kitzmiller. I owe special thanks to Ann Sigmund of *Antiques* for many hours spent in checking references for me.

Bryan Holme, director of Studio Books, Viking Press, has brought an enthusiasm to the making of this book which has been encouraging to me through the delays affecting my part of the work, and his suggestions regarding the handling of text and descriptions have greatly benefited their final form.

ILLUSTRATIONS. I am grateful for the privilege of showing many subjects which have appeared in *Antiques*, and particularly for use of color plates of the hall at Hempsted House, the living room in the home of Mr. and Mrs. William C. Harding, the Great Chamber at Mount Pleasant, the Red Room at the White House, and the Victorian parlor at Fountain Elms.

My thanks go to the Macmillan Company for permission to illustrate subjects from Joseph Downs' *American Furniture, Queen Anne and Chippendale periods, in the Henry Francis du Pont Winterthur Museum* (1952).

The color photograph of the japanned highboy at the Metropolitan Museum in plate III has been kindly made available through the courtesy of the Shell Oil Company.

Gilbert Ask has taken all photographs at the Winterthur Museum except No. 411; Charles Baptie, interiors at Woodlawn Plantation; Samuel Chamberlain, No. 414, from the Heyward-Washington House, Charleston; James R. Dunlop, No. 344, from Mount Vernon; Louis H. Frohman, interiors at Van Cortlandt Manor, Sleepy Hollow Restorations; Ned Goode, furniture at the Chester County Historical Society, West Chester, Pennsylvania; Gottscho-Schleisner, No. 411 at the Winterthur Museum, and interiors in the home of Mr. and Mrs. Mitchel Taradash, and at Marlpit Hall, Morristown, New Jersey; Hopf, interiors at the Hunter House and furniture in the Newport Loan Exhibition, 1953; Robert J. Kelley, interiors of Hempsted House, New London, Connecticut; Frank Kelly, No. 5, from the Currier Gallery of Art, Manchester, New Hampshire; Richard Merrill, interiors at the Harrison Gray Otis House, Boston, and the Barrett House, New Ipswich, New Hampshire; Holmes I. Mettee, furniture in the collection of Mr. and Mrs. Sifford Pearre; Charles T. Miller, furniture and interiors from the Henry Ford Museum and Greenfield Village; W. F. Miller and Company, furniture in the collection of Mr. and Mrs. Frederick K. Barbour; Charles Mills and Sons, furniture in the collection of Mrs. W. Logan MacCoy and Dr. W. S. Serri; Einars J. Mengis, furniture and interiors at the Shelburne Museum; J. H. Schaefer and Son, the dining room at the Hammond-Harwood house, Annapolis, Maryland; E. T. Simons, furniture in the collection of Frank L. Horton; Richard Averill Smith, interior at Philipsburg Manor, Upper Mills, Sleepy Hollow Restorations; Taylor and Dull, all subjects from Old Deerfield, the Garvan Collection at the Yale University Art Gallery, the collection of Mrs. Giles Whiting, and interiors at Fountain Elms, Utica, New York. Wadsworth Atheneum photographs are by E. Irving Blomstrann. Colonial Williamsburg photographs are by John Crane, Delmore A. Wenzel, and Thomas L. Williams. The work of staff photographers of other museums is also acknowledged with appreciation.

Plate I, the hall at Hempsted House, is by Louis H. Frohman. Plate II, the living room in the home of Mr. and Mrs. William C. Harding, is by Taylor & Dull. Plate IV, the Great Chamber at Mount Pleasant, is by A. J. Wyatt. Plate V, the Pennsylvania-German room in the home of Mr. and Mrs. Mitchel Taradash, is by Gottscho-Schleisner. Plate VI, the drawing room in the home of Mrs. Giles Whiting, is by Henry Fullerton. Plate VII, the Red Room at the White House, is by Charles Baptie. Plate VIII, the Victorian parlor at Fountain Elms, is by Taylor & Dull.

# Index

*(Figures in bold-face type are illustration numbers. An asterisk indicates that only one example is indexed.)*

Acanthus*: Jacobean, **47**; "oak-leaf," **446**; ruffled, **265**; spiral, **537**; tattered, **264**

Adam, Robert (1728-1792): in Italy, 192

Adam style: 192; **433, 471, 499, 500, 502, 503, 507**

Adams, Lemuel (ac. by 1792): 206; **427**

Adams and Todd (in partnership 1798): 206; **548**

Aesop's fables motif: **312, 377**

Acroteria: **413**

Affleck, Thomas (1740-1795; ac. 1763): 130; **248, 255-56, 264, 317, 369, 388**

Aitken, John (ac. by 1775): 206; **449**

Albany Institute of History and Art, Albany, N.Y.: bed, **410**; looking glass, *Sheraton*, **508**; kneehole chest of drawers, **382**; table, *Empire*, **560, 585**, gate-leg, **125**

Albany mirror: **508**

Alden, Mrs. Eliot, coll. of: **295**

Allison, Michael (ac. 1800-1845): 206; **559**

Allyn, Mary (inscribed chest): **55**

Alston, Governor Joseph (sideboard): **515**

American Museum in Britain, Claverton Manor, near Bath, England: **282**

Anderson, Elbert (ac. 1789-1800): 206; **428, 510**

Anthemion: 192; **413***

Antiquarian and Landmarks Society of Connecticut: **6, 21**, Color Plate I

Appell, Mrs. Louis J., coll. of: **572**

Applied turning: 16; **51***

Arcaded chest: **47***

Arched skirt: **70***

Arched-panel door: **336***

Architectural mirror: **344***

Architecture: Adam style (in America), 205; and furniture design, 117; Gothic Revival, 275; Greek Revival, 205; Palladian style, 116; Tuscan Revival, 276

Arm*: concave (support), **148**; continuous, **527**; horizontally rolled, **347**; looped, **150**; mushroom, **33**; ram's-horn, **38**; vertically rolled, **249**

Ash, Gilbert (1717-1785): 130; **260**

Ash, Thomas (ac. 1815): **460**

Astragal: **334**

Bachman, John (1746-1829): 130; **335**

Badlam, Stephen (1751-1815): 206; **423**

Ball family chair: **424**

Balloon-back chair: 283; **632***

Baltimore Museum of Art, Baltimore, Md.: chair, **283, 458**; Baltimore Loan Ex., **421, 429, 435, 437, 481, 484, 527, 532, 553-554, 564-65, 580**

Baluster: 16; **106***; ringed, **76***

Banister-back chair: 18; **38***

Bar-back chair: **445***

Barbour, Mr. and Mrs. Frederick K., coll. of: **117, 306, 326, 398, 575**

Barnhart, John (c. 1814-1815), decorator: 208; **458**

Bartol, Samuel (c. 1765-1835), decorator: **459**

Barwell, Bartholomew (ac. 1749-1760): **188**

Baudouine, Charles A. (ac. 1845-1900): 285; **650**

Baumstone, Teina: **198, 401**

Bayard, William, chair for: **451**

Bayou Bend collection, Houston, Texas: chair, *William and Mary*, **44**; *Queen Anne*, **149, 153, 171, 174**; *Chippendale*, **257, 258, 260**; chest, **54, 55, 65**; chest of drawers, **296, 299**; daybed, **89, 195**; desk, **324, 490**; desk and bookcase, **329, 330**; high chest, **311, 315**; lowboy, **221**; piano, **509**; settee, **350**; sofa, **528**; table, *William and Mary*, **132**; *Queen Anne*, **215, 216, 233**; *Chippendale*, **365, 366, 369, 373, 386, 388, 390, 392, 393, 400**

Beaded edge: **374***

"Beau Brummel(l)": **571**

Bed: field (or tent), **140, 406**; folding-trestle, **3, 4**; high-post, 15, **138, 235-37, 407, 408, 409**; low-post, 15, **1, 139, 238**; pencil-post, **237**; "sleigh," **410, 411**; trundle, **6**; Victorian, **628, 644, 655**

Beirne, Mrs. Francis F., coll. of: **514**

Belding, Samuel (1633-1713) and Allis, John (1642-1691): 21; **56**

Belter, John Henry (1804-1863): 285; **636-49**

Bench: 15; "forme," **7**; garden, **659**; upholstered, **11, 413**; window, **358, 412-13**

"Bended back": 72; **28**

Benjamin, Asher (c. 1772-1845): 205

Benkard, Mrs. Harry Horton, coll.: **495**

Bellflower: **429***

Berkey and Gay Co.: **628**

Beveled molding: **64***

Beverley, Mr. and Mrs. W. Welby, coll. of: **278**

Bible box: **12-15**

Bissell, Mrs. Alfred P., Jr., coll. of: **241**

Blagojevich, Col. and Mrs. Miodrag, coll. of: **137**

Blair, Mrs. J. Insley, coll.: **38, 43, 64, 77, 111, 155, 277, 310, 451, 503, 570**

Blaney, Richard, coll. of: **469**

Blin, Peter (ac. c. 1675-1725): **53, 54, 81**

Blockfront: 127; Connecticut, **299***; Massachusetts, **297***; Newport, **298***

Bombé shape: **329***

Bonnet top:* **200**; closed, **315**

"Book" inlay: **549***

Bookcase: **239-40, 414, 416, 612, 617**

Borland, Francis, table owned by: **373**

Boss: **80***

Boston, Museum of Fine Arts: chair, wainscot, **23**; cupboard, press, **78, 81**; dressing chest of drawers, **472**; *M. and M. Karolik coll.*, chair, *classical period*, **426, 433, 436, 439, 441, 443**; chest-on-chest, **471**; commode, **470**; desk, **321, 323, 488**; desk and bookcase, **200, 494**; looking glass, **204, 502, 506**; sideboard, **518, 523**; sofa, **534**; stand, **540, 543, 544**; table, *Chippendale*, **402**, *classical period*, **540, 543, 544, 558, 591, 592**; wine cooler, **419**

Bowfront: **465***

Bowl turning: **121***

Box, book or desk: 15; **12-15**

Bradford, William (1589/90-1657): **16**

Breakfront: **239-40, 414-15**

Brewster chair: 15; **16, 17**
Brigham, Ezékiel (ac. 1816): **485**
Brooklyn Museum: bed, **237**; chair, *Queen Anne*, **166**, *Chippendale*, **266**, *Victorian*, **626, 647**; chest-on-frame, **58**; clock, **188**; couch, **536**; dressing chest of drawers, **302**; kneehole chest of drawers, **381**; Milligan Library, **612**; Milligan Parlor, **635**; ottoman, **413**; table, *Empire*, **587**; *Victorian* dressing room, **627**; Victoriana Ex. alcove, **628, 638**; whatnot, **618**
Brooks, Louis E., coll.: **37, 244, 248, 263, 297, 393, 500**
Brooks, Thomas (1811-1887): 285; **626-27**
Brown, Gawen (1719-1801): **187**
Bruner, Henry, New York, c. 1850: **612**
Buckland, William (1734-1774): 116; **567**
Budd, John (ac. 1817-1840): 206; **497**
Builders' guides: 116, 205
Bulfinch, Charles (1763-1844): 205
Bulbous support: **74**\*
Bureau: **627, 628, 649, 653**
Burling, Thomas (ac. 1769-1775): 130
Burnham, Benjamin (ac. 1769-1773): 131
Butler, Joseph T., coll. of: **623, 624, 642, 643**
Butler's desk: **491**\*
Butterfly table: 19; **117-18**
Byard, J. K., coll. sale: **121, 232, 452**

C-scroll: **264**\*
Cabinet: Plymouth, **73**; spice, **241-242**; wall, **87**; *see also* bookcase, cupboard
Cabinetmaking: 17
Cabochon: **369**\*
Cabriole leg: 73, 282; **142**\*; ridged, **261**\*
Candlestand: **102, 209-11, 353-54, 539, 542, 545-46**
Cane furniture: 16, 18; **36**\*
Carpenter, Mr. and Mrs. Ralph E., Jr., coll. of: **177**
Carroll, Charles, of Carrollton, chair owned by: **429**
Carver chair: 15; **18, 20, 29**
Caryatid support: **586**
Cast-iron furniture: **658-63**
Caylus, Comte de (1692-1765): 191
Cellaret: **141, 243, 418-19**
Chair: banister-back, 18, **38-42**; bar-back, **445-46**; Boston rocker, **462**; Brewster, 15, **16, 17**; cane,

18, **36, 37, 142**; Carver, 15, **18, 20, 29**; chair-table, **22**; corner, **45, 152-54, 257**; "Cromwellian," 15, **27**; drapery back, **424-25, 442**; easy, 18, **43, 44, 155-56, 249-52, 421**; "Elizabethan," **651-652**; "fancy," 203, **458-60**; Gothic, 272, **613-15**; heart-back, **430-431**; Hitchcock, **461**; klismos, 198, **452**; Lambert family, **265**; Livingston family, **171**; Martha Washington, **438, 577**; oval-back, **436-37**; painted, **436, 458-59, 656**; papier-mâché, **664**; patent, **658**; Pennsylvania-German, **291**; "pretzel-back," **281**; Rhode Island, **433**; ribbon-back, **266**; "Salem," **258**; "sample," **275**; Senate, **427**; shield-back, **423-29**; slat-back, 15, **30-35**; Spanish-foot, **37, 46**; Speaker's, **256**; square-back, **441-50**; tall-back, **36**; tassel-back, **262-63**; transition, 196, **422**; trellis-back, **443**; turned great, **19**; Van Rensselaer family, **247**; wainscot, 15, **23-25**; windsor, 129, **284-90, 463-64**
Chair-back settee: **350**
Chapin, Aaron (1753-1838): 131; **331, 486, 512**
Chapin, Eliphalet (1741-1807): 131; **261, 314, 331, 434**
Charleston Museum, Charleston, S.C.: bookcase, *Hepplewhite*, **414**; chest-on-chest, *Chippendale*, **309**
Chest: 14; arcaded, **47**; Connecticut, **53-55**; diamond-panel, **48**; double, on frame, **307**; dower, **219-92**; dressing, **303**; dressing, kneehole, **380**; fourteen-panel, **50**; geometric, **51**; Guilford, **67**; Hadley, **56**; high chest, **69-72, 181-184, 310-15**; one-drawer, **52, 65, 66**; Pennsylvania-German, **291-92**; six-board, **49**; Sunflower, **53, 54**
Chest-on-chest: **305, 306, 308, 309, 471**
Chest-on-frame: **57, 179**; painted, **58**
Chest of drawers: 14; **59-64, 68, 178**; bombé, **296**; bowfront, **465-66**; blockfront, **297-300**; dressing, **302**, with attached mirror, **472-75**; kneehole, **380**; oxbow, **295**; serpentine, **294, 467-468**; swellfront, **469**
Chest of drawers on frame: **301**
Chester County Historical Society, West Chester, Pa.: chest of drawers, **178**; desk-on-frame, **92**; wardrobe, **86**

Chicago, The Art Institute of: cabinet, Pilgrim, **73**; chair, child's, **17**, *classical period,* **432**, windsor, **289**; chest, painted, **180**; chest-on-frame, **57**; desk-on-frame, **90**; Hudson Valley kas, **82**; table, gateleg, **123**, *Hepplewhite,* **583**
Chinese influence: 118; Chinese-Chippendale fret, **334**\*; lattice, **276**\*; pierced fret, **361**\*; straight leg, **387**\*
Chip carving: **13**\*
Chippendale, Thomas (c. 1718-1779): 119
Chippendale style: American, 120; English 117
Christopher, Mr. and Mrs. T. B., coll. of: **322, 335, 476, 516, 552**
City Art Museum, St. Louis: stand, *Hepplewhite,* **541**; table, *Chippendale-Hepplewhite* transition, **364**
Claggett, William (ac. 1720-1740): **186**
Classical period: European background, 191; furniture forms, 197; style characteristics, 192, 194, 196; style names in America, 195
Claw-and-ball foot: 118
*Cleopatra's Barge,* chairs: **459**
Clock: banjo, **479**; bracket, **318**; girandole, **482**; mantel, **663**; "pillar and scroll," **483**; tall, **186-88, 316-17, 476-77, 480-481**; wall, **478**
Clothes press: **82-84, 86, 404, 405**
"Clover-leaf" top: **557**\*
Clustered columns: **566**\*
Cockbead: on drawer front, **294**\*; on frame, **71**\*
Cogswell, John (ac. 1769-1818): 131; **329**
Cole, Henry (1802-1883): 277
Colonial Dames of America in the State of Virginia: sideboard at Wilton, **521**
Colonial Williamsburg, Williamsburg, Va.: bed, *Chippendale,* **238**; chair, open-arm, **253**, side, **275**, *Queen Anne-Chippendale* transition, **176**; desk, fall-front, **96**; press, china, **192**; sofa, Marlborough, **348**; table, five-stretcher, **134**
Colonnettes: **470**\*
Column support: **563**\*
Commode: **470**
Concertina action: **215**
Conch shell, inlaid, **495**\*
Connecticut chest: **53, 54**

Connecticut Historical Society, Hartford, Conn.: chair, *Chippendale-Hepplewhite,* **422,** Senate, **427,** *William and Mary,* **39;** desk and bookcase, **486;** table, draw, **110;** *George Dudley Seymour coll.;* chair, *William and Mary,* **28, 34;** chest, seventeenth century, **48;** chest of drawers, **465;** double chest of drawers, **62;** stand, **104;** table, hutch, **129,** porringer, **131,** tavern, **136**

Connelly, Henry (1770-1826): 206; **442, 517**

Conner, Robert (ac. 1842-1858): 281

Constitution mirror: **344***

Convex foot: **542***

Coons, Mr. and Mrs. G. Dallas, coll. of: **301**

Cooper, Peter (1791-1883): **657**

Cooper Union Museum, New York: chair, *Empire,* arm, **456,** *Victorian,* **648, 657;** hot-air circulator, **661;** sofa, *Victorian,* **636;** table, *Empire,* center, **563**

Copland, H.: 118, 120

Corner cupboard: 74; **189, 191, 319**

Cornucopia motif: **538***

Couch: **533, 535-36, 639;** *see also* daybed

Court cupboard: 14; **74-76**

Cradle: **1, 2, 5**

Cresting: eared, **263***; hoop (yoke), **166***; serpentine (bowed) **248***; voluted, **244***

Crocket: **613***

"Cromwellian chair": 15; **27**

Crosman, Robert (1707-1799): 81; **180**

Crown crest: **38***

Crystal Palace Exhibition, London: 277

Cup turning: **70***

Cupboard: china press, **192;** clothes, **82-84, 86, 404, 405;** corner, **189, 191, 319;** court, 14, **74, 76;** kas, **82-84;** kitchen, **85, 190, 192-93;** Pennsylvania-German, **320;** press, 14, **77-81;** wall, **87**

"Cupid's bow" splat: **147***

Currier Gallery of Art, Manchester, N.H.: desk and bookcase, **332;** double chest on frame, **307**

Curtis, Lemuel (1790-1857): **482**

Curule support: **454***

Cylinder closing: **489***

Cyma curve: **71***

Dates: 20, 80

Davis, Alexander J. (1803-1892): 276, **613**

Daybed: 16, 18, 73; **88, 89, 194-195**

Deerfield: *see* Old Deerfield

Dennis, Thomas (c. 1638-1706): 20; **24, 47, 57, 78-80**

Dentil: **328***

Derby family, furniture owned by: **419, 426, 436, 439, 470, 471, 473, 505, 540**

Design books:
Ackermann, Rudolf, *Repository of the Arts,* 195
Adam, Robert, *Ruins of the Palace of the Emperor Diocletian at Spalatro,* 192
Anon., *Gothic Album for Cabinetmakers,* 281
Benjamin, Asher, *American Builder's Companion; Country Builder's Assistant,* 205
Campbell, Colen, *Vitruvius Britannicus,* 117
Caylus, Comte de, *Recueil d'antiquités,* 192
Chambers, Sir William, *Designs of Chinese Buildings, Furniture, Dresses, Machines and Utensils,* 119
Chippendale, Thomas, *The Gentleman and Cabinet-Maker's Director,* 120
Darley, Matthew, *New Book of Chinese, Gothic and Modern Chairs,* 119
Downing, Andrew Jackson, *Architecture of Country Houses; Cottage Residences,* 276
Edwards and Darley, *A New Book of Chinese Designs,* 119
Gibbs, James, *A Book of Architecture,* 116
Halfpenny, William, *New Designs for Chinese Temples,* 119
Halfpenny, William and John, *The Modern Builder's Assistant,* 116
Hall, John, *The Cabinet-Maker's Assistant,* 277
Hepplewhite, George, *The Cabinet-Maker and Upholsterer's Guide,* 193
Hope, Thomas, *Household Furniture and Interior Decoration,* 193
Langley, Batty, *Gothic Architecture Improved,* 119
Langley, Batty and Thomas, *City and Country Builders and Workman's Treasury of Designs,* 116

Lock, Mathias, *A New Drawing Book of Ornaments,* 118
Lock, M., and Copland, H., *A New Book of Ornaments,* 118
London. *The Cabinet-Maker's London Book of Prices,* 197
Loudon, J. C., *Encyclopaedia of Cottage, Farm and Villa Architecture,* 281
Manwaring, Robert, *The Cabinet and Chair-Maker's Real Friend and Companion,* 117
Mésangère, Pierre la, *Album, (Meubles et objets de goût),* 195
Nicholson, Peter and Michael Angelo, *The Practical Cabinet-Maker, Upholsterer and Complete Decorator,* 195
Percier (Charles) and Fontaine (Pierre), *Recueil de décorations intérieures,* 194
Piranesi, Giambattista, *Diverse maniere d'adornare i camini,* 192
Sheraton, Thomas, *The Cabinet-Maker and Upholsterer's Drawing Book; The Cabinet Dictionary; The Cabinet-Maker, Upholsterer and General Artist's Encyclopaedia,* 193
Smith, George, *The Cabinetmakers and Upholsterers' Guide,* 195; *A Collection of Designs for Household Furniture,* 193
Stalker (John) and Parker (George), *A Treatise of Japanning and Varnishing, 1688,* 119, 314n27
Swan, Abraham, *Designs in Architecture,* 116
Tatham, Charles Heathcote, *Etchings of Ancient Ornamental Architecture,* 193
Ware, Isaac, *Complete Body of Architecture,* 116
Wood, Henry, *A Series of Designs of Furniture Decoration,* 281

Desk: 18, 74; butler's, **491;** fall-front, **96, 498;** lady's, **487-89;** slope-front, **95, 197, 321-27, 484-85;** tambour, **490;** -on-frame, **90, 93, 196, 198**

Desk and bookcase: 73; **98, 200, 201, 328-38, 486, 493-96, 597-598;** on frame, **202**

Desk box: **12-15**

Detroit Institute of Art, Detroit, Mich.: Desk box, seventeenth century, **14**

Diagonal dentil: **81***

Diagonal stretcher: **119***

Diamond splat: **260***

Dillehunt, Mr. and Mrs. H. B., Jr., coll. of: **554**
Directoire style: 194
Disbrowe, Nicholas (1612/13-1683): 20; **55, 59**
Dished seat: **16***
Dished top: **230***
Dog's-paw foot: **412***
Doggett, John (1780-1857): 207
Dolan, John T. (directory, 1811): 207; **557**
Doll's dressing table: **616**
Dolphin foot: **410***
Double-arch molding: **95***
Downing, Andrew Jackson (1815-1852): 276
Drapery-back chair: **424***
Drawing table: **570**
Dresser: **193, 320**
"Dressing box": 16
Dressing chest: **303, 380**
Dressing glass: **501**
Dressing table: 17; **119-21, 219-225, 374-82, 571, 616**
Drop handle: **61***
Dunlap family of cabinetmakers (late eighteenth, early nineteenth century): 131; **307**

Eagle: carved, **506**; inlaid, **484**; New England, **550**
Eastlake, Charles L. (1836-1906): 277
Easy chair: origin of, 18
Ebonized turning: **80***
Egerton, Matthew, Sr. (died 1802): 207
Egerton, Matthew, Jr. (ac. in own shop, 1785; died 1837): 207; **511**
*Églomisé* glass: 317n58; **489, 494, 500, 503, 508, 564**
Elfe, Thomas (ac. 1747-1775): 131; **240, 309, 338**
Egyptian influence: 194; **452***
Elizabethan (Victorian) style: 281
Elliott, John, Sr. (1713-1791): 131; **340-41**
Empire style: in America, 198; France, 196; late, 196, 203
Essex Institute, Salem, Mass.: candlestand, *Sheraton,* **539,** polescreen, **545**; chair, *Hepplewhite,* **432,** wainscot, **24**; desk and bookcase, **328**; dressing chest of drawers, **473, 475**; overmantel mirror, **507**; table, console, **228,** work, **594**
*Etagère:* 283; **619, 621-22**
Evans, Edward (c. 1707): **96**

Fales, Mr. and Mrs. Dean A., Jr., coll. of: **474**
Fan: **314***

Feather motif: **436***
Federal style: 196
Finial*: basket-of-flowers, **308**; corkscrew, **332**; flame, **337**; phoenix, **344**; pierced cartouche, **311**; pineapple, **525**; urn, **305**
Finlay, John and Hugh (ac. 1799-1833): 207; **532**
Firescreen: **351, 545-47**
Fisher family, side table: **390**
Fithian, Philip Vickers (1747-1776): 115
Folwell, John (ac. 1762-1780): 132
Flemish scroll: 17; **36, 88**
Fluted arches: **75***
Fluted pilaster: **328***
Foliation: **47***
Foot*: ball, **61**; bracket (blocked ogee) **305,** (flaring) **468,** (ogee) **294,** (straight) **295**; brass paw, **470**; "button," **472**; claw-and-ball, **171**; convex, **542**; dog's-paw, **412**; dolphin, **410**; hoof, **613**; lion's-paw, **525,** (bracketed) **537**; pad, **154**; pierced claw, **392**; "rat" claw, **397**; "snake," **541**; spade, **431**; trifid, **148**; web, **208**; scrolled toe, **275**; slipper, **165**
Form (bench): 14; **7**
Franklin, Drs. C. Ray and Winifred Hope, coll. of: **431**
"French chair": **253**
French influence: 198, 283; **410, 420, 490, 492, 526, 560, 585**
Fretwork (Victorian): **620**
Fretwork mirror: **340***
Friesland (Friesian) carving: **15**
Frothingham, Benjamin (1734-1809): 132; **304**
Fueter, Lewis (ac. 1770): mounts by, **339**
Fulton, Robert, chair owned by: **431**

Gaines, John (1677-c. 1750) of Ipswich: 21; **37**
Gaines, John (1704-1743) of Portsmouth: 21; **46**
Galusha, Elijah (1804-1871): 285; **622, 635**
Gaming table: **578**; *see also* table, card
Garden furniture: **658**
Gateleg table: 19; **122-27**
Geddes, Charles, New York (c. 1773): **318**
Geesey, Titus C., coll.: **320**
Gentleman's chest: **303**
Geometric chest: **51***
Geometric paneling: 16
Gesso: **344***; and wire, **503***
Gillim, Charles (d. 1727): **67**

Gillingham, James (1736-1781): 132; **268**
Ginsburg & Levy: **161, 183, 203, 280, 375, 397, 423**
Girandole: **506**
Goddard, John (1723-1785): 80, 132; **221, 394**
Goddard, Stephen (1764-1804) and Thomas (1765-1858): 207
Goddin, Mr. and Mrs. John C., coll. of: **225**
Gostelowe, Jonathan (1745-1795): 132; **294**
Gothic style: *Chippendale,* 119; fret, **385***, splat, **270***; Victorian, 278, 281; **605, 606, 609-616**
Graining: **563**
Grand Rapids Public Museum: **628**
Grapevine motif: **368, 426, 523**
Grant, Ulysses S., desk of: **327**
Gratz family, lowboy: **376**
"Great chair": 15
"Grecian squab": **533***
Greco-Roman influence: 191, 194; **452, 454**
Guilford chest: **67**
Guilloche: **47***

Hadley chest: 20; **56**
Haines, Ephraim (1775 to after 1811): 207; **445, 516**
Hairy-paw foot: **274***
Half-daisy motif: **530**
Hall, John (1840): 277
Hamilton, Dr. Alexander (1712-1756): 71
Hammond-Harwood House Assn., Annapolis, Md.: cellaret, **243**; dining room, **567**
Hancock, John, table owned by: **363**
Harding, Mr. and Mrs. William C., coll. of: Color Plate II
Hardware*: Chippendale brasses, **295**; drop handle, **61**; lion-mask handle, **470**; loop handle with engraved backplate, **71**; ring handle enclosing Bilston enamel, **490**
Harrison, Mr. and Mrs. James D., coll. of: **421**
Hart, Ware & Co., Philadelphia, c. 1850: **653**
Haskell, Mrs. J. Amory, coll.: **266, 413, 569**
Heart-and-crown crest: **41***
Henry Ford Museum and Greenfield Village, Dearborn, Mich.: bookcase, **609**; candlestand, **210, 354, 542**; chair, *Jacobean-William and Mary,* **35, 37, 40**; *Queen Anne,* **148, 167**; *Chip-*

*pendale,* **244, 248, 251, 252, 256, 263, 271;** *classical period,* **438, 440, 444, 445, 447, 450, 453, 461, 462;** *Victorian,* **615, 640, 662;** chest, **67, 293;** chest of drawers, **297, 300, 466;** chest-on-chest, **304;** clock, **186, 187, 480, 663;** couch, **533, 639;** cupboard (press), **80;** daybed, **194;** desk, **95, 199;** desk and bookcase, **202;** *étagère,* **621;** high chest, **182;** looking glass, **345, 500, 501;** polescreen, **547;** "Salem secretary," **415;** sideboard, **525;** sofa, **349;** table, *Queen Anne,* **218, 226;** *Chippendale,* **363, 370, 371;** *classical period,* **555, 559;** *Victorian,* **600;** wardrobe, **405**

Henry Ford Museum and Greenfield Village interiors: Plympton house, **42;** Secretary house, **158**

Henry Francis du Pont Winterthur Museum, Winterthur, Del.: bed, **236;** box (desk), **13;** candlestand, **209;** chair, *Queen Anne,* **142-43, 145-47, 154, 165, 168;** *Chippendale,* **250, 262, 265, 270,** *Empire,* **457;** desk and bookcase, **334, 493;** looking glass, **100;** lowboy, **223, 376;** stool, **212;** table, *Queen Anne,* **213, 217, 227, 230;** *Chippendale,* **360, 372, 383, 385, 387**

Henry Francis du Pont Winterthur Museum interiors: Banister Stair Hall, **162;** Cecil Bedroom, **138;** Chippendale Bedroom, **173;** Empire Bedroom, **411;** Empire Hall, **492;** Federal Parlor, **434;** Franklin Room, **406;** Gold and White Room, **409;** Hardenbergh Bedroom, **84;** Hardenbergh Parlor, **105;** Hart Room, **106;** Kershner Parlor, **291;** Morattico Hall, **11;** Oyster Bay Room, **29;** Queen Anne Bedroom, **139;** Readbourne Parlor, **156;** Seventeenth-Century Room, **7;** Vauxhall Room, **151;** Walnut Room, **4**

Hepplewhite, George (d. 1786): 193

Hepplewhite style: 193, 196

Herreshoff, Norman, coll. of: **305**

Herringbone inlay: 63*

High chest: 16, 17, 73, 121; **69-72, 181-84, 310-15**

Highboy: 17

Historic house museums:
 Allen house, Old Deerfield, Mass., **127**
 Asa Stebbins house, Old Deerfield, **520**

Ashley house, Old Deerfield, **190, 220**

Barrett house, New Ipswich, N.H., **519**

Bartow, Pelham Bay Park, N.Y., **206**

Brush-Everard house, Williamsburg, Va., **348**

Campbell house, St. Louis, Mo., 285

Corbit house, Odessa, Del., 117

Dumbarton house, Washington, D.C., 205

Fountain Elms, Utica, N.Y., **588, 596-99, 606-608, 622, 633, 644, 650,** Color Plate VIII

General Salem Towne house, Old Sturbridge, Mass., **574**

Governor John Langdon house, Portsmouth, N.H., 205

Governor's Palace, Williamsburg, Va., **134, 192**

Gunston Hall, Lorton, Va., 116

Hammond-Harwood house, Annapolis, Md., 117; **243, 567**

Hempsted house, New London, Conn., **6, 21,** Color Plate I

The Hermitage, near Nashville, Tenn., 285; **609**

Harrison Gray Otis house, Boston, Mass., **408, 568**

Heyward - Washington house, Charleston, S.C., **309, 414**

Hunter house (Wanton-Lyman-Hunter house), Newport, R.I., **249, 396**

Jeremiah Lee house, Marblehead, Mass., 117; **397**

Lady Pepperrell house, Kittery Point, Me., 116

Marlpit Hall, Middletown, N.J., **189**

Moffatt-Ladd house, Portsmouth, N.H., 205

Mount Morris (Morris-Jumel mansion), New York, 117

Mount Pleasant, Fairmount Park, Philadelphia, 116; Color Plate IV

Mount Vernon, Mount Vernon, Va., 116; **281, 344**

Peirce - Nichols house, Salem, Mass., 205; **507**

Philipsburg Manor, Upper Mills, North Tarrytown, N.Y., **5, 193, 279, 504, 529, 577**

Pingree house, Salem, Mass., 205; **473**

Raleigh Tavern, Williamsburg, Va., **96**

Rosalie, Natchez, Miss., 285

Secretary house, Greenfield Village, Dearborn, Mich., **158**

Stenton, Philadelphia, Pa., 72

Stratford Hall, Westmoreland Co., Va., 72

Strawberry, Fairmount Park, Philadelphia, 205

Sweetbrier, Fairmount Park, Philadelphia, 205

Sunnyside, Irvington-on-Hudson, N.Y., 284; **602, 603, 614, 616, 654-56, 659-60**

Trent house, Trenton, N.J., 72

Van Cortlandt Manor, Croton, N.Y., **94, 128, 163-64, 205, 273, 288**

Warner house, Portsmouth, N.H., 72; **239**

Wickham-Valentine house, Richmond, Va., 205

Wilton, Richmond, Va., **521**

Woodford, Fairmount Park, Philadelphia, 116

Woodlawn Plantation, Mount Vernon, Va., **455, 531**

Hitchcock, Lambert (1795-1852): 207; **461**

Hodgkins, Thomas (ac. 1790): **545**

Holland, Henry (1746-1806): 193

Hook, William (1777-1867): 207; **475**

Hope, Thomas (1769-1831): 193

Horsehoe-shaped (compass) seat: **151***

Horton, Frank L. coll.: bookcase, **240;** chair, **20, 254, 424, 448;** chest, **52;** chest of drawers, **468;** court cupboard, **76;** desk, **487;** desk and bookcase, **98, 338;** lowboy, **224, 379;** sideboard, **515;** table, **576**

Howe family highboy: **312**

Hunt board: **580**

Husk motif: **429**

Hutchins, F. W., New York, c. 1850: **633**

Imbrication: **115***

Independence Hall: Speaker's Chair, **256;** windsor chair, **290**

Inlay*: "book" ("tambour"), **549;** crossbanding, **556;** geometric, **553;** herringbone, **63;** lunette, **548;** mitred panels, **513;** rope ("barber pole"), **552;** stringing, **220;** thumbprint, **548;** variegated star, **220**

Inset quarter-columns: **308**

Irving, Washington, furniture owned by: **603, 614, 659**

Jackson, Andrew, breakfront owned by: **609**

Jacobean style: American forms,

14; design sources, 13; characteristics, 16

Jamieson, Mr. and Mrs. Malcolm, coll. of: **303**

Japanning: 314n27; **184-85, 606,** Color Plate III

Jelliff, John (1813-1893): 286; **625, 634**

Jeremiah Lee house (table): **397**

Johnson, Edmund (ac. 1793-1811): 207; **415**

Johnson, Sir William, table owned by: **125**

Johnston (Johnson), Thomas (ac. 1732-1766): 80; **184-85**

Jones, Inigo (1573-1652): 116

Josiah . . ., Kentucky cabinetmaker: **496**

Kalm, Peter (1716-1779): 115

Karolik coll. *See* Boston, Museum of Fine Arts

Kas: **82-84**

Kaufmann, Edgar, Jr., coll. of: **658**

Keeping room (hall): **7, 21,** Color Plate I

Kelly, Robert, furniture owned by: **604, 611, 617, 630-32**

Kemble, Gouverneur, foundry: **659**

Kent, William (1686-1748): 116, 119

Kettle-base: **296***

Klinkowström, Baron Axel (1775-1837): 204

Klismos (chair): 194; **452***

Kneehole chest of drawers: **380**

Kneeland and Adams (1792-1795): 207

Knife case: **339**

Knight, Sarah Kemble (1666-1727): 71

Kylix motif: **433***

La Rochefoucauld-Liancourt, F. A. F., duc de (1747-1827): 204

Ladd, Arthur B., coll. of: **172**

Lady's work table: **592***

Lambert family chair: **265**

Laminating: 282; **640***

Lannuier, Charles-Honoré (1779-1819): 198, 207; **410, 560, 585-87, 589**

Lattice pediment: **337***

Leg*: cabriole, **142;** Marlborough, **348;** reeded, **439;** ridged cabriole, **261;** "saber," **533;** straight, **385;** stump, **245;** tapering, square, **431**

Leiter, Mrs. Frederick, coll. of: **437**

Lemon, William (ac. 1796): 207; **471**

Lewis, Reginald M., coll.: **256,**

**271, 300, 337, 345, 447, 450**

Lewis, Mrs. Reginald M., coll. of: **565**

Lincoln, Abraham: furniture owned by: **638-640**

Lion's-paw foot: **525***

Lip molding: **93***

Livingston family, furniture owned by: 171, **529**

Lock, Matthias: 118, 120

Lockwood, Luke Vincent, coll.: **54, 380, 593**

Looking glass: 19, 122; **99, 100, 203, 204, 205, 340-45; 499-508**

Loop handle: **71***

Lorimer, George Burford, coll.: **381**

Los Angeles County Museum, Los Angeles, Calif.: chair, *Chippendale,* **261,** windsor, **463;** chest of drawers, **295;** *étagère,* **619;** sideboard, *Sheraton,* **522;** table, tripod, **234, 590**

Louis XVI style, influence of: **420, 526**

Lowboy: 17; **119-21, 185, 219-225, 374-79**

Lunette: **59***

Lunette inlay: **548***

Luquer, Lea S., coll. of: **116**

Lyre splat: **412***

McComb, John (1763-1853), table designed by: **584**

MacCoy, Mrs. W. Logan, coll. of: **317**

McIntire, Samuel (1757-1811): 208; **426, 444, 471, 528, 540**

Manwaring, Robert: 117

Manwaring-type chairs: **172, 258, 432**

Marble-top table: *see* Table, slab

Marlborough leg: **348***

Martha Washington chair: **438, 577**

Martha Washington mirror: **344***

Maryland Historical Society, Baltimore, Md.: chair, *Hepplewhite,* **435;** clock, **481;** "musical glasses," **573;** table, corner, **564**

Maynard, R. W., coll. of: **152**

Mechanization: effect of on design, 276

Meeks, Joseph, and Sons (1797-1868): 286; **605, 609, 665**

Metal furniture: Victorian, 283; **657-63**

Metropolitan Museum of Art: bed, **1, 3;** chair, *Jacobean-William and Mary,* **19, 26, 27, 36, 43;** *Queen Anne,* **144, 155;** *Chippendale,* **246, 259, 272, 274, 284;** *classical period,* **428, 460;**

chest, **47, 292;** chest of drawers, **59, 60, 64, 298;** clock, **478;** cradle, **1;** cupboard, **77;** desk and bookcase, **495;** desk-on-frame, **91;** firescreen, **351;** high chest, **69, 71, 72, 184,** Color Plate III; knife case, **339;** looking glass, **343;** lowboy, **185;** settee, **206, 207, 346;** settle, **9, 10;** sofa, **537, 637;** stand, **103;** stool, joint, **108;** table, *Jacobean–William and Mary,* **111, 112, 124, 130;** *Queen Anne,* **229;** *Chippendale,* **367, 384, 389, 403;** *classical period,* **586;** *Victorian,* **646**

Miles, Mrs. Clarence, coll. of: **580**

Millhiser, Mr. and Mrs. E. Ross, coll. of: **141**

Milligan (Robert) house: library, **612;** parlor, **635**

Mills and Deming (1793-1798): 208

Mirror-back pier table: **585***

Molding*: beveled, **64;** cockbead, **71;** convex, **389;** double-arch, **95;** lip (ovolo), **93;** mitred, **51;** rope, **256;** serrated, **73;** single-arch, **94;** thumbprint, **66**

Monmouth County Historical Assn., Freehold, N.J.: chair, wainscot, **25;** cupboard in Marlpit Hall, **189**

Monopodia: **609***

Mount Vernon Ladies' Association, Mount Vernon, Va.: chair, side, **281;** looking glass, **344**

Munson-Williams-Proctor Institute, Utica, N.Y.: bookcase, **617;** chair, **631, 632;** desk, **633;** desk and bookcase, **597-98;** Fountain Elms interiors, **596, 599, 608, 622, 644,** Color Plate VIII; sofa, **630;** table, **604, 606, 607, 611, 650**

Museum of the City of New York: bed, Sheraton, **407;** chair, banister-back, **38,** *Chippendale,* **277,** *classical period,* **451, 454,** *Victorian,* **613, 651, 664;** desk, *Empire,* **498;** looking glass, *Sheraton,* **503;** sofa, *Victorian,* **641;** table, *Sheraton,* writing, **497,** *Victorian,* **601;** wardrobe, **605**

Mushroom arm: **33***

"Musical glasses": **573**

Myer, Mr. and Mrs. John Walden, coll. of: **333**

National Trust for Historic Preservation: Woodlawn dining room, **455;** parlor, **531**

Needles, John (1786-1878): 286; **610**

Nelson, Mrs. Lucian D., coll. of: **496**

Nelson, Mrs. Pennington, coll. of: **429**

Nelson Gallery of Art: *see* William Rockhill Nelson Gallery of Art

New England Antiquities, Society for the Preservation of, Boston, Mass.: Harrison Gray Otis house bedroom, **408**, dining room, **568**; Barrett house, New Ipswich, N.H., dining room, **519**

New Hampshire Historical Society, Concord, N.H.: *Prentis coll.*, daybed, **88**; chair, corner, **45**; side, **46**; stool, *William and Mary*, **109**

New York City Museum: *see* Museum of the City of New York

New-York Historical Society: chair, arm, banister-back, **41**; desk, *Chippendale*, **325**; high chest, *William and Mary*, **70**, *Chippendale*, **310**; table, side, **584**

Newark Museum, Newark, N.J.: chair, *Victorian*, arm, **625**, side, **652**; writing cabinet, **634**

Newport County, Preservation Society of, Newport, R.I.: easy chair, *Chippendale*, **249**; Hunter House during loan exhibition, 1953, **396**

Nicholson, Peter and Michael Angelo (1828): 195

Ogee curve: **71***

Old Deerfield, Deerfield, Mass.: chair, **175**; chest, geometric, **51**, one-drawer, **66**; cupboard, kitchen, **190**; desk and bookcase, **331**; lowboy, **220**; sideboard, **520**; table, card, **548**, dressing, **571**, Spanish-foot, **127**

Old Sturbridge Village, Sturbridge, Mass.: cabinet, wall, **87**; chair, *Hepplewhite*, **430**; windsor, **287**; chest, six-board, **49**; Sunflower, **53**; chest-on-frame, **179**; clock, banjo, 479, girandole, 482, "pillar and scroll," 483; cupboard, kitchen, 85; desk, *Hepplewhite*, **485**; General Salem Towne house parlor, **574**

Ormolu mounts: **294, 410, 498, 560, 585**

Ottoman: 283; **413**

Ovolo molding: **93***

Oxbow: **295***; blocked, **304***

Pabst, Daniel (mid-nineteenth century): 286; **629**

Painted decoration: 16; **58, 64-67,** **83, 84, 100, 409, 436, 473, 630-32, 653-56**; Pennsylvania-German, **292-93, 405**

Palladian style: 116

Palladio, Andrea (1518-1580): 116

Palmate panel: **47***

Papier-mâché: **664**

Parcel gilding: **380***

Parmenter family court cupboard: **75**

Patent furniture: 284; **658**

Peabody Museum, Salem, Mass.: chairs from *Cleopatra's Barge*, **459**

Pearre, Mr. and Mrs. Sifford, coll. of: **341, 358, 551, 578, 581**

Pediment: broken-scroll, **184***; broken triangular (pitch), **338***; lattice, **314***; triangular (pitch), **334***

Peirce-Nichols house (mirror): **507**

Pembroke table: 121; **359-62, 574-79**

Pencil post bed: **237***

Pendent drop ("pendill"): **80***

Pennsylvania - German furniture: 129; **291-93, 320, 404, 405**

Pepperrell family looking glass: **100**

Percier, Charles (1764-1838) and Fontaine, Pierre (1762-1853): 194

Petre, Miss Constance, coll. of: **267**

Philadelphia Museum of Art: bureau, painted, 653; chair, *Chippendale*, **245, 268**, *Louis XVI style*, **420**, *Sheraton*, **446**, *Queen Anne*, **150, 170**; chest-on-chest, **308**; chest of drawers, **294**; couch, *Late Empire*, **535**; cupboard, Pennsylvania-German, **320**; highboy, **312**; desk and bookcase, **336**; looking glass, **340**; sideboard, *Sheraton*, **517**, *Victorian*, **629**; sofa, *Chippendale*, **347**, *Louis XVI style*, **526**; table, card, **556**; dressing, **374**; wardrobe, Pennsylvania-German, **404**; whatnot, **620**

Phyfe, Duncan (1768-1854): 196, 198, 208; **406, 412-13, 451, 453-54, 491, 509, 525, 533-34, 558, 570, 591**

Piano case: **509**

Pierced cartouche finial: **311***

Pilaster*: Corinthian, **498**; fluted, **328**; Ionic, **329**; simulated, **520**

Pilgrim period: 13

Pilgrim Society, Pilgrim Hall, Plymouth, Mass.: William Bradford's chair, **16**

Pineapple finial: **525**

Pingree house (dressing chest): **473**

"Pinwheel": **306***

Platform support: **566***

Platt, Isaac (c. 1830), New York: **588**

Poignand, David (ac. 1788): 208; **364, 541**

Polescreen: **547***; with dropleaf shelf, **545***

Power, Mr. and Mrs. Raymond C., coll. of: **191, 418**

Prentis coll.: **45, 46, 88, 109**

Press: china, **192**; clothes, **86**

Press cupboard: 14; **77-81**

Prince, Samuel (d. 1778): 133; **327, 334**

Prince, Thomas, Rev., chest of drawers owned by, **63**

Prince-of-Wales feathers: **505***

Projecting: back rail, **457***; Colonnettes, **469***; top, **498***

Proud, Joseph, Newport (c. 1762): **386**

Pugin, Augustus Welby Northmore (1812-1852): 278, 281

Punched ground: **14, 244**; star-punched, **528**

Quarter fans: **510***

Queen Anne style: 72, 73

Quervelle, Anthony (ac. 1835-1849): 286; **597-98**

Ram's-horn arm: **38***

Randolph, Benjamin (ac. 1760-1790): 133; **269, 275-76**

Récamier couch: **533***

Reclining chair: **658**

Red Room, The White House: **589**, Color Plate VII

Reeded frame: **533***

Reeded leg: **451***

Regency style: 193, 196; influence, **452, 497, 566**

Regional characteristics: 74, 127, 203

  Annapolis, **514**

  Baltimore, 204; **421, 429, 435, 447-48, 484, 489, 495, 513, 527, 551, 553-54, 564-65, 578, 580, 583**

  Boston, **183-85, 200, 230, 304, 322, 416, 419, 439-40, 450, 470, 490, 505, 506, 518, 520, 522, 543-44, 548, 556, 592**

  Charleston, 128, 204; **224, 240, 254, 309, 338, 371, 414, 424, 555, 576**

  Chester County, Pa., **92, 197, 242**

  Connecticut, 127; **53-55, 67, 81, 101, 117, 136, 140, 142, 166, 182, 198, 202, 236, 261, 299, 300, 306, 314, 326, 331, 378,**

398, 427, 465, 512, 571, 575,
Essex County, Mass., 23, 24, 57,
78-80, 111
Hudson River Valley, 82-84, 128,
146, 163
Kentucky, 496, 524
Long Island, 193, 231
Maryland, 223, 266-67, 283,
358, 573
Massachusetts, 79, 122; 61, 62-
63, 75, 93, 95, 114, 123,
132-33, 157, 213, 215, 217,
226, 230, 246, 258, 272, 280,
295-97, 321, 323, 328-29,
350, 353, 363, 373, 380, 397,
485, 488; see also in this entry: Essex County; Plymouth
New England, 203; 1-4, 6-8, 12-
19, 21-24, 28, 30, 32-34, 39-
41, 44, 47-51, 59, 60, 64-66,
68, 85, 88, 100, 110, 113,
118-21, 124, 126, 129-30,
131-32, 135, 145, 155, 181,
196, 219-20, 346, 393, 430,
459, 466, 469, 493, 523, 550,
594
New Hampshire, 45, 46, 109,
199, 307, 332, 466
New Jersey, 25, 26, 222, 511
New York, 79, 127, 203; 69, 91,
94, 116, 122, 125, 144, 147,
159, 161, 171, 203, 205, 207,
229, 247, 250, 257, 259-60,
262, 273, 277, 279, 302, 327,
333-34, 339, 349, 367-68,
382, 384, 387, 391, 399, 407,
410-13, 431, 441, 451-54,
456-57, 460, 491, 497-99,
509, 510, 529-30, 533-34,
537, 557-60, 566, 570, 572,
584-87, 589-91, 595
Newport, 79, 127; 143, 152,
154, 160, 172, 175, 177, 201,
212, 216, 218, 221, 228, 235,
249, 298, 305, 315, 324-25,
330, 351-52, 354, 356, 361,
365-66, 381, 386, 392, 396,
549
North Carolina, 98, 362, 521
Pennsylvania, eastern, 86, 89,
241-42
Philadelphia, 79, 128, 204; 96,
139, 148, 148-51, 153, 156,
165, 167-70, 176, 194-95,
233-34, 244-45, 248, 251-53,
255-56, 263-65, 268-71, 274-
276, 281-82, 294, 308, 310-
313, 317, 336-37, 340-41,
343, 347-48, 355, 360, 369-
370, 374-77, 388-90, 395,
400, 401, 402, 403, 420, 436,
442, 446, 449, 516-17, 526
Plymouth, Mass., 73, 77
Rhode Island, 203; 138, 433

Salem, 203; 408, 415, 426, 432,
443-44, 469, 471, 473-75,
523, 528, 539-40, 545, 552,
594
South Carolina, 515
Southern, 52, 76, 134, 141, 191-
192, 225, 243, 278, 379
Taunton, Mass., 180
Virginia, 74, 301, 303, 418,
468, 487
Renaissance (Victorian) style: 281;
623-29
Renshaw, Thomas (listed 1814-
1815): 208; 458
Restauration influence: 603
Revere-Little family furniture: 51,
280
Rhea, Robert (c. 1695): 25
Rhode Island chair: 433*
Rhode Island School of Design,
Providence, R.I.: bed, Chippen-
dale, 235; chair, Chippendale,
side, 160, 264; chest-on-chest,
305; desk and bookcase by Job
Townsend, 201; stand, 356; table,
Chippendale, card, 368
Ribbon-back chair: 266
Ringed baluster: 76*
Rittenhouse, David (1732-1796):
317
Roberts, Aaron (1758-1831): 133;
306
Rocking chair: 462, 657
Rococo style: 117; design books,
118; Victorian, 282; cabochon,
369*; pierced cartouche finial,
311*; rockwork, 265*; tattered
acanthus, 264*
Romanesque (Victorian) style: 281;
617
Roth, Mrs. Herbert de, coll. of:
532


S-scroll: 12*
"Saber" leg: 453*
Sack, Israel, Inc.: 140, 169
"Salem": chair, 258*; secretary,
415*
Saltire stretcher: 645*
Sample chair: 275
Sanderson, Elijah (1752-1825) and
Jacob (1758-1810): 208
Savery, William (1721-1788): 133;
176
Schrank: 404, 405
Sconce: 341*
Screen: 351, 545-47
Scrolled toe: 275*
Secretary: see desk and bookcase
Senate chair: 427*
Serrated molding: 73*
Serri, Dr. William S., coll. of: 355
Settee: 74; 206, 207, 346; chair-

back, 350; painted, 532; see also
Sofa
Settle: 15; 8, 9, 10
Seymour, George Dudley, coll.:
see Conn. Historical Society
Seymour, John (c. 1738-1818) and
Thomas (1771-1848): 208; 416,
419, 450, 470, 472-73, 490,
518, 520, 522, 543-44, 556,
592
Shaw, John (1745-1829): 209; 514
Shearer, Thomas: 197
Shelburne Museum, Shelburne, Vt.:
chair, slat-back, 33, windsors,
285, 286, 464; chest of drawers,
61, painted, 68; lowboy, William
and Mary, 119, Chippendale,
378; stool, Chippendale, 357;
table, spider gateleg, 391; splay-
leg, 133
Shell: conch, 551*; inset, 150*;
intaglio, 220*; rococo, 336*; vo-
luted, 249*
Sheraton, Thomas (1751-1806):
193
Sheraton style: 193, 196
Shoemaker, Jonathan (ac. 1757-
1793): 133; 245
Short, Joseph (1771-1819): 209
Shuttle lunette: 48*
Sideboard: 193; 510-25, 599, 628
Sideboard table: 580
Single-arch molding: 94*
Six-board chest: 49*
Skillin, Simeon, and Sons. Simeon,
Sr. (1716-1778); John (1746-
1800); Simeon, Jr. (1757-1806):
133
Skirt*: arched, 70; scrolled, 131
Slab table: see Table, slab
Slack, Mrs. Harry R., Jr., coll. of:
527
Slat-back chair: 15; 30-35
Sleepy Hollow Restorations, Tarry-
town, N.Y.: Philipsburg Manor,
Upper Mills, Beekman Parlor,
504, 577; cradle, 5; chair, 279;
dresser, 193; sofa, 529; Sunny-
side, Guest Bedroom, 654-55,
chair, 603, 614, 656; doll's
dresser, 616; garden bench, 659;
hall stand, 660; sofa, 602; Van
Cortlandt Manor, chair, 163,
273; desk, 94; dining room, 205;
ferry-house bar, 128, 288; old
parlor, 164
"Sleigh" bed: 410*
Slipper chair: 175*
Sloan, Samuel (1815-1884): 277
Slover and Taylor (1802-1804):
209; 530
"Small panel" style: 57
Smith, George (ac. 1808-1828):
193, 195, 196

Smithsonian Institution: chair, **449**; high chest, **313**; *Greenwood Gift*, chair, **30**; chair-table, **22**; chest, **50**; chest of drawers, **63**; desk-on-frame, **93**; table, **114, 115**

"Snake" foot: **541***

Sofa: 74, 121; **208, 347-49, 526-531, 534, 537-38, 602, 610, 630, 636-37, 641**

Sofa table: **589***

Spanish foot: **37, 40, 43-45, 109, 127, 132-33**

Speed Art Museum, The, Louisville, Ky.: sideboard, **524**

Spice cabinet: 16; **241-42**

Spindle turning: **51***

Spiral gadroon: **369***

Spirals, late classical: **535***

Splat: diamond, **236***; pierced, **264***; scrolled, **160***; vase-shape, **163***

Splay front: **24***

Splay-leg table: **132***

Stand: basin, **352, 543**; bedside, **544**; candle, **102, 209-11, 353-354, 539, 542, 545-46**; cross-base, **102, 105**; dropleaf, **103**; firescreen, **351, 545-47**; kettle, **355-56**; tilt-top, **541**; trestle, **101**; triangular, **103**; urn, **540**; with drawer, **104**

State House chair: **440**

Stein, Mr. and Mrs. Charles F., Jr., coll. of: **484**

Stenciled decoration: **536***

Stewart, Mr. and Mrs. Alexander M., coll. of: **553**

Stitcher and Clemmens (c. 1804): **209**; **481**

Stockwell, David: **242, 276**

Stool, joint: 14; **106, 107, 108**; upholstered, **109, 212, 356**

Stop-fluting: **235***

Stout, Mrs. Andrew Varick, coll. of: **412**

Strapwork: **24***

Stratton & Seymour, New York (c. 1837-1843): **661**

Stretcher*: arched, **373**; block-and-spindle, **249**; diagonal, shaped (cross, X-shape), **119**; high (five-), **134**; inset, **429**; flat, **116**; rectangular, **115**; saltire, **645**; shaped, **69**

Stretcher table: 14; **113-16**

Sturbridge: *see* Old Sturbridge Village

Sunflower chest: **53, 54**

Svinin, Pavel Petrovitch (1787/88-1830): 204

Swiss export top: **130**

Table: breakfast, **213-14, 359-62**; butterfly, **117-18**; "buttress," **393**; card, **215-16, 363-71, 548-61**; center, **217, 372, 562-63, 600, 606, 645-46**; china, **373**; console, **228**; corner, **383, 564**; dining, **218, 384, 565-69, 599, 611**; draw, **110**; drawing, **570**; dressing, **119-21, 219-25, 374-82, 571, 616**; dropleaf, **117-18, 122-127, 213-14, 218, 383-84, 391, 600**; five-stretcher, **134**; folding-top, **111**; gaming, **578** (*see also* card); gateleg, **122-27**; harlequin, **572**; handkerchief, **383**; hutch, **128-29**; kneehole dressing, **380**; mirror-back pier, **601**; mixing, **130, 226**; "musical glasses," **573**; pembroke, **359-62, 574-579**; piecrust, **233, 400-402**; pier (*see* side); porringer, **131, 227**; side, **228-29, 385-90, 581-88**; sideboard table, **580**; slab, **217, 229, 385-87**; sofa, **589, 610**; Spanish-foot, **127, 132-33**; spider gateleg, **391**; splay-leg, **132-33**; stretcher, **113-16**; tavern, **135-36**; tea, **137, 230-34, 392-402**; trestle, **112**; trestle gate, **122**; tripod, **233-34, 396-402, 590**; work, **591-95**; writing, **403, 497**

Tall-back chair: 16; **36**

Tambour closing: **490***

"Tambour" inlay: **549***

Taradash, Mr. and Mrs. Mitchel, coll. of: **83, 122, 395**, Color Plate V

Tassel-back chair: **247***

Tatham, Charles Heathcote (1772-1842): 193

Tea table: 19, 73; **137, 230-34, 392-402**

"Tear-drop" panel: **553***

Terry, Eli (1772-1852): **483**

Thumbprint molding: **66***

Tinges, Charles (ac. 1787-1816): **481**

"Tortoise shell" ground: **184***

Townsend, Job (1699-1765): 133; **201, 325**

Townsend, John (1732-1809): 134, 209; **298, 352, 361**

Townsend-Goddard cabinetmakers: **305, 315-16, 324, 330, 356, 365-66, 381, 392**

Tracy, Ebenezer (1744-1803): **287, 463**

"Transition" chair: **422***

Trefoil (splat): **268***

Trellis-back chair: **443***

Trotter, Daniel (1747-1800): 134; **282**

Trumpet turning: **71***

Tufft, Thomas, (ac. 1772-1778): 134; **270, 374**

Tufted upholstery: **631**

Tulip motif: **14***

Turning*: ball, **27**; ball-and-ring, **123**; baluster, **106**; block-and-vase, **28**; bowl, **121**; cup, **70**; knob, **61**; sausage, **34**; spindle, **136**; spiral (twist), **26, 497**; spool, **57**; vase-ball-and-ring, **105**

"Turret" ends: **369***

Upholstery: over seat frame, **274***; with nail heads, **422***; tufted, **631***; *Victorian,* 282

Upjohn, Richard (1802-1878): **604, 617, 630-32**

Urn-and-drapery back (chair): **442***

Van Cortlandt family, chair owned by: **147**

Van Rensselaer family, furniture owned by: **247, 367, 382, 410, 560, 585**

Vase pedestal: **558***

Vase-shaped splat: **163***

Venable, Mrs. Edward, coll. of: **532**

Veneering: 16; with burl, **63***; crotch mahogany, **416***; walnut, **71***

Verplanck family, furniture: **229, 259, 537**

Victorian collections: 284

Victorian styles: Elizabethan, 281; Gothic, 278; Renaissance, 281; Romanesque, 281; rococo, 282

Victoriana exhibition, 1960: **638**

Vine trail: **59***

Volute: **244***

Wadsworth Atheneum, Hartford, Conn.: **512**; *William B. Goodwin coll.,* table, **359**; *Wallace Nutting coll.,* chair, **18**; court cupboard, **74, 75**; cradle, **2**; looking glass, **99**; lowboy, **120**; stand, **101, 102**; stool, joint, **107**; settle, **8**; table, **113, 126, 135**

Walton, John S.: **214, 219, 239, 319, 511**

Wardrobe: **86, 404, 405, 605**

Warner house (breakfront): **239**

Washington, George, chair owned by: **281**

Washington, Martha, mirror owned by: **344**

Waterleaf: **453***

Wax inlay: **404***

Weaver, Holmes (1769-1848): 209

Wharton-Lisle highboy: **311**

Whatnot: 283; **618, 620**

Wheat-ears: **426***

White House, Washington, D.C.: **589**, Color Plate VII

Whiting, Mrs. Giles, coll. of: **118**, **197**, **342**, **416**, **417**, **491**, **595**, Color Plate VI

Willard, Aaron (1757-1844): **477**

Willard, Simon (1753-1848): **476**, **478-79**

William and Mary style: 17

William Rockhill Nelson Gallery of Art and Atkins Museum, Kansas City, Mo.: chair, upholstered side, **255**; cupboard, press, **79**; table, *Hepplewhite* card, **549**

Williamsburg: *see* Colonial Williamsburg

Wilmerding, Henry A., coll. of: **499**

Wilmerding, William (ac. 1785-1794): 209; **499**

Window seat: **358**, **412**

Windsor chairs: 129; **284-90**, **463-464**

Winged support: **560**\*

Winterthur Museum: *see* Henry Francis du Pont Winterthur Museum

Wire inlay: **560**\*

Wood: 74, 282

Wren, Sir Christopher (1632-1723): 116

Writing chair: **603**

Yale University Art Gallery: *C. Sanford Bull coll.*, Hadley chest, **56**; *Mabel Brady Garvan coll.*, chair, *Chippendale*, **269**, *Hepplewhite*, **425**; chest of drawers, **467**; high chest, **314**; clock, **477**; looking glass, **505**; lowboy, **222**; sideboard, **513**; sofa, **538**; tea table, **231**